Great *Commanders*
—*and Their Battles*—

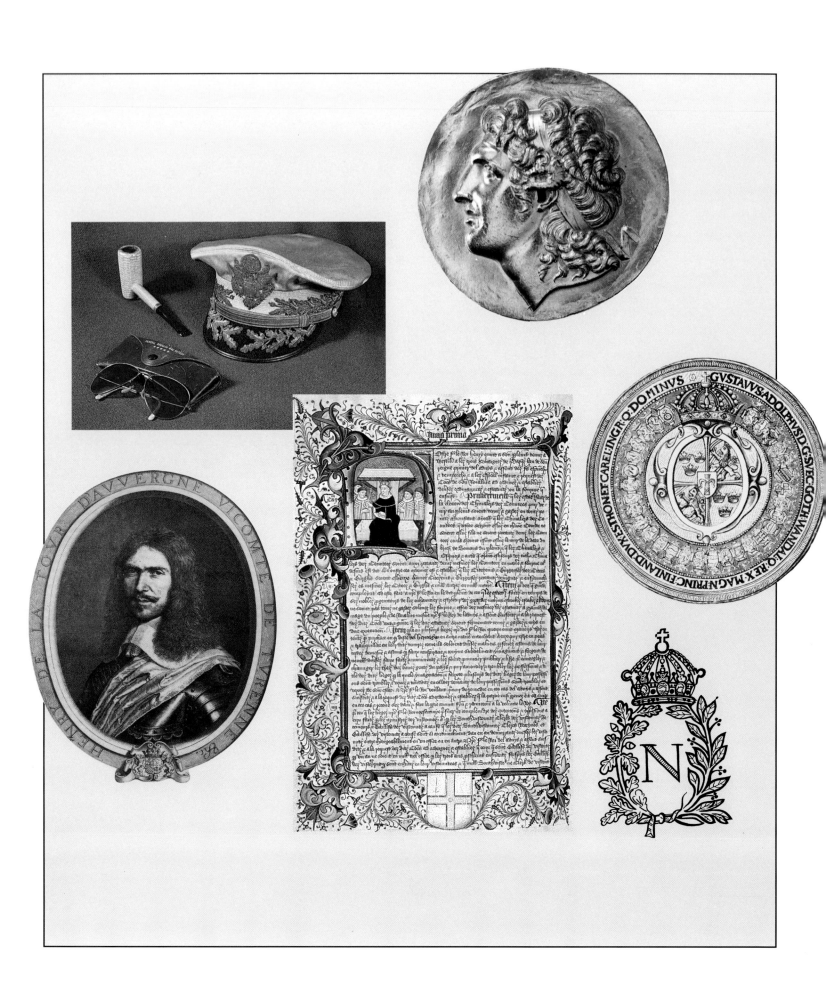

Great Commanders
—and Their Battles—

Anthony Livesey

Randal Gray, Consulting Editor
Foreword by General Sir John Hackett

an imprint of Running Press
Philadelphia, Pennsylvania

Canadian representatives: General Publishing
Co., Ltd., 30 Lesmill Road, Don Mills, Ontario
M3B 2T6.

9 8 7 6 5 4 3 2 1

Digit on the right indicates the number of this
printing.

ISBN 1-56138-330-9

Library of Congress Cataloging-in-Publication
Number 93-70593

This book was conceived, edited, and designed by
Marshall Editions Limited
170 Piccadilly
London W1V 9DD

Cover design: **Toby Schmidt**
Editor: **Gwen Rigby**
Assistant Editor: **Louise Tucker**
Editorial Assistants: **Pat Hunter**
                    Louise Bostock
Consulting Editor: **Randal Gray**
Art Director: **David Goodman**
Picture Research: **Annie Horton**
Production: **Janice Storr**
Illustrator: **Harry Clow**

Printed in Singapore

Published by Courage Books, an imprint of
Running Press Book Publishers
125 South Twenty-second Street
Philadelphia, Pennsylvania 19103

CONTENTS

FOREWORD BY GENERAL SIR JOHN HACKETT

Much has been said and written over the centuries about the 'art of war'. Parallels have been drawn with music, with the performance of orchestral music in mind, under the baton of a conductor. And there are associations with sculpture: Michelangelo, for example, seeing in a great and brutal block of stone the peerless, imprisoned figure of David. The general, it might be said, will also seek a form hidden in raw stone, a form he must strive to discern and free.

The art I should choose as offering the nearest likeness to command in battle is painting. The commander and the painter each have a mass of more or less disorderly material to reduce to an order of their own choosing.

The materials before the artist in command include men, weapons and machines – on both sides, of course, not just his own. The painter too has materials – colours, brushes, tools, instruments, fluids, surfaces. When he approaches a blank surface and sets about placing upon it a composition which uses his materials in an order of his choice, he is trying to do precisely what the commander tries to do on the battlefield.

All arts have to take account of developments in materials and techniques, with the danger that artists may find themselves dominated by the means put at their disposal. Leonardo had to grind and prepare his own paints; today the artist's colourman would do all that for him. While the painter's responsibility has been reduced, there remains the area of choice in which his powers are paramount.

Similarly, in military command, electronic data processing may suggest the possibility of involving an automatic response – firing missiles, for example – without the intervention of the human will. This has to be resisted most firmly; the availability of information may be used to reduce the area within which only an intuitive decision by the human mind is valid, but not to eliminate it. The power of discrimination can be concentrated; the colours though are ready-mixed.

Every artist, be he general or painter, musician or sculptor, is, like every other human being, unique. His work cannot fail to reflect his own character. In this book we are looking at twenty artists – generals – in the context of twenty masterpieces – battles.

We can ask the same questions as we would about painters. What was he like as a person? How did he get that way? What made him do it? Was he innovative, thus influencing the consequent practice of his art? Could things have turned out differently?

My suggestion here that military command is not unlike painting may offer a rewarding point of entry to its study. For testing its merit, this book is a fascinating canvas.

General Sir John Hackett, GCB, CBE, DSO, MC, soldier and scholar, with Oxford degrees in Classics and in Medieval History, ended a military career (three times wounded and with three decorations for gallantry in World War II) as Commander of NATO's Northern Army Group before returning to university life. A devoted supporter of the Atlantic Alliance, he has particularly close affinities with US forces. His two books on a Third World War have sold more than two million copies worldwide.

INTRODUCTION BY MAJOR-GENERAL SIR JEREMY MOORE

When Britain dispatched a task force to recover the Falkland Islands after they had been invaded and garrisoned on the orders of the military junta in Argentina in the northern spring of 1982, it was manned and commanded, almost exclusively, by men without the actual experience of war. A number of us had taken part in minor operations at section and platoon or, in a few rare cases, company level.

All of us, except perhaps a few 'old salts' in some of the civilian-manned ships which did such sterling work, were too young to have had any part in the great battles of 1944 and 1945; most had not been born when the Second World War, or even that in Korea, came to an end. Yet a principal attribute of the members of that Task Force, acknowledged alike by friend and foe, and interested observer, was the great professionalism with which the campaign was so quickly, effectively and, furthermore, relatively cheaply, completed.

Soldiers of earlier centuries have frequently had the opportunity to study the elements of their calling at first hand, through a lifetime of fighting, sometimes under the command of, or alongside, their future enemy. For instance, Marlborough, at the age of 24, fought with the French under the great Marshal Turenne at the battles of Sinzheim and Enzheim. But for the British serviceman in the second half of the twentieth century, the only opportunity to learn his craft has been by study at second hand. For as long as it remained practicable, the training of British Army officers at the Staff College included visits to the battlefields of Normandy, with many of the participants in those battles, to learn how they had seen events and to hear of their experiences.

A successful commander must have a clear insight into all three of the elements in which he deals: men, material and ground. None of these is simple and the art of applying the first two to the last at the time, in the way and in the place where they will have the most devastating effect must be diligently learned. Without the benefit of actual participation, the ingenuity of the instructors who devise peacetime exercises, map studies, telephone battles simulating war in a classroom, tactical studies on the ground (the famous Tactical Exercise Without Troops, or TEWT) and occasional large-scale manoeuvres, though all very valuable in their own ways, are not enough. Future commanders must largely glean their 'experience' from history.

This book gives the reader as balanced a view of all the elements of command as the science and art of publishing can achieve in a single volume. It has always, for me, been one of the most fascinating facets of the study of the ground to visit battlefields and to try to envisage what the great commanders saw (and often were unable to see, but must have divined) to be able to achieve their great feats. In some cases, for instance at Blenheim and Ramilles, simply seeking a good place from which to view the scene draws one naturally to the place where a Eugène or a Marlborough stood, and helps one toward an understanding of the appreciation of ground. In others this is not possible, and in these circumstances, or for those who are unable to study battles except from an armchair, the combination of technology and art in this book will provide new insights.

Jeremy Moore

Major-General Sir Jeremy Moore, KCB, OBE, MC, was the victorious Commander of the British Land Forces in the Falkland Islands in May–July of 1982. As a career soldier in the Royal Marines he saw action in Malaya, Cyprus, Brunei, Sarawak and Northern Ireland during his 35-year span of service.

Alexander the Great *356-323 BC*

A lexander the Great was the supreme commander, the model of many of history's most talented tacticians and military leaders. Like all great commanders, Alexander inspired intense loyalty in his subordinates. His insistence on sharing every danger with his men, and the constant care he showed for their wellbeing, led them to proffer the same devotion and follow him for a decade on his campaigns through Persia and India. His magnetism, his charm, his physical beauty and his generosity bound almost all of them to him for life.

Alexander stands on the threshold of modern history as a figure at once brilliantly illuminated and tantalizingly elusive. He was below average stature, it was said, but remarkably handsome; certainly he was blond and had the luminous grey eyes of the visionary. And his vision was stupendous – no less than the conquest of the East. When he and his army crossed the Hellespont into Asia, Alexander's first act was to plunge his spear into the soil, thereby laying claim to the entire continent, and his life was dedicated to this end. At his death, his massive empire stretched from Illyria in the west to Kashmir in the east. He was 32 years old.

In childhood and youth, Alexander, heir to the Macedonian king, Philip II, had every educational and social advantage. The Greek philospher Aristotle was his tutor and had an abiding influence on him; his companions were chosen for their intelligence and standing, and the young Alexander was meticulously prepared for his future profession of soldier and king. Yet there was another, more sinister side to his upbringing, for his parents loathed each other. His mother Olympias entertained a possessive love for Alexander, while his father constantly belittled his achievements. Why the child, torn between his parental loyalties, did not develop into an unstable adult, as did the Roman emperor Nero, remains a mystery.

One result of Philip's attitude toward his son was that Alexander formed a passionate resolution to outshine his father in everything he did, and it was probably this that fuelled his ambition and drove him throughout his life. His childhood miseries may also have affected his adult sex life, for open, lasting relationships with other men were more important to him than any of his liaisons with women. On the death of Hephaestion – a young man of arresting appearance, whom he met in adolescence, and who became both a distinguished soldier and his boon companion – Alexander's grief was so extreme that the commander's generals feared, for a time, for his reason. By contrast, Alexander appears to have been only briefly infatuated with Roxane, a beautiful Persian girl who became one of his several wives.

Though a soldier's general, Alexander was also an aesthete. He was a lover of the theatre, of music, and especially of books, a collection of which he carried with him on his campaigns. But when the occasion demanded, Alexander was quick to show the ruthless side of his nature. In 330 BC, when a conspiracy was uncovered against him, supposedly led by the son of Parmenion, Alexander ordered the execution not only of the guilty son but also of the innocent father.

Inevitably Alexander, like any great historical figure and man of power, has his detractors. He has been portrayed as a sexual monster, and it has been rumoured that he fathered only one son because his potency was chronically diminished by alcohol. In his defence it must be said that Alexander was a young man who, according to his contemporaries, usually sat up over the wine with his commanders and friends for his pleasure of the discussion, on subjects ranging from warfare to philosophy. Equally, occasional drinking to excess was accepted by the Greeks as normal behaviour. Indeed, nothing that has been said about Alexander in malice can detract from his supremacy as a leader and a soldier.

Alexander the Great. This marble head, dating from the 2nd century BC, *was found at Pergamum in Turkey.*
Bronze statuette of the Roman Imperial Period, thought to represent Alexander.

BC	
356	*20/21 July* Born at Pella, son of King Philip of Macedonia.
340/ 339	Regent of Macedonia; defeats the Thracians and Illyrians.
338	*2 August* Leads the Macedonian cavalry at the Battle of Chaeronea against the Athenians.
336	*July* Succeeds Philip, aged 20.
335	Campaigns in Thrace and on the Danube; destroys rebellious Thebes.
334	Crosses the Hellespont into Asia. *May* Wounded at the Battle of the Granicus. Takes Miletus and Halicarnassus.
333	*November* Defeats King Darius III of Persia at the Battle of Issus (wounded).
332	*January–July* Takes Tyre and, *September*, Gaza (wounded). Reinforced in Egypt and Syria by troops from Greece
331	*1 October* **Battle of Gaugamela**. Enters Babylon and, *December*, Susa.
330	*January* Storms the Persian Gates, enters Persepolis and pursues Darius until *July*. Campaigns south of the Caspian Sea.
329	Operations near Maracanda (Samarkand) and in Afghanistan.
328	Campaigns in Bactria and Sogdiana (Russian Turkestan); marries Roxane.
327	Takes the Aornos Rock (Pir-Sar).
326	Invades India. *May* Defeats and captures King Porus at the Battle of the Hydaspes. *July* Mutiny at the River Hyphasis.
325	Sails down the River Indus to its mouth by *July*. *August–November* Crosses the Gedrosian (Makran) Desert; *20 December* meets his fleet near Hormozia (Hormuz).
324	*Summer* Stops the mutiny of the Macedonian veterans at Opis.
323	*10 June* Dies at Babylon, aged 32.

Battle of Gaugamela/*1 October 331 BC*

ALEXANDER'S GRAND STRATEGY may be simply stated. Since his army was small and his territorial ambitions great, he needed first to lure the Persian Army into battle and then destroy it. Ideally, he also needed to capture or kill Darius, the Persian king, since if he did the disparate tribes of the empire would probably accept him as Darius's successor.

Darius, the grandson of Artaxerxes II who had ruled Persia from 404–359 BC, had himself been raised to the throne only in 336 BC, when he was about 50 years old, by the eunuch Bagoas. This ambitious and unscrupulous man had previously murdered the two possible rivals for the Persian kingdom.

Alexander had defeated the Persian Army at Issus in 333 BC, two years before the Battle of Gaugamela. But at Issus Darius had fled and made good his escape. Now Alexander had to try again.

In July or early August 331 BC, Alexander and his army reached the city of Thapsacus on the Euphrates. He did not know exactly where Darius was, but calculated – in the event, correctly – that he would be raising and training a new army in the region of either Arbela or Babylon. These two cities were obvious targets for Alexander, so Darius had to guard them.

Conflict between Greece and Persia

The Greek City-States, though independent and frequently at war, were nevertheless loosely united, since all their citizens considered themselves to be Hellenes and all shared the same religious beliefs. Alexander united the City-States in a common cause – the conquest of Persia.

Between 500 and 449 BC, there was a series of wars between the City-States and the Persian Empire. Alexander's exploits, more than a century and a half later were a logical extension of this conflict.

In the time of King Darius I (r521–486), Persia controlled all of western Asia and Egypt and the king decided to annex Greece as well. But in 490 BC, despite earlier successes, the Persians were defeated by the Athenians at Marathon. However, Darius's son and successor, Xerxes I (r486–465 BC), renewed the struggle. Although Athens was captured in 480 BC, the Persian fleet was destroyed shortly afterwards by the Greeks near the island of Salamis.

The following period of stability enabled King Philip II of Macedonia (382–336 BC), who had reorganized his army and trained it in the phalanx formation, to make himself supreme in Greece by defeating the Athenians and the Thebans at the Battle of Chaeronea in 338 BC. Having consolidated his power, secured a lasting peace throughout Greece and laid the foundations of a formidable army, Philip then conceived the plan of removing Persian influence from Greek affairs for ever by invading the empire. He was preparing to march when he was assassinated.

Philip's success at home made possible the great achievements of his son. His plans had been for only a limited invasion; Alexander's to conquer Asia, an ambition that would take him to Gaugamela.

There were two possible routes for an army to take from Thapsacus to Babylon: either directly down the River Euphrates or northeast across Mesopotamia and then down the east side of the River Tigris. Darius and his staff calculated that it was overwhelmingly probable that Alexander would take the first route. He made his dispositions accordingly, expecting to meet Alexander in battle somewhere on the plains north of Babylon. Typically, Alexander chose the improbable option,

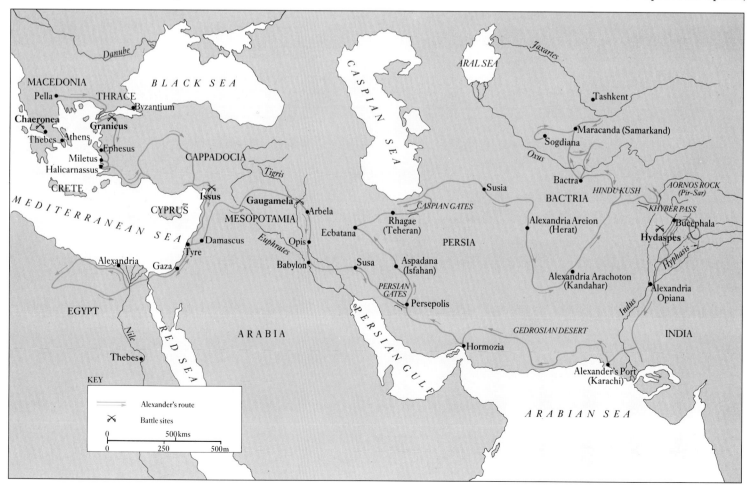

KEY

⟶ Alexander's route

✕ Battle sites

that of crossing Mesopotamia and coming south down the River Tigris.

Darius's first plan had, therefore, to be abandoned and a new one devised. Although his second plan was strategically sound, it was difficult to implement. Scouts were to observe Alexander's movements and calculate which ford on the Tigris he was making for. Once this had been established for certain, word was to be sent to Mazaeus, the Persian satrap of Babylon, who commanded an advance force. His orders were to march to the appropriate ford and make a show of defending it. Meanwhile, Darius's main army, which was already marching north via Arbela, would also hasten to the ford and destroy Alexander's army as it was making, or soon after it had accomplished, the crossing.

There were four possible crossing points from which Alexander could choose. From north to south, they were Jazirat-ibn-Omar, Abu Dhahir, Abu Wajnam and Mosul, the last being the most southerly ford and the one closest to Arbela. The Persians calculated that he would try to cross at Mosul on the hot river plain – indeed, that was the only point they had any hope of reaching in time. Typically again, Alexander confounded his enemies by taking the longer route, marching through the cooler northern uplands and making an unexpected crossing, although which of the three fords higher upstream he used is uncertain. What is known is that he was over the Tigris before the Persians had even found out which ford he intended to use.

The Persians' revised plan was, therefore, as redundant as their first. It is only possible to speculate, but the probability is that Darius was by now thoroughly off balance and his staff unsure. If so, this was the first dividend to accrue from Alexander's strategy.

Darius, however, still had one strong card to play. Because his army lay between Alexander's in the north and its target, Babylon, to the south, he could at least choose the battleground. The site he selected was a plain near Gaugamela and he quickly ordered the rough outcrops to be levelled to facilitate the passage of his chariots when they charged. The site was well chosen – or perhaps he came across it merely by chance – but it had one drawback: some 5km/3mls or so to the northwest was a range of hills, which the oncoming Alexander could use as a lookout post.

Early on the night of 30 September 331 BC, the armies were within striking distance of each other. There was great

The taming of Bucephalas
This bronze statuette of Alexander taming Bucephalas dates from the 4th century BC and is one of the earliest representations of this fabled event.

It seems that the fiery charger was offered to King Philip at a great price but refused to be mounted. The king, therefore, deemed him useless, but Alexander, then only eight or nine years old, insisted that the horse was unsurpassed. His father offered him a challenge: if Alexander could mount the steed, it would be bought for him; if he failed, he must pay for it himself. Legend has it that the boy, noticing the horse was startled by its own shadow, turned it into the sun and vaulted on to its back, winning the bet.

Bucephalas – 'Oxhead' – appears to have placed instant trust in Alexander, and as long as he lived would allow no one else to sit on his back.

War chariots
Chariot warfare originated in Mesopotamia soon after 3500 BC, when cities such as Ur relied upon two-wheeled and four-wheeled chariots as their main striking force. Drawn by onagers, or wild asses, these first chariots were heavy and clumsy and were probably used for frontal assault. With the invention of the lighter spoked wheel, chariots became more manoeuvrable, particularly when horses were introduced around 2000 BC.

The gradual growth of horsed cavalry, especially Persian, due to better breeding

Persian war chariot; detail from the 4th-century BC marble Alexander Sarcophagus.

and improved bits, downgraded the chariot everywhere in the ancient world to a vehicle for hunting and racing. By the time of Gaugamela, chariots were outmoded as a weapon of war, except in south India. Here the best horses were kept for chariots, and they persisted as a weapon for 700 years after Gaugamela, despite the fact that only five years later the 80-100 chariots used against Alexander at the Hydaspes by King Porus simply stuck in the mud.

The Issus Mosaic, found at Pompeii, was copied from a contemporary painting and shows the crucial moment of the Battle of Issus, with Alexander preparing to attack Darius in his war chariot. On this occasion, Darius fled to fight again and meet his ultimate defeat at Gaugamela.

Legends surrounding Alexander became more bizarre with each succeeding age, with fact and fantasy inextricably mixed. In this medieval French manuscript painting by Vauquelin, Alexander is portrayed in hose and doublet, seated on a mythical Bucephalas who has grown a unicorn's horn and a peacock's spreading tail.

disparity in their numbers. The Persian host comprised at least 100,000 infantry and 34,000 cavalry, many of high quality, notably the Cappadocians, who were newly equipped with link armour, a longer sword than hitherto and a spear instead of a javelin. Alexander's force, though it was the biggest he had ever commanded, comprised only, it is estimated, 40,000 infantry and 7,000 horsemen.

Alexander made a reconnaissance in person of the enemy's strength and dispositions and, despite the eagerness of most of his generals, he decided against an immediate night attack. Instead, he retired to his tent to devise his strategy. He ordered his troops to be well fed and then to rest. Darius, on the other hand, mindful of Alexander's unpredictable manoeuvres, ordered his army to stand to

throughout the night in readiness for a surprise attack. It is certain that the alertness of one side and the fatigue of the other played at least some part in the outcome of the battle next day.

Alexander worked late in his tent that night; then, his tactics clear in his mind, he retired to sleep. In the morning – he had ordered his troops to be ready to move before dawn – his generals found him

Macedonian heavy cavalry

The Companion cavalry, the king's own horseguard, originally numbered only 600; by 338BC they numbered 1,800. Initially they were equipped with white cuirasses made from linen-covered metal plates, Phrygian helmets, optional greaves and boots. They carried straight stabbing swords and the long cavalry spear, or *xyston*, that outreached Persian weapons. Dress included long-sleeved purple tunics and purple-bordered golden-yellow cloaks. Alexander replaced the Phrygian helmet with the broader Boeotian type, which protected the face and shoulder as well as giving better all-round vision. The Companions were born horsemen and, like all riders in the ancient world, rode without saddle or stirrups. Each man had a groom and marched on foot to spare his horse.

The Companion cavalry was divided into eight territorial squadrons, seven numbering 200 men, and the first, or Royal Squadron, being double strength. It was always posted on the right and contained Alexander's personal companions, led by Alexander, in battle mounted on Bucephalas. Each squadron was made up of four troops of 49 men, with a leader.

Battle formations adopted by the Companion cavalry included the square, the diamond and the wedge. The latter, invented by Philip, was most favoured, for the troop could be drawn up in the wedge with its leader at the apex, allowing a concentrated attack to be made on a narrow front.

Companion cavalryman

Boeotian helmet

The Macedonian phalanx

Foot companion

This pike-armed infantry formation, 16 men deep, was part of Alexander's military inheritance from his father. For more than 300 years Greek battles had been fought by formations, or phalanxes, of *hoplites*, usually eight men deep. These troops, named after their metal-covered round shields, were armed with spears up to 3.6m/ 12ft long, a sword and a *sarissa*, a two-handed pike originating from the Balkans which was about 4.8–5.5m/15–18ft long.

Alexander's phalanx, known as Foot Companions in recognition of their élite status, was 9,000 to 12,000 strong. They were divided into six regiments, each made up of three battalions of 512 men, who were deployed in 32 files, each of 16 men. The battalions were further divided into two *syntagma* of 256 men: 16 files of 16 men.

Constant drilling made the Macedonian phalanx formidable in action and able to adopt various formations. They advanced

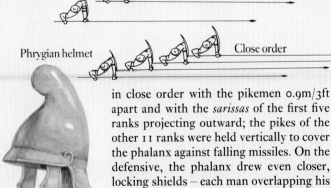

Advancing in open order

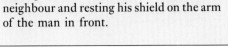

Phrygian helmet

Close order

in close order with the pikemen 0.9m/3ft apart and with the *sarissas* of the first five ranks projecting outward; the pikes of the other 11 ranks were held vertically to cover the phalanx against falling missiles. On the defensive, the phalanx drew even closer, locking shields – each man overlapping his neighbour and resting his shield on the arm of the man in front.

13

'sleeping like a child'; he had, indeed, to be shaken to be awakened. Such is the confidence of the supreme commander.

The Persian Army, outnumbering the Macedonians five to one, was drawn up in a line running west to east, with two powerful cavalry wings: on the right, the western cavalry, including the Cappadocians commanded by Mazaeus; on the left, cavalry from the eastern provinces commanded by Bessus, satrap of Bactria and Darius's cousin. Darius stationed himself in the centre, with 1,000 horseguards ahead of him, then 50 scythed chariots and, in front of these, 15 war elephants. Why these elephants were not eventually used in the battle is one of the minor imponderables of military history.

There were a further 100 scythed chariots on his left centre and 50 on his right centre. Scythed chariots, once effective but long discarded, had been reintroduced by Darius but there had not been enough time to train the charioteers fully.

The Macedonian line, being less numerous, was much shorter. Indeed, when the deployment was completed, Alexander, who stationed himself on the right wing, was almost immediately opposite Darius in the Persian centre. It was certain that Darius would try to outflank him and that the front line of Persian cavalry and chariots would attack early. Alexander had, therefore, no alternative but to adopt a defensive stance. Thus he stationed his phalanx in the centre, strongly supported on its flanks by deep formations which were turned back at an angle of 45 degrees at their extremes to prevent encirclement.

On the left, Parmenion commanded the Thessalian cavalry, on the right, Philotas commanded the Companion cavalry, half the Macedonian archers and – shortly to be a disposition of crucial importance – units of javelinmen. Since Alexander could be outflanked with comparative ease, his line being only half as long as that of the Persians, he deepened his flanks with reserves, who were ordered to turn about if encirclement seemed likely.

In this disposition, the Companions were opposite the scythed chariots. Alexander started moving to the right so that the infantry, who were far less vulnerable to a chariot charge, were opposite them. This manoeuvre had the additional advantage of reducing the Persian overlap. He continued moving units to his right until the outermost formations reached the end of Darius's area of flattened ground, beyond which rough going would inhibit the progress of chariots. The trap had been set; it was now to be sprung.

Silver coin issued by Ptolemy, showing Alexander wearing an elephant head-dress.

Alexander appears as a Roman emperor on this gold medallion from Abukir in Egypt.

Gold medallion from Abukir: Alexander wears the horns of the Egyptian god Ammon.

For Darius had little option but to attack Alexander's right wing to maintain his overlap. Darius launched his Scythian cataphracts (heavy armoured cavalry), then his Bactrian cavalry, against Alexander's extreme right. A heavy fight ensued but they were held off.

Soon afterward, in support of the Bactrians, Darius ordered the 100 chariots on his centre left to charge. Now the Macedonian javelinmen came into their own. A flurry of javelins threw the charioteers into confusion; many were killed, most of the horses shied away and bolted. The remaining chariots, those which reached the phalanx, were borne remorselessly forward through a well-disciplined opening formed by the infantry ranks – only to be eliminated by the second line of Macedonian infantry.

Darius now saw that Alexander was – or appeared to be – fully engaged on his right flank and judged the moment opportune to order the entire line of Persian cavalry to advance in two – hopefully decisive – enveloping attacks. This optimism was misplaced. Had Darius concentrated his attack against the Companions, the battle's outcome might have been different; but the blow was aimed toward the far right of the Greek Army, and a gap developed in the Persian front.

This was Alexander's moment. Planning and preparation, guile, manoeuvring, foresight – all are necessary in battle, but the crowning mark of a supreme commander is the ability to seize, not with conscious thought but by instinct, the absolute second at which to commit himself. Alexander now led the Companions in a ferocious charge straight at King Darius himself.

As Alexander, at the apex of the charge, had almost reached the royal chariot, Darius lost heart and nerve. His charioteer wounded, the king seized the reins, turned the chariot about and was the first to leave the field. The Persian centre, mistakenly thinking the wounded charioteer to be Darius, began to disintegrate.

The battle was not yet over, however. The advance of the Companions and battalions of the phalanx in their wake had left a gap in the Greek centre, which Darius's Persian Guard and Indian cavalry quickly penetrated. Had they then turned right against Parmenion, who was hard pressed, the entire Greek left would have been in peril. Instead, they galloped on to loot Alexander's baggage train some distance in the rear.

Parmenion was nevertheless obliged to send urgently to Alexander for assistance. As Field Marshal Viscount Montgomery later wrote, it is 'an indication of Alexander's extraordinary control that he succeeded in turning the Companions immediately, and led them across to the other side of the battle.' Before Alexander reached Parmenion, however, he was obliged to fight a cavalry action with the Persian Guard returning from looting his base camp. When he finally reached Parmenion, he found that the Thessalians had beaten off the Persian right and the situation had been restored.

Many Persians were by now aware that Darius had fled, and they lost heart. Mazaeus felt, with justice, that his obligations to the Great King were at an end and extricated his men as best he could. Bessus and his force on the Persian left also deserted the field.

It now only remained for Alexander to order a general pursuit to ensure that the Persians could never re-form as an army. His chase of 56km/35mls to Arbela was so fierce that, it is said, 1,000 horses perished. Darius's abandoned chariot was found, but the king himself had vanished. No matter. Alexander now held Darius in such contempt that he would not demean himself by seeming to value his capture.

The Chigi Relief, from which this drawing was made, is a small yellow marble panel about 14cm/5½in long by 9cm/3½in wide. It dates from AD 14–37, the time of the Roman Emperor Tiberius. Discovered by Prince Chigi in 1780, it is now kept in the Palazzo Chigi in Rome. The inscription in Greek across the top explains that the circular medallion depicts the battle between Greek and Persian cavalry at Gaugamela. Below is an altar dedicated to Alexander. The two draped figures represent Europe and Asia and signify Alexander's empire, linking the two continents.

Alexander, riding Bucephalas, is shown attacking Persian warriors in this relief from the Alexander Sarcophagus.

Instead, he at once began to lay plans for campaigns to extend his empire eastward.

Gathering up his army, Alexander marched to Babylon, where he accepted the surrender of Mazaeus and rested his troops. He then marched on to Susa and through the Persian Gates to Persepolis, remaining there for four months and finally looting and burning Darius's palaces. Early in 330 BC, his pursuit of Darius took him northeastward; after Darius's death and the surrender of one of his murderers and erstwhile generals, Nabazarnes, Alexander pressed on

Battle of Gaugamela/4

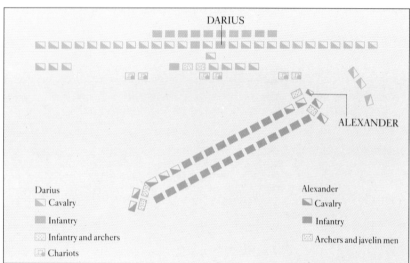

Dispositions before Alexander's attack

Alexander's army was outnumbered five to one, so he needed to lure Darius into an attack, which would exhaust the Persians and give him the opportunity for a decisive riposte. This tactic of attack from a defensive position, brilliantly executed by Alexander, was also successfully used by Henry V at the Battle of Agincourt and by von Manstein at Kharkov. Darius had previously had a great area of ground cleared and flattened so that his charging chariots would not be hampered.

Alexander's response was to march his army from its original disposition steadily to the right, at an angle, to prevent Darius's much larger army from enveloping his right flank. By moving his force to the extreme edge of the flattened ground, Alexander provided a safe anchor for his right wing.

Darius, (2) confident that Alexander was preoccupied with the fighting on his right wing, judged the moment opportune to order his cavalry wings to charge in two enveloping manoeuvres.

Alexander (1) had made his dispositions in anticipation of precisely this move, for by again attacking Alexander's right wing, Darius could not prevent a gap forming in his own left wing. The moment had come for Alexander's own decisive charge.

Mounted on the 24-year-old Bucephalas, Alexander at once led his Companion cavalry **(4)** in a fierce charge straight at Darius, an imposing figure, 2m/6½ft tall. Alexander had almost reached the royal chariot when Darius, fearing for his life, seized the reins from his fatally wounded charioteer, turned the chariot about and fled the field of Gaugamela.

The Battle of Gaugamela opened early in the day on 1 October 331 BC, when Darius launched his Scythian cavalry against Alexander's extreme right wing and almost succeeded in turning the Macedonian line. The Persians were, however, disconcerted to find infantry among Alexander's horse who brought them to close combat.

2

At the same time, the 100 scythed chariots on Darius's centre left were loosed. But as a result of Alexander's move to the right, they were now opposite the Macedonian infantry, who were far less vulnerable to a chariot charge than were cavalry.

Alexander's archers let fly their arrows, and his javelinmen (3) advanced to meet the charge. With a flurry of their long javelins, they threw the chariots into confusion, killing or wounding many drivers and horses. Some of the horses shied and bolted to left and right; others had their bridles seized by javelinmen, and drivers were torn from their positions. Many chariots passed harmlessly through well-disciplined openings formed by the ranks of infantry, to be destroyed in the Macedonian rear.

The Persian centre, who had witnessed the scene, at first thought Darius had been killed and began to disintegrate. Soon, however, they and troops on both wings of the Persian Army realized that the king had fled; they, too, lost heart and gave up the fight.

Alexander ordered a general pursuit. Darius's chariot was found abandoned, but the king had escaped.

Macedonian losses at Gaugamela were put at no more than 500; the lowest figure for Persian casualties has been given as 40,000.

through Bactria, beyond the River Oxus, in pursuit of Bessus, the second murderer. Bessus himself was betrayed by his own men when they heard of Alexander's approach, tried in a Persian court as a common criminal and executed.

Alexander was now indisputably head of the Persian Empire, and was regarded as such by the people. Many of his soldiers were, however, dissatisfied with the prospect of further campaigning after their many years of soldiering far from home; moreover they resented Alexander's adopting Persian customs and attire, fearing that he might in turn become as despotic as the Persian kings had been.

Nevertheless, Alexander now advanced deep into Sogdiana, and it was here that he encountered and married Roxane, the daughter of a local chieftain. For a time he seems to have been captivated by her, but the marriage scandalized some among his Macedonians, and a plot was hatched to kill Alexander. It failed, and once again in supreme command over his army, Alexander mobilized to march east into India. He overran the Punjab, defeating the Indian King Porus at the Battle of Hydaspes. Beyond that point, however, his men refused to go; it was eight years since they left Greece; they had fought numerous battles and marched some 27,400km/17,000mls.

Accepting the ultimatum from his men, Alexander prepared to turn his back on India. He had already built a fleet of ships and now took it down the River Indus to its mouth; from there he sent it under Nearchus on the uncharted voyage to the Persian Gulf. Meanwhile, he and his army marched homeward across the desert region of southern Persia, with a small force under Craterus taking a more northerly route. On 20 December 325, he met his fleet at Hormozia (Hormuz) and returned to Babylon. Here, early in 323 BC after a campaign against the Cossaean

Alexander's funeral procession.

The signs of hardship, sickness and grief can be seen in the face of Alexander the warrior, depicted on this gold medallion from Abukir.

nomads, he settled down to plan an attack on Arabia, but contracted a fever, probably from drinking polluted water, from which he died on 10 June.

Alexander's funeral car was magnificent. It took nearly two years to make and cost was not considered. The coffin was of gold; on the pall of embroidered purple were displayed Alexander's helmet, armour and arms. Ionic columns of gold on the sides of the catafalque supported a roof of gold, set with jewels and surmounted by a massive wreath of olive leaves in gold. At each corner of the roof was a golden figure of Victory, holding a trophy.

Beneath the cornice hung a painted frieze on which were depicted elements of Alexander's life: war elephants, ships, and cavalry, and Alexander himself in his chariot with his Persian and Macedonian bodyguards. The entire edifice was embellished with precious stones and the entrance guarded by gold lions.

It took 64 mules, each adorned with a crown and a collar studded with gems, to pull the massive catafalque on which rested Alexander's embalmed body. On its ponderous, 1,600km/1,000ml journey across Asia it inspired admiration and awe in all who beheld it. And when it reached Egypt, Alexander was entombed in similar splendour at the city that still bears his name; whether his tomb remains buried under the débris of time, is not known.

Darius III, King of Persia r336–330 BC

Darius's decisive defeats at Issus and Gaugamela derive from many factors, not least his failure to delegate command, even though he had capable officers in Mazaeus and Bessus. Thus he matched himself alone against Alexander's genius, and although he was a sometimes daring and ingenious commander, he lacked Alexander's drive and his ability to seize the propitious moment. At Gaugamela, Darius's advantage in numbers, both in cavalry and infantry, was dissipated by his losing the initiative and failing to attack early with his right wing; in addition, his reliance on scythed chariots, already outmoded weapons, was misplaced.

Darius fled from both battles. At Issus there was justification, since he personified the Persian Empire and his death or capture would have heralded its disintegration. He fled to raise a new army and to fight another day, although his whole family was captured. But at Gaugamela his premature flight ended any hope for Persia's future under his

Persian gold coin showing Darius III running and bearing a bow, the symbol of authority.

rule; during the following six months he managed to raise only 3,000 cavalry and 34,000 infantry.

Alexander remained at Persepolis for four months, then pursued Darius north toward Ecbatana (Hamadan). There he heard that Darius had fled northeast through the pass in the Elburz Mountains known as the Caspian Gates. Alexander continued his chase and at Rhagae, near modern Teheran, learned that his enemy, now demoralized and ineffectual, had been imprisoned by Bessus and Nabarzanes, two powerful commanders disillusioned with his rule. Darius's hitherto loyal Persian Guard, seeing the hopelessness of resisting Alexander further, had abandoned him.

Alarmed that Darius might, under duress, confer legality on a successor by abdicating in favour of either man, Alexander led a troop of horsemen overnight at a wild gallop across some 64km/40mls of sandflats to intercept the Persians. In the morning they sighted a line of carts in the distance. Darius was not with the caravan, but later they found him in an abandoned wagon, murdered. Alexander wrapped the corpse in his own cloak and had it taken to Persepolis for royal burial.

The influence of Alexander

Alexander's empire did not long survive his death, in part because he had not named a successor, and his son by Roxane, the future Alexander IV, was as yet unborn. His generals quarrelled among themselves, each seeking to carve out a greater sphere of influence for himself. Three major powers resulted: Macedonia, dominant in Greece; the Seleucid kingdom, comprising much of the old Persian Empire; and Egypt, where the dynasty founded by Alexander's friend and biographer, Ptolemy, remained supreme for almost 300 years, until it was extinguished by the venom of Cleopatra's asp in 30 BC.

Although Alexander's empire proved ephemeral, its impact on world history was profound and lasting. Alexander had founded some 70 cities, many bearing his name, both as strongholds and cultural and trade centres, thereby spreading Greek ideals and knowledge eastward as far as China. Evidence of the extent of Hellenistic influence is still being found: an ancient city, dating from Seleucid times or even from the time of Alexander, was uncovered at Ai Khanum in Afghanistan during the 1960s. Here there is a theatre, an *agora* (market place), a gymnasium, colonnades and temples – all the elements of a great Greek city that flourished for centuries. Even some early Buddhist sculptures found in India shows stylistic characteristics drawn from Greek work.

Alexander's interests had been almost limitless, among them warfare, medicine, botany, zoology and astrology – subjects which would be taught in many universities he established. One of the most prestigious seats of learning was at Alexandria in Egypt, where a great library grew up also and where many famous scholars taught, including the mathematician Euclid.

When Rome gained control of the Hellenistic world after 190 BC, Greek culture rapidly infused that of Rome, and together they formed the basis of modern western culture.

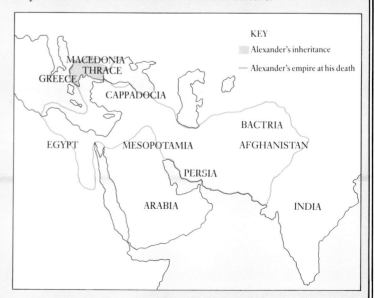

KEY
▓ Alexander's inheritance
— Alexander's empire at his death

MACEDONIA
THRACE
GREECE
CAPPADOCIA
EGYPT
MESOPOTAMIA
PERSIA
BACTRIA
AFGHANISTAN
ARABIA
INDIA

Scipio Africanus *236-183 BC*

B y curious chance, the first recorded incident in the life of Publius Cornelius Scipio – known as Scipio Africanus following his victories in North Africa – was at the cavalry action on the River Ticinus in 218 BC, the first engagement fought on the Italian mainland by his later rival, Hannibal. Scipio was 17 years old at the time, and an incident during the battle was to influence his conduct in warfare all his life.

Scipio's father, the leader of the Roman force, had given his son command of an élite body of cavalry to ensure his safety. But when the young Scipio saw that his father was wounded and cut off by the Carthaginians, he urged his squadron to the rescue. They refused because of the overwhelming numbers of the enemy; whereupon Scipio galloped toward the foe alone. Shamed by the youth's courage, his horsemen followed, and the elder Scipio was saved. Having once demonstrated his bravery, however, Scipio never again exposed himself to danger in battle.

We next hear of the young Scipio in a political role. His elder brother Lucius was a candidate for the aedileship – the first step to the higher Roman magistracy – but had little hope of election. Scipio, seeing that his brother's prospects were forlorn but could probably be realized if they both stood, told his mother that he had experienced two identical dreams in which she wept with joy and kissed both her sons on their election to aedileship. Scipio implored her to provide him with a white toga, the garment worn by candidates, which she did despite his extreme youth.

In the event, both brothers were elected and, astonished and overjoyed, their mother greeted them with tears and embraces, just as foretold in Scipio's dreams. From this stemmed two important consequences. Scipio was credited with powers of divination, which both then and later he neither encouraged nor denied, leaving the Romans to think what they would. It also provoked the beginnings of that jealous enmity in his contemporaries that was always to plague him.

Scipio's military and political promotion was rapid. In about 211 BC he volunteered for, and was elected to, the proconsulship in Spain, where the Roman forces had been shattered by the Carthaginians and forced to retreat north of the River Ebro. There were three widely dispersed Carthaginian armies in the peninsula. Most commanders would have attacked first one then the next. But Scipio, with an astuteness astonishing in one so young, saw with clarity the overall situation and struck both on land and by sea at the Carthaginian base and lifeline, the great depot of New Carthage, today's Cartagena. He took it in a single day.

Several aspects of Scipio's character were revealed by this successful operation. Not only did it demonstrate his command of both strategy and tactics but his foresight and humanity, for he offered lenient surrender terms and, on his orders, the inevitable massacre was limited. Indeed, the historian Polybius wrote that, after the city had fallen, some Roman soldiers brought an attractive young girl to Scipio as a gift. Although struck by her beauty and much enamoured of women, Scipio at once handed her to the man of her choice. When in gratitude the parents pressed gifts on him, he gave these too to the bridegroom, as a dowry. This act was as shrewd as it was kindly, for his troops and the local population, who quickly heard of it, held him in even greater regard for his forbearance.

Of the Roman leaders who are commonly known, few were without blemish. Scipio comes nearest to fulfilling the Roman ideal: proud but not haughty; ambitious only for his country; and a consummate commander who took the longer view – that magnanimity in victory was more likely than vengeful oppression to secure lasting peace.

BC	
236/5	Born into a patrician Roman family.
218	*November* Commands cavalry against Hannibal at the Battle of the Ticinus under his father, whom he saves from death.
216	*August* Survives the Battle of Cannae as a military tribune.
211	Appointed to command in Spain, with proconsular powers.
209	Captures New Carthage (Cartagena) in a surprise attack.
208	Defeats Hasdrubal, Hannibal's brother, at the Battle of Baecula.
206	Fights the Battle of Ilipa, which ends Carthaginian rule in Spain; defeats Spanish tribes at the Battle of the Ebro.
205	Returns to Rome in triumph. Elected consul; based on Sicily, where he raises a volunteer army. Takes Locri from Hannibal.
204	Invades North Africa and defeats the Carthaginian cavalry at the Tower of Agathocles, but fails to take Utica.
203	*June?* Defeats the Carthaginians at the Battle of the Great Plains; Hannibal is summoned back to Carthage.
202	*October* Defeats Hannibal at the **Battle of Zama**.
201	Returns to Rome, is granted a formal triumph and takes the name Africanus. Retires into private life.
194	Elected consul for the second time.
184	Forced into exile by a plot against him led by Cato the Elder.
183	Dies at Liternum, aged 52/3.

Scipio Africanus, as he must have appeared at the time of Zama; late 3rd- or early 2nd-century carving on a gold signet ring by the sculptor Herakleidas.
Marble relief of an armed cavalryman found in the forum at Rome; 2nd century BC.

Battle of Zama/*October 202 BC*

WITHIN A FEW years of his swift capture of New Carthage in 209 BC, Scipio had defeated the Carthaginians in Spain. In 205 BC, as consul, he advocated carrying the war to Africa, but his enemies in the Roman Senate, motivated by jealousy and spite, granted him leave to go only as far as Sicily and did not provide him with an army. Once there, however, Scipio raised and trained a volunteer force and the following year was given leave to invade Africa. At Zama, late in 202 BC, he was to achieve the victory that stamped him for all time as one of the world's great commanders.

Scipio established his base at Utica, northwest of Carthage. When he learned that Hannibal and his army had landed at Hadrumentum, to the southeast, he began to advance westward from Utica up the Bagradas Valley, the rich and fruitful interior region from which Carthage harvested its supplies.

This strategic move has often been cited as the supreme example of Scipio's military genius, for it achieved several objectives simultaneously. Not only did Scipio overrun the Carthaginian economic base, while still protecting his own, but he lured Hannibal away from Carthage. As the military historian Sir Basil Liddell Hart

Rome and Carthage at war

War between the empires of Carthage and Rome seems, at first glance, to have been unlikely and unnecessary. The Carthaginians were traditionally traders, the Romans, farmers and there was, apparently, no great conflict of interest. They were, however, suspicious of each other, and Rome was alarmed at Carthage's growing hold on the western Mediterranean.

The First Punic War (264–241 BC) grew out of a quarrel between the Sicilian cities of Messana (Messina), backed by Carthage, and Syracuse, backed by Rome. Since the Strait of Messana, separating Sicily from Italy, was of great strategic importance, hostilities became inevitable. The war, fought mainly at sea, dragged on, with the new Roman Navy generally victorious, and eventually the Carthaginians sued for peace.

The Second Punic War (218–201 BC), provoked by Carthaginian expansion in Spain, was sparked off by their general Hannibal's siege and capture in 219 BC of Saguntum, a city allied to Rome. This success opened the way for Hannibal to make his celebrated crossing of the Alps into Italy. His triumphant campaigns there lasted for 16 years, and it was not until Scipio was given permission by Rome to implement his grand strategy of invading North Africa and threatening Carthage that Hannibal was obliged to evacuate Italy to go to the defence of the city.

observed: 'The more one studies and reflects on this manoeuvre, the more masterly does it appear as a subtly blended fulfilment of the principles of war.'

Within a few days, Hannibal and his army reached Zama, southeast of Scipio's position. From there he sent out scouts to locate and reconnoitre the Roman camp. Three of the scouts were captured and taken before Scipio who did not punish them as generals ordinarily did, but showed them all the Roman dispositions and then sent them back to Hannibal's camp with an escort. This – as it was intended to do – demonstrated both to Hannibal and his troops Scipio's great self-confidence.

Before battle was joined, Hannibal asked Scipio for a parley. Whether he solicited this out of curiosity to meet so

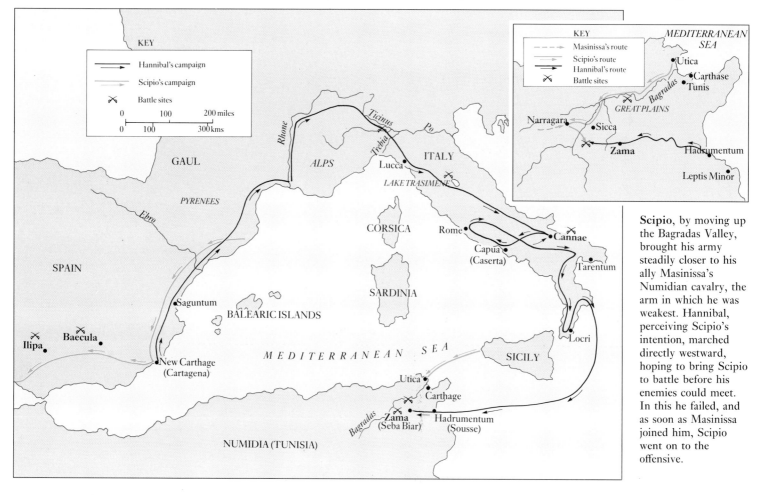

Scipio, by moving up the Bagradas Valley, brought his army steadily closer to his ally Masinissa's Numidian cavalry, the arm in which he was weakest. Hannibal, perceiving Scipio's intention, marched directly westward, hoping to bring Scipio to battle before his enemies could meet. In this he failed, and as soon as Masinissa joined him, Scipio went on to the offensive.

unusual a commander, or whether it was a sagacious move on his part to secure peace terms, since he was deficient in cavalry, the arm that had always brought him victory, is uncertain. What is known, however, is that Scipio agreed, though prudently delaying the meeting until Masinissa and his cavalry had reached him. During the intervening period, Scipio moved his camp to a site close to the town of Narragara that had running water nearby. Hannibal also moved his army forward to occupy a commanding hill, but by doing so distanced his troops from water; this was later to give Scipio a considerable advantage.

The weight of evidence suggests that Hannibal's request for parley was a serious peace initiative rather than mere curiosity, for there was another crucial factor in his situation and one over which he had no

War elephants

The first recorded use of war elephants was their deployment by Darius at Gaugamela. The Indian elephants, complete with towers containing several soldiers, so impressed Alexander and his successors that, from 326 BC onward, Hellenistic armies generally included them. Thus the Carthaginians first encountered elephants in 272 BC when King Pyrrhus of Epirus invaded Sicily, and they rapidly phased out their chariots for the new weapon.

Hannibal took 37 elephants on his great march over the Alps, but only seven survived the Battle of Trebia in 218 BC, and of these just one lived through the winter. Although in 215 BC Hannibal was sent more animals for use during his Italian campaigns, their part is seldom recorded. By

Silver coin from New Carthage.

202 BC the stables at Carthage, with room for 300 elephants, were empty, so 80 new, untrained beasts were rapidly collected for Hannibal's army.

control: Rome had command of the Mediterranean Sea. Thus Scipio had less to lose in defeat, for another Roman army could in time be raised and ferried to Africa, and everything to gain in victory, since Carthage would then be at his mercy. Hannibal, on the other hand, had less to gain in victory, for he would inevitably have to fight another battle sooner or later, but absolutely everything to lose in defeat. Put another way: a Carthaginian victory would merely prolong the war, but a Carthaginian defeat would end it in Rome's favour.

It is not certain what Hannibal's peace terms were – probably that Carthage

would withdraw from Italy if Rome withdrew from Africa – but Scipio rejected them and battle was joined the next day.

The dispositions of the rival forces comprised some original features. To consider Scipio's deployment first. In the front line, he placed his two legions of Roman heavy foot and to either side of them his cavalry – Laelius and his Italian horse on the left wing, Masinissa and the Numidians on the right. The infantry was drawn up in the customary three lines: the *hastati* in the van, the *principes* behind them and the *triarii* at the rear. But in their respective dispositions, Scipio introduced a subtle and effective innovation.

Scipio, and Hannibal parleying before Zama; tapestry by the Flemish maker Van der Streecken in the Palazzo Quirinale, Rome.

Roman generals normally stationed their maniples – subdivisions of a legion comprising either 120 or 160 men – in much the same way as the black and white squares on a chequerboard: those of the second line were positioned behind the intervals in the front line and so on. At Zama, however, Scipio stationed the middle and rear lines of maniples immediately behind those of the front line. This produced lanes between the cohorts, through which he hoped Hannibal's 80

Battle of Zama/2

At the Battle of Zama, Hannibal tried to disrupt the Roman Army by launching his elephants at its centre. Successful penetration of the enemy's centre offers the prospect of his encirclement on both right and left. If the move is to have any hope of success, the attacker's flanks must usually be dangerously weakened to provide sufficient impact at the point of attack.

If the attack fails, as Hannibal's did because Scipio anticipated his move and because his elephants stampeded, the attacker may find his army thrown into confusion and demoralized.

Hannibal opened the Battle of Zama, on a hot, windless, early autumn day, by ordering his 80 elephants, stationed in the centre of his army ahead of his front line of infantry (6), to charge the Roman centre.

These now-extinct forest elephants from the Atlas Mountains stood only some 2.5m/ 8ft at the shoulder and carried one, or at most two, javelinmen or archers in addition to the driver.

Scipio, stationed to the rear of his army, ordered a blare of trumpets along his entire front line when the charging elephants were almost on top of his men. This strident noise terrified the animals, most of which turned and careered back into the Carthaginian troops. Many crashed into Hannibal's best cavalry, the Numidians on his left (7), who were about to charge, and threw them into confusion, panicking the horses.

Scipio had deployed his *hastati*, heavy infantry, with the maniples (2) one behind the other so as to leave lanes between them (3). These afforded obvious routes of escape for the elephants, all now terrified and many wounded by the javelins of the *velites* (4). Those that did not turn back, passed through the Roman lines to the rear.

Numidian horsemen fought on both sides at Zama, for although Numidia, Land of the Nomads (present-day Algeria), was traditionally the ally of Carthage, Scipio had won over King Masinissa, who brought with him 4,000 cavalry and 6,000 infantry.

The Numidians, (1,7) were the finest horsemen in the world at the time; they rode bareback with only a simple rope neck harness to direct their sturdy, fleet mounts.

The horsemen wore short, sleeveless tunics, tied with a belt of rope, and carried small round shields and a number of javelins, which they used in hit and run attacks.

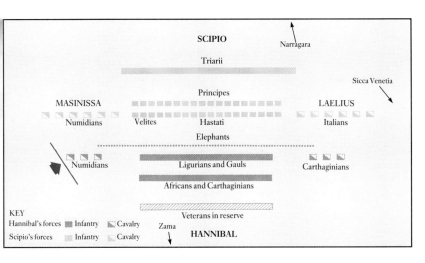

King Masinissa on the Roman right, seeing the confusion among the Carthaginian cavalry ahead of him, immediately ordered his Numidians (1) to charge and drove the enemy from the field. The stampeding elephants created almost equal confusion on Hannibal's right, and the Italian cavalry under Laelius seized the opportunity to strike. Both cavalry wings of Hannibal's army were thus routed within minutes of the first attack.

Elephant drivers were equipped with a hammer and spike (5), which they drove into the animal's brain if it ran amok. In the confusion following the Roman's blare of trumpets, the drivers did not have time to destroy their mounts before they smashed back into their own soldiers.

Of Hannibal's 80 elephants used at Zama, 11 were killed and the others either bolted to safety or were captured and later paraded at Scipio's formal triumph in Rome the following year.

The Carthaginian and Roman infantry were evenly matched, and the fighting between them that followed was inconclusive. But Scipio won the day at Zama when his two cavalry wings, having driven off the Carthaginian cavalry and scattered them, returned at the crucial moment and took Hannibal's army in the rear, before he had a chance to use his veterans from Italy.

elephants, if spurred by Roman javelins, would pass harmlessly to his rear, since elephants, like horses, will always take the easiest route of escape. Scipio had already encountered some 36 elephants at the Battle of Ilipa in Spain, where they had presented no problem.

There was a further advantage to this disposition: the *velites*, or skirmishers, whom Scipio placed in the spaces in the front line and who were to open the action, could retire either to the rear or laterally, behind the second line of infantry.

The Carthaginian disposition, since Hannibal was outnumbered in cavalry, was devised to make maximum use of his 80 elephants. A single elephant might disrupt an army, 80 must surely destroy it; such was Hannibal's thinking. He therefore placed his elephants in the centre, ahead of the front line of infantry. Behind the elephants were Ligurian and Gallic infantry, with Numidian cavalry to their left and Carthaginian cavalry to their right. Behind the infantry in the centre was ranged a line of Carthaginian and African infantry levies; these, having been hastily raised, were Hannibal's least reliable troops. His élite force, veterans of his Italian campaigns, were kept in the rear as the third line, to protect them from Roman attacks until such time as Hannibal saw fit to employ them.

Numerical strengths are not precisely known, but the probability is that the total Carthaginian force numbered a little more than 50,000, the Romans about 35,000. The conflict, which was to prove one of the decisive battles of history, fell into three phases. Hannibal's plan was to break his enemy's front and for this, in the early stages, he relied heavily on his elephants. In the event, they were his undoing.

The first major encounter followed Hannibal's order to the elephant drivers to charge the Roman centre. A scene of the utmost pandemonium shortly ensued. As the charging elephants neared the Roman line, Scipio ordered a blare of trumpets and cornets along his entire front. The effect was dramatic. Terrified at the unexpected, strident noise, most of the elephants turned about and careered back toward their own lines. The majority turned about left, crashing into Hannibal's best cavalry, the Numidians. Masinissa, on the Roman right, seeing the confusion ahead of him, immediately charged Hannibal's left-wing cavalry and drove it from the field.

Other elephants, many now wounded, lumbered to safety through the openings in the Roman lines – just as Scipio had hoped – and still others turned about right

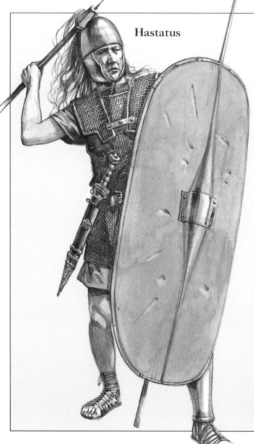

Hastatus

The Carthaginian Army
Carthage relied principally on African, Spanish (after 342 BC) or Celtic mercenaries for her army, rather than on her own citizens, who rowed her warships instead. Zama, where Hannibal's second line consisted of 12,000 Carthaginian and African levies, was an exception. The one standing unit was the 2,500-strong Sacred Band of cavalry, drawn from the city's best families, which served also as an officer training unit. Although not specifically mentioned at Zama, it could have comprised most of Hannibal's 2,000 right-wing heavy cavalry.

Unlike those of Rome, Carthage's forces were not heterogeneous in organization or armament and their quality depended entirely on their own leaders and the general in overall command. Hannibal's third line of veterans, mainly Bruttians from the toe of Italy, had long been equipped largely with captured Roman mail shirts, shields and javelins, and they fought in maniples. The troops from Carthage may have had Greek-type shields, pikes and helmets.

The Roman Republican legion
The army Scipio led to victory in the Second Punic War had evolved from Camillus's reforms in the 380s BC. He paired the legion's 60 centuries, each with 60 men, into maniples, which became the new tactical unit of 120–160 men. The legion was to fight not as a phalanx but in three lines of 10 maniples each. Men aged 17 to 46 were eligible for service, according to property qualifications.

In front were the poorest and youngest, acting as *velites*, light troops armed with javelins 1.2m/4ft long and 1m/3¼ft leather shields. The first line of *hastati* (spearmen) were more experienced and, like the second line *principes* (leaders), were armed with two 2.1m/7ft *pila*, or throwing javelins – one light and one heavy – and a short cut-and-thrust sword of Greek origin. Lastly came the veteran *triarii* (third liners), with only 60–80 to the maniple, carrying the original long 4m/13ft spear. All legionaries carried a 1.2m/4ft oval shield and wore a mail shirt. Attached to each legion were 300 cavalry, and an equal number of allied troops, organized in a similar legion.

engagement – opened. The opposing first line formations advanced upon each other, but Hannibal's Gauls and Ligurians, though at first having the best of it, could not break the Roman *hastati*. Then the weight of Roman infantry began to force them back. The Carthaginian and African levies in the second line, to keep their formation intact, failed to support the Gauls and Ligurians who, feeling they had been betrayed, turned and fled.

Hannibal's second line of infantry then threw back the Roman *hastati*, who were struggling forward across ground littered with corpses and abandoned weaponry and by now slippery with the blood of the fallen. At this point, however, officers of the *principes* ordered their men forward in support. Because the Roman line was longer than that of the Carthaginians, the latter became hemmed in and were cut down. Now they, like the Gauls and Ligurians before them, fled to the safety of the rear.

But Hannibal now had another enemy – time. He must have known that Scipio's superlative control of his troops would ensure that his cavalry commanders would return to the battle as soon as they had seen off the Carthaginian and Numidian cavalry. Their reappearance must therefore be expected – and sooner rather than later. Though for Hannibal speed was of the essence, all was certainly not yet lost

and crashed into Hannibal's right-wing cavalry. This formation was likewise thrown into disorder, and Laelius immediately ordered a charge, driving them from the field also. Thus both Hannibal's protective flanks were broken.

Now the second phase – the infantry

for the Carthaginians. Hannibal's 24,000 veterans from Italy were in perfect order and unfatigued by combat – and they were under Hannibal's personal command.

A most remarkable episode marked the beginning of the third phase of the battle. In the heat and confusion, Scipio recalled his leading infantry and re-formed them: a tribute indeed to his overall control. He closed up his *hastati* in the centre, then each half of his *principes* and *triarii* on either flank, to form a compact force. Violence of attack was now his objective; hitherto it had been length of line to provide maximum striking power.

Polybius wrote that 'the two lines charged each other with the greatest fire and fury. Being nearly equal in numbers, spirit, courage and arms, the battle was for a long time undecided, the men in their obstinate valour falling dead without giving way a step.' Then, the outcome still unresolved, the cavalry of Masinissa and Laelius returned to the scene, took the Carthaginians in the rear and cut them down without difficulty.

Both Polybius and the later Roman historian Livy put Carthaginian losses at 20,000 dead and as many taken prisoner. Roman losses are not known with any certainty but a likely estimate is 2,000. Hannibal did not quit the field until all hope had gone, then he escaped with a few horsemen to Hadrumentum. Scipio, with his usual generosity of spirit, is reported as saying that Hannibal 'acquired the fame of having handled his troops on that day with singular judgement.'

Hannibal and Scipio were so evenly matched in talent and resources that historians have long debated why the one lost at Zama and the other won. Writing some 60 years later, the Greek historian Polybius said of Hannibal that 'good man that he was, he met another better.' This simplistic view is however untenable.

Although Hannibal's strategy in Italy of repeatedly defeating Roman armies to bring about the disintegration of the confederation failed entirely, the British historian J.F. Lazenby has observed that no other strategy 'could have brought Carthage as near success . . .'.

Hannibal was defeated at Zama by three factors: some unreliable infantry levies; insufficient cavalry; and an unwise reliance on untrained elephants. Even so, he nearly won the day; it was only the return of Scipio's cavalry that turned the battle so decisively against the Carthaginians.

After the defeat at Zama, Hannibal became chief magistrate at Carthage and reorganized the system of tax collection to pay the tribute imposed by Rome. In 195 BC he was falsely denounced for conspiring against Rome and fled to King Antiochus the Great of Syria. That the two generals of Zama continued to respect each other is shown by the tale of an alleged meeting

between them at Ephesus in 193 BC. Scipio asked Hannibal whom he considered the three greatest generals of all time and received the reply, 'Alexander, Pyrrhus and myself.' Slightly piqued, Scipio queried 'What would you have said if you had defeated me?', to which Hannibal deftly and flatteringly answered that he would then have placed himself before everyone.

The Syrians were, however, soon at war with Rome themselves, and Hannibal fled again to Bithynia. In 183 BC, knowing he was about to be handed over to the Romans, he took poison.

Carthaginian silver triple shekel.

Genghis Khan *1167–1227*

I n the last quarter of the twelfth century there arose a Mongol leader whose name has become synonymous with pitiless cruelty and an insatiable ambition for conquest – Genghis Khan. As a youth of about seventeen, he became hereditary leader of a small Mongol group; within 10 years he had been accepted by vast numbers of Mongols as khan, or king. How was this possible?

Genghis Khan (he had been named Temujin and took the name Genghis only on his election to khanship) was a great-grandson of Kabul Khan, leader of the Mongol nation, who had been poisoned, it was said, by the Tartars. During succeeding decades, the Mongols were repeatedly defeated in battle until, by the time Temujin was born in about 1167, they were scattered, leaderless and militarily impotent.

Temujin's small group of people and some few goats and sheep were isolated in a cruelly inhospitable terrain and encompassed by enemies. But by forming alliances and defeating his rivals in battle, his reputation was so enhanced that within a few years individuals, groups, whole tribes flocked to his banner to share the comradeship, the sense of unity and purpose and, above all, the plunder that his wars of expansion offered.

That he earned such absolute loyalty from so many thousands of people is not difficult to understand. By his early twenties he was of commanding appearance: tall by the standards of his time, with, it is said, a wide forehead, powerful physique, long, imposing red beard and piercing grey-green eyes like a cat's.

Temujin had many other attributes that served him and his cause well, notably the ability to make use of the talent of others. Though himself illiterate, he took into his service any who were scribes. This he also did with craftsmen, for although he usually slaughtered all his enemies, he was always careful to spare any who might be useful to him.

Though his army consisted of nomadic warriors, he organized it on a sound military basis. As a strategist he stands in the first echelon and, like all great strategists, he was forever innovative. Thus, as his empire expanded, he came across great cities that he dared not by-pass and so had to subdue. Siege warefare was unknown to the Mongols, whose tactics were designed for the vast steppes of Asia. Genghis Khan applied himself to the problem and soon made himself a master of this military art.

Despite his high intelligence and many gifts, Genghis Khan is remembered in history primarily for his cruelty, of which there is no question. Indeed, it was by this very cruelty that he spread the terror that was crucial to his military success. When one city which he had spared rose once more against him, he ordered the population's extermination: of some 100,000 citizens fewer than 50 escaped.

How much of the cruelty of this terrible figure was deliberate policy and how much the product of his race and his times is impossible to judge. Certainly the Afghans were as cruel, one of their delights being to hammer nails into the ears of Mongol prisoners. Cruelty did not cease at the Khan's death. Every living thing in the path of the cortège was destroyed as his corpse was taken in solemn procession to be buried, probably near the River Onon at Burkhan-Khaldhun in Mongolia. He had once rested under a tree there and had selected it as his burial place, saying, 'This place is fit for my last rest. Let it be noted.'

Genghis Khan was a nomad whose home throughout his life was a tent, albeit a vast and sumptuously furnished one. Though his life in the field was frugal and hard, here he held imposing state, as this Persian miniature shows. No one might pitch his tent before that of the Khan, whose view to the farthest distance must be uninterrupted.
This Chinese portrait of Genghis Khan depicts him in old age, when his red hair had turned grey; but the eyes remain as wary and distrustful as in youth.

1167	Born, son of chieftain Yesügei.
c1184	Marries and makes an alliance with Toghrul, Christian khan of the Keraits.
c1196	Battle of Dalan-baljut, forced to retreat by Jamuqua.
c1198	Defeats the Tartars with Chin and Kerait help.
1201	Wounded in the neck by an arrow at the Battle of the Onon.
1202	Battle of Dalanhemürges wipes out the Tartars.
1203	Drawn battle with Jamuqua and the Keraits; destroys the latter at the Battle of Jeser-Undur.
1204	Defeats the Naimans and Merkits.
1206	Proclaimed Khan of Khans; takes the name Genghis Khan.
1207/ 1210	Twice defeats the Tanguts. Besieges Erikaya, gains Tangut submission.
1211	Invades the Chin Empire in North China. Battle of Huan-ertsi.
1213	Battle of Wei-Chuan destroys a Chin army. Devastation of North China.
1215	Sacking of Peking by Mukali.
1219	Invades Kwarazmian Empire. Crosses the Syr Darya (Jaxartes) and the Kizil Kum Desert.
1220	*February* or *April* Storms Bokhara and, *March* or *May*, takes Samarkand.
1221	Destroys Balkh. *24 November* **Battle of the Indus.**
1223	*March* Falls from horse while boar-hunting near Tashkent.
1226	Defeats the Tanguts at the Battle of the Yellow River.
1227	*June* Surrender and razing of Tangut city of Erikaya. *24 August* Dies of fever near Chung-shi in East Kansu mountains, aged 60.

Battle of the Indus/*24 November 1221*

'THE GREATEST DELIGHT for man is to inflict defeat on his enemies, to drive them before him, to see those dear to them with their faces bathed in tears, to bestride their horses, to crush in his arms their daughters and wives.' Such was the lifelong philosophy of Genghis Khan.

When he was still in his teens, probably about 17, Genghis Khan made his first alliance, one that was to set him on his stupendous path of conquest. The alliance was with Toghrul, khan of the Keraits, his father's oath- or blood-brother. Genghis Khan's father had supported Toghrul when his rule was threatened by an ambitious neighbour; now Genghis claimed support from Toghrul.

From this time forward, about 1184, more and more warriors came to Genghis's standard, enabling him to embark first on consolidating his position, then on a course of unsurpassed expansion lasting about 40 years. With the help of the Keraits and Chin troops, he defeated the Tartars in about 1198. Then, in 1201 or 1202, with Toghrul's Keraits, he destroyed the army of Jamuqua, a rival khan.

In 1202, he was again ready to confront the Tartars, and at Dalanhemürges, near the River Khalkha in eastern Mongolia, he surrounded and then annihilated them in his first great battle of extermination. It is testimony to his shrewd leadership that he forbade his troops to take any booty until victory was won, and he confiscated the spoils of two relatives who disobeyed him.

By 1204, having reorganized his army, he was master of Mongolia and two years later he was proclaimed Universal Ruler,

War of revenge

By 1216, the dominions of Genghis Khan bordered on the Islamic empire of Khwarazm, a sprawling Persian and Turkish area which had been seized from the Seljuk sultans in the previous century. Muhammed II, Ali ad-Din, was its third shah, and his authority was absolute from the north of the Caspian Sea to the Indus Valley and the Persian Gulf. His empire contained some of the richest Muslim cities, founded on trade, which straddled the routes of central Asia. Small wonder he was called 'the chosen prince of Allah'.

Relations between Khwarazm and the Mongols had been almost cordial. Then Inalchik, governor of the city of Utrar, wantonly seized a Mongol caravan of some 500 camels and killed all the merchants. Shah Muhammed did not merely condone the banditry; he murdered Genghis Khan's ambassador, who was sent to demand justice. Genghis replied simply but with fearful implications: 'You have chosen war. That will happen which will happen and what is to be we know not.' What was to happen was the Battle of the Indus.

Khan of Khans, at a great *quriltay*, or assembly, of chieftains. There he hoisted his famous standard of nine white yak tails for the first time and was designated God's representative on Earth.

The ten years of virtually constant campaigning provided Genghis Khan with a tough, experienced army. Although drawn from all 31 Mongol tribes, the army was no longer organized on a tribal basis; moreover, his bodyguard, once comprising merely 150 warriors, now numbered 10,000, each man chosen on merit.

Genghis Khan was next intent on invading China. In the spring of 1211, before the heat of summer, the Mongols crossed the Gobi Desert along three routes. There were at least 180,000 troops in the three armies, with 20,000 left to garrison Mongolia. This was few enough when compared with the Chin Empire's half a million, of whom 120,000 were

mounted archers. But Genghis Khan had secured the alliance of the Onguts, living north of the Great Wall of China, and this enabled him to cross the daunting defensive barrier without having to fight.

Now began the period of his most annihilating victories. Two enormous Chin field armies, hastily trying to build defences south of the Great Wall, were surprised and defeated, in part because deserters had told the Mongols of their whereabouts. Genghis Khan exploited his victory with a ruthless pursuit, cutting down all stragglers and plundering the plain to within 40km/25mls of Peking. Capturing the capital, however, proved beyond the Mongols capabilities. This pattern was to be repeated during the next three years: absolute victories in the field but an inability to take the stronger cities.

Genghis Khan now applied himself to mastering siege warfare, a craft wholly

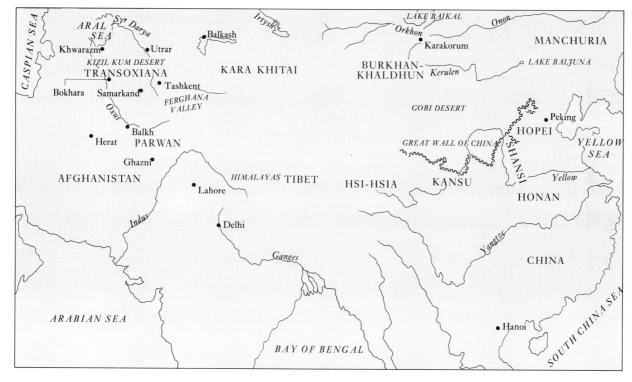

Genghis Khan ruled one of the most extensive empires of all time. He occupied the greater part of the Chin Empire of north China, conquered Turkestan, Transoxiana and Afghanistan, and reached as far west as the Dnieper River in eastern Europe.

The Mongol soldier

The horse was the single most important element in Mongolian life. Infants were taught to ride even before they could walk; horse thieves were put to death. Moreover, the Mongols had saddles and stirrups which, together with cruppers, gave riders great stability when firing their arrows.

Mongol cavalrymen were equipped with a short, composite bow, which had a range of more than 320m/350yds. Arrows, of which each man carried at least 60 in two quivers, were of two types: light arrows for firing at a distance and more heavily tipped arrows for use at close quarters. Some arrows had incendiary heads.

Warriors were also equipped with a small sword (heavy cavalry carried scimitars), two or three javelins, and a dagger strapped inside the left forearm. They also carried a shield of wickerwork or skin and a lariat.

Every soldier wore a raw Chinese silk undershirt. This would wrap itself around a penetrating arrow, lessening its impact and allowing its quick, relatively painless removal. Over their tunics they wore a protective lacquered leather jerkin.

In addition to weapons, each man was equipped with a waterproof hide saddlebag, which could be inflated for river crossings. This contained a change of clothing, fishhook and line, a hatchet, arrow-sharpening files, an iron cooking pot, two leather bottles – one for water, the other for milk – and a needle and thread. Rations consisted of yoghurt, millet and smoked meat. In this way, every one of Genghis Khan's warriors could operate as an entirely independent unit.

The Chinese drawing, *left*, dating from the Han Dynasty (202 BC–AD *c*220) shows that the Mongols' equestrian skills were renowned long before the time of Genghis. Their mounts were notorious for their evil temper, as the fine painting, *below*, suggests.

unknown in Mongolia. Chinese prisoners, proficient in engineering, were coerced into building siege engines for him and to instructing his troops in their use. Huge shields to protect the besiegers, scaling ladders and battering-rams were also employed by them for the first time. Moreover, Genghis Khan made ruthless use of prisoners as frontal cover in his assaults on the cities of Hopei, Shantung and Shansi, all of which fell to his new siege tactics.

Nevertheless, Peking held out until 1214, when sheer exhaustion brought the Chinese emperor to accept abject terms. Genghis accepted a princess of the blood royal as a wife, together with 1,000 child slaves, 3,000 horses and gold, silver and silk. Within a year the emperor had fled, part of his army had mutinied, and the depleted, starving garrison of Peking opened its gates to the Mongols. A terrible massacre and sacking ensued.

It was a sign of his confident ability to delegate power that Genghis left Mukali, one of his generals, to carry on the war in China for the rest of his reign, while he himself returned to his new capital of Karakorum in 1216. Then, following the murder of the merchants in a Mongol

Organization of the army

Genghis Khan's army was supreme if not always invincible. Other armies had conquered great areas, and other armies – notably those of the Parthians, Persians, Arabs and Byzantines – had been based on the mounted archer and armoured lancer combination, but none achieved such spectacular results nor in so short a time. The army's coordination, speed and flexibility in some ways foreshadowed twentieth-century tank warfare, used in the German blitzkriegs of World War II.

One factor above all brought about the Mongol Army's great success: its strict organization. The Imperial Guard, or *Keshik*, comprised 10,000 men: 7,000 lifeguards, 1,000 day guards, 1,000 night guards and 1,000 quiver-bearers. They wore black tunics with red facings and black armour; their mounts, all black, were equipped with red leather bridle and saddle.

The Army itself was subdivided on the decimal basis. The smallest unit, the troop or *arban*, comprised 10 men, the leader being elected by the others. Ten troops formed a squadron or *jagun*, the leader elected by the *arban* leaders. Ten squadrons made a regiment or *mingan* and 10 *mingans* a division or *tumen*. An army, or 'horde', comprised three *tumen*.

At the Battle of the Indus, Shah Jalal ad-Din tried to turn the Mongols' left flank. Gonzalo de Córdoba used this ploy to great effect at the Battle of the Garigliano in 1503, but the Shah's manoeuvre brought him disaster for his opponent, Genghis Khan, anticipated the move. Thus, when the Shah weakened his left flank to reinforce his right for the enveloping ploy, Genghis Khan attacked the Shah's denuded left.

The two armies were of roughly equal strength, each comprising some 50,000 men. The Shah is thought to have drawn up his force in a strong position, with his left flank pinned on the foothills of a mountain range and his right on the River Indus. Genghis Khan advanced at dawn on 24 November 1221, bringing the two lines face to face.

Genghis Khan took station in the middle of his army. His changing positions during the battle were always known to his men through his highly visible standard of nine white yak's tails (5).

Mongol squadron leaders, each of whom commanded 100 men, had their personal standards, which acted as rallying points, and black and white flags for transmitting orders. A similar use of flags to convey orders and information was made more than 700 years later by British tank crews without radios in the North African desert during World War II.

The Mongols used trumpets and kettledrums of bronze and iron, mounted on camels (7), to sound an assault. At night, flaming arrows and torches conveyed information throughout the Mongol Army.

Mongol tunics were of blue with red facings or brown with light blue facings. Boots were made of felt or leather. Their quilted caps had two red ribbons and were trimmed with fur. Cloaks were of different colours, according to the *tumen*.

Shah Jalal ad-Din (1) was the first to deploy when he ordered Emir Malik (8), on his right wing, to attack. The charge drove back the Mongol left.

As the Shah judged the Mongol right to be no immediate threat, he depleted his left flank in order to reinforce Malik's successful charge on the right. To make victory certain, he then personally led a massive charge at the Mongol centre.

The Mongols were in danger of defeat. To Genghis Khan (4), however, the situation offered nothing but opportunity. Leaving his hard-pressed centre (3) to cope as best it might, he led his black-clad Imperial Guard (6) in a charge so ferocious that it drove Emir Malik's force back in confusion.

Unknown to the Shah, a Mongol *tumen* (2) had been detached from the right wing to ride behind a ridge in the foothills. They completed their move undetected and fell on the Shah's much-reduced left flank.

At the same time, Genghis Khan, having driven Malik back, turned inward to encompass the Shah's cavalry in the centre.

The encirclement was spectacularly successful: a mere 700 of the Shah's troops escaped slaughter.

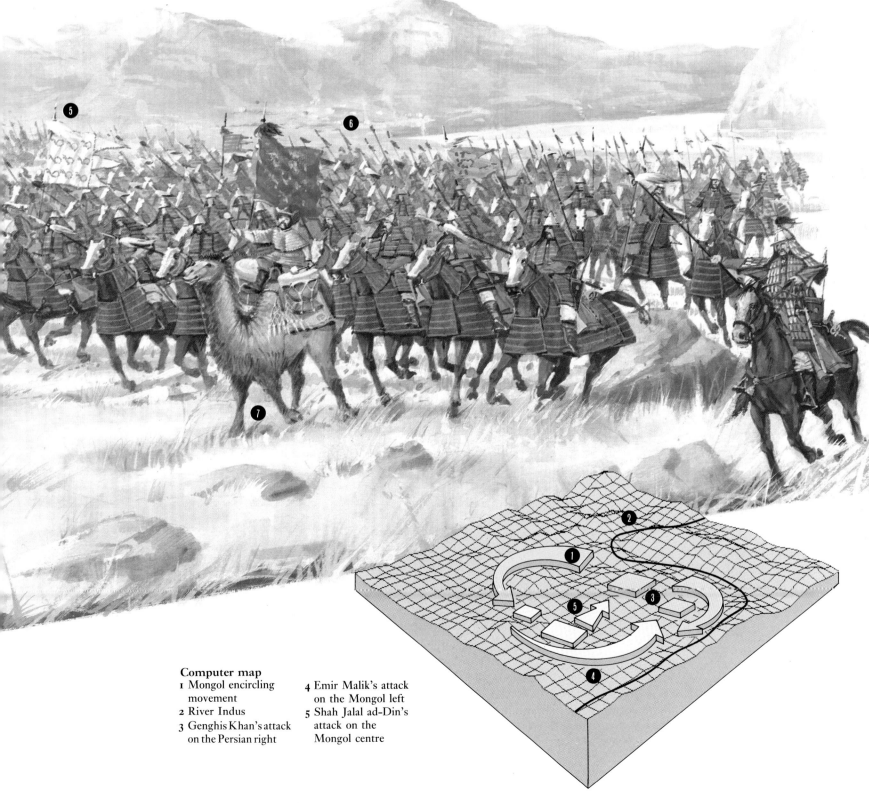

Computer map
1 Mongol encircling movement
2 River Indus
3 Genghis Khan's attack on the Persian right
4 Emir Malik's attack on the Mongol left
5 Shah Jalal ad-Din's attack on the Mongol centre

camel caravan by Inalchik, governor of the city of Utrar, war between the Islamic empire of Khwarazm and the Mongols became inevitable.

Mongol men aged 17–60, together with some allies, were mobilized, to muster 150,000 troops on the upper River Irtysh in the summer of 1219. They included 10,000 Chinese siege engineers, with their dismantled catapults and their ammunition carried on yaks and camels. Muslim interpreters were assembled for intelligence work and detailed logistic preparations undertaken, including the building of a road and bridges broad enough for two carts to travel side by side along the route to be taken. Supply dumps of dried meat were established.

Shah Muhammed deployed 300,000 well-equipped troops along 805km/ 500mls of the Syr Darya (Jaxartes) River, his northern border. He distrusted his generals and, trying to garrison all the towns, left himself weak everywhere. Genghis's strategy was to keep him on the defensive. Three *tumen* under Chepe, one of his best generals, advanced from Kharakhitai to threaten the Shah's right flank in the Ferghana Valley. The Shah sent one of his sons, Jalal ad-Din, with 50,000 men to meet the threat. The battle forced the Mongols to fall back to Kashgar, but they had succeeded in shielding their main body's advance to the Syr Darya River.

In the autumn of 1219, Genghis Khan advanced 966km/600mls and fell upon the city of Utrar, where his ambassador had been murdered, at the very time Chepe began to advance again from Kashgar. Leaving his younger sons to wreak vengeance on Utrar, Genghis ordered his eldest son, Jochi, to attack the cities at both ends of the great river. Khojend fell, and Chepe in the south, this time defeated an army of 50,000 men.

Meanwhile, Genghis and his 40,000 men crossed the supposedly impassable Kizil Kum desert, crossed the River Oxus and then, from the west, struck at Bokhara, to the bewilderment and dismay of his enemy, who had no reserves.

A garrison of between 20,000 and 30,000 Turks fought for three days. Then they made a sortie, their only remaining option, but were annihilated. Bokhara submitted and its inhabitants were forced to help capture their own citadel. Genghis ordered the city to be depopulated and destroyed by fire.

Within three weeks the royal 'horde' had united with the other columns in front of Muhammed's capital, Samarkand. There Genghis Khan spent two days in

Arrow messengers

All great commanders have known that battles cannot be won through the eyes of others. Napoleon customarily travelled in the rear of his army but, once an engagement seemed imminent, he moved rapidly to the front to see with his own eyes the terrain and the deployment of his enemy. Genghis Khan's empire was so vast that for him this was not always possible. But he needed accurate, detailed information of everything that was happening in his far-flung domains. To this end, he devised a system of relay messengers.

Here, as in battle, the sturdy Mongol ponies came into their own: tough, sure-footed and agile, they had the twin advantages of stamina and speed. Mounted on these ponies, Genghis Khan's messengers, their bodies bandaged against the friction of riding and the fierce, freezing winds, scoured his empire, by means of their relay system often covering as much as 160km/ 100mls in a day. Stations, sited some 40km/ 25mls apart, had been established on all the major roads, where the arrow messengers, bells on their saddles announcing their arrival, could collect food and change horses. The information gleaned was then returned by relay to the Great Khan.

Exact numbers are unknown, but a reasonable hazard is that Genghis Khan's organization comprised more than 250,000 ponies and some 10,000 stations. By this means, the Khan received news, it was said, within the space of a day and night that would ordinarily have taken a month to reach him. This is certainly an exaggeration, but the value he placed on his messengers is not in dispute: they were granted absolute authority when about their duties and were handsomely rewarded.

detailed reconnaissance, which enabled him, on the third day, to ambush and destroy 50,000 Tajik infantry who had come out of the city to engage him. On the fifth day, the Shah's uncle and commandant, Tughai Khan, led out 30,000 Kangli mercenaries to change sides, and the city opened its northwest Prayer Gate to the besiegers. All Transoxiana had fallen and the Shah fled west from Balkh, pursued by three *tumen*, to a lonely death in 1221 on an island in the Caspian Sea.

In the summer of that same year, Genghis himself advanced across the Hindu Kush to track down Shah Jalal ad-Din, Muhammed's son, who was trying to raise fresh forces around Ghazni in Afghanistan. Genghis sent nearly 40,000 men ahead on reconnaissance. At Parwan the Mongols unwisely fought a battle on broken terrain with Jalal ad-Din's host, twice the strength of their own, and were beaten. Genghis reached Ghazni with his main body by forced marches in two days. Jalal ad-Din, his army now halved by the defection of his Turkish forces, fell back to the Indus Valley.

By forced marches again, Genghis caught up with the Khwarazmian army at night, as it was making preparations to cross the River Indus the following day. Jalal ad-Din was obliged to prepare his 50,000 men for battle against nearly the same number of Mongols.

Details of the battle are not precisely known because contemporary accounts are incomplete. Scholars disagree on the exact position of the rival armies, for

Further evidence of Mongol horsemanship is provided by the lively painting of cavalry, *below*, whose skill and daring is echoed by the performance of present-day circus riders.

example, but certain aspects of the conflict are generally acknowledged.

The Khwarazmian position was strong, with their left flank resting on mountain ridges and their right upon the Indus. Genghis advanced at dawn, but Jalal ad-Din charged first with his right wing, under Emir Malik, and drove back the Mongol left. Since the Mongols' right wing appeared to offer no threat, the Shah weakened his left flank to reinforce Malik's success. Having done this, he led a massive charge at the Mongol centre, with the object of gaining quick victory by killing Genghis Khan himself.

Unknown to the Shah, Genghis Khan had, however, ordered a *tumen* to scale the heights around the Khwarazmian left. Meanwhile, leaving his centre to fend for itself, he led his Imperial Guard in a ferocious charge that routed Malik's force. Then he swung inward on Jalal ad-Din's cavalry, who had charged his centre.

At almost the same time, the *tumen* that had been ordered to trek across the ridges had beaten the Shah's now token left flank, taken his camp and cut off his retreat to the south. Jalal ad-Din, his army disintegrating, cut his way through to the Indus with his last 700 men and escaped.

Genghis Khan had more battles yet to fight, but the Battle of the Indus must remain among his greatest strategic and tactical achievements, in which he turned a potentially deadly enemy charge to his advantage and destroyed an entire army.

The Annual Hunt

In the brief interludes when the Mongols were not at war they were training for war. Men and women had separate responsibilities. The warriors were obliged to have their weapons always ready, the women to provide food for their husbands and sons and to sew their sheepskin cloaks and boots.

Hunting was more than an economic necessity to the nomadic Mongols; it epitomised their life style, and Genghis Khan, who in his youth had been reduced to hunting even mice and other small creatures to remain alive, was one of its keenest followers. Indeed, it was while hunting in 1223, in old age, that he was thrown from his horse and incapacitated for several months. The Mongols used corn to a limited extent, but their chief foods were mutton and mares' milk.

The most intensive training for Mongol warriors came through sport in the Annual Hunt. A vast area was circumscribed; then, at a given time, Mongol horsemen, without weapons, drove every living creature inward, until they were packed tight within a small confine. The creatures – boar, leopards and tigers, as well as smaller game – were by then terrified, starving and at a bewildered, nervous pitch of ferocity. Once more armed, the horsemen then began the kill, slaughtering every animal. In this way Genghis Khan's apprentice warriors learned how to work in unison in difficult terrain and how to use their weapons.

Chinese drawing of a Mongol archer hunting small game.

Shah Jalal ad-Din ?–1231

There is apparently no portrait of Shah Jalal ad-Din, defeated by Genghis Khan at the Battle of the Indus. He is a shadowy figure of whom little is known save his spectacular courage in the moment of his defeat. His cause lost, he cast aside his armour, mounted a fresh horse, spurred to the banks of the Indus and, still carrying his standard, leaped from a cliff variously given as 6–18m/20–60ft above the torrent and so escaped.

Genghis Khan hastened to the spot and said, marvelling, 'Fortunate should be the father of such a son!' His admiration for the Shah did not induce him to show mercy to his captured children, however. All – the eldest was only 8 years old – were tossed into the Indus and drowned.

Disintegration of the Mongol Empire

At his death, Genghis Khan left his army and his empire, both intact, to his sons. For many years expansion for the Mongols continued, though they were now divided into four khanates. These were the Great Khanate, comprising all of China and most of eastern Asia, which came to be known as the Yuan Dynasty; the Jagatai Khanate in Turkestan; the Kipchack Khanate of the empire of the Golden Horde in most of Russia and a khanate in present-day Iran.

Like all empires, both before and since, that of the Mongols reached its greatest extent and then, divided and lacking leaders of the first quality, contracted. By 1382 the Mongols were completely expelled from China. They soon reverted to their pastoral ways and lapsed into obscurity, though their influence on Asia and much of Europe left an indelible legacy, notably in the art of rapid, mobile warfare.

Henry V *1387-1422*

When Henry V ascended the throne of England in 1413, he was 25 years old. He was considered handsome, in the fashion of the day, with a long pointed nose, strong chin, large hazel eyes and full red lips. His life was devoted to soldiering and, like all soldiers of the period, he shaved his thick brown hair on the sides and back of his head so that his helmet would fit more comfortably.

Little is known of Henry's childhood, but his education was not neglected, despite the fact that even as a youth he was engaged in his father's campaigns. He knew Latin and could write in English and French. He played the harp well and was fond of poetry. He delighted in reading (indeed, he always took a small library with him on campaign) and both encouraged and advanced musicians, writers, theologians and other men of learning. It is probable, also, that he spent some time at Oxford University.

The picture of Henry as a wild and dissolute youth has been much exaggerated, notably by Shakespeare in his plays *Henry IV*, Parts 1 and 2. According to this version, on becoming king, Henry at once gave up the life of a libertine and became a sober, solemn ruler. However, the well-documented change in his style of life refers not so much to the abandoning of youthful excess as to the gravity with which he undertook his great new responsibilities.

The reign of his father, Henry IV, had seen numerous rebellions among the nobles as well as conflicts with Wales and Scotland; at his death, the country was at peace, but the Crown was heavily in debt. Though the wars of Henry V were eventually to increase that debt substantially, they were at first profitable and enjoyed both parliamentary and national support. Certainly, Henry established civil order and gave his subjects a spirit of national pride.

It is likely that Henry genuinely believed in his right to the throne of France. He was a profoundly orthodox king and no dissembler. He also, throughout his life, held strong, orthodox religious beliefs, and when he claimed God's favour for his cause, it was done in all sincerity. There can, in any event, be no doubt that he always behaved as if he were the rightful King of France. For example, when he laid siege to Rouen in 1418 and the starving inhabitants sought surrender terms, he replied that the city was his, and they could not bargain with its lawful lord.

This and other incidents, such as his slaughter of prisoners during the Battle of Agincourt, have been cited as examples of his brutality. In fact, Henry was a compassionate man by prevailing standards and resorted to harshness only when military or political considerations demanded it. As, for instance, when he allowed 12,000 women, children, old and sick to perish between the lines at Rouen because his own army had barely enough food to survive the winter.

But Henry is remembered above all as a soldier, an undefeated military genius, who displayed brilliant daring in action, sound strategy and diligent attention to detail, all supported by a high degree of diplomatic skill. These were the qualities, together with his personal courage and skill at arms – he was said to wear his armour 'as though it were a cloak' – his sense of justice and spontaneous generosity, that enabled him to raise an army, hold it together under dreadful conditions and in fearful danger, and lead it to victory against huge odds. In the words of William Shakespeare, in his play *Henry VI*, he was:

'. . . too famous to live long.
England ne'er lost a king of so much worth.'

The carved wooden effigy of King Henry V appears on his tomb in the Chantry Chapel dedicated to him in Westminster Abbey, London.
Henry V and some of his courtiers are depicted within the illuminated letter H on this page of the Cartae Antiquae, *a late 15th-century collection of statutes belonging to the Corporation of the City of London.*

1387	*16 September* Born at Monmouth, son of the future Henry IV.
1399	*15 October* Made Prince of Wales.
1403	First campaign against Owen Glendower *21 July* Wounded at Shrewsbury.
1405	*March* Captures Glendower's son.
1408	Captures Aberystwyth Castle.
1410/ 1411	Heads the King's Council. Sends a force to France to aid the Duke of Burgundy.
1413	*21 March* Becomes King of England.
1415	*11 August* Sails for France from Southampton. *August-September* Besieges and captures Harfleur. *25 October* **Battle of Agincourt.**
1416	*15 August* Signs the Treaty of Canterbury with Sigismund, the Holy Roman Emperor.
1417	*30 July* Sails for Normandy; lands at Touques. *August-September* Besieges and takes Caen.
1418/ 1419	*February* Falaise falls after a 4-month siege. *July* Besieges, and *January*, captures Rouen.
1420	*21 May* Becomes regent and heir to the French throne by the Treaty of Troyes. *June-July* Takes the castle of Montereau. *July-November* Besieges and captures Melun. Returns to England.
1421	*10 June* Sails to France on his final campaign. *July-August* Captures Dreux, relieves Chartres. *September* Storms Beaugency on the Loire.
1422	*2 May* Captures Meaux after a 7-month siege. *31 August* Dies from dysentery at Bois de Vincennes, near Paris, aged 34.

Battle of Agincourt/*25 October 1415*

ON 11 AUGUST 1415, Henry V set sail for France in his flagship *Trinity Royal*. Some 1,500 ships of all types had been assembled in Southampton Water to transport his invasion force. All the nobility of England was there. There were about 2,000 men-at-arms and 6,000 archers, half of them with horses; there were pages, armourers, smiths and engineers, and Henry's own retinue of nearly 900 men.

The fleet anchored two days later off the Chef de Caux (Cap de la Hève), 4.8km/3mls below the fortress of Harfleur. This citadel was Henry's first objective since it was the key to Normandy and, if not taken, would remain a menace to his rear. Subduing Harfleur, however, proved a costly and lengthy undertaking, for it was strongly defended and the small River Lèzarde, having been dammed, had flooded the surrounding contryside.

On 17 August, Henry moved his army up to the town to undertake a formal siege, but progress was slow and it was not until 16 September, the king's birthday, that the English seized one of the bulwarks of the fortifications. The city eventually surrendered its keys on 22 September.

Although successful, the siege had cost Henry dear in both time and men, for although few had perished in the assault on the city, fever and dysentery had reduced the ranks of the English. This, with some desertions which infuriated the king, left him with at most 900 men-at-arms and some 5,000 archers.

What was he to do? Honour demanded that he should not merely capture one strongpoint and then retire; on the other hand, an attempt to march on Rouen and Paris was clearly impossible. His decision to march through northern Normandy – 'my duchy', as he termed it – and then embark from his citadel of Calais has been much criticized by armchair historians for the dangers entailed in having to pass through some 240km/150mls of enemy-held territory. But Henry was confident he could beat a French army in the field and set out from Harfleur on 6 October. His men had provisions for only eight days, and Henry was fully aware that the outcome of this 'most foolhardy and reckless adventure' would leave him either dead, a prisoner held for ransom, or England's hero-king.

By 8 October, all his army was on the move. To the southeast, as Henry knew, lay a French advance guard at Rouen and the main body of the French Army, still assembling at Vernon. But he was nearer to Calais than his enemies and had the advantage of about two days' march, so he had a chance of reaching it before them.

The Hundred Years War

The origins of the Hundred Years War between England and France (1337–1453) lay in William the Conqueror's victory over the English at Hastings in 1066, for he was Duke of Normandy and technically a vassal of the King of France. Matters were further complicated in 1152, when one of his descendants, Henry II of England, married Eleanor of Aquitaine, the divorced wife of France's King Louis VII. By this marriage, Henry acquired the regions of Poitou, Gascony and Guienne, which made him lord over as great an area of France as the king himself.

During the ensuing years, the English lost much of this territory, including Normandy in 1204, but it was largely regained by Edward III, great-grandfather of Henry V. Subsequently, however, English power again declined, and by 1375 they retained only Calais and small areas around Bordeaux.

Internal discord prevented the next two English kings – Richard II and Henry IV – from reasserting what they considered their rights in France. This situation changed when Henry V became king, for he quickly restored order and peace at home. The time to press the English claim to the French throne was ripe for other reasons as well.

The then King of France, Charles VI, was for much of his life insane, and his madness led to murderous struggles for power between various factions, especially those led by John, Duke of Burgundy, who held vast tracts of land in the north, and the Armanacs under the Dukes of Orléans, who had powerful interests in both central and southern France.

But there was another, more urgent, reason for Henry's invasion of Normandy. His title to the crown of England, deriving as it did from his father's deposition of Richard II, the undisputed king, was suspect, and many of the nobles supported the rival claims of the House of York. By making common cause of his assault on France, in which all English noblemen joined him, Henry could minimize the prospect of rebellion at home.

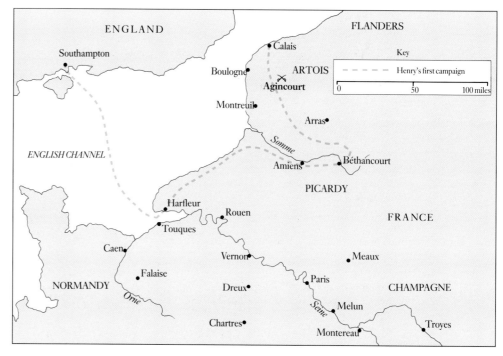

Between Henry and Calais, however, lay the River Somme, an obstacle that was nearly to prove his undoing. He intended to cross the river by the same ford near its mouth that his great-grandfather King Edward III used on his march to Crécy. However, a captured Frenchman told him that the river was defended and staked at the crossing, so Henry had no choice but to turn inland and seek another ford.

Within the space of a few hours his whole strategy had been disjointed. His depleted army, exhausted by their march and their sufferings at Harfleur, were already reduced to meagre rations which would shortly run out.

Moreover, Henry was now obliged to move toward the vanguard of the French Army under Charles d'Albret, the Constable of France, and Marshal Jean de

Men-at-arms

The standard late medieval soldiers, of whom the knights formed only the élite, were the men-at-arms. Knights or higher nobles led their own contingents of armoured men under their own banners. Each man-at-arms was served by a squire and one or two pages. Their horses were of the large, hunter-type, but after the Battle of Poitiers in 1356, it had become more usual to fight on foot. Henry V paid his men-at-arms a shilling a day.

By 1415, full plate armour with the egg-shaped, visored helmet was worn, with padded clothing underneath to prevent bruising. Chain mail covered the groin and armpit. Although weighing 27–32kg/60–70lb and stuffy to wear, full plate armour, with its glancing surfaces, gave good protection and allowed considerable agility. The wearer was only in danger if he fell over, for it took two men to pick him up.

The man-at-arms wore a jewelled belt with his sword on the left and dagger on the right. The sword could be used two-handed, since no shield needed to be carried. Other weapons were maces, battle-axes and the lance (shortened for foot use by the French at Agincourt).

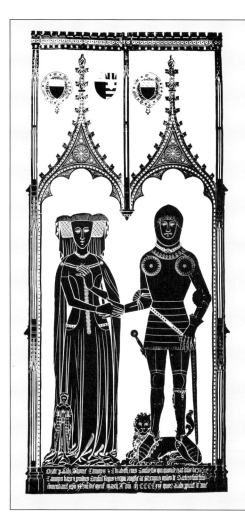

Brass rubbing from the tomb of Lord Camoys in the church at Trotton, Sussex

English longbowmen

Almost 70 years after the English archers' victory at Crécy, the longbow remained a matchless weapon. Usually made of yew, it was about 1.8m/6ft long and needed a pull of 36kg/80lb. Each sheaf of 24 goose-feathered arrows, up to 91cm/37in long, contained 8 light flight arrows, with a maximum range of around 275m/300yds, and 16 of the heavier but shorter armour-piercing variety. These were only 70cm/27in long and could travel about 155m/170yds; they were accurate against individual targets at 73–91m/80–100yds. A skilled archer could fire ten arrows a minute, but constant practice was required.

An archer's secondary weapons might include a sword, dagger, lead mallet, club or billhook, sometimes used with a small buckler, or shield. Well-off archers might have a mail shirt or metal-plated leather jerkin, while headgear could be a kettle helmet or just a felt hat. They were paid six pence a day.

English longbowmen; 'Life and Acts of Richard Beauchamp, Earl of Warwick' c1485.

Boucicaut, who were marching north, rather than ahead of them and away to safety. Bridges all along the Somme had been dismantled or heavily defended, and the river staked. On the opposite side of the river he caught occasional glimpses of a shadowing force. And a far larger force was gathering, for the fall of Harfleur had awakened the French from their lethargy and many great dukes had rallied to the standard.

The English situation seemed doomed. But on 18 October, Henry found two fords at Béthencourt and nearby Voyennes that were practicable, although the approaches were through marshland and the causeways over it had been destroyed. He at once set his troops to demolishing the houses and sheds in the area and to gathering sticks from the woods to provide timber to repair the causeways. On 19 October, the entire English Army managed to cross the Somme in safety. Soon afterward, however, heralds came from the French lines, announcing that the princes and dukes of France meant to offer battle on the road to Calais. This they duly did near the small village of Agincourt.

The position of the English, on 24 October, with the men outnumbered and starving, seemed hopeless, but Henry personally bolstered their spirits. When one of his knights, Sir Walter Hungerford, fearful of the battle's outcome, lamented there were not another 10,000 English archers, the king rebuked him. 'I would not have one more, even if I could. This people is God's people; He has entrusted them to me today and He can bring down the pride of these Frenchmen . . .'. Henry's confidence and faith were to be sorely tested the next day.

The battlefield of Agincourt was roughly diamond-shaped. At the four points were heavily wooded villages; between them lay an open field some 3km/2mls long and 1.2km/¾ml wide, which had been ploughed and sown with winter wheat. It rained hard for several hours during the stormy night. Toward first light on 25 October, however, the weather began to clear, and the two sides could view each other's dispositions.

The little English Army was drawn up in line, four deep across the field, stretching between the southernmost tips of the woods of Agincourt and Tramecourt. The Duke of York commanded the right wing and Lord Camoys the left, while the king stationed himself in the centre. Each of the three divisions comprised bodies of men-at-arms, with archers in wedge-shaped formation on either side of them. Every man, including the king, was to fight on

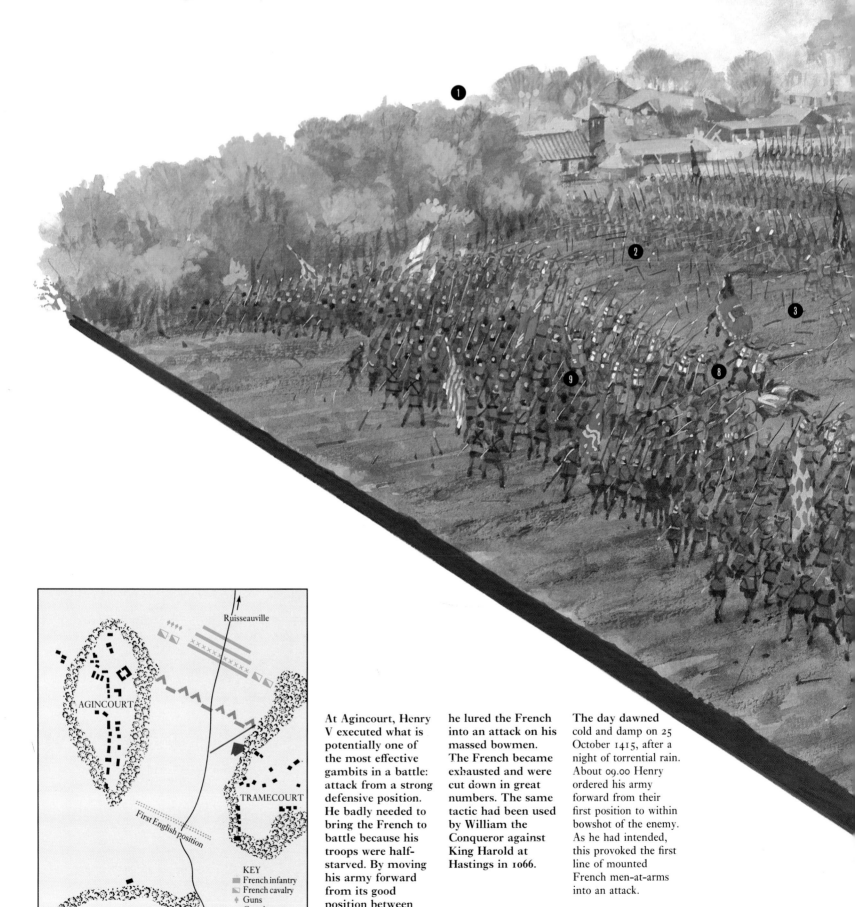

At Agincourt, Henry V executed what is potentially one of the most effective gambits in a battle: attack from a strong defensive position. He badly needed to bring the French to battle because his troops were half-starved. By moving his army forward from its good position between two woods to one equally strong but nearer the enemy, he lured the French into an attack on his massed bowmen. The French became exhausted and were cut down in great numbers. The same tactic had been used by William the Conqueror against King Harold at Hastings in 1066.

The day dawned cold and damp on 25 October 1415, after a night of torrential rain. About 09.00 Henry ordered his army forward from their first position to within bowshot of the enemy. As he had intended, this provoked the first line of mounted French men-at-arms into an attack.

Ruisseauville

AGINCOURT

TRAMECOURT

First English position

KEY
- French infantry
- French cavalry
- Guns
- × Crossbowmen
- English men-at-arms
- ▲ English archers

MAISONCELLES

Blangy

Henry himself (9), also fighting on foot, was surrounded by a pack of 18 French knights, but the attack was beaten off by his men-at-arms (8). Henry's helmet, dented in the fray and with one of the fleurons missing from the encircling crown, can still be seen in Westminster Abbey.

As the archers ran out of arrows, they threw down their bows and fought hand-to-hand. Unencumbered, they clambered over the piles of fallen French knights, raised their visors and stabbed them through the eye, or smashed in their helmets with clubs.

Horses were shot and fell, pitching their riders to the ground, where they lay, unable to move under the weight of their armour. Those horses that reached the English lines ran up against the sharp stakes (3), which the archers had driven into the soft earth.

Hemmed in by the woods at Agincourt (1) and Tramecourt, most of the terrified animals turned (6) and bolted back into the second line of men-at-arms (2), who were struggling through the mud on foot. Under the rain of arrows, men fell on top of those already on the ground, and many suffocated inside their visored steel helmets.

The third line of the French Army (5), watching from a helpless distance and seeing the carnage, began to melt away; the crossbowmen and guns (4) also played little part in the action. Within about an hour the battle was over: some 11,000 Frenchmen were killed and, it is estimated, only 100 English. As they had at Crécy in 1346, the longbowmen won the day.

Hampered by the heavy mud of the ploughed field, their charge faltered, and horses and riders became easy targets for the wedge-shaped formations of English longbowmen (7). Henry, recognizing the worth of his archers in battle, had spent more than two years preparing them for his Normandy campaign; and the accuracy and speed of their shooting devastated the enemy.

Plunder and ransom

'The gains of war' might be obtained by an invading army in one of two ways: plunder or ransom. Since the sole aim of a volunteer army was to reap profit, disputes over prisoners and stolen goods were common, and a code of conduct became necessary.

The Crown reserved to itself all that was immovable – land, cities, castles – together with ransom payable for captured noblemen. This was augmented by a 'tax' of one-third of the plunder won by captains and a third of the third they received when their men took prisoners.

There were no rules governing what might be taken and anything movable might be pillaged. Since some soldiers were better placed to take prisoners and ransack than others, simply by chance of circumstance, small groups often agreed to divide whatever was taken between them. In the same way, if one of them were seized for ransom, they would pay the negotiated sum as a unit. If they could not raise the fee, they would stand surety as hostages while their comrade returned home to raise the money.

Henry's army was, in many aspects, little better than a band of robbers. Gain was

their object, and anything that might be turned to profit was taken. After the Battle of Agincourt, Henry's men loaded themselves with so much spoil that they could not transport it, and he ordered much of the plunder to be used to make a funeral pyre for the English dead.

Plunder was one of the perquisites of a victorious medieval army; the soldiers took anything movable, from food and drink to household goods, as this illumination in a manuscript dating from *c*1398 shows.

foot. The baggage train was sited to the rear and was only lightly defended. This small force, cold, soaked and starving, faced an army estimated to have been at least four times its strength.

The French were drawn up on slightly rising ground about 1.6km/1ml north of the English. Because the space between the woods at Agincourt and Tramecourt was so narrow the large French Army was forced to form up in three dense masses, one behind the other. The front line, comprising a picked body of heavily armoured lords and knights bearing spears and lances 3.7–4.3m/12–14ft long, was commanded by Charles d'Albret and Jean Boucicaut. A second, similar formation was commanded by the Dukes of Bar and Alençon. Those not of gentle birth were relegated to the third line.

The determination of the nobility to be first in action and so win all the anticipated glory for themselves led to several tactical errors. The knights were packed so tightly together they could use their long weapons only with difficulty, and the crossbowmen, positioned behind the front line, consequently proved useless. Cavalry units were stationed at each side of the front line, with a few guns placed behind the cavalry on the right wing, where, like the crossbowmen, they were largely unusable, although at least one unlucky

English archer was killed by 'uno gune'.

For three hours, from dawn, the two armies faced each other. This inactivity boded disaster for Henry: he had insufficient numbers to attack; his road forward was barred and retreat through hostile country, harried by a mighty army, would mean death or starvation. His only hope was to lure the French into action and settle the matter without delay.

Shortly after 09.00, therefore, he gave the order 'Forward banners'. The whole English line, with the baggage train following, advanced some 640m/700yds through the deep mud to within bowshot range of the enemy, and the archers drove sharpened stakes at an angle into the ground to deflect the French cavalry. The tactic produced the result Henry had hoped for: a glittering shiver passed along the French cavalry lines as lances were brought to the horizontal for a charge.

The French planned to charge the archers, drive them back and then roll up the main English force by weight of numbers. The attack, however, proceeded at a slow pace, for the horses carrying the knights in their great weight of armour were soon up to their fetlocks in mud. Most of the mounted knights were shot down before they were anywhere near the English; those that reached the archers' stakes were killed by concentrated fire at

close range. The few men surviving were carried by their terrified horses back toward their own lines.

Meanwhile, the first line of unmounted men-at-arms was advancing with extreme difficulty, since under the weight of their armour they, too, sank into the mud. Within the first few minutes of the action, the French were already in disorder. By a supreme effort, the vanguard reached the English men-at-arms and bore them back a spear's length. But, being crowded together into ever narrower columns and exhausted, their attack faltered.

Henry then ordered his archers to throw aside their bows and take on the French knights in hand-to-hand fighting. The archers laid about them with axes, mallets and swords, and soon these unarmoured, often barefooted, men had knocked most of the knights to the ground, where they lay as many as three deep.

Meanwhile, the second line was advancing, but also became exhausted in the mud, and seeing the fate of their comrades, soon broke under arrow fire and turned tail. At this moment in the battle, messengers brought news that a fresh French force had attacked the English baggage train, where many of the prisoners were held. Since the number of French prisoners far exceeded the strength of the English Army, Henry at once ordered them all to be killed. As prisoners meant ransom, his troops were at first reluctant to obey, but then a rumour spread that the French intended to cut off the right hand of every archer they captured, and all joined in with ferocious alacrity. Soon, dead French knights lay in their thousands, and the third French line, witnessing the slaughter from a distance, began to melt away.

Later it proved that the attack on the baggage train had been carried out by a local squire intent on plunder. Despite the criticism of Henry for ordering the slaughter of prisoners, his action was not really unreasonable in the circumstances. Absolute victory was his only hope of survival; to have spared the many prisoners would have left the battle still in the balance.

The English were left undisputed masters of the field, and Henry's road to Calais was open. Through tactical incompetence and a misplaced belief in their superiority, the French had paid a terrible price.

Jean Boucicaut c1365–1421

Miniature from Boucicaut's Book of Hours.

One of the great soldiers of the age of chivalry, Boucicaut was a champion of the tournament, a crusader and the founder of a chivalric order. His whole life was spent under arms, first against the Flemish, then against the Turks.

He was made a marshal by the French King Charles VI in 1391, and later was prominent in the 1398–9 defence of Constantinople against the Turks – unwisely they had ransomed him after his capture at the Battle of Nikopolis in 1396.

Boucicaut was again captured at the Battle of Agincourt, but Henry V spared his life in recognition of his chivalry, courage and rank. He died in England some six years later, still waiting to be ransomed.

Siege cannon

Cannon had been known in Europe for 75 years before Henry began his military career, but he used them with a new intensity and effectiveness – his later campaigns consisted entirely of sieges.

Siege cannon were cumbersome guns, weighing up to two tons and measuring up to 3.7m/12ft long, with calibres up to 60cm/24in; they fired 181–226kg/400–500lb stone balls. These guns had to be lifted by muzzle rings and breech loaded, so rate of fire was counted in shots per day.

Another loading method was to insert a movable box, or chamber, of which each gun had two or three weighing 4.5–30kg/9–66lb. These were filled with gunpowder, using a spoon, and had a tube through which a heated taper, or lunt, was inserted to ignite the charge. The chamber mouth was sealed with a softwood tampion, or bung, rammed in with a pusher.

The box was then lifted into the breech by its handle and clamped with a flail or iron rod. Each gun was packed into an elm or oak gun carriage with pulleys, levers and chains for lifting. Field forges were on hand for the frequent repairs needed.

Against Harfleur Henry used 12 guns, including the 'London', 'Messenger' and 'King's Daughter', and employed round-the-clock bombardment.

Henry V besieging a French city; 'Life and Acts of Richard Beauchamp, Earl of Warwick' c1485.

England's short-lived triumph

Henry V's victory over the French at Agincourt, despite the daunting odds, was absolute, yet his immediate gains were minimal. However, Harfleur had been taken and Calais made doubly sure; moreover, the French never again dared attack Henry in the field. His newfound European prestige enabled him to negotiate an alliance with the Holy Roman Emperor, Sigismund, in August 1416; and a year later Henry again invaded Normandy and began a systematic conquest of his duchy. The capture of Rouen in 1419 and the murder of John, Duke of Burgundy, led to the Anglo-Burgundian alliance that Henry had sought since 1411.

This was the keystone to Henry's success in France. It gave him Paris and, through marriage to Catherine of Valois, made him Regent and heir to the throne of France by the Treaty of Troyes in 1420. But Henry died of dysentery contracted during his campaign at Meaux before he could consolidate his gains and begin the awesome task of conquering the Dauphin's France

south of the Loire. He was succeeded by his infant son, Henry VI, who was to grow into a saintly but inept ruler.

Once Henry V was dead, the French renewed their efforts to recapture their territory, aided from 1428 by the bizarre but inspiring figure of Joan of Arc. This enterprise was assisted by domestic strife in England, for with the death of Henry's able brother the Regent, John, Duke of Bedford, in 1431 and the ending of the Burgundian alliance in 1435, the great nobles again became disputatious.

Eventually, partly as a consequence of the ultimate loss of France, they took rival sides in the civil war known as the Wars of the Roses. By 1453 the English had again been driven out of France, save for the city-fortress of Calais. The great victory of Agincourt, it eventually turned out, achieved nothing more than to place the English Crown hugely in debt and unnecessarily prolong the Hundred Years War. Yet to this day, mention of Agincourt can still conjure up a vision of medieval English glory.

Gonzalo de Córdoba *1453-1515*

G onzalo de Córdoba was fortunate that he lived at a time when his great abilities could find profitable employment. After the union of Aragon and Castile, brought about by the marriage of Ferdinand and Isabella in 1479, Spain became an expanding power. It was Isabella, particularly, who encouraged and financed the voyages of exploration by Christopher Columbus; and it was 'the kings' who presided over the expulsion of the Moors from their last stronghold in Spain, Granada.

Born in Montilla in southern Spain, Gonzalo Fernandez de Córdoba was the son of a prosperous Castilian citizen, and he and his elder brother were brought up in Córdoba under the tutelage of a certain Diego Carcomo. It was this gentle and educated man who has been credited with inspiring Gonzalo with the 'generosity, greatness of soul, the love of glory, and all those virtues which subsequently marked his glorious career.'

These admirable qualities were Gonzalo's only inheritance, for the entire family estate descended to his elder brother. Spain was then not far from ruin; the cities were ungoverned, the nobility discontented, the people oppressed, and, worst of all, the country was wracked by civil war. The dire conditions, however, were to give Gonzalo the opportunity to distinguish himself as he craved, and his early experiences of warfare were in junior command during the civil wars. But it was in the service of Aragon and Castile, in the war against the Moors, that Gonzalo's military skills in both mobile and siege warfare were perfected. He repeatedly played a courageous and energetic part, and when Granada itself was finally liberated in 1492, his name was already widely known and held in high esteem.

His advancement at court was rapid, on account of his ability and handsome, engaging presence. Inevitably, his success, his great physical strength, his superlative horsemanship – an accomplishment much prized by the Spaniards – and prowess in all military exercises inspired envy in some of his contemporaries, but admiration in most.

He was particularly noted for his style: his furniture, his table, and especially his personal attire, were both elegant and luxurious, even on the battlefield. Gonzalo was, too, a deeply religious man – throughout his life he carried on his person a small image of the Holy Child – who showed a natural mercy to his defeated enemies. Thus, when he besieged a city, he would always try to persuade the military and civic authorities to come to honourable surrender terms, rather than see their homes and livelihoods destroyed. This attitude was hitherto unknown in European warfare; usually it was taken as a matter of course that a fallen town should be sacked, not only for the plunder but to provide revenue with which to pay mercenaries. In these diplomatic negotiations Gonzalo's appearance and dignified, courtly manner were more effective than cannon.

Estates and titles were lavished on Gonzalo – he was created Duke of Terranova and became the Viceroy of Naples – but his position was suddenly imperilled by the death in 1504 of Queen Isabella, who had been his staunchest supporter. In Spanish eyes, Ferdinand appeared lacklustre when compared with the resplendent figure of the 'Great Captain'. Aware of this and always suspicious of Gonzalo's power, the king, encouraged by Gonzalo's enemies at court, made him the object of insults and insinuations and ordered him to return to Spain in 1507. Distressed at the king's animosity and suspicion, Gonzalo, whose loyalty had been absolute, withdrew into private life. In 1515, at the age of 62, he died in bitterness and solitude at Granada from malaria contracted in Italy. As Scipio Africanus had discovered before him, Gonzalo found that the reward for loyal service is not always affection and gratitude.

The statue of Gonzalo de Córdoba in the church of St Jerome in Granada – scene of his early triumph over the Moors – shows him as a pious, armour-clad knight.
Spanish arquebusiers of the 16th century are commemorated in this frieze of tiles at the palace of the Marqués de Santa Cruz at Azulejos in Spain.

1453	*1 September* Born at Montilla.
1474/	Castilian War of Succession.
1479	Fights against the Portuguese at the Battle of Albuera.
1482	Final war with Muslim Kingdom of Granada: plays a prominent part at the capture of Tajara, Illora and Monte Frio.
1483/ 1487	Takes part in the Spanish military reorganization.
1487	*May-August* At the siege of Malaga.
1489	At the capture of Almeria.
1491	*April* Siege of Granada begins.
1492	*2 January* Negotiates the surrender of Granada.
1495	*6 May* Lands at Reggio di Calabria in southern Italy. *28 June* First and only defeat at the Battle of Seminara.
1496	*21 July* Captures the town of Atella and the French C-in-C, the Duke of Montpensier. Receives the sobriquet the 'Great Captain'.
1497	Clears the French out of the Kingdom of Naples, captures the French garrison at Ostia.
1498	*August* Returns to Spain.
1500	*December* With the Venetians, captures the Turkish-held islands of Cephalonia and Zante.
1502	*August* Defends Barletta against the second French invasion of the Kingdom of Naples.
1503	*26 April* Wins the Battle of Cerignola. *May-June* Retakes Naples. *June-October* Besieges Gaeta. *29 December* Wins the **Battle of the Garigliano**.
1504	*1 January* Surrender of Gaeta. Created Viceroy of Naples.
1507	Recalled to Spain.
1515	*1 December* Dies from malaria in Granada, aged 62.

Battle of the Garigliano/*29 December 1503*

IN 1495 FERDINAND and Isabella ordered Gonzalo to southern Italy to defend Spain's interests there against the French invasion. His army, whose pay was usually in arrears because of Ferdinand's reluctance to send funds, comprised 1,500 crossbowmen, 500 genitors (light cavalry), 100 men-at-arms, a few sword and buckler men, and arquebusiers.

At the Battle of Seminara in June 1495, which Gonzalo was obliged to fight against his better judgement, he was defeated for the first and only time by a French army of 800 men-at-arms and Swiss pikemen. The battle's chief interest lies in the effect it had on Gonzalo's tactical thinking, for it convinced him that the key to future success lay in the arquebus. Shortly thereafter he reorganized his army and equipped the bulk of his force with these handguns, calculating that *en masse* they could frustrate attacks from great numbers of crossbowmen, pikemen and even cavalry, as the English longbowmen had earlier done at Agincourt. He virtually dispensed with crossbowmen and men-at-arms.

His new tactics were first employed against the French at the Battle of Cerignola in April 1503. Here he stationed his arquebusiers, with pikemen behind them for hand-to-hand fighting in counter-attacks, on the lower slopes of a hill. At its foot a ditch was dug out and the spoil used to form a low rampart, with vine stakes driven into the top, to protect the arquebusiers. Gonzalo then positioned his artillery right opposite the French heavy cavalry on his left.

Gonzalo opened the battle by sending out his genitors to provoke the Duke of Nemours into attacking without prior reconnaissance. This he shortly did, only to have his cavalry halted by the ditch, while every charge of the pikemen and crossbowmen was brought down by the fire of the arquebusiers and he himself was killed. Each side had entered the conflict with about 8,000 men; the French lost about half their number, the Spaniards a mere 1,000.

The Battle of Cerignola, though of little significance politically, revolutionized European warfare. Gonzalo had turned the infantryman, armed with an arquebus, into the most important element in his army and in the space of an hour's fighting had threatened the last vestige of medieval knighthood and chivalry.

Gonzalo's great gifts as strategist and tactician were again displayed toward the end of the same year at the Battle of the Garigliano. This was to be his last battle but his most perfectly executed.

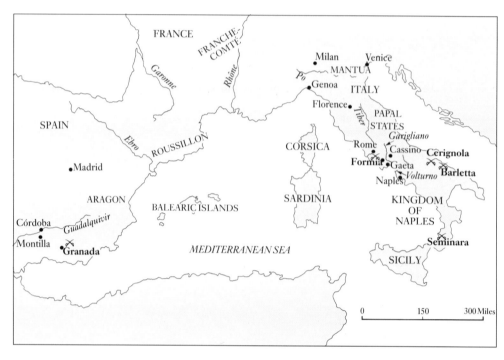

The remnants of the French Army so decisively beaten at Cerignola had collected in the fortress of Gaeta, situated on a headland on the coast north of Naples. Gaeta thus became the Spaniards' prime target. Yet even the talent and industry of Pedro Navarro, Gonzalo's specialist in the use of artillery and the construction of trenches in siege warfare, could make only insignificant progress against so well-sited and so strongly defended a citadel. A citadel, moreover, that could be replenished and reinforced by sea, since the French navy controlled the western Mediterranean Sea.

After several fruitless assaults, Gonzalo withdrew about 8km/5mls inland to Castellone, for fear of being caught between the impregnable fortress and an advancing French relief force. The French Army, together with Swiss and Italian levies hired on their southward march, numbered some 20,000 men.

Moving south from Rome, this army could take an inland road, the old Via Latina, or go along the Via Appia which followed the coastline. The French, under the Marquis of Mantua, opted for the inland route. On hearing of this, Gonzalo prudently moved inland to San Germano, close by Monte Cassino of World War II fame. Here, in 524, St Benedict had founded his order, and over the intervening centuries it had been turned into an enormous, fortified monastery.

It was now late October, however; rain seemed never to cease, cavalry and wagons could move only with great difficulty. The winter landscape offered no provisions and many soldiers in the French Army were dying of dysentery. The Marquis of Mantua therefore resolved to move westward to the Via Appia and thence to Gaeta, where provisions were abundant.

Gonzalo and his army, little more than half the number of the French, trailed their enemy along the southern bank of the River Garigliano, and early in November 1503 the two formations were facing each other near the sea, with the flooding river between them. The Marquis of Mantua brought matters to a head by building a bridge and getting his cavalry across the river. When about 1,000 of his men were over, Gonzalo attacked them; many of the French fled back, others were drowned and the bridge itself was destroyed by cannon fire, some of it inadvertently from the French side.

Further French efforts to cross the river, after they had rebuilt the bridge, also failed. The weather was now deteriorating rapidly, and Mantua decided to abandon operations until the Garigliano subsided and drier conditions would enable his cavalry to operate effectively. Indeed, conditions were so bad that the Marquis found it convenient to claim he was suffering from a fever and to withdraw from the scene, handing over command to his deputy, the Marquis of Saluzzo.

There ensued a period of six weeks deadlock, during which, as the British historian Sir Charles Oman has observed, conditions were very similar to those in the trenches on the Western Front during World War I. Mud lay everywhere and men could move only on 'duckboards'; food was scarce and the soldiers lived at best in improvised hovels of wattle twigs.

The Italian Wars

Europe suffered two grievous setbacks during the 14th century, notably the Black Death, which claimed roughly one-third of the population, and the sudden climatic deterioration (the 'Little Ice Age') that ended the earlier agricultural boom. The revival, which started about 1450, coincided with the growth of strong monarchy in most of Europe.

The Hundred Years War came to an end in 1453 when Charles VII finally expelled the English and gained control over the greater part of present-day France. Civil war in Spain ended with the union of Castile and Aragon in 1479; and in 1492 the Moors were driven from their last foothold in Granada in southern Spain. The advent of the Tudors in England in 1485 led swiftly to monarchical control and a centralized state. Only in Italy was it otherwise.

Despite the strong government of such able rulers as Lorenzo de Medici in Florence and Ludovico Sforza in Milan, the country remained fragmented in City-States, with a large central area under Papal control. These regions, with their wealth and treasures created by the Renaissance, offered plump prizes for the newly consolidated monarchies.

The so-called Italian Wars (1494–1559) began when Charles VIII, the vainglorious, pleasure loving young king of France, invaded Italy and seized Naples. His was a wild dream of grandeur, not based on any sound strategical judgement. In order to free himself for the exercise, he had first had to neutralize his potential enemies.

Charles ceded to Ferdinand of Aragon the Pyrenean states of Roussillon and Cerdeña, on the understanding that he should not be disturbed in his designs by the Spanish. He returned Franche-Comté and the Artois to the Emperor Maximilian on the same understanding. And he secured the neutrality of Henry VII of England by paying him 620,000 escudos in gold.

In this way, the impetuous and impolitic French king ceded territory which could not have been taken from him in a bid to conquer territory he could not possibly hold. Though his advance into Italy – more an excursion than a military campaign – was initially hugely successful, it immediately brought about a coalition against him of the Holy Roman Empire, the Papal States, Venice, Milan and – ominously – Spain, soon to be the leading military nation in Europe.

The war that followed devastated vast areas of Italy and enabled Gonzalo de Córdoba to earn the well deserved accolade of 'The Great Captain'.

This bitter period of trench warfare, and great suffering for both sides, but notably for the Spanish who lacked the provisions available to the French from Gaeta, is especially remarkable for the contrasting conduct of the respective commanders and their officers. While the Marquis of Mantua departed for pleasanter surroundings, Gonzalo lived in a hut only 1.6km/1ml back from the front. He visited his forlorn troops daily, thereby keeping his soaked and mud-bound army intact, though sullen. The French officers, following the example of their recently departed leader, lost interest in the proceedings and retired to the comforts and pleasures of the nearest town. Thus, though the Spaniards suffered the privations of a particularly cruel winter, they remained a united fighting force, while the leaderless French became dispirited and mutinous.

The last thing the French expected was that Gonzalo, who was known to possess inferior numbers, and numbers suffering disproportionately because they lacked a supply base, would launch a general attack during the last, freezing snowy days of December. But once he had ascertained how weakly the French lines across the river were manned, Gonzalo saw his long-awaited opportunity.

His tactical foresight was such that for some weeks, about 24km/15mls behind

Swiss pikemen

By 1503 Swiss mercenaries had dominated European battlefields for more than 30 years. They owed this position to their bravery, superior training and ferocity. Originally equipped with 2.4m/8ft halberds, they soon turned largely to 3m/10ft pikes to counter Austrian and Burgundian cavalry. By the 1490s, the shaft had been lengthened to 5.5m/18ft, with a 25.5cm/10in steel spike on the end. Most pikemen were unarmoured, only the front rank wore half or three-quarter armour and helmets, with the result that they could move rapidly. In attack, the pike was held with both hands well in front of the butt, at head height, but with the point slightly lowered.

The Swiss advanced swiftly, usually in three deep columns ranged in echelon from either right or left, with the pikes of the first four ranks projecting and those in the centre held erect – in much the same way as the Macedonian phalanx had done. A tenth of their number were deployed as arquebusier skirmishers in front.

They were organized in companies of 200 men, each headed by an elected captain and a standard-bearer. Each canton supplied a contingent, and there were often bitter rivalries between them. Regular pay

Massed pikemen were a formidable sight, as is shown in this clash with mounted knights at the Battle of Marignano in 1515 on the tomb of the French King Francis I. Used in combination with arquebusiers, they were a dominant force until 1700.

– *point d'argent, point de Suisses* – was essential to keep them from changing sides or going home.

The onslaught of pikemen, with banners waving and horns sounding, could be irresistible. At the Garigliano, although forming 40 per cent of the French Army, they did not get the chance even to form up and so fared badly in the Spanish pursuit.

Battle of the Garigliano/2

Gonzalo de Córdoba's opening move at the Battle of the Garigliano was a masterly example of attacking, then turning, a single enemy flank. This tactic, which Rommel employed successfully at Gazala, and Gustavus Adolphus might have achieved at Lützen had fog not suddenly descended, offers great rewards. It does, however, entail a commander exposing himself to danger when – as he must – he depletes other sectors of his front to provide numerical superiority at his point of main attack.

At the Garigliano, Gonzalo neatly solved this problem by deploying on his left flank a force sufficient to seize from the French the sole existing bridge – albeit a temporary one – across the river. Thus his centre and left were secure when he launched his heavily reinforced right wing in the attack at the town of Sujo.

The Spanish rout of the French at the River Garigliano reads like a modern surprise river crossing – indeed the British 56th Division crossed the river at much the same place in January 1944 during their advance on Rome.

On 29 December 1503, at dawn, in freezing cold and torrential rain, Bartolomeo de Alviano at the head of a force of 3,000 men, mainly cavalry, attacked the French in the village of Sujo. Gonzalo de Córdoba had chosen this spot for the crossing because the river here was relatively narrow, the banks were fairly firm, and they were not overlooked by the enemy.

Pedro Navarro, the expert siege engineer, had designed a pontoon bridge (1) that could be rapidly assembled on the spot. Construction began during the night of 28 December, after pontoons, precisely measured planks and lengths of rope, already prepared some 24km/15mls to the rear, had been brought up to the river on the backs of mules.

The drunken Norman infantrymen, asleep in their billets on the outskirts of Sujo (9), were taken completely by surprise when Alviano's men descended upon them and set fire to the barns and outhouses. They fled along the muddy river banks pursued by Spanish cavalry and pikemen.

Gonzalo de Córdoba himself (2), in command of the main body of Spanish infantry (3) and men-at-arms, as well as his own bodyguard, crossed over the bridge after Alviano's men. They made a splendid sight with their burnished armour and flags and banners, but there were few French left to see them. Afraid that all the enemy might escape him, Gonzalo sent a body of light horse ahead (8) to harass them as they retreated.

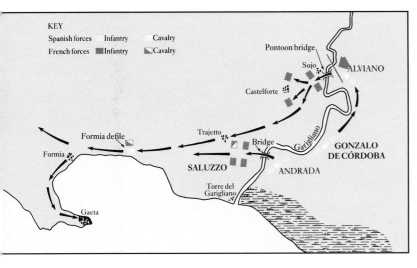

Down-river, some 8km/5mls away (**4**), all was confusion as the French tried to dismantle the bridge they had built in November and to carry off their artillery pieces in the small boats on which it floated. But before they could do so, Fernando Andrada led his cavalry across the river. The French, under the Marquis of Saluzzo, abandoned all their belongings, including nine cannon, and even their wounded, and under cover of a cavalry charge made an orderly retreat toward Formia.

Near Formia the road passes through a narrow defile; here the Marquis of Saluzzo rallied his cavalry and a fierce battle took place with the cavalry of the Spanish van. This was the only real fighting of the day, but despite gallant attempts by the French – it is said that the Seigneur de Bayard lost three horses killed under him – they were beaten back late in the day and retreated to Gaeta (**7**).

The French held the fortified port of Gaeta and also the small fort at the mouth of the river, the Torre de Garigliano (**5**). In addition, the French fleet (**6**) had been moored off the coast since November, ensuring them a safe supply route. This meant that they were in a strong bargaining position when the truce was negotiated with de Córdoba after the battle. All the French troops were allowed to go free, and all prisoners were released.

the front, he had been preparing materials for a bridge to enable him to get his army across the river to engage the enemy. He judged the moment right to attack when he received reinforcements comprising 1,400 light horse and 4,000 Italian foot, led by the redoubtable Bartolomeo de Alviano, whose faction, the Orsini, had concluded a treaty with Spain.

There seems to have been a truce of some sort between the two armies during the Christmas period of 25 and 26 December. The French, however, continued their celebrations, giving Gonzalo the opportunity on 27 December to bring up his pontoons from the rear on mules to a site opposite Sujo, on the French left flank. On the same day he also began to move up part of his army, with Alviano in charge, to the same point. He himself took command of the main force farther south. The remaining division, under Fernando Andrada, was left stationed opposite the French bridge on the Spanish left, with orders to hold the bridge and then, if matters farther upriver went according to plan, to attack across it.

The Battle of the Garigliano, which began on 29 December, fell into four distinct phases. At first light, the Spanish pontoon bridge was swiftly laid without opposition, for the French on the other side of the river were not yet under arms. Moreover, many of their officers were absent. Alviano's light cavalry, banners unfurled, brushed the French aside, then

The arquebus was the decisive factor in the Spanish triumph over the French at Pavia in 1525; after that, all European armies adopted it.

Siegecraft and fortifications

By the time Charles VIII and Gonzalo invaded Italy, cannon balls were made of iron, not stone; they were propelled by coarser gunpowder and could be fired faster. Trunnions enabled guns to be elevated and wheeled gun carriages meant guns could be rapidly deployed.

One of the most effective inventions was the gunpowder mine, since fortress walls could now be blown apart, rather than undermined and propped up with wood, which was then fired; the walls collapsed but left a huge barrier of rubble. Pedro Navarro, Gonzalo's expert siege engineer, used mines to spectacular advantage when he blew up Castel Uovo near Naples.

These developments stimulated the inventive Italian engineers. Defence in depth became the rule, with walls backed by ditches and ramparts of earth. Low-lying pointed bastions became platforms for artillery and small arms, and covered works within the ditches provided points from which to pour lateral fire on the enemy. The surest way to subdue a fortress was again starvation, guile or treachery.

The development of the arquebus

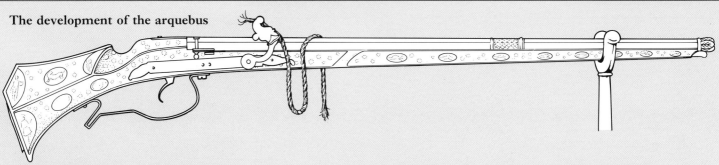

This heavy but portable matchlock gun was invented in Germany around the middle of the 15th century. The name comes from the French *arquebuse* or German *Hakenbüchse*, meaning literally 'hook gun', and is variously thought to derive from an anti-recoil hook, used when it was fired from a wall, or even from a hook on the gun by which it was attached to a support when fired. But it is more likely to refer to the curved butt.

There was no standard size for the arquebus in the early 16th century, but most guns were about 1.06m/3½ft long and weighed about 4.5kg/10lb. The weapon was often fired held against the cheek or chest. A target range set in 1508 in Augsburg is known to have measured 207m/226yds, so effective battle range was probably 137m/150yds or so.

The Spanish Army under Gonzalo de Córdoba was the first non-Turkish army to employ the arquebus in great numbers.

How the matchlock worked

The matchlock was a cheap and simple mechanism whereby a metal serpentine clipped to the gun held a smouldering 'match', or cord soaked in liquid saltpetre. When the trigger was pulled, the serpentine swung over so that the match sparked the gunpowder in the priming pan, setting off the main charge. This consisted of wadding and a 42g/1½oz ball, which were rammed down the barrel.

smashed through the village of Castelforte and on down the right bank of the river at such speed that the enemy had no opportunity to form a front. Meanwhile, Gonzalo moved his command up to the pontoon bridge and then over it.

The Marquis of Saluzzo tried to establish a front at Trajetto, indeed he ordered a cavalry charge at the advancing Spanish horse. It was in vain: nothing, it seemed, could now stop the Spanish onrush, and the French, in panic and disorder, fell back to a defile just east of Formia.

The third phase of the battle opened when the French managed to establish a line at the defile, a pass between the mountains and the sea, and fierce fighting ensued for about an hour. Saluzzo belatedly ordered the destruction of the French bridge on the lower reaches of the Garigliano, but by then Andrada, knowing that the attack was going as planned, had successfully stormed the crossing and seized most of the French artillery on the northern bank. Gonzalo's entire army was thus safely over the river.

Though the French were still fighting stubbornly at the defile, they were finally broken when Andrada's cavalry reached the scene. The Spanish horse, in the final phase of the battle, chased the shattered French, slaughtering their infantry and capturing their guns, all the way to Gaeta.

The Battle of the Garigliano was a remarkable achievement by any standard but especially when it is remembered that the original French force numbered more than 20,000 men and the Spanish less than 15,000. Gonzalo's victory was absolute.

Marquis of Mantua   Marquis of Saluzzo   Seigneur de Bayard

Francesco Gonzaga, Marquis of Mantua, (1466–1519) had handed over his command of the French Army to his deputy, Ludovico, Marquis of Saluzzo, (1438–1504) before the Battle of the Garigliano began. Saluzzo, whose tiny marquisate was known as the 'Doorkeeper of the Alps', was a noted *condottiere* – one of those commanders who during the previous 200 years had led bands of mercenary troops in the wars between the Italian City-States. But, like Mantua, he was an Italian and the French troops resented his being in command.

Though Saluzzo had a respectable record in the field, he lacked the ability to inspire his men, a particularly serious deficiency in the dreadful conditions prevailing in the Garigliano campaign. He himself died in Genoa of fever contracted there.

The fearless Pierre du Terrail, Seigneur de Bayard (c1473–1524), stood out as the most dedicated and appealing

Seigneur de Bayard

of the French commanders. After the Battle of Seminara, when Gonzalo was besieged in the city of Barletta, the French constantly taunted the Spanish with their alleged cowardice. Stung by their contempt, the Spaniards issued a challenge: 11 knights would fight an equal number of French knights outside the city walls. The French accepted;

Bayard was to be their champion.

The combat began at midday and was to end at sunset if not brought to a conclusion earlier. At first charge, seven French knights were unhorsed because the Spaniards aimed their lances at mounts not riders – an unchivalrous tactic in Bayard's view. Nevertheless, at sunset the four remaining Frenchmen, Bayard among them, were still fighting, and a draw was declared.

Bayard was one of the commanders at Gaeta after the French defeat at the Battle of Cerignola and gallantly commanded cavalry at the defile of Formia during the Battle of the Garigliano. He met a soldier's death in 1524, cut down by a ball from an arquebus in a hopeless charge against pursuing Spanish troops near Milan. He was among the last of the knights of the Age of Chivalry, 'sans peur et sans reproche', a breed finally rendered obsolete by the battle tactics of Gonzalo with his superlative use of the arquebus.

Destruction of the French Army

After the Battle of the Garigliano, the position of the French in Gaeta, though perilous, was by no means hopeless. They could hold off assaults no matter how hard pressed, and could be reinforced by sea. Gonzalo, therefore, readily accepted their surprising offer of surrender.

Under the terms of the truce reached on 1 January 1504, French troops in Gaeta were allowed to quit the city unmolested, by land or by sea, provided they swore never to fight in Italy again. Gonzalo released all prisoners without the payment of ransom.

More French elected to leave by sea than to undertake the long land march, but neither party found much fortune. Those that boarded the ships provided by Gonzalo without charge, among

them the Marquis of Saluzzo, perished in great numbers on the passage to Genoa. They died either from 'marsh fever' – malaria – contracted on the Garigliano or from debilitation caused by the long winter campaign.

Those who marched homeward up the length of Italy, notably the Swiss contingents, were attacked by the peasants whom they had earlier plundered and terrorized. Many died from starvation, and of those few who reached Rome most finally succumbed to fever. Barely a third of the French Army reached home.

French interest in the rich pickings to be had in Italy did not however cease, and later armies again clashed with the Spaniards. But Gonzalo's combined force of arquebusiers and pikemen had become the accepted fighting unit in the Spanish Army, and it continued to be successful against both cavalry and all types of infantry. After the rout of Swiss pikemen at Bicocca in 1522 and French cavalry at Pavia in 1525, all the European armies rapidly adopted the winning combination that Gonzalo had introduced.

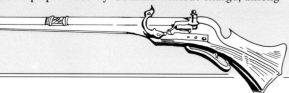

Gustavus Adolphus *1594-1632*

Gustavus Adolphus has been called the 'Father of Modern War'. Certainly, good organization, training, high morale and the effective all-arms combination of horse, foot and guns made the Swedish Army the most advanced of its day; and much of Gustavus's success in the field derived from his grasp of planning and administration.

When he came to the throne of Sweden in 1611, Gustavus Adolphus was not yet 17 years old, but his education had been dauntingly comprehensive. He was well versed in Latin (then still the language of diplomacy), knew some Greek, and was fluent in English and German. By the end of his life he was said to be at least acquainted with eight languages. Gustavus was also instructed in law, history and theology – he was a devout Lutheran, but unbigoted. His grounding in the military arts, however, was theoretical. In the practical aspects of his profession, Gustavus was largely self-taught, but his approach was original and innovative; for instance, he was among the first commanders to use the newly invented telescope.

Gustavus was a man of great personal courage, tall by the standards of the time, but broad shouldered so his height seemed less. His pointed beard and short hair were brownish-yellow, earning him the sobriquet 'Lion of the North'. Being heavily built, he was somewhat clumsy but could swing an axe with the strongest of his men. He took pride in sharing their hardships and, on campaign, lived much as his troops did. Even his dress was as simple as theirs, except that he habitually wore a scarlet sash or cloak.

Yet Gustavus was a king above all else – autocratic, self-confident, and with a will that brooked no defiance. Here, in part, lay the secret of his military success. As king, he could dispose his forces as he wished: he was his own commander-in-chief. This gave him, as it was later to give Frederick the Great and Napoleon, complete freedom of action, a boon vouchsafed to few modern commanders.

Although open and soldierly, Gustavus was a complex character. Ambassadors, misled by his simple friendliness, were soon brought to an appreciation of his knowledge – both theoretical and practical – and the agility of his mind, which enabled him to make rapid and sound judgements. He had also one of the essential attributes of the great commander: he understood human nature and so was able to surround himself with trustworthy and talented men, even among his Scottish and Irish mercenaries. And while he was abrupt in his dismissal of inefficient officers, he would readily promote the lowest footsoldier on merit. Above all, he inspired abiding loyalty in almost all who served him.

Of no one was this more true than of Axel Oxenstierna, the Swedish Chancellor, who had been adviser to the king from his youth. Taciturn and scholarly, Oxenstierna was the only man from whom Gustavus would accept both advice on great issues and criticism of himself without reproof or anger. Their bond endured throughout the king's life, for they exactly complemented each other. Gustavus had the impulsive passions of the genius, Oxenstierna the sober judgement of the great administrator. Each placed an absolute trust in the other. When Gustavus was killed at Lützen, his troops embarked on frantic, grief-stricken revenge against Wallenstein's men; Oxenstierna disguised his distress and carried out the king's plans as he had intended them.

One of the greatest tributes to Gustavus came from the Scottish captain, Robert Munro, who later wrote: 'For though he had bin no King, he was a brave warriour, and which is more, a good man, magnificent, wise, just, meeke, indued with learning, and the gift of tongues, and as he had strength of body, and a manlike stature, he had also the ornaments of minde, fitting to a brave commander.'

King Gustavus Adolphus c1630; this painting is attributed to Albert Cuyp.
Gustavus's seal bears the words 'Lord Gustavus Adolphus, by the grace of God, King of the Swedes, Goths and Vandals, Crown Prince of Finland, Duke of Estonia and Karelia'.

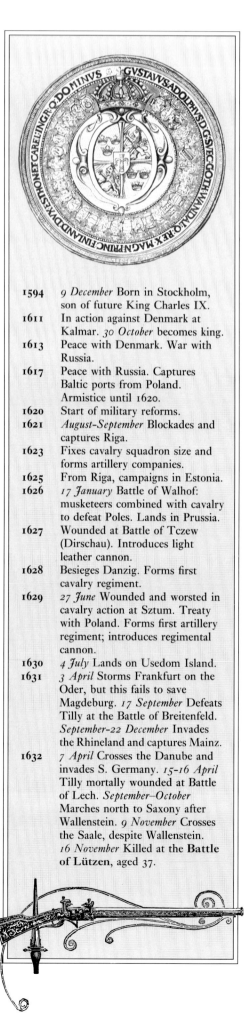

1594	*9 December* Born in Stockholm, son of future King Charles IX.
1611	In action against Denmark at Kalmar. *30 October* becomes king.
1613	Peace with Denmark. War with Russia.
1617	Peace with Russia. Captures Baltic ports from Poland. Armistice until 1620.
1620	Start of military reforms.
1621	*August-September* Blockades and captures Riga.
1623	Fixes cavalry squadron size and forms artillery companies.
1625	From Riga, campaigns in Estonia.
1626	*17 January* Battle of Walhof: musketeers combined with cavalry to defeat Poles. Lands in Prussia.
1627	Wounded at Battle of Tczew (Dirschau). Introduces light leather cannon.
1628	Besieges Danzig. Forms first cavalry regiment.
1629	*27 June* Wounded and worsted in cavalry action at Sztum. Treaty with Poland. Forms first artillery regiment; introduces regimental cannon.
1630	*4 July* Lands on Usedom Island.
1631	*3 April* Storms Frankfurt on the Oder, but this fails to save Magdeburg. *17 September* Defeats Tilly at the Battle of Breitenfeld. *September-22 December* Invades the Rhineland and captures Mainz.
1632	*7 April* Crosses the Danube and invades S. Germany. *15-16 April* Tilly mortally wounded at Battle of Lech. *September–October* Marches north to Saxony after Wallenstein. *9 November* Crosses the Saale, despite Wallenstein. *16 November* Killed at the **Battle of Lützen**, aged 37.

GUSTAVUS ADOLPHUS LANDED on Usedom Island on 4 July 1630 with an army of only 13,000 men; arrayed against him were Imperialist forces totalling some 100,000. But within two weeks he had occupied Stettin, the capital of Pomerania, and the Dukes of Pomerania and Mecklenburg shortly became his allies.

At this early stage of his campaign, Gustavus derived unexpected benefit from an astonishing decision taken by the Emperor, Ferdinand II. He had become overconfident and thought he could dispense with his commander Albrecht von Wallenstein, whose power he had come to fear. With Wallenstein's dismissal, half of Gustavus's enemies withdrew from the war, and the Swedish king was now confronted only by an army of 40,000 under Count von Tilly.

Despite this good fortune, Gustavus at first made only slow progress. The German princes, or Electors, wished above all to preserve their own territories and did not look with much enthusiasm on Gustavus. Their reluctance to fight was modified by the tragedy that shortly befell the Protestant city of Magdeburg. Tilly's army lacked provisions and ammunition, so he and his subordinate general, Pappenheim, determined to relieve their distress by capturing the well stocked and strategically important city of Magdeburg.

By May 1631, Gustavus was ready for battle and marched to the relief of the city, but the Protestant Elector, John George of Saxony, refused him leave to march across his territory. Tilly renewed his siege, and on 20 May the city at last fell.

The results were not what Tilly had planned. His victorious troops, after weeks of siege warfare on short rations, became rapidly out of control. Pappenheim had fired one of the great gates during the final assault, but whether this, or the drunken disorderly soldiers, was the cause of what ensued is unknown. At about midday, however, flames suddenly erupted in some twenty places at almost the same moment. Fanned by gusty winds, the raging fires soon converged and the entire city was consumed; of the 30,000 inhabitants, only about 5,000 survived. Here for all Europe to see was a Catholic atrocity of horrible proportions. Protestant states became resolute for war, and Gustavus emerged as their natural champion.

Tilly's position was now desperate, for the burning of Magdeburg left him still without provisions. The need for supplies became his sole preoccupation and at the end of August he invaded Saxony to

The Thirty Years War 1618–48

When Gustavus Adolphus, the Swedish king, intervened in the Thirty Years War in 1630, his objectives were many. His aim, he told his Royal Council, was 'to guarantee Sweden's position for a few years to come.'

The origins of the Thirty Years War lie in the religious disputes of the previous hundred years. The materialism and opulent lifestyle of the popes and higher clergy, together with their financial abuses, fired revolt, and in 1517 Martin Luther hammered his list of 95 theses on the church door at Wittenburg. The spirit of Protestantism exercised a vast appeal, particularly in England, Switzerland and much of Germany, and by 1560 only just over a quarter of the Holy Roman Emperor's subjects were still Catholics.

In 1618, however, politics rather than religion became the driving force toward a European war. In essence, it was a struggle between German Protestant princes, with their Protestant allies (at various times, Denmark, England, Sweden and the Netherlands) and the Habsburg empire.

Revolt against Emperor Ferdinand II began in May 1618 in Prague when two royal officials were unceremoniously thrown from a window by Protestant members of the Bohemian Diet, or parliament. The insurrection in Bohemia was savagely repressed, but fighting rapidly spread to the Palatinate.

At first the Habsburgs carried all before them. Then, in 1625, King Christian IV of Denmark, fearing the Catholics' growing power, entered the war. Opposed by two formidable commanders, Wallenstein and Tilly, the Danish advance foundered, and in 1629 the Danes withdrew from the war.

Gustavus's invasion of north Germany the next year was strategically sound. Sweden's population – and therefore its army – were small in comparison with that of the European powers. It would thus be impossible to guard the country's enormous coastline from a Habsburg invasion. In addition, if Gustavus could seize Silesia it would enable him to neutralize the power of Poland. It was a bold, sagacious decision.

pillage. It seemed as if he might destroy Leipzig as he had Magdeburg.

John George, Elector of Saxony, hastily signed a military pact with Gustavus. The two armies met at Duben and advanced to relieve Leipzig to the south. At Breitenfeld, on 17 September 1631, the Protestant and Imperialist forces faced each other. Tilly relied on the well-tried Spanish formation of weight, with massed pikemen guarded by musketeers; Gustavus on the newly devised manoeuvrability of his army. The result was decisive: The Holy Catholic League lost 13,000 men, the Swedes fewer than 3,000.

In April 1632, Gustavus again defeated the Imperial forces at the Battle of the Lech, where Tilly was mortally wounded. Gustavus then marched toward Munich, south of the Danube, and Ferdinand, now greatly alarmed, recalled Wallenstein. Gustavus had calculated that his southward march would draw his opponent away from Saxony in pursuit. Wallenstein, however, saw through this ploy and invaded Saxony.

As Gustavus was preparing to besiege Ingolstadt on the Danube, he received news on 8 October that the main Imperialist Army had crossed the Saxon frontier from the east three days earlier. This meant that Wallenstein would soon be astride Gustavus's lines north to the Baltic and on to Sweden. The situation was too perilous to tolerate. Gustavus, therefore, left small detachments in Bavaria and marched northward to Erfurt in Saxony — some 260km/162mls in 18 days.

From Erfurt, Gustavus moved to Naumburg on 31 October, and here he entrenched his army. Wallenstein, meanwhile, had advanced, but more slowly, to Leipzig. The armies were now just 40km/25mls apart. But the early days of November proved suddenly and unexpectedly cold, so Gustavus moved some of his soldiers nightly into billets in Naumburg. This confirmed Wallenstein's belief that the Swedish king did not intend to fight that year, and he allowed Pappenheim and his cavalry to move west and occupy Halle for the winter. Wallenstein was left with an army comprising some 20,000 men; Gustavus had roughly 12,000 foot and 7,500 horse. Wallenstein withdrew toward Lützen to establish his winter camp.

Now Gustavus resolved on battle, for though he was as yet without Saxon support, Wallenstein was without Pappenheim. It was essential to act quickly, but here luck turned against the Swedes. Rudolf von Colloredo, an Imperialist cavalry commander, stumbled upon Gustavus's advancing army. He realized

Reorganization of the Swedish Army
In 1620 the king introduced conscription for all healthy Swedish males up to the age of 50; with a minimum of 20 years at the age of 15. These soldiers were constantly drilled and well disciplined, and they were given not only uniforms but regimental badges, an innovation that enhanced morale and gave them a sense of belonging to a truly national army. The manpower shortage meant that Gustavus had also to rely on mercenaries, mainly Scots, Irish and German, but they were organized and equipped on Swedish lines.

Gustavus's tactical brilliance was evinced in his understanding of two crucial aspects of warfare: an army's mobility and its firepower. He increased the ratio of musketeers to pikemen, making the musket his chief weapon. Under this reorganization, in around 1620, a company comprised 72 musketeers but only 54 pikemen. Four companies made a battalion, eight battalions a regiment. By 1630, permanent brigades, known by colours and consisting of two, three or four regiments, made up the main battlefield formation.

Gustavus shortened the musket to 1.2m/42in, so removing the need for a firing rest, and lightened it to 6.8kg/15lb; the ranks were reduced from 10 to 6 to provide more linear firepower. Musketeers were trained to fire two- or three-rank salvoes, rather than rolling fire, and the 5.5m/18ft weapons of the pikemen were used to exploit the effect of this firepower, rather than simply for defence.

The cavalry, a large proportion of whom were Baltic volunteers with small horses, were divided into cuirassiers, armed with sword and pistol, and dragoons, or mounted musketeers. Drawing on his experience of aggressive Polish lancers, the king taught his light cavalry to charge home at the gallop with swords drawn; pistols were now definitely the secondary weapon. A further innovation was the employment of civilian engineers, miners and sappers as ancillaries, on hand whenever needed.

Swedish Field Artillery
Gustavus's greatest military innovation was, perhaps, in the area of artillery for, quite apart from equipment, in 1629 he formed the first artillery regiment. The 16 earlier types of gun were standardized into three calibres, and the king also sought a light gun to back up his new infantry regiments – a 'support weapon'.

In 1629, too, he brought out a 4-pounder of 66mm/2½in calibre and 272kg/600lb weight that could be drawn by two horses. By wiring the ball to a powder charge in a primitive cartridge, their rate of fire could be increased to three times that of guns which still needed powder ladled into them. With 9.4 guns to 1,000 men, Gustavus had unique, highly integrated and mobile firepower that could outshoot and overwhelm his foes. More than 40 of these regimental guns were in action at Lützen.

Swedish gun of the 17th century

that they were intent on attack, warned Wallenstein, and fought a delaying action behind the Rippach, a small stream that lay astride Gustavus's path to Lützen. By the time the Swedes were across the stream, it was mid-afternoon; battle could not be joined that day. Wallenstein now had time to call in his troops from their bivouacs and to summon Pappenheim, with his 8,000 men. Worst of all, Gustavus had lost the element of surprise.

Wallenstein, who thought soldiering was over for the winter, had been astonished, at 10.00 on 15 November, to hear three cannon shots, the prearranged signal by which Colloredo announced that the enemy was advancing. In desperate haste, he wrote to Pappenheim, still 56km/35mls march away, 'Sir, let everything else be, and hurry with all your force and artillery back to me.' That freezing night the two armies faced each other, every regiment 'lying down in the same order that they had marched.'

Between the two armies on the plain of Lützen, one of the flattest in Germany, ran the road to Leipzig to the northeast. At this point it had been constructed on a causeway, to either side of which were ditches which Wallenstein's soldiers laboured all night to deepen so that they could safely shelter his musketeers. About 3km/2mls northeast of Lützen, the road crossed a small canalized stream known as the Flossgraben.

Wallenstein deployed his army in a

Battle of Lützen/2

At Lützen, Gustavus Adolphus set out to envelop Wallenstein's vulnerable left flank, so as to drive his army back on Lützen and to prevent it seizing the Leipzig road, along which Gustavus was expecting the Elector of Saxony's troops to come to his assistance.

This tactic of enveloping a single flank entails engaging the enemy's attention with diversions, such as skirmishing or artillery fire, in one sector of the field before launching the main attack elsewhere.

The main danger is that in detaching formations to strengthen one wing, other points on the front are weakened. If the opponent sees this taking place, or anticipates the manoeuvre as Genghis Khan did at the Battle of the Indus, the results can be catastrophic.

But unforseen circumstances may also play a part: at Lützen, Gustavus's initial success could not be exploited at the crucial moment, when the manoeuvre seemed on the point of achieving its aim, because fog suddenly came down. As a result, overall command became impossible, and the Swedes were not able to take full advantage of their great opportunity.

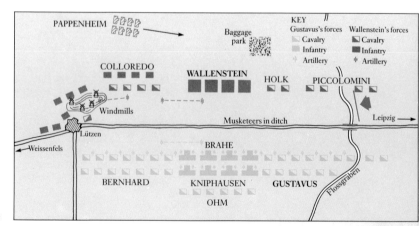

On the morning of 16 November 1632, thick fog shrouded the plain outside Lützen, where the armies of Gustavus Adolphus and Wallenstein were drawn up opposite each other.

The Swedish army (2) was ranged in two lines of cavalry and infantry, with their field guns, and a reserve force; Wallenstein's in a single line with the Spanish-style *tercios* (6) – great squares of pike and musket men – in the centre.

Wallenstein had earlier set fire to the town of Lützen (4) to cut off that line of retreat for his troops and to prevent the Swedes sweeping round and taking him in the right flank. On the slight rise known as windmill hill (5), he had positioned his nine heavy guns.

The fighting began with artillery fire and sporadic cavalry charges from both sides all along the line. After about an hour, the Swedes had pressed forward to the edge of the Leipzig road. During the previous night, Wallenstein's men had dug out the ditches on either side of the raised road, and these were lined with musketeers (3).

At about 11.00, the fog lifted and a weak sun shone through. This was the moment Gustavus had been waiting for. Without armour and wearing his familiar red sash, the king (8) led his right-wing cavalry (1) in a ferocious charge and overwhelmed the musketeers.

The king was wounded almost at once, but he stayed at the head of his men and took on Piccolomini's heavy cavalry (7). In spite of determined opposition, Gustavus's horsemen drove them back, and only the arrival of Pappenheim with reinforcements prevented a rout.

Then the fog again descended; in the confused fighting that followed, both Pappenheim and Gustavus were killed. When the Swedes heard of their beloved leader's death, they pursued their attack in a spirit of savage vengeance. Finally they overran the guns on windmill hill, and in the late afternoon Wallenstein retired to Leipzig.

single line, north of the road. His right wing was pinned on a group of windmills on high ground just north of Lützen, his left on the Flossgraben. He divided his army into three sections: centre, left and right. The centre comprised massed infantry; to the right and left were cavalry. His guns, probably a little more than 30 in number, were posted in two batteries, one in front of his right wing, the other in front of his centre right.

Gustavus advanced at first light, but the November mist was so dense that he was obliged to halt, even though he knew that every minute was bringing Pappenheim nearer to the scene of battle. Gustavus's principal object was to cut off Wallenstein from Leipzig, which lay to the northeast. This would not only deprive Wallenstein of a base to which he could retreat but would also open the road for John George, Elector of Saxony, whose force of some 1,500 men Gustavus expected hourly.

Gustavus deployed his army in two lines, one behind the other. In the centre

of both lines he stationed infantry and on either side positioned his cavalry. He himself commanded the right wing, Bernhard of Saxe-Weimar the left. Behind the whole deployment was a reserve of cavalry and in front of the infantry he posted, in the centre and left, his 26 field guns.

Gustavus's tactical problem may be simply stated: he had to dislodge Wallenstein from a defensive position of his own choice before Pappenheim and his cavalry arrived on the scene. He therefore posted his elite troops – Finnish and Swedish horse – on his right, with the object of turning Wallenstein's weak left flank.

Despite the fog, which descended and dispersed in unpredictable fashion, Gustavus's army was in position to attack at about 08.00. But shortly after 10.00, thick fog descended again, and the army had to stand to for another fretful hour. A little before 11.00, however, the sun at last broke through and Gustavus – three hours behind schedule – could attack.

Gustavus led forward his right-wing

cavalry and swept aside the Imperialist musketeers lining the causeway. Almost immediately, he was shot through an arm and his horse was wounded in the neck. He nevertheless charged on toward Piccolomini's heavy cavalry on Wallenstein's left flank, quickly driving it backward. Just then, Pappenheim arrived on the scene and restored order among the Imperialist forces in that sector of the battle, although in his charge against Gustavus he was mortally wounded. At this, panic caused his men to falter; then whole regiments began to flee.

Meanwhile, the cavalry on Gustavus's left flank, had charged and pushed back Colloredo's cavalry. At almost the same time, Gustavus's infantry in the centre advanced and seized Wallenstein's central battery of guns, taking seven and turning them on the Imperialists. Swedish victory seemed assured; but at precisely this crucial stage, the mist again descended. Not only did it prevent organized, disciplined fighting but it hid from the Swedes their dominance of the Imperial left and prevented their exploiting this advantage.

Meanwhile, Bernhard's attack faltered and the Swedish infantry were shortly thrown back, losing the artillery they had earlier captured – a repulse that was to cost Gustavus his life. No two contemporary accounts of the next few moments accord because the dense fog reduced visibility to a few yards. There is general agreement, however, that Gustavus, hearing that his centre was in retreat, galloped toward it with the Småland regiment of horse. He became separated from his force in the fog and, with only three companions, rode into a unit of Imperialist cavalry.

Gustavus's own plan for the disposition of his troops at Lützen, *right*, differs slightly from the order he finally adopted. Von Matthäus Merian's contemporary engraving, *below*, clearly shows the massed *tercios* of the Imperial Army and the much smaller, more mobile Swedish force, as well as the gun positions.

Almost immediately, he was shot; his careering horse bore him into further enemy cavalry, and another horseman shot him in the back. He fell to the ground and was dispatched, face downward, by a bullet in the head. His bloodstained horse bolted back to the Swedish lines, thus announcing the king's death to his troops.

Gustavus's death served to inspire his men to greater efforts. Nevertheless, by about 14.00 the battle was turning against the Swedes. Bernhard of Saxe-Weimar, upon whom the Swedish command had devolved, resolved to make a final, supreme effort to win the day.

His ferocious attack took the windmills one by one, together with all Wallenstein's guns. But by about 17.00, when dusk began to fall, the issue still appeared undecided. In reality, the outcome was clear. Wallenstein had lost his right-wing base and all his artillery; complete rout was avoided only by the stubborn resistance of his infantry, who were joined by Pappenheim's foot from Halle.

Wallenstein, ill with gout and fearful of the arrival of John George's force, whose number he wrongly exaggerated, could cope no more: he retired to Leipzig, leaving the field to the Swedes. Both sides were exhausted, out of ammunition and reduced to wielding musket butts; pursuit by the Protestants was impossible.

Losses can only be hazarded. Authorities suggest that the Imperialists suffered 10,000 killed, wounded or taken prisoner; the Swedes probably lost 5,000–6,000 men. The forces of Gustavus Adolphus were robbed of absolute victory by the cruel presence of fog and the war dragged on for another 16 years.

Albrecht von Wallenstein 1583–1634

Twice generalissimo of the Imperial forces, Wallenstein was a man of relatively humble origins who, by military skill, financial manipulations and extortion, acquired vast territories and a huge fortune. He built his power by augmenting his original lands with those of his rich bride, by purchase and later by requisition, until he held sway over the greater part of Bohemia. His enormous wealth enabled him to raise armies and to lend the Emperor Ferdinand vast sums of money, so placing him hugely in his debt.

In return, the Emperor allowed Wallenstein such freedom of action that he was not obliged to refer to Vienna before taking military action. The result was inevitable: enemies proliferated at the Imperial Court.

In 1630, when Ferdinand began to fear his growing power, he dismissed Wallenstein, but his strategic skill and combat success had made him indispensable and his enemies could not prevent his recall in 1631. Within two years, however, his defeat at Lützen and his scheming had left him distrusted and without allies. His health began to deteriorate rapidly and his always volatile mental state to degenerate into madness.

In January 1634, Wallenstein caused alarm and indignation at the Imperial Court by exacting an oath of personal loyalty from his colonels. He was also known to be in contact not only with Ferdinand's allies but his enemies,

providing excellent ammunition for his own many enemies. In February 1634, the Emperor ordered Wallenstein to be brought to Vienna for questioning or, if that were not possible, he was to be murdered. Hearing of the plot, Wallenstein fled to the fortress of Eger near the border of Saxony, and on arrival took to his bed.

On the evening of 24 February, just as four of Wallenstein's closest associates finished their meal, some of the Emperor's dragoons forced their way into the castle and cut them down. A moment later, the officers burst into Wallenstein's room: he was speared to death as he lay helpless in bed.

The Peace of Westphalia

Had either of the great commanders, Gustavus Adolphus or Wallenstein, lived, the war would probably have been ended quickly. In the event, it dragged on for a further 16 years and eventually embraced most of Europe. France, guided by the scheming and powerful figure of Cardinal Richelieu, entered openly into the conflict alongside Sweden in 1635; Spain joined the Imperialist side. The war was now in reality a struggle between the Habsburg and Bourbon dynasties, with the original religious disputes largely forgotten.

By 1644, however, it was clear that neither side could achieve outright victory, and in 1648 a compromise solution was evolved at the Peace of Westphalia. Religious toleration was granted to German Lutherans and Calvinists, although not within Habsburg territories, which remained staunchly Catholic. Austro-Spanish efforts to restore Roman Catholicism throughout central Europe had failed; and France emerged as the strongest military power in Europe.

The real loser was Germany itself. In the land over which the war had mainly been fought, the devastation was dreadful. The city of Marburg, for example, was occupied 11 times, Magdeburg besieged 10 times. Yet city dwellers could often survive, whereas peasants had no option but to flee. Agriculture, therefore, collapsed and famine ensued.

Some eight million people in Germany perished. It has been estimated that the German cities lost one-third of their population, and the rural areas as much as two-fifths. In Bohemia alone, of the 35,000 original villages, only 6,000 survived. As well as her agriculture, Germany's commerce and industry were ruined.

The Holy Roman Empire became little more than a name, and the might of the Habsburgs was greatly reduced. However, the Peace of Westphalia did mark the end of European warfare for religion's sake, and the political boundaries that were drawn remained unusually stable.

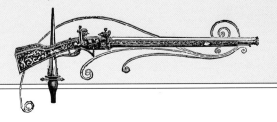

Vicomte de Turenne *1611-1675*

Henri de La Tour d'Auvergne was the second son of the sovereign prince of Sedan and Elizabeth of Nassau, daughter of William the Silent, both staunch Protestants. In youth, Turenne displayed none of the attributes commonly associated with a great commander. He appears to have had a sluggish mind and his tutor found him unable to express his thoughts; moreover, he was physically delicate and seemed unsuited for a rigorous military life. But even at the age of 13 he possessed great determination, and his every ambition was focused on succeeding in the profession of arms.

He devoted himself with discipline and perseverence to physical exercise and in this manner developed a robust constitution. Then, to prove that he was capable of enduring the hardships of war, unknown to his companions, he spent a winter's night on the ramparts of Sedan. In the morning he was found asleep on a gun platform, none the worse for his experience. When Turenne was 15 years old, he was strong enough to be sent to Holland by his mother to learn the arts of soldiering under his uncles, Maurice and Frederick Henry of Nassau. There he endured all the labours and privations of a common soldier before being given command of a Dutch infantry company.

He himself directed his soldiers through their exercises and supervised every detail of their training until, it was said, his company was the finest and 'best disciplined of the whole army'. This attention to detail was characteristic of his entire military career. Another of his qualities emerged at this period: he dealt with his men justly. He demanded much of them but was not brutal in his punishments and was liberal in his rewards. Thus, at an early age, he learned how to gain the respect and affection of those who served under him.

Turenne had nothing to recommend him as a courtier. He was of medium height, with broad shoulders and a large head, which he carried a little thrust forward. He had a ruddy complexion and, immediately noticeable, extremely thick eyebrows. He was simple in manner and, while being jealous of the respect due to his high birth, was without haughtiness and both disliked and distrusted ostentation. Turenne had, in fact, no liking for court life and remained with his troops in winter quarters as long as he could. When on campaign he lived a life of the utmost simplicity, in strong contrast to the pleasure-loving customs of most commanders of the period. One important emissary recalled being offered rabbit stew on a tin plate for dinner at Turenne's headquarters.

In almost every respect the Protestant Turenne was the opposite of the Catholic Condé, who was 10 years his junior. Turenne was excessively proud of his noble birth, but beyond that seems to have been free from vice. Nor was he a schemer, unlike Condé. Perhaps the most remarkable aspect of his career is that his military talents consistently grew, so that every campaign found him bolder and more masterly than before. He never attained Condé's capacity for instant decisions followed by prompt action, but he compensated for this by the correctness of his reasoning, which with time became more subtle and swifter. One Frenchman wrote: 'In speaking of a single campaign, we speak more enthusiastically of what Monsieur the Prince [Condé] did; but when it is over, we enjoy longer the fruits of what Monsieur Turenne did.'

Turenne's personal courage and his care for the safety and comfort of his troops won him their affection; his diligent, thorough preparations before battle and his masterly use of the elements of mobility and surprise earned the admiration of his king and contemporary commanders, as well as of many later commanders, notably Napoleon.

In this atmospheric painting of the Battle of the Dunes, painted by La Rivière in 1837, Turenne is shown directing the action; the besieged Dunkirk lies in the distance. A nineteenth-century engraving of Turenne after a portrait by Champaigne.

1611	*11 September* Born at Sedan.
1625/ 1629	In Dutch Army; rises to captain.
1630	Given command of a French infantry regiment.
1634/ 1635	Colonel in the Lorraine campaign; wounded at the siege of Saverne.
1636	Defeats Imperialists at Jussey and covers the siege of Jonville.
1638	As lieutenant-general helps take Breisach on the Rhine.
1639	Proposes raising of French dragoons; carried out from 1650.
1639/ 1641	Italian campaigns under Harcourt. Wounded at the siege of Turin (1640).
1643	*16 November* Made a Marshal of France, aged 32. Reorganizes the Army of the Rhine.
1644/ 1645	With Condé wins at Freiburg and Nördlingen.
1646/ 1648	Joins the Swedes in Germany and forces Bavaria out of the Thirty Years War.
1648/ 1653	In the *Fronde* Civil Wars changes sides, twice defeats Condé; saves Louis XIV and Mazarin from capture at Bléneau.
1654	Relieves Arras from Condé and the Spanish.
1656	*15–16 July* Forced by Condé to raise the siege of Valenciennes.
1657	Forced by Condé to raise the siege of Cambrai.
1658	*14 June* **Battle of the Dunes**.
1660	*5 April* Created the first Marshal-General of France.
1667	Invades the Spanish Netherlands.
1672/ 1673	Invades Holland. Outmanoeuvres the Imperialists on the Rhine.
1674	*16 June* Wins the Battle of Sinsheim across the Rhine.
1675	*5 January* Wins the Battle of Türckheim to crown his winter campaign in Alsace. *27 July* Killed at Salzbach by a cannonball, aged 63.

Battle of the Dunes/14 June 1658

THE GREAT QUESTION during the final years of the Franco-Spanish conflict was which side Oliver Cromwell would take. Following his victory in the English Civil Wars (1642–51), he had at his command, in the New Model Army, the finest military instrument in Europe, despite its being relatively few in numbers.

Though eagerly courted by both France and Spain, Cromwell's ultimate choice was almost inevitable. He lacked the acumen to see that the wars of religion were essentially over and that a new period of nationalistic wars had opened. But his final decision to join the French was not due solely to his hatred of the Spanish and of Catholicism, a hatred most Englishmen had shared since the time of the Armada, but also to his need for money, for England's coffers were empty. The prospect of obtaining some of Spain's great riches in the New World beckoned.

In 1654 Cromwell sent an invasion force to occupy Santo Domingo in the West Indies. Unaccountably for a commander of Cromwell's stature, the force was hastily assembled and the troops were undisciplined and, within a short time of landing, many men began to die from disease. Though Jamaica was taken, the expedition ended in fiasco, but it had a diplomatic effect of the utmost importance. Spain, naturally enough, became

The 'Frondes'

During the minority of King Louis XIV of France, between 1648 and 1653 there were two revolts against the government of Cardinal Mazarin, the chief minister, and the regent, Louis' mother, Anne of Austria. These came to be called the *Frondes*. The first, instigated by the *Parlement* of Paris, sought to limit the power of the hated Italian Mazarin and that of the Crown, and was supported by the great mass of the people, who suffered punitive taxation. The streets of Paris were barricaded, and Mazarin and Anne were forced to submit.

The Thirty Years War, fought mainly in Germany between Protestant and Roman Catholic powers, but with France supporting the Protestants for political advantage, was ended by the Peace of Westphalia in 1648. This released the French royal army, under the Prince de Condé, and enabled it to blockade Paris. But Condé's arrogance led ultimately to his arrest by Mazarin and Anne, which gave rise to the '*Fronde* of the Princes'. The uprising was finally subdued, but Condé, when he was released, took service in the cause of Spain, which had remained at war with France since 1635.

The King of Spain did not sign the Peace Treaty of Westphalia because he did not consider himself beaten; moreover, the *Fronde* had left France ill governed, a situation in which the Spanish king saw nothing but opportunity for himself. When Oliver Cromwell, Lord Protector of England, allied himself with France in 1657, further campaigning became inevitable.

passionately hostile to Cromwell and at once offered her support to his greatest enemy, Charles Stuart, the future King Charles II of England.

Cromwell was then obliged to make a treaty with France, which in March 1657 was extended into an offensive and defensive alliance. Under the terms of the Treaty of Westminster, Cromwell was committed to sending 6,000 English infantry, or 'Ironsides', to Flanders, where

the fighting with Spain was most severe, and to keeping a fleet stationed off the Flemish coast.

The plan was that an Anglo-French army should besiege Dunkirk, Mardyk and Gravelines. The first two towns, when taken, were to become English possessions, while the last would be kept by the French. Though Mardyk and some small towns fell, Marshal Turenne – who commanded the Anglo-French force – prudently declined to besiege Dunkirk until the following year, 1658, when Cromwell sent him two more regiments, each comprising 1,000 of his Puritan soldiers.

On 27 May 1658, Turenne duly laid siege to Dunkirk. Don Juan of Austria, the younger, Captain-General of the Spanish Army of Flanders stationed at Brussels, became alarmed and marched to its relief. The Prince de Condé repeatedly warned Don Juan not to advance without his full complement of field guns, which were laborious to move over muddy terrain and would take time to bring forward, nor without all his infantry. However, Don Juan elected to ignore the great Condé's advice, with calamitous results.

The two armies were of roughly equal strength, but whereas Turenne was a commander of the first rank, Don Juan was indolent, unobservant and without imagination. The Army of Flanders, moreover, was commanded by a motley group: the 29-year-old Don Juan himself, Condé, the Marquis of Caracena and James, Duke of York, (brother of Charles Stuart and later England's King James II) who had been reluctantly drawn away from serving with Turenne and into the Spanish camp when Cromwell made his two treaties with France

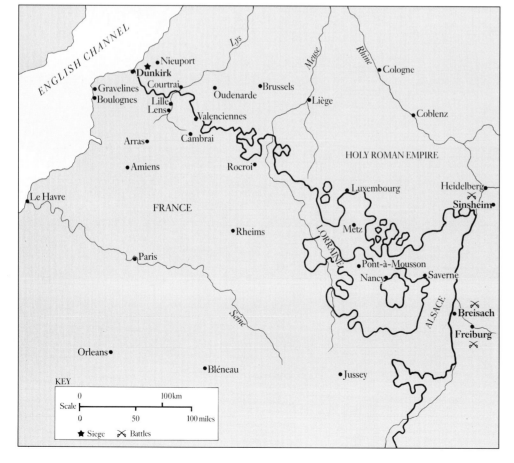

KEY

Scale		
0		100km
0	50	100 miles

★ Siege   ✕ Battles

The 'Ironsides'

The New Model Army, England's first standing army, was formed in 1645 by Sir Thomas Fairfax with 12 infantry regiments, each 1,200 strong, made up of one-third pikemen and the rest musketeers. The 'Ironsides' wore red coats, which remained the uniform of the British Army until the formal adoption of khaki in 1902. The New Model Army had won the first Civil War by 1646 and, under Cromwell, was victorious throughout the British Isles in the second Civil War of 1648–51.

Cromwell's 1657 expeditionary force to aid the French was unusual in consisting entirely of infantry and in being all-English, at French insistence. Ironically, the French Dillon Regiment was composed of Irish fugitives from Cromwell's wrath.

The group of Commonwealth soldiers depicted below in the uniforms of 1658 appears to be a parleying party. The mounted officer, bearing a document, wears a 'lobster' helmet, with the tail dipping down to cover the back of his neck. The morion helmet of the pikeman, who carries a halberd to which a white truce flag has been attached, closely imitates the style of the contemporary Spanish helmet, while the drummer has the more usual felt hat.

Both forces comprised some 14,000 men: Turenne had 8,000 foot, 6,000 horse and 10 guns; Don Juan had no guns and only 6,000 foot, but 8,000 cavalry. However, Don Juan's superior strength in cavalry – often the decisive arm in battle – was of little advantage on the terrain near Dunkirk, for the sand dunes were exhausting for the horses, especially when they carried the considerable weight of an armoured rider and his weapons.

When he decided to give battle, Turenne reached his full complement of men only by summoning from Mardyk his English allies under Sir William Lockhart, Cromwell's Scottish-born ambassador to France. Turenne had given his messenger a letter to Lockhart, explaining his reasons for doing battle with the Spanish Army at that time. Lockhart's confidence in his superior was such that he did not bother to read the letter, remarking, 'I take the reasons for granted; it will be time to hear them when the battle is over.' He immediately ordered Major-General Thomas Morgan, the infantry commander, to march to Turenne's assistance.

At 05.00 on 14 June 1658, Turenne's army moved out of its positions to take station for attack about 5km/3mls east of the besieged fortress, on what were to be the Anglo-French evacuation beaches in 1940. Both James, Duke of York, and Condé told Don Juan that Turenne's army was assembling for attack and advised an immediate retreat, but he dismissed his opponent's manoeuvre as no more than a move to drive in his light cavalry screen, positioned to his front to watch enemy movements and dispositions. Condé, infuriated by this incompetent reasoning, turned to the young Duke of Gloucester, the third son of Charles I, and asked if he had ever seen a battle. The Duke, at that time only 18 years old, replied that he had not. Condé caustically replied, 'Then within half an hour you shall see us lose one.'

It was some time before Don Juan finally realized that he was indeed about to be attacked. He accordingly made his dispositions, though the Spanish – who were meticulous but ponderous in manoeuvre – were in confusion. Don Juan drew up his army between the seashore on his right and the Bruges-Furnes Canal on his left, with all his infantry in front.

On his extreme right was a sandhill that rose higher than the others; rightly judging this to be the crucial feature in his front, he garrisoned it strongly with four Spanish infantry regiments. To their left he positioned Charles Stuart's five Royalist regiments – 2,000 English, Scottish and

Irish infantry – commanded by the Duke of York; while to the left of them, stretching to the canal, were battalions of Germans and Walloons under Caracena's command. Behind the infantry, Don Juan massed his own cavalry wing, while Condé held the left, but he was so close to the canal that his cavalry had to form six lines.

Turenne's dispositions were altogether different. In his front line he deployed 11 squadrons of French cavalry both on the right and the left, with 11 battalions of infantry (four of which were English) between them. His second line, although less numerous, was deployed in the same manner: cavalry right and left, with seven infantry battalions between. Further troops of horse were placed between the two lines and to the rear. On his right he also sagaciously sited four or five pieces of field artillery in anticipation of a Spanish cavalry charge. His other five guns were on his left, in support of the English.

Already the unobservant Don Juan had made a tactical miscalculation, and one which Turenne would be quick to exploit. The Spanish commander, when pinning his right flank on the sea, had failed to take into account that it was past high tide and that shortly, as the water receded, Turenne could, if he chose, envelop his right flank. Moreover, this right flank, which incorporated the strong defensive position of the high sandhill, was shortly to be subjected to bombardment from three frigates of the English fleet that had been brought up from their blockading duties off Dunkirk.

Turenne's assault began at about 08.00, when the English infantry under Morgan charged toward the strongly held sandhill, projecting 100 paces in front of the Spanish right. While musketeers from Lockhart's Regiment poured fire on the top of the sandhill from both right and left, pikemen advanced to the foot of it, where they briefly halted and re-formed. Then, with a great shout, they launched themselves up the side of the dune, hauling each other up in the steepest places.

Many officers were killed by Spanish fire but the pikemen pressed gallantly on. Stiff fighting ensued, and Don Gaspar Boniface's Spaniards were ultimately driven from the dune in confusion. The Duke of York, careless of his own safety, charged at Morgan's triumphant regiment with his single troop of 50 horsemen. But he was driven back, after breaking into a Cromwellian regiment that resisted with musket butts and refused quarter.

As this fierce struggle was in progress, the Spanish right continued to be bombarded by the English fleet. Then, when

At the Battle of the Dunes, Turenne employed one of the most often used and effective opening moves – trying to turn one of the enemy's flanks, as Gonzalo de Córdoba did with such spectacular success at the Battle of the Garigliano in 1503 and Gustavus Adolphus almost succeeded in doing at the Battle of Lützen in 1632. The danger with this tactic comes if the opponent anticipates the move, as Genghis Khan did at the Battle of the Indus in 1221.

The battle opened at about 08.00 on 14 June 1658, when Lockhart's regiment of English infantry, under Lieutenant-Colonel Fenwick, advanced from their position on the French left centre to attack the heavily defended sandhill on the Spanish right. The incline was so steep that Fenwick ordered his men to pause at its base for a minute or two to get their breath. Meanwhile, the musketeers accompanying the pikemen maintained a steady fire on Don Gaspar Boniface's Spanish *tercio*, comprising pikemen, (4), and musketeers, (5), stationed on the top of the sandhill.

Fenwick's pikemen (2), on his order, then struggled up the side of the sandhill, each man hauling up a comrade from behind him, and in turn being hauled up himself. Many officers, including Fenwick, were killed or wounded but the troops pressed on, reached the summit and at once engaged the enemy. Despite being exhausted by their advance and climb, and despite stiff resistance from the Spanish, who were fresh, they drove the enemy from the sandhill in disorder.

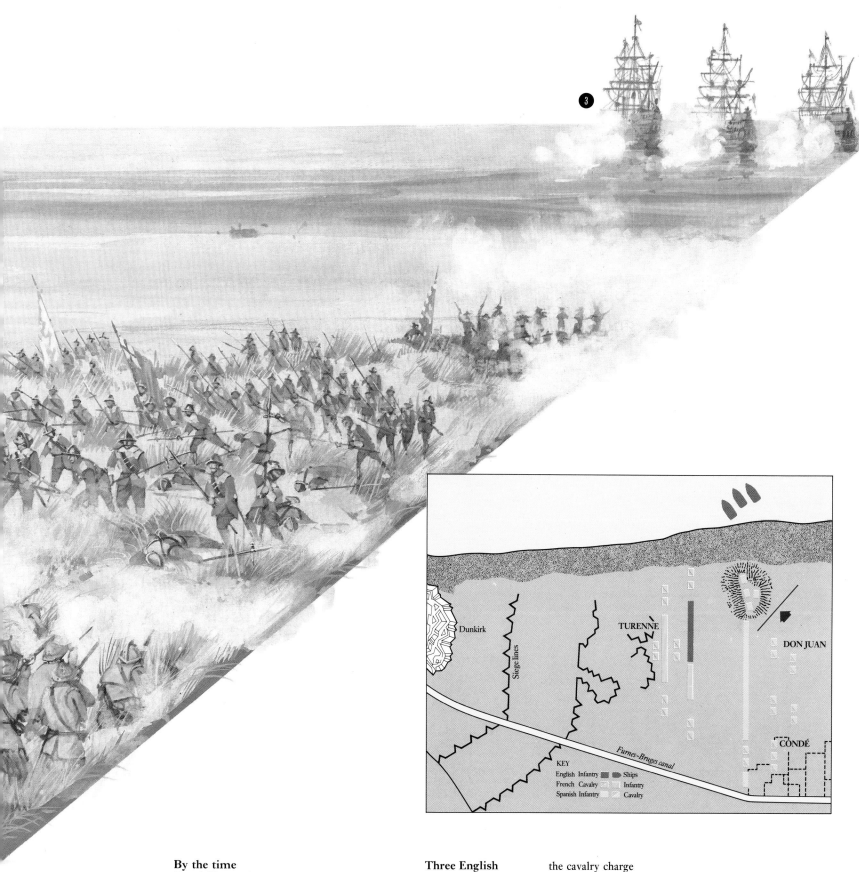

By the time
Fenwick's men had
reached the top of the
dune, the tide was
going out. Turenne
then ordered the
Marquis of Castelnau
and his 1,300-odd
French cavalry (1) to
charge along the
strand and take the
Spanish right in flank.

**Three English
frigates** (3) seeing
the opening moves of
the battle, and
correctly judging the
Spanish right to be the
crucial point of
conflict, opened fire
on them, causing
heavy enemy losses.
   These three moves
– taking the sandhill,

the cavalry charge
along the strand, and
the supporting naval
bombardment –
caused the Spanish
right to disintegrate
and virtually assured
French victory.

the confusion was at its greatest, Turenne ordered the Marquis of Castelnau, commanding the French cavalry on his left, to charge along the strand exposed by the ebbing tide and take the Spanish right in the flank. Soon the entire Spanish right wing was enveloped and began to disintegrate.

Meanwhile, as the French infantry in the centre were slowing pushing their opposite numbers backward, the Spanish left flank was suffering heavy losses, inflicted by Turenne's four strategically sited guns. Condé threw his troops at the French right with the object of saving the day and reversing Turenne's ascendancy by reaching Dunkirk. Three times he charged and drove back the French cavalry, but a battalion of French Guards sited in the dunes fired remorselessly into his right flank and wrought havoc among his squadrons. Many officers were cut down and Condé's horse was killed under him; though he quickly mounted another, he only narrowly escaped capture.

Turenne, who expected the Spanish charges, hurried to the danger spot and assailed Condé's cavalry. Once more Condé rallied his horsemen, charged and even fought hand-to-hand himself. But the day was lost, for though fresh French troops came to Turenne's support, there were none available to Condé.

Great commander that he was, Condé accepted defeat – which might have been avoided had he, not Don Juan, had overall command of the Army of Flanders. As best he could with his much reduced, demoralized and defeated cavalry, he conducted a covering retreat to enable the remnants of the Spanish Army to escape eastward. In the centre, the 300-strong King's Royal Regiment of Guards, English ancestor of the 1st Foot or Grenadier Guards, stood its ground but had to submit when the French took two of its officers on to a sandhill and showed them that the Army of Flanders had fled the field. They surrendered, provided they were not handed over to the Cromwellians.

The battle had lasted a mere four hours and Turenne's triumph was complete. Although Don Juan, Condé, Caracena, and the Dukes of York and Gloucester

The Spanish 'tercio'

Between 1534 and 1704, most of Spain's infantrymen were organized into *tercios*. The forerunner of all modern regiments, this was the first permanent, sizeable and named infantry formation in Europe since the Roman legion. At the beginning of Philip IV's reign in 1621, there were 35 *tercios* in the Spanish Army. On paper, each numbered 3,000 men in 12 companies. From 1636, the company was reduced to 200 men and constituted 11 officers, 30 musketeers, 60 arquebusiers and 99 pikemen. But the famous 20 *tercios* destroyed by Condé at Rocroi in 1643 averaged only 1,000 men each, and more heavy losses were suffered at Lens in 1648.

Typically, the *tercio* was a massive troop formation consisting of a central block of pikemen surrounded by musketeers who also formed squares at the corners.

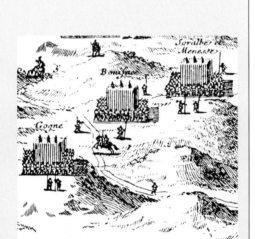

Don Gaspar Boniface's 'tercio', routed by the English infantry, appears in the centre of this detail from an old pictorial map of the battle.

Condé is depicted at Freiburg, throwing his marshal's baton into the enemy's trenches; he then commanded his troops to bring it back, so forcing an attack.

Prince de Condé 1621–1686

Seventeenth-century commanders were liable to change their allegiance without inhibition. Thus Louis II de Bourbon, Prince de Condé, at one time served Louis XIV, then later Philip IV of Spain, before returning to his original loyalty.

Condé, dubbed 'The Great Condé', was a commander of the highest order whose military gifts were evident at an early age, for he was only just 21 when he defeated the Spanish Army of Flanders at Rocroi in 1643, during the Thirty Years War. Condé and Turenne combined to win several hard-fought victories in Germany between 1643 and 1645. In 1646, Condé besieged and took Dunkirk for France for the first time; ironically, in view of later events. At Lens in 1648, Condé inflicted another defeat on the Army of Flanders.

After the *Fronde* of the Princes and his release from imprisonment by Mazarin in 1651, the aggrieved Condé allied himself with Spain. As a result, he and Turenne found themselves opposing each other for seven successive campaigns, chiefly memorable for their manoeuvring skill and fluctuating fortunes. After his defeat at the Battle of the Dunes, and having been pardoned by Louis XIV, Condé returned to French service. In 1668 he overran Franche-Comté; he defeated William of Orange at the Battle of Seneff in 1674; and, fittingly, he restored the situation on the Rhine after Turenne was killed at Salzbach. In the same year, 1675, he retired to Chantilly.

Although many of his contemporaries found him unreliable and insufferable on account of his constant scheming and extravagant pride, Condé and Turenne remained friendly. Indeed, Turenne wrote admiringly of 'his personality, his courage, and his leadership.'

managed to escape, the Spanish and their allies lost about 1,000 men killed and nearly 4,000 taken prisoner. At least 500 of the casualties were English Royalists. Turenne's losses have been estimated at no more than 400, most of whom were among the courageous English contingent that had stormed the sandhill.

That night, Turenne wrote to his wife an account of the day: 'The enemies have come upon us; thank God, they have been beaten! I have worked somewhat hard all day, so I shall wish you good night and go to bed.' It was a laconic, modest description of a victory so complete that it virtually ended a war of 23 years' duration.

The young King Louis, accompanied by Turenne and his victorious army, enters Dunkirk on 25 June 1658.

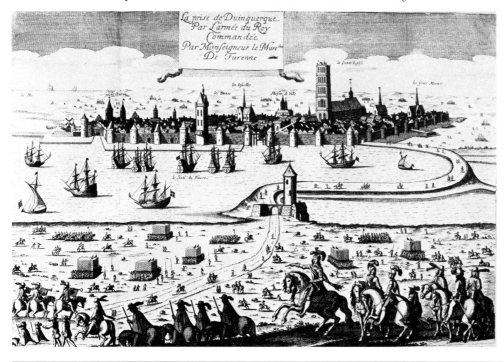

French Army logistics
By 1658 the French Army was beginning to benefit from some far-reaching reforms in supply, or logistics (the word ultimately derives from the French *loger*: to quarter troops). The architect of this reform was Michel Le Tellier (1603–85), who had been *intendant*, or supply officer, to the Army of Italy in 1640–2 under Turenne; he strove to obtain regular pay for the troops and to root out corrupt contractors.

In April 1643, Le Tellier became Secretary of War and, as such, instituted four main reforms: ration scales according to rank; standard contracts, escorts, payment and compensation for the sutlers who supplied each company; a wagon train with reserve rations for the army in the field; and the formation of a corps of *intendants*.

Turenne's 1643 Rhine campaign benefited from food magazines at Metz, Nancy and Pont-á-Mousson. In 1644 Le Tellier set up a cavalry magazine with the vast amounts of fodder (9kg/20lb per horse per day) needed at the first siege of Dunkirk.

The Le Tellier-Turenne partnership worked admirably in 1658. A magazine at Calais supplied the besiegers of Dunkirk by sea; and after the port's capture, Turenne's inland advance was supplied with bread and ammunition by river and canal barges.

The Peace of the Pyrenees
After the Battle of the Dunes, the great object of French strategy was to take Dunkirk and then present it to the English, as they were obliged to do under the terms of their treaty with them. Three days after the battle, Turenne's regiment, having returned to its investment of the town, gained a footing on the counterscarp – the sloping wall of the ditch surrounding the town.

The governor still held out resolutely, but on 23 June he died from a wound received earlier, and his 3,000-strong garrison lost heart and opted for surrender. On 25 June the defenders marched out of Dunkirk as prisoners of war, watched by the 19-year-old Louis XIV, who duly handed over the town to the English.

Napoleon, commenting on the campaign, criticised Turenne for not immediately marching – as he himself would have done – on Brussels, the administrative centre of Spanish government in the Low Countries. Political considerations were the cause of Turenne's decision, for the relinquishment of Dunkirk had caused unrest in France. To restore good order and renew confidence in his administration, Mazarin needed the army to take Gravelines, before the English – who were committed to help in its investment provided it began before September 1659 – withdrew. Strongly besieged, Gravelines fell on 27 August 1658, as shortly did numerous other towns of strategic and economic importance in Flanders, notably Oudenarde.

Turenne was preparing to renew the campaign in 1659, but his great victory at the Dunes had induced Spain to seek peace terms. The Peace of the Pyrenees was concluded on 7 November, after a

In 1662, having bought Dunkirk back from the English King Charles II for £5 million, Louis again rode into the city, which he refortified and turned into a naval base.

truce had earlier been agreed. France kept almost all her conquests in Flanders, and the young Louis XIV gained as his bride the Infanta Maria Theresa of Spain, Philip IV's daughter.

This union was intended to prevent further discord between the two countries; in fact, it was to lead to dynastic complications that would, 42 years later, bring about the War of the Spanish Succession. But already the magnitude of Turenne's achievement at the Battle of the Dunes was evident: Spain, once the supreme military power, had been supplanted by France.

Duke of Marlborough *1650-1722*

John Churchill, Duke of Marlborough was perhaps the most outstanding commander Great Britain has ever produced. Certainly, only Wellington stands comparison. True, neither was an innovator, both seeking rather to make the most efficient use of current weaponry and technical expertise. But there any valid comparison ends, for Wellington, save in the Waterloo campaign, never bore the great diplomatic burdens that were Marlborough's lot. Throughout the long war against Louis XIV, Marlborough alone held the shaky Allied coalition together by his political, diplomatic and military skills. Were it not for Marlborough, the power of France might not have been broken.

Born the son of an impoverished Royalist squire, John Churchill became a page to the Duke of York, later James II, in 1665. He entered the army in 1667 and was rapidly promoted under the duke's patronage. His marriage to Sarah Jennings in *c*1678 was to have important consequences for his career, for she had been a childhood friend of James's daughter, the Princess Anne, and remained an influential and close confidante when Anne became Queen in 1702.

Churchill served James well, but eventually became antagonized by his fanatical Catholicism and treasonably corresponded with William of Orange, later William III, and supported his cause in the 'Glorious Revolution' of 1688. Though William, on his accession, created Churchill Earl of Marlborough, he soon became jealous of his military talents, while Marlborough resented William's treatment of the Princess Anne. Now he made tentative moves to change sides again and corresponded with James in exile. The correspondence was discovered, and Marlborough fell from favour. In 1702, however, Anne, who had remained loyal to Marlborough, became queen, and he was given the fullest scope for his genius in the War of the Spanish Sucession.

By the time of Oudenarde, Marlborough was turning grey; but he retained his good figure, bright eyes, even teeth and healthy complexion. Though of only medium height, he was an imposing figure in his scarlet uniform and Garter star and ribbon, although he was usually careless of his dress. Marlborough was a devoted husband and father; he also had great charm and was socially agreeable. Sophia, Electress of Hanover and mother of the future George I of England, wrote of him after their first meeting: '. . . his manners are as obliging and polished as his actions are glorious and admirable'. He could, however, dissemble when occasion arose, as his changing loyalties to James II and William III showed. And while amassing a great fortune, he was notoriously frugal, not to say mean: on campaign he dined in turn with his various senior officers to get to know them well, but never returned their hospitality.

Despite his great victories, Marlborough was falsely accused of misappropriating public funds and early in 1712 was dismissed. The reasons were wholly political. Queen Anne had favoured the Whigs, the political party that supported the war. Unfortunately for Marlborough, his wife quarrelled with the Queen, who then came under the influence of Abigail Masham, cousin of Robert Harley, one of the anti-war Tory leaders. In 1710, the Whigs fell and Harley came to power. The war was expensive, and Marlborough – again, falsely – was accused of deliberately continuing it for his personal aggrandisement and to finance the building of his great new home, Blenheim Palace.

Marlborough returned to England only in 1714, on the accession of George I, when he was again given command of the army. But disillusioned and ageing, he took little further part in public life.

John Churchill, Duke of Marlborough, wearing the blue sash and insignia of the Order of the Garter; painted by Sir Godfrey Kneller c1700.
The quarterings, crest and supporters of the First Duke of Marlborough.

1650	*5 June* Born in Devonshire, son of the cavalier Winston Churchill.
1667	*24 September* Ensign in the Foot Guards, King's Own Company.
1672	*8 June* In naval Battle of Solebay; promoted captain.
1673	*17 June–8 July* Siege of Maastricht.
1674	Serves under Turenne at the Battles of Sinzheim and Enzheim.
1678	Becomes colonel of Foot.
1685	*6 July* Major-General; second in command at the Battle of Sedgemoor.
1689	*24 February* Created lieutenant-general and Earl of Marlborough. *27 August* In the Battle of Walcourt near Namur.
1690	*September–October* Irish campaign; takes Cork and Kinsale.
1692/ 1698	In disgrace and dismissed from the army.
1701	*12 June* General over all Foot Forces in Holland.
1702	*March* Becomes C-in-C Holland, Master-General of the Ordnance and Captain-General of Her Majesty's Land Forces. *April–October* Takes Liege and five other fortresses. *November* created Duke of Marlborough.
1703	Takes Bonn, Huy and Limburg.
1704	March to the Danube. *2 July* Battle of Schellenberg. *13 August* Battle of Blenheim.
1705	*17–18 July* Forces the Lines of Brabant at Elixhem.
1706	*23 May* Battle of Ramillies.
1708	*11 July* **Battle of Oudenarde.** *13 August–9 December* Siege of Lille. Retakes Ghent and Bruges.
1709	*11 September* Battle of Malplaquet.
1710	Takes Douai, Béthune, St Venant and Aire.
1711	*August–September* Forces the Lines of Ne Plus Ultra and takes Bouchain.
1712	Dismissed by Queen Anne.
1714	Returns to England and is reinstated as Captain-General.
1722	*16 June* Dies at Windsor Lodge, aged 72.

Battle of Oudenarde/*11 July 1708*

THE DUKE OF Marlborough was well aware that the inconclusive soldiering of 1707 in Flanders, the main theatre of war, had put the alliance of Great Britain, Holland and the Empire in jeopardy. It was imperative to gain a decisive victory over the French, and Marlborough's entire strategic thinking during the campaign of 1708 was directed to bringing the enemy to battle.

In one respect, Marlborough had a great advantage: the commander of the Empire's army was the 45-year-old Prince Eugène of Savoy, a soldier of immense talent. The two men had first met in 1704 and had immediately formed a deep friendship and what was to prove one of the most successful and enduring partnerships in military history. They were known as the twin Princes.

The joint French commanders – the Dukes of Vendôme and Burgundy – were almost always in disagreement. Vendôme was an experienced, gifted and successful commander of 54; Burgundy a young man of 26, religious, proud and little versed in war. Louis XIV's decision to put his eldest grandson jointly in command after Vendôme's successful solo tenure in 1706–7 was to prove a misjudgement of the first magnitude.

Marlborough and Eugène conferred at the Hague and devised a simple strategy: when their two forces were ready, Eugène would march westward from Coblenz,

War of the Spanish Succession 1701–14
This conflict was brought about by the ambition of Louis XIV to make France's power absolute. Its immediate causes were dynastic: Charles II of Spain was both childless and in poor health, and a successor had to be named who would be acceptable to the major European powers. There were three possible contenders. First, Louis XIV, who claimed the throne of Spain on behalf of his eldest son who, by virtue of Louis' marriage to the Infanta Maria Theresa in 1660, was a grandson of Philip IV of Spain and nephew of Charles II. Second was Joseph Ferdinand, the Electoral Prince of Bavaria, a great-grandson of Philip IV; and, last, Leopold I, the Holy Roman Emperor, who had married one of Philip's daughters and claimed the succession for his son, the Archduke Charles.

The dynastic subtleties and the political implications of the final choice, exercised the minds of most European statesmen over a long period. Finally, in 1698, the First Partition Treaty was signed, by which Joseph Ferdinand was named as the principal heir, although the other claimants received territorial compensation. Joseph Ferdinand's unexpected death nullified the treaty, and a second treaty was agreed to in 1700, by which the Archduke Charles received most, though not all, of the Spanish possessions.

But Spanish statesmen, determined to keep the Spanish territories intact, persuaded the dying King Charles to name Louis XIV's grandson his sole heir. The prospect of France and Spain being united was intolerable to England, Holland and the Holy Roman Empire; so these three formed an alliance to combat France's growing military and commercial power, and in 1701 war broke out.

some 240km/150mls distant, to join the duke, and since their armies outnumbered the French, they would bring them to battle at the earliest opportunity. If they did not succeed in joining up, Marlborough would deal with the French alone, despite being outnumbered.

During May, Marlborough assembled his army of 90,000 men (112 battalions of infantry and 197 squadrons of horse) just south of Brussels. Eugène began to assemble his force, but he had to recruit men and train them, so the procedure took longer.

By the end of May, a French army numbering more than 100,000 soldiers (130 battalions and 216 squadrons) had assembled near Mons. The commanders

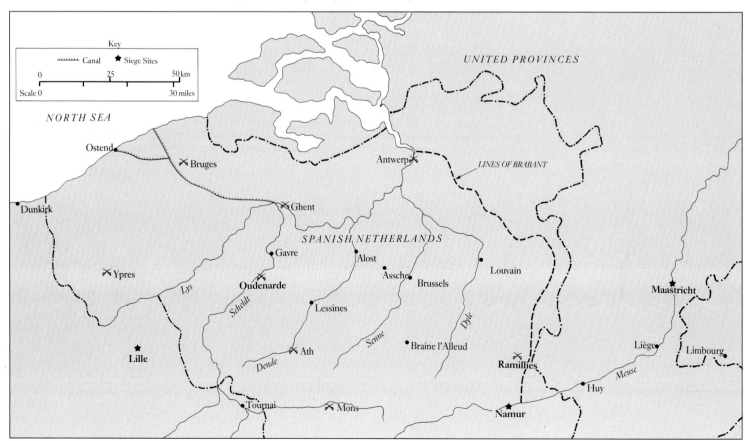

The flintlock musket

By 1703, the old combination of matchlock and pike had been replaced in both the British and French armies by the flintlock musket. This was more expensive, but also more reliable, more weatherproof and lighter. Although all muskets carried a socket bayonet roughly 40cm/16in long, Marlborough's troops had no standard type of weapon – barrel lengths varied considerably, and English-made muskets were supplemented by purchases from the Dutch. Probably the most common was the King William III Land Musket of c1696, the forerunner of the 'Brown Bess', 1.6m/ 5ft long and weighing 5.2kg/11½lb.

The French *fusil ordinaire* weighed a little more (5.4kg/12lb) yet had a significantly smaller calibre of only 17–22mm/ 0.68–0.85in, and the ball weighed 18g/⅔oz to the British 28g/1oz. Both sides carried 24 cartridges and could fire two or three rounds per minute for short periods.

Platoon firing

British and French infantry battalions had 12 companies of 60 men and one grenadier company with 50 men. The platoon firing system, which may even have dated from Gustavus Adolphus, was adopted by British troops from 1700, and also by the Dutch and some German troops. It gave Marlborough's infantry fire superiority over their enemies.

In battle, the battalion was split into four grand divisions of four platoons each, with two flanking platoons of grenadiers: a total of 18 platoons with about 40 men in each, drawn up into three ranks. They were distributed along the line in three firings of six platoons each, ensuring that a third of the battalion was always ready loaded.

Sometimes whole platoons fired separately in a pre-set order to produce a rippling volley; or the first rank's fire could be reserved entirely to produce a fourth firing. To correct the tendency to fire high, the men were often ordered to aim at the enemy's belts or even their shoes; and they trained with live ammunition.

French troops being dressed by a sergeant in preparation for firing.

were already in dispute. Vendôme was keen to march east to besiege the fortress of Huy on the River Meuse, since this might draw Marlborough in pursuit. In the open country of the area, Vendôme could capitalize on having a much greater force of cavalry. Burgundy, on the other hand, favoured marching into Flanders, in the expectation that this would cause many important cities, where Dutch rule was profoundly disliked, to revert to their French allegiance. Vendôme's and Burgundy's heated exchanges in public inevitably lowered the morale of their staff. In the event, on instructions from Louis XIV, Burgundy's plan was adopted.

The French Army started to move in the direction of Brussels on 26 May and eight days later halted at Braine l'Alleud, from where they were poised to attack either Brussels or Louvain. Marlborough, as in a game of chess, moved his army to just south of Louvain, a position that enabled him also to cover both cities.

For the better part of June no further military move was made, but then, for the only time in the entire campaign, Marlborough was badly wrongfooted. He was, at this period, in constant danger from Vendôme's larger force and it was not until 29 June that Eugène's 15,000-strong army, gathering on the Rhine, began to move. Eugène was so seriously behind in his schedule that Marlborough sent him an urgent request to bring up his cavalry with all speed, ahead of his infantry.

Then suddenly the French ended the long period of inactivity. Without having given any sign of their intention, they broke camp and marched westward toward Bruges and Ghent. French sympathisers in the two cities had been forewarned, and both cities quickly fell on 5 July, although some 300 British soldiers in the citadel of Ghent managed to hold out for a few days.

Marlborough was dumbfounded. He had not expected any such manoeuvre and the loss of the two cities at no cost to the French seems temporarily to have demoralized him. His spirits did not revive until after Eugène, who had spurred ahead of his advancing army, was at his side. Morale in the Allied army had also plumeted. Marlborough's despair, once overcome, appears however to have inspired him, for there shortly ensued one of the most tactically brilliant marches in the history of the British Army.

Vendôme and Burgundy by now had control of the entire length of the River Scheldt from the French border to Ghent, with the sole exception of the fortified town of Oudenarde. If they could secure it, Marlborough's army would be cut off from the coast and Flanders – and therefore from contact with England.

Marlborough judged their objective correctly and also the method by which they would seek to achieve it. He discounted the possibility that they might march straight along the Scheldt and then lay siege to the town because, during such a manoeuvre, his own army could always threaten them. It was more likely that they would march south down the east bank of the river, then leave a covering force between his army to the east and Oudenarde to the west. The obvious place to do this was at Lessines on the River Dende, and a race developed to see who could get there first.

On 8 July the bulk of the French Army began marching from Alost toward Lessines. Marlborough was at Assche when he heard the news and set out at 02.00 hours on 9 July in his race to reach Lessines ahead of the French. By midday, after great exertions, his army was nearing Enghien, from which, that same evening, he ordered eight squadrons of horse and eight battalions to make a forced march to seize the prize. This they did without difficulty, and by noon on 10 July the bulk of Marlborough's army had reached the town, after a march of some 48km/30mls in 36 hours, mostly at night.

The tactical situation had changed decisively. Had the French reached Lessines first, they would have been stationed

Marlborough at the Battle of Blenheim is depicted in this vast tapestry, *right*, one of a series at Blenheim Palace, the great baroque house built on land given to him by Queen Anne as a tribute after his famous victory. Work began in 1705 to plans by Vanbrugh and Hawksmoor, and the finest artists and craftsmen were employed to decorate and embellish it.

between Marlborough and Oudenarde, 24km/15mls away. They could then have left a large force in Lessines to hold up the Allies while the rest of the army marched westward and besieged Oudenarde at some leisure.

The duke's forced march, carefully prepared for (double rations had been issued to every soldier) and faultlessly executed, had frustrated French plans. Vendôme and Burgundy, hearing that Lessines was already occupied and their way to the bridge at Oudenarde therefore barred, turned northwest to Gavre, where there was another bridge over the Scheldt. The race to Lessines now became a race to the Scheldt, for whichever army crossed the river first would gain the prize.

Marlborough's grasp of command, and the high esteem in which he was held by his troops, inspired the weary army to make another forced march. Marlborough sent forward an 11,000-strong advance guard under his Quarter-Master General, William Cadogan, a formidable Irish cavalry officer whom Marlborough often used in an advance position to survey enemy dispositions. He was only 32 years old, but greatly experienced, and had been at Marlborough's side since 1702. Cadogan's task was to establish five pontoon bridges downstream of Oudenarde as

quickly as possible, and then to hold the crossing point until the main army came up. He had laid the bridges by 10.30 next day, 11 July, before the French – who were fully engaged in crossing the Scheldt at Gavre – could prevent him. Indeed, it was some time before the French had any idea what Marlborough was about.

The writer Hilaire Belloc, in describing the march, recalls Marshal Ferdinand Foch's famous remark, 'It was not the Carthaginians who crossed the Alps, it was Hannibal.' Certainly Marlborough's success in predicting his enemy's intentions and then moving his army so far and so fast

---

Prince Eugène of Savoy 1663–1736

Eugène was already renowned as one of the outstanding commanders in Europe when he and Marlborough met in 1704. He had entered the service of Leopold I, the Holy Roman Emperor, in 1683 at the age of 20, after Louis XIV had refused to commission him in the French Army, and was implacably opposed to France all his life.

Fighting always with great personal bravery, Eugène saw action against the Turks in 1688, at the relief of Vienna and at the capture of Belgrade. Later, in 1697, he overwhelmed the Turks at Zenta.

Eugène's appearance belied his ability, for he was short, slouched and had pock-marked cheeks. He was short-tempered and notoriously tactless, yet was, paradoxically, a gifted diplomat, and was renowned as a patron of the arts. Although his strategic thinking lacked ingenuity and daring, his coolness and strength in the field equalled Marlborough's.

Prince Eugène and Marlborough reconnoitring; from an engraving by the Flemish artist Camsvelt.

A bluecoated footman delivers a message to Marlborough; detail from a tapestry.

during two days of relentless marching was a military achievement of the first order and ranks among the grand marches of history. His reward was great: by mid-afternoon on 11 July his entire army, some 90,000 men, was safely across the river without loss. He had, moreover, denied Vendôme his most fervent wish – to line the west bank of the Scheldt to prevent an Allied crossing while he besieged Oudenarde – and had brought about what he himself most desired: a major battle.

The first shots were now about to be fired. Cadogan's eight squadrons of Hanoverian dragoons, advancing down the left bank of the river, came to the crest of a small hill. From there they could see French troops foraging among the hamlets sited between the green fields, streams, woods and hedgerows of the lush terrain. It was infantry ground and unsuitable for cavalry, but it was units of Cadogan's mounted force that were first engaged.

Cadogan had left four battalions to protect the pontoon bridges and had led the rest of his advancing force toward the Diepenbeek stream. He himself then made a reconnaissance of Eyne. Here he encountered French advance units, probing up the west bank of the Scheldt from Gavre, and immediately ordered dragoons under the command of Jorgen Rantzau, a Danish major-general of proven worth, to advance to take prisoners for interrogation. Many of the French escaped and fell back to warn the commander of the 8,000-strong vanguard, Lieutenant-General the Marquis de Biron, of the unexpected and unwelcome presence of Allied troops on the west bank of the river.

Biron advanced with 12 squadrons to reconnoitre, while Rantzau prudently retired behind the left flank of Cadogan's infantry, now nearing Eyne. Biron must have been most disagreeably astonished to find not a foraging party, as he had supposed, but a formidable force. Then, from raised ground, he saw an even more unwelcome sight: an uninterrupted column of cavalry moving down to the guarded pontoon bridges and, farther east, dust clouds caused by the rapidly advancing Allied Army. He hurriedly sent back messengers to the French HQ.

Vendôme, who had crossed the river and was having lunch, found the news unbelievable. But soon, from a vantage point, he too saw the clouds of dust drawing closer. Vendôme probably became aware of the nearness of the Allied Army some time between 13.30 and 14.00. By then a battery of six guns had been positioned on Cadogan's left, near the village of Schaerken.

The French Army, as it crossed at Gavre, was drawn up in line on a ridge north of the River Norken, about 5km/3mls from Oudenarde. Vendôme and Burgundy had two options: they could hold their strong defensive position – virtually impregnable, given their superiority in numbers – and slip away in the night, or they could fight. Vendôme, knowing that most of the Allied Army was still on the other side of the Scheldt, opted for immediate attack but Burgundy overruled him.

Nevertheless, Vendôme ordered Biron to attack Cadogan's position. As Biron,

with his squadrons, approached the Allied line, he saw with dismay that Cadogan had been able to call up the four battalions that had originally guarded the pontoons and that his reinforced line of 16 battalions now stretched from the Scheldt to the village of Schaerken. Having only seven Swiss battalions and 20 squadrons himself, Biron, with good reason, hesitated.

At almost that moment, Lieutenant-General the Marquis de Puysegur, of Burgundy's staff, rode up. He was an officer of wide experience and was thought to be thoroughly familiar with the terrain, but his opinion was, almost of itself, to cost the French the battle. In his view, the marshy land around the Diepenbeek was impassable to cavalry; Vendôme, who had been bringing down reinforcements to support Biron's attack, accepted the advice and turned his troops westward to the incline near Huysse.

While these limited manoeuvres were in progress, Marlborough and Eugène, with 20 squadrons of Prussian cavalry under Major-General Dubislaw Natzmer had galloped to the Scheldt; and by 13.00 the Prussians had crossed the river. As the various formations crossed, Marlborough directed them to the points where they would be of most use.

The rest of the intended right-wing cavalry was stationed across the Oudenarde to Ghent road, between Bevere and Eyne, to watch the northern flank in case the French called off their

crossing of the river. The left-wing cavalry had been ordered to cross the Scheldt by the two stone bridges at Oudenarde, where two pontoon bridges had also been laid. Marlborough had reserved the nearer pontoon bridges for his approaching infantry, who had footslogged over 80km/50mls in 60 hours. The twin Princes themselves crossed at about 14.00.

Just before 15.00, the leading British brigade from the infantry units under the Duke of Argyll, a largely inexperienced but resolute and gifted young man, was crossing the river, and Cadogan, with Marlborough's authority, attacked the seven battalions of Swiss mercenaries to his front. These units had been ordered forward by Vendôme when he had earlier instructed Biron to attack and had, through oversight, been ignored.

Cadogan's attack overwhelmed the Swiss, and he occupied the village of Heurne. Rantzau's dragoons, the future King George II of England among them, had also charged to good effect. They drove back not only the Swiss but Biron's squadrons, until they crashed into a great force of French cavalry; then, heavily outnumbered, they were forced to retire. The tactical effect of this assault was slight, but it gained time for more Allied units to cross the river.

There was another, most significant result of the attack: Burgundy, stung and humiliated at the defeat of the Swiss by so small a force, decided on a general attack

By mid-afternoon, Marlborough had the bulk of his army over the River Scheldt (4), and fighting along the Marollebeek (7) and Diepenbeek streams was fierce. Eugène, on the Allied right, was hard pressed. To relieve him, at about

18.15, Marlborough executed a skilful, disciplined manoeuvre: he directed units of Hanoverian and Hessian infantry, newly across the Scheldt, into Major-General Lottum's force on his left.

He ordered Lottum's troops to withdraw through pre-arranged intervals and march (5) to support Eugène.

This manoeuvre not only gave him fresh troops for his left wing but Lottum's men some respite from the

fighting. Marlborough's right wing now outnumbered his enemy's left (6). Meanwhile, Burgundy (2) remained inactive, as did the large body of French cavalry and infantry (3) stationed on rising ground north of the River Norken (1).

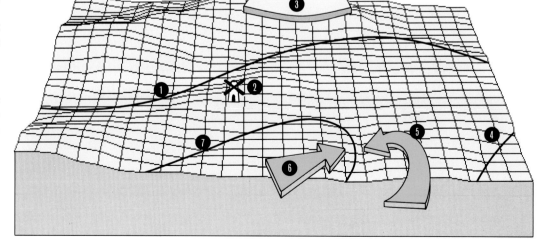

Duke of Vendôme 1654–1712

By the time of Oudenarde, Louis Joseph de Bourbon, Duke of Vendôme, was a hugely experienced commander who had served with Turenne at the same time as Marlborough in 1674. He was a great-grandson of Henry IV of France, and although he was descended from one of the king's illegitimate children, he was nevertheless of royal blood. Despite this, his personal habits were filthy – he wore the same tobacco-stained clothes for weeks at a time – and few sought, and fewer still could stomach, his company.

Although a debauched and cynical man, he had notable qualities as a commander, high among them being his ability to see early on how a battle could best be fought. But he never comprehended the great value of detailed reconnaissance, and he so greatly enjoyed personal combat that he often became embroiled in a particular sector of an action, rather than directing the whole, as a commander ought.

Perhaps no man understood his nature better than Prince Eugène, a cousin, who had fought against him in Italy at the indecisive Battle of Cassano in 1705. When asked by Marlborough for his assessment of Vendôme, Eugène wrote; 'He is beloved by the common soldiers, and once he has taken a

decision he adheres to it, so that nothing whatever can shake him . . . If his plans are at all upset, he finds it difficult to adjust himself even in an action, and leaves the remedy to chance.'

This penetrating estimate of his character neatly explains Vendôme's conduct at the Battle of Oudenarde: he could call up great devotion and energy from his men, but he could not adapt his tactical thinking to changing circumstances, clinging doggedly to his original plan of battle.

Though his dissolute and objectionable behaviour and his defeat at Oudenarde made him many enemies at court, he was still employed by Louis XIV, and in 1710 was sent to Spain, where his victories at Briheuga and Villaviciosa helped the Sun King's grandson, Philip V, to retain his precarious throne. Of Vendôme's success there, Louis made a telling remark: 'Yet, after all, there was only one man more with the army.'

---

while the Allies were still relatively few in number. Vendôme, who had earlier been ardent to attack, thought that now, at about 15.30, it was too late in the day. He was overruled. The French right wing, therefore, began to cross the River Norken and close on the Allies in Eyne. A satisfactory explanation has never been found as to why the French left wing remained stationary near Huysse.

By about 16.00, most of Argyll's troops were across the river and deploying on Marlborough's instructions. The Allied advanced formations were then positioned in two adjoining halves, facing north and west. Twenty-eight Prussian and Hanoverian squadrons were drawn up north of Eyne in a line running east to west from the Scheldt to the village of Groenewald. The cavalry's left flank was joined, at a right angle, by the right flank of Cadogan's infantry. Thus the cavalry could guard the infantry's right flank and prevent its being encircled, while the infantry, now facing west, was to receive the impending French attack, which began at about 16.00.

Burgundy ordered an assault on Groenewald, but this, though pressed hard, was repulsed by Prussian regiments. Then Vendôme, hearing the sound of fire, committed an act of astonishing folly for a commander of his experience and ability. Instead of consulting Burgundy, whose headquarters were now close by the

Royegem windmill, and together forming a new plan, he collected 12 regiments and personally led the next attack on Groenewald and Herlegem. Soon he himself was fighting hand-to-hand with a 2.7m/9ft half-pike. Thus, within a short time of the main battle's opening, one French commander was sited far to the rear, little more than an impotent observer, the other embroiled in close fighting, where he had no opportunity to exercise overall control.

Nevertheless, at this moment – roughly 17.00 – the French had victory within their compass. In their left wing, they had some 30,000 troops, of all categories, as yet uncommitted. If this considerable formation had attacked the Allied right flank, it could – and probably would – have rolled it up. Meanwhile Vendôme, though heavily engaged at Groenewald, could have enveloped the Allied left wing toward Schaerken before the rest of Marlborough's army crossed the Scheldt.

However, Vendôme's request for the French left wing to move was overruled by Burgundy, who had accepted Puysegur's incorrect assessment that the marshy ground in front of it was impassable. Burgundy conveyed his refusal to Vendôme by messenger, who failed to deliver it. Thus Vendôme maintained his attack on Herlegem and Groenewald in the expectation of an attack by the French left

which, in the event, never materialized.

Meanwhile, more of Argyll's infantry regiments were across the pontoons and these, on Marlborough's orders, were fed into the perilous gap between Cadogan's extreme left and Schaerken. But this brought only temporary relief, for the French line was continually extending to the right and once again threatened to overlap the Allied left.

One physical factor greatly assisted the duke at this juncture: as the Allied lines, in response to French moves, shifted steadily westward, the distance between the pontoons and the left flank was reduced, so troops arriving there could be in the battle more quickly.

This was the crux of the battle, but Marlborough continued to display his exceptional gifts as a commander throughout the rest of the day. At about 18.00, he decided to divide his command. Seeing that his left flank would shortly be the point of decision, he moved his personal headquarters there, leaving the right under the command of Eugène. Then, perhaps a quarter of an hour later, conscious that Eugène was under intense pressure, he executed with finesse and total success one of those manoeuvres for which he is so rightly famous.

Another 18 battalions of Hanoverian and Hessian infantry had recently crossed over the pontoons, and these he fed into

Marlborough's plan at Oudenarde was to envelop both French flanks; he might well have been successful had not the collapse of the two pontoon bridges in Oudenarde delayed Overkirk's force by about an hour.

Without great numerical superiority, this tactic can be dangerous because the enveloping arms may become attenuated and vulnerable to counter-attack. If successful, as it was in the instance of Genghis Khan at the Battle of the Indus, the complete destruction of the enemy is assured.

At about 18.00, knowing that his left flank would be the crucial sector if double envelopment of the enemy was to be achieved, Marlborough moved to that sector, leaving Eugène in command on the right wing.

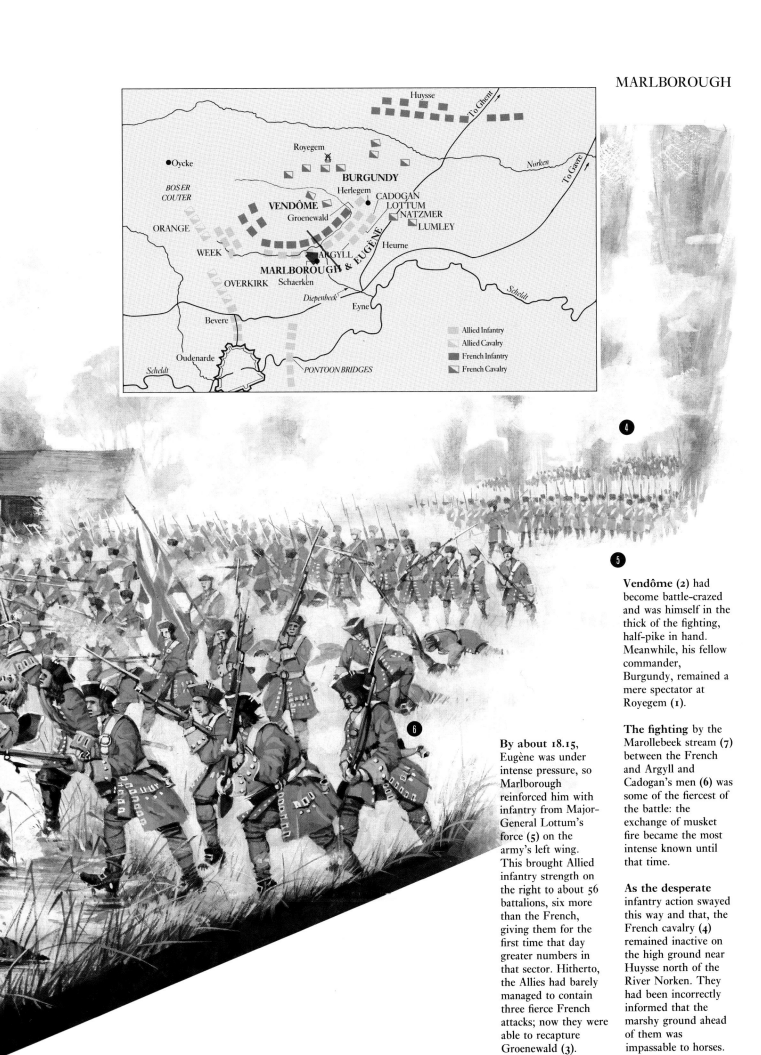

Map legend:
- Allied Infantry
- Allied Cavalry
- French Infantry
- French Cavalry

Vendôme (2) had become battle-crazed and was himself in the thick of the fighting, half-pike in hand. Meanwhile, his fellow commander, Burgundy, remained a mere spectator at Royegem (1).

The fighting by the Marollebeek stream (7) between the French and Argyll and Cadogan's men (6) was some of the fiercest of the battle: the exchange of musket fire became the most intense known until that time.

As the desperate infantry action swayed this way and that, the French cavalry (4) remained inactive on the high ground near Huysse north of the River Norken. They had been incorrectly informed that the marshy ground ahead of them was impassable to horses.

By about 18.15, Eugène was under intense pressure, so Marlborough reinforced him with infantry from Major-General Lottum's force (5) on the army's left wing. This brought Allied infantry strength on the right to about 56 battalions, six more than the French, giving them for the first time that day greater numbers in that sector. Hitherto, the Allies had barely managed to contain three fierce French attacks; now they were able to recapture Groenewald (3).

the 20 infantry battalions of the Prussian Lieutenant-General Carl von Lottum's force on his extreme left flank on the Diepenbeek. But this was a ruse to deceive the French, for Marlborough then ordered Lottum's troops to withdraw through pre-arranged intervals and march to the support of Eugène on the right.

This manoeuvre, which demonstrated not only the genius of Marlborough but the discipline and confidence of his men, achieved a number of objectives, notably that the fresh Hanoverian and Hessian troops were deployed on his left where they were most needed. And Lottum's exhausted men, though obliged to march at their best pace to support Eugène, were at least temporarily withdrawn from the fighting. Now Eugène had at his command 56 battalions, with 50 of which he stemmed Vendôme's assaults, while Marlborough himself had at his disposal a mere 18. But the moment of his masterstroke was at hand – or so he thought.

Count Hendrik Overkirk, an extremely experienced 67-year-old Dutch field marshal and Marlborough's companion in arms over many years, had been ordered to cross the bridges at Oudenarde with the Dutch Army. He was to march northward to the high ground, known as the Boser Couter, on the extreme left of the field, and then to turn eastward and envelop the French right. Unhappily for Marlborough, however, the pontoon bridges at Oudenarde had collapsed; so Overkirk had no option but to take his entire force over the two stone bridges in Oudenarde itself. This entailed a delay of about an hour.

At about 19.00 the battle entered its final phase, as Marlborough attempted his tactical plan of double encirclement,

Queen Anne's head appears on this medal, which was later struck to commemorate Marlborough's victory at Oudenarde. On the reverse, French captives are shown, chained to a column flanked by flags.

although always watchful of the great mass of stationary French troops to the north, who might, for all he knew, attack at any moment. Natzmer, now under the command of Eugène on the right, charged not long after 19.00, smashing the French cavalry to his front as he made for Royegem and Burgundy's headquarters.

This charge was ultimately driven back, after heavy loss, by the French Household Cavalry, the Maison du Roi. Nevertheless, it further demoralized the French and temporarily gave protection to the Allied right wing. Meanwhile, Marlborough divested himself of cavalry to send to Eugène, whose flank was thereby made reasonably secure.

With his small numbers, Marlborough could do no more than hold the French in the centre; but Overkirk's forces on the extreme left were now assembled. Earlier, at Marlborough's order, eight Dutch battalions of Overkirk's command had wheeled right, roughly half-way on the route from Oudenarde to Oycke, to take the French right in flank.

At about 19.30, Marlborough launched his encircling move, when he ordered Overkirk to attack the French rear from the high ground of the Boser Couter. This force, comprising 12 squadrons and 16 Dutch battalions, took the French wholly

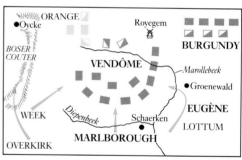

After Oudenarde

The French Army did not recover throughout 1708 from the serious reverse it had suffered at Oudenarde. 'It is most certain', Marlborough wrote shortly after the battle, 'that the success we had at Oudenarde has lessened this army at least 20,000 men, but that which I think our greatest advantage consists in the fear that is among their troops, so that I shall seek all occasions of attacking them.'

To this end, Marlborough devised a dramatic, potentially deadly strategic plan, which he at first communicated to Eugène alone. This was to use Abbeville as a base to receive supplies from England, while his army, bypassing and ignoring the great fortresses on the French frontier, marched on Paris and brought the war to a swift and victorious conclusion.

English and Dutch fleets could provision the great army, which would total some 100,000 men; the French garrisons on the frontier would be forced to abandon their fortresses and march in pursuit, as would Vendôme's force in Ghent, so offering the

duke yet another opportunity to defeat the French in the field. Most tempting of all – the move would obviate the need for a costly and prolonged siege of a French frontier fortress.

To implement his plan, however, Marlborough needed the enthusiastic cooperation of his illustrious fellow-captain, Eugène. For once, however, Eugène could not bring himself to accept so colossal, so audacious a strategy as that conceived by the British Captain-General. He saw only the logistical problems and the dangers. Without Eugène's approval, Marlborough's plan was doomed. He was, therefore, obliged to turn to the lesser adventure – the siege of a fortress, which, if successful, would be a strategic gain but could not bring the war to an end.

Marlborough organized two vast convoys of provisions, cannon and ammunition to be brought up from Brussels toward the French frontier. This manoeuvre enabled him to confuse the French as to whether he meant to invest the fortresses of Ypres, Tournai or Lille. His plan, in fact, was to take Lille.

by surprise and soon their entire right wing began to disintegrate; by then it was well past 20.30. Despite courageous resistance, the French were clearly beaten, and by 21.00 at the latest, in light rain, those who still could were trying to break out of the closing Allied ring and make off northward to Huysse. Burgundy, Vendôme and their staff took the same route.

Marlborough was deprived of the total victory that he had sought – and to which his plans and conduct of the battle entitled him – by the failure of the bridges at Oudenarde. This had left him insufficient hours of daylight to complete his great design of double envelopment. Nonetheless, his achievement was stupendous. The French had lost at least 13,750 men, half of whom were taken prisoner, 4,500 horses and 25 guns; the Allies lost not more than 2,975, of whom only 175 were British infantry.

Two scenes, shortly after the battle, may in some measure explain its outcome. While Marlborough and Eugene, in harmonious accord, discussed their plans for the morrow, Burgundy and Vendôme were locked in heated and profitless recrimination. In the event, at Burgundy's insistence, what remained of the French Army withdrew to the safety of Ghent, with Vendôme arguing with his ostensible superior to the last.

The siege of Lille

Captain Robert Parker, who served with Marlborough throughout his campaigns, wrote of him that he 'never fought a battle he did not win, nor besieged a town he did not take'. In 1708 he won a great battle at Oudenarde and followed it with the greatest and, at 120 days, almost the longest of his 30 sieges: that of Lille.

This fortress-city was the masterpiece of the brilliant French siege engineer Marshal Sébastian Vauban. Between 1668 and 1674 he had refortified it, using 60 million bricks to build huge zigzagging outer walls that enclosed a moat, in which there were island bastions, and a vast inner wall with more bastions. The citadel itself was star-shaped, with two outer walls and two moats before the main wall could be reached.

The Allied siege train of 18 heavy guns and 20 mortars needed 16,000 horses and 3,000 ammunition wagons to move it the 113km/70mls from Brussels by road. It stretched for 24km/15mls and had to be protected all along the route from menacing French forces to north and south.

Marlborough, with a field army, was to cover the siege from any attempt by the French to relieve the city, while Eugène, with a force of 35,000, conducted the siege. This started officially on 13 August, and within two weeks some 16km/19mls of circumvallation – earthworks surrounding the city – had been completed and trenches forward to the ramparts begun. On 27 August, from about 550m/600yds, 88 guns began firing their great iron balls at the outer defences covering the northern gates.

The 16,000-strong garrison, with 150 guns, was commanded by the veteran Marshal Louis Boufflers, who had once served with Marlborough under Turenne. On 26 August he made a sortie out of the city, and again on 5 September, while Marlborough and Eugène were engaged in outfacing 100,000 French troops just southwest of Lille. But try as he might, Marlborough could not bring the French to battle. The siege dragged on, the guns making no impression on the massive walls.

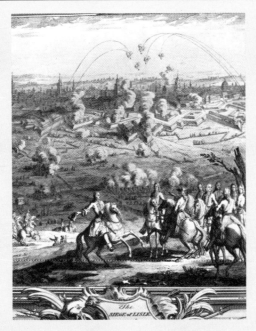

Prince Eugène and Marlborough watching the bombardment of Lille, *above*. The plan of the citadel of Lille, Vauban's masterpiece, *below*, was drawn by a German captain during and after the siege and later presented to Prince Eugène.

By 27 September both sides had only four days' gunpowder supply left. But Boufflers received nearly 18 tons when 2,000 dragoons succeeded in riding through with a 22kg/50lb bag apiece; and then a convoy fought through from Marlborough's new supply base at Ostend with 111 tons for the besiegers. These men were down to a two-thirds bread ration by 16 October, when their guns finally created a 107m/350ft gap in the main city wall. Boufflers surrendered the town on the 22nd, to prevent its ransack, and was given three days in which to evacuate 5,000 fit troops and 4,000 sick and wounded. The Allies suffered almost 7,000 casualties.

On 26 October, Eugène opened trenches against the pentagonal citadel, and at the end of November Marlborough defeated an attempted diversion by the French Army; on 4 December, it went into winter quarters. Now, with no hope of relief, and his foes having sapped their way in very close with numerous batteries, Boufflers surrendered on 9 December.

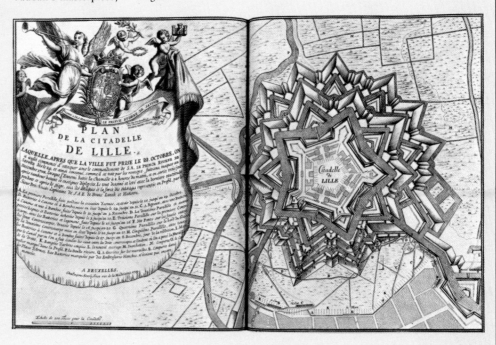

PLAN
DE LA CITADELLE
DE LILLE

Frederick the Great *1712-1786*

'Hats off, gentlemen – if he were still alive, we should not be here.' The tribute paid to Frederick at his tomb in 1806 by Napoleon, the greatest ever French general, would have gratified 'Old Fritz', for his passions in life were all things French, his army and, incongruously it might seem, the flute.

The quirkiness and contradictions in Frederick the Great's character stem at least in part from his father's brutal, contemptuous treatment of him as a youth. Frederick William I of Prussia, an industrious but coarse and domineering man, suffered from the rare and painful disease porphyria which drove him into periodic madness. He despised his son's liking for French art and literature and took delight in humiliating him in public. At the same time, Frederick was not above provoking and taunting his ailing father – pitying him but also loathing him.

In 1730, when Frederick was 18 years old, his father's insults and brutality drove him to attempt escape. His wild scheme was discovered, and Frederick was imprisoned and forced to watch his accomplice and special friend Lieutenant von Katte executed. Within two weeks, realizing that his situation was hopeless, Frederick submitted to his father. Three years later, largely so that he might be able to set up his own establishment, he married Elizabeth of Brunswick. He made his attitude clear in a letter to his sister Wilhelmine: 'I . . . will marry the lady; but then it will be good day, Madame, and good luck to you', and they soon separated; thereafter he showed almost no interest in women. However, he thoroughly enjoyed his home, Rheinsberg, with its library and garden. It was only on his father's death that Frederick displayed that ruthless leadership that was to be his principal characteristic throughout his life.

Frederick was slightly taller than average but stooped, and this, together with his sway back and broad hips, gave him an ungainly appearance; his most remarkable feature was his penetrating, watchful eyes. He usually dressed in a simple uniform and was careless of his everyday attire, wearing the same snuff-covered clothes until they were in tatters.

It is impossible truly to understand Frederick's character, for he was a man of great contradictions. He was profoundly interested in the arts and held celebrated dinners at Sans Souci, his palace at Potsdam, to which came artists, writers and thinkers – Voltaire among them – from all over Europe. He played the flute well, composed military marches, and wrote illuminatingly on politics and the military arts.

Yet he was wholly unscrupulous; he broke treaties without compunction and regarded all humans as merely adjuncts to his will. He studied the wellbeing of his soldiers only because they would otherwise be incapable of forming the efficient army his ambition demanded, but could not bear to witness savage military punishments meted out. And he attempted to relieve the conditions of his serfs, encouraging education, building roads and canals and creating new industries. He tolerated all religions, while professing himself an aetheist.

Frederick was, however, a commander of genius and, apart from Alexander, was the outstanding exponent of ceaseless attack. Napoleon claimed that Frederick attempted stratagems even he would have hesitated to perform and studied his battles in the greatest detail. His words form a fitting epitaph for Frederick: 'It is not the Prussian Army which for seven years defended Prussia against the three most powerful nations in Europe, but Frederick the Great.'

Frederick the Great, portrait by J.G. Glume; he wears the orange sash and embroidered silver star of the Order of the Black Eagle, the senior Prussian award, which had been established in 1701.
Uniforms of the No 12 Prussian Infantry Regiment c1752; left to right: grenadier-sergeant, grenadier and grenadier-corporal.

1712	*24 January* Born at Berlin, eldest surviving son of King Frederick William I of Prussia.
1721	Put in command of 100 cadets.
1727	Major in the Potsdam Guards.
1731	Arrested for attempted desertion.
1734	Serves with Prince Eugène on the Rhine at the siege of Phillipsburg.
1740	*31 May* Becomes King of Prussia.
1741	Invades Silesia. *10 April* His infantry wins Battle of Mollwitz.
1742	*17 May* Wins Battle of Chotusitz.
1744	Invades Bohemia. *2 September* Captures Prague.
1745	*3–4 June* Wins Battle of Hohenfriedberg and, *30 September*, Soor. *25 December* Treaty of Dresden.

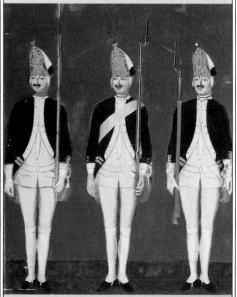

1756	*29 August–10 September* Invades Saxony and occupies Dresden. *1 October* Wins Battle of Lobositz and takes over Saxon Army.
1757	*6 May* Wins Battle of Prague. *18 June* Loses Battle of Kolin. *5 November* Wins Battle of Rossbach. *5 December* **Battle of Leuthen.**
1758	Fails in siege of Olmütz. *25 August* Just wins Battle of Zorndorf. *14 October* Loses Battle of Hochkirch.
1759	*12 August* Loses Battle of Kunersdorf.
1760	*15 August* Wins Battle of Leignitz and, *3 November*, of Torgau.
1762	*5 January* Death of Elizabeth of Russia saves Frederick. *May* Peace treaties with Russia and Sweden. *21 July* Wins Battle of Burkersdorf.
1763	*16 February* Retains Silesia under Treaty of Hubertusburg.
1778/ 1779	Indecisive 'Potato War' of the Bavarian Succession.
1786	*17 August* Dies at San Souci, aged 74.

Battle of Leuthen/*5 December 1757*

FREDERICK'S PRE-EMPTIVE INVASION of Saxony in August 1756, and his capture of Dresden on 10 September, spurred the Allies to immediate retaliation. He won the Battle of Lobositz on 1 October but, when the campaigning season of 1757 opened, Frederick was decisively defeated by Field Marshal Leopold von Daun at the Battle of Kolin. He found himself, with at most 68,000 men, confronted by Allied armies, numbering in total some 350,000, moving to attack Prussia from west, south and east.

Frederick, however, was at his best in adversity and always struck first when opportunity afforded. On 5 November he brought a superior Franco-German force to battle near Rossbach and signally defeated it. Prussian losses have been put at fewer than 200 killed and 400 wounded, while the Allies lost 3,000 killed and wounded, some 5,000 prisoners, some 70 guns and almost all their supplies. Great Britain, Prussia's ally, rejoiced and a subsidy of more than £1m was voted to Frederick by Parliament.

Yet Frederick remained in peril, for he was still unsafe in Silesia. An Austrian army, under Prince Charles of Lorraine and Field Marshal Daun, so Frederick learned, had advanced to Lissa, almost certainly thinking that he had abandoned campaigning for the winter. He, however, resolved to force a battle.

The Austrian Army was drawn up west of the small Schweidnitz River, a strong position except that their line was overextended and risked envelopment. Prince Charles's force consisted of 85 battalions of infantry, 125 cavalry squadrons and 210 light guns; the army comprised some 65,000 men, against whom Frederick could deploy no more than

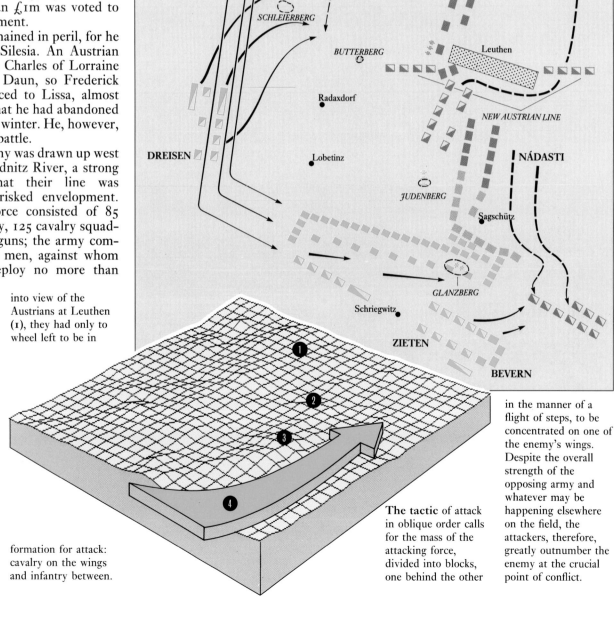

Frederick's plan of attack entailed making a feint against the Austrian right while his main force (4) marched south behind low hills, which hid them from the enemy.

The Prussians had begun their march in 'wings' – five parallel columns, cavalry on the flanks and infantry between them. Now they re-formed into 'lines' – two parallel formations with cavalry to front and rear.

When the Prussians emerged near Lobetinz (3) and Judenberg (2)

into view of the Austrians at Leuthen (1), they had only to wheel left to be in

formation for attack: cavalry on the wings and infantry between.

The tactic of attack in oblique order calls for the mass of the attacking force, divided into blocks, one behind the other

in the manner of a flight of steps, to be concentrated on one of the enemy's wings. Despite the overall strength of the opposing army and whatever may be happening elsewhere on the field, the attackers, therefore, greatly outnumber the enemy at the crucial point of conflict.

Austria's quarrel with Prussia

On 29 August 1756 Frederick the Great of Prussia led an army of 70,000 men into Saxony: the Seven Years War, the first of the world wars, had begun. The reasons for the conflict can be found in the War of the Austrian Succession (1740–8) that shortly preceded it.

The Archduchess Maria Theresa of Austria, wife of Francis I, the Holy Roman Emperor, and dowager empress after his death and the accession of her son Joseph II in 1765, was a daughter of the Holy Roman Emperor Charles VI. By the Pragmatic Sanction of 1713, Charles had sought to make his daughter heir to the Habsburg possessions. During his lifetime, this was accepted not only within the Habsburg territories but by the main European powers. At his death, however, the great powers speedily reneged with effortless facility and formed a coalition against her. Frederick of Prussia, with neither warning nor scruple, seized the Austrian province of Silesia.

After the Treaty of Aix la Chapelle that ended the war, Maria Theresa's gifted chancellor Prince von Kaunitz sought to convince the French, Austria's traditional enemy, that the true enemy of both was indeed Prussia. Thus, although Frederick guaranteed the Pragmatic Sanction and had his acquisitions in Silesia likewise guaranteed, he gained only a temporary truce, for Maria Theresa was determined to recover Silesia from Prussia.

While Kaunitz was reaching agreement with France, Maria Theresa formed an alliance with Elizabeth of Russia; later Sweden joined the grouping. Meanwhile, war broke out between Great Britain and France in North America and Britain signed the Treaty of Westminster with Frederick, by which he guaranteed Hanover, then a possession of the English King George II. Thus the scene was set: Prussia and Great Britain on one side, the allies – Austria, France, Russia and Sweden – on the other.

Frederick knew that Elizabeth of Russia was urging Maria Theresa to hasten Austrian mobilization and that most of Europe was already ranged against him and would stigmatize him the aggressor even if he remained inactive. He therefore resolved to strike before his enemies were in the field.

33,000 soldiers (48 battalions and 129 squadrons). But he had always maintained that an oblique attack was possible even if outnumbered three to one.

The Austrians were drawn up with their right wing, under General J. Lucchese, pinned on the bogs around Nippern in the north. Their left wing, under General F.L. Nádasti, curved back behind the village of Sagschütz, a little more than 6.4km/4mls to the south. In the centre of the Austrian line lay the village of Leuthen. Behind Leuthen, Prince Charles stationed his left cavalry wing, the right wing being farther north, near the hamlet of Guckerwitz.

Frederick knew the terrain intimately, since in peacetime his army performed their autumn manoeuvres there. The open grassland, with a light covering of snow, was quite flat, except for a ridge of low hills stretching from Borne to Lobetinz, which could hide Prussian movements from Austrian view.

Frederick took the undefended village of Borne and from a nearby rise, the Schönberg, studied the dispositions of the entire Austrian Army. He conceived his plan quickly: he would make a feint at the Austrian right, while manoeuvring the bulk of his force south in the dead ground provided by the hills to take their left by an oblique attack.

This, however, entailed reorganizing his advancing troops, before wheeling them to the south so that they would come into action against the Austrian left wing in their proper deployment. Frederick's army had been advancing on Borne by 'wings' – that is, a formation generally of four or more parallel columns, followed by an equal number of columns and so on throughout the entire army, with the cavalry on the flanks and the infantry between them.

At this moment, Frederick's insistence on his army's being repeatedly drilled during peacetime to bring them to disciplined perfection paid great dividends. He saw the parade formations solely as a discipline that could be employed in war. Thus, at this moment immediately prior to the fighting, he was able to re-form his advancing army into 'lines' – that is, two parallel lines of troops with cavalry to front and rear, and infantry between. When these troops wheeled into oblique attack, they were in precisely the right formation: cavalry on the wings, infantry in the centre.

As Frederick was busy directing the bulk of his army southward, an incident at Borne played into his hands. The hazy early morning sunlight was beginning to

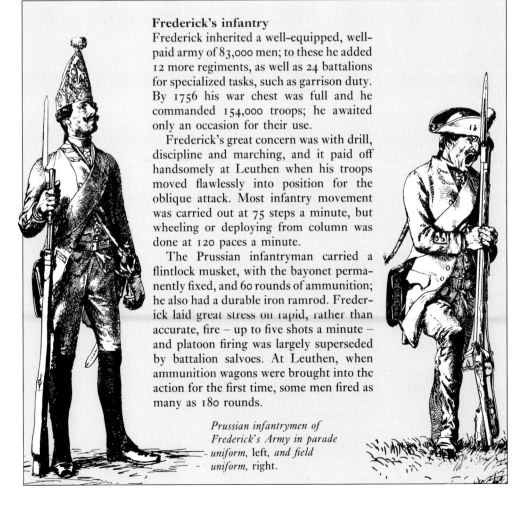

Frederick's infantry

Frederick inherited a well-equipped, well-paid army of 83,000 men; to these he added 12 more regiments, as well as 24 battalions for specialized tasks, such as garrison duty. By 1756 his war chest was full and he commanded 154,000 troops; he awaited only an occasion for their use.

Frederick's great concern was with drill, discipline and marching, and it paid off handsomely at Leuthen when his troops moved flawlessly into position for the oblique attack. Most infantry movement was carried out at 75 steps a minute, but wheeling or deploying from column was done at 120 paces a minute.

The Prussian infantryman carried a flintlock musket, with the bayonet permanently fixed, and 60 rounds of ammunition; he also had a durable iron ramrod. Frederick laid great stress on rapid, rather than accurate, fire – up to five shots a minute – and platoon firing was largely superseded by battalion salvoes. At Leuthen, when ammunition wagons were brought into the action for the first time, some men fired as many as 180 rounds.

Prussian infantrymen of Frederick's Army in parade uniform, left, and field uniform, right.

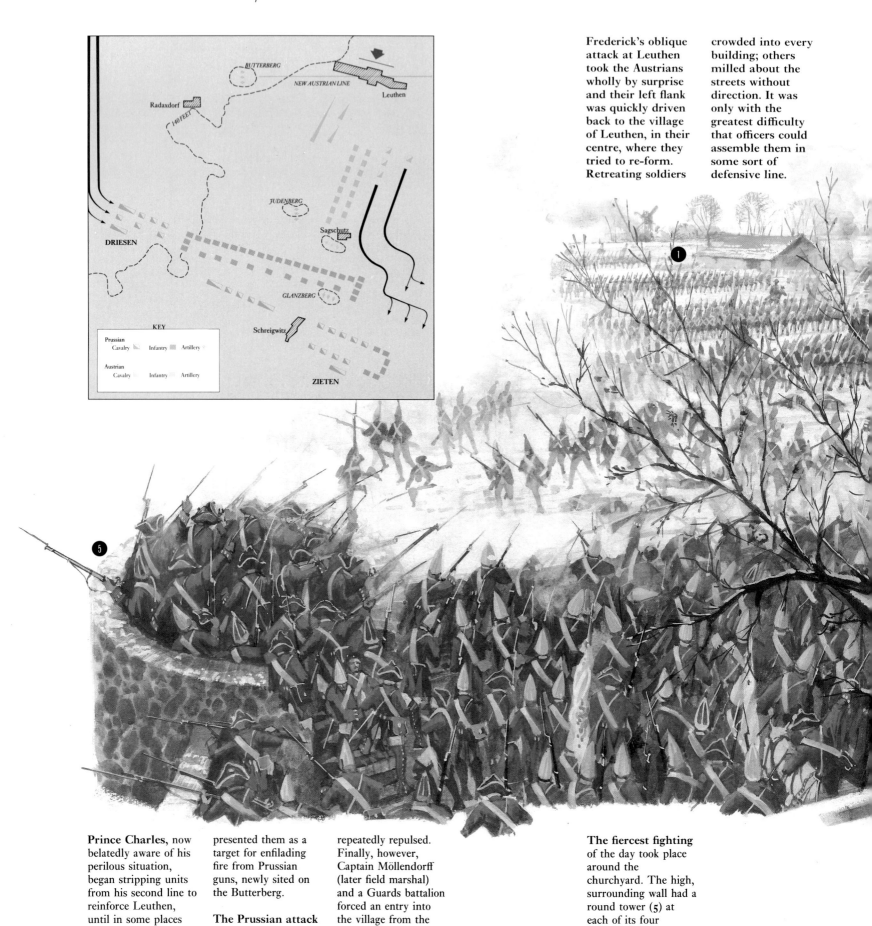

Frederick's oblique attack at Leuthen took the Austrians wholly by surprise and their left flank was quickly driven back to the village of Leuthen, in their centre, where they tried to re-form. Retreating soldiers crowded into every building; others milled about the streets without direction. It was only with the greatest difficulty that officers could assemble them in some sort of defensive line.

Prince Charles, now belatedly aware of his perilous situation, began stripping units from his second line to reinforce Leuthen, until in some places the Austrians stood 40 and more deep. This, however, merely presented them as a target for enfilading fire from Prussian guns, newly sited on the Butterberg.

The Prussian attack on Leuthen began at about 15.30, but at first the infantry were repeatedly repulsed. Finally, however, Captain Möllendorff (later field marshal) and a Guards battalion forced an entry into the village from the south through a group of stables.

The fiercest fighting of the day took place around the churchyard. The high, surrounding wall had a round tower (5) at each of its four corners; all were occupied by infantry.

The church and churchyard were defended by a German battalion of Roth Würzberg, allies of the Austrians. They were crammed tight, the front rows standing on barrels, ammunition boxes and waggons to fire over the wall. Others (3) climbed on to the church roof and into the belfry to secure a vantage point.

The advancing Prussians (1) were fired on from either side by snipers (2) with muskets sited in stables, barns and houses. Both forces suffered heavy losses.

Resistance was so stiff that the Prussians had to bring up an artillery piece to breach the churchyard gate (4). This accomplished, the Prussians penetrated the churchyard, forcing the enemy to withdraw. After 30 minutes of fighting, the whole of Leuthen was abandoned by the Austrians, who fled and formed another defensive line north of the village.

illuminate the plain of Leuthen when Frederick's advance formations encountered enemy cavalry under General Nostiz. These were dispersed and driven back to the Austrian right wing, many men being killed or taken prisoner. Lucchese, on the Austrian right wing, believing himself the chief object of Frederick's attention, asked and received support from the Austrian left flank – just as Frederick must most fervently have hoped.

While the Austrians were redeploying cavalry units to meet this supposed main attack, Frederick ordered units advancing on Borne to wheel right and head southward, behind the curtain of rising ground, toward the enemy left. The mixture of Prussian cavalry and infantry thus disappeared from Austrian view. Prince Charles and Marshal Daun could not understand these movements and mistakenly thought that the small Prussian Army – the 'Berlin watch-parade' as the Austrians called it – having seen the Allies great numerical superiority, were in hasty retreat.

They were soon to be disabused, for shortly after 12.00 the leading Prussian formations were seen wheeling northward near Sagschütz and threatening the Austrian left, which had earlier been much reduced in strength to reinforce the right wing. Thus the depleted Austrian left wing, in unexpected and unwelcome manner, was faced with the full weight and ferocity of the main Prussian Army.

Frederick was now in position to attack in 'oblique' order. This manoeuvre is simple on paper but extremely complex in practice. It calls, above all, for discipline and precision of troop movement – and Frederick's soliders were the best drilled in Europe. He had often tried this manoeuvre, but always with incomplete success; now he was to employ it with overwhelming impact.

Nádasti, commanding on the Austrian left, seeing the advancing Prussian force (which greatly outnumbered his own) about to strike, sent urgently to Prince Charles for reinforcements. It was much too late, for by then Sagschütz had been taken and a battery of six guns brought up by the Prussians. Moreover, most of the Austrian cavalry was on the right wing, nearly 8km/5mls to the north.

Nádasti, in desperation, charged the advance squadrons under General Hans Joachim von Zieten, Frederick's trusted, veteran commander. Although at first successful, Nádasti merely drove Zieten's cavalry back to the next 'step' of troops in Frederick's oblique formation; shortly he in turn was charged and his men dispersed

Prussian firepower at Leuthen

By 1756 Frederick had two artillery battalions, totalling 2,747 troops, 1,700 horses and 250 field guns. In 1731 calibres of guns had been standardized at 3-, 6-, 12- and 24-pounders. Frederick experimented with two additional light 3-pounders and a light 6-pounder, but the battles of 1757 convinced him that these were inferior to the more powerful Austrian guns. There was, too, a light 12-pounder, 29 of which were lost at Breslau two weeks before Leuthen, so Frederick brought up some older 12-pounders from Glogau. These Bruemmers proved devastating and, unusually, 24-pounder siege guns were also used in the battle.

The Prussian artillery, with 167 guns, really came of age at Leuthen. A 12-pounder battery accompanied the advance guard, knocking out two Austrian cannon and then providing effective fire support from the Glanzberg. The heavy battery on the Judenberg completed the oblique crossfire converging on the Austrian left wing. And when the Austrian line redeployed, both formations of guns moved rapidly to the Butterberg to pour devastating enfilading fire into it.

Frederick's greatest contribution was, perhaps, in the area of shell-flinging howitzers. To the 18-pounder of the previous reign he added a 10-pounder and a new 18-pounder in 1743–4. The year after Leuthen, a 7-pounder battalion weapon appeared and by 1762 every battalion had one. The Prussian Army's capacity for high-trajectory indirect fire at defences and hill positions was thus unrivalled.

Frederick conferring with his generals before the Battle of Leuthen. The artist has made the scene more snowy than is historically accurate.

and driven in disarray into the woods around Rathen.

Within half an hour of Nádasti's charge, the left wing of the Austrian army was thus disintegrating, whole formations fleeing northward to the supposed safety of Leuthen. This large village had, however, been only lightly defended and now Prince Charles, belatedly aware of the extreme peril in which he had been placed, speedily recalled the cavalry which he had been deceived into thinking was needed on his right flank. While they made their way southward, all he could do was feed into Leuthen any infantry units he could safely detach from the centre.

Pour le Mérite

Prussia's highest award for valour was founded by Frederick in June 1740 to supplement the somewhat devalued *Ordre de la Générosité*. Although intended as a more military decoration, it could be won for an invention or a smart parade: even the most unmilitary Voltaire received one. Up to the end of World War I, during which it was won by officers such as Ludendorff and Rommel, the elegant blue-enamelled cross was much coveted. At Leuthen it was given to 15 officers of the spearhead Meyerinck Infantry Regiment.

On an officer's promotion to the rank of lieutenant-general, it was handed back in return for the large embroidered silver star of the Order of the Black Eagle.

In this way, the Austrian Army turned at right angles to its original position – that is, straddling east to west through Leuthen, rather than north to south as before – in an attempt to hold the northward advance of Frederick's attack. The fiercest fighting of the day ensued.

The effect of all this uncoordinated and panic-ridden manoeuvring by the Austrians was that Leuthen and its environs soon became crammed with bewildered and uncertain troops. Nevertheless, the Austrians put up a stout resistance in the town – notably around the churchyard, which the Prussians penetrated after artillery bombardment – and were driven from it only after half an hour of intense close-quarter fighting.

The Austrians rallied and made a further stand under the protection of a battery sited to the north of Leuthen. As they re-formed, again west to east, Frederick moved his heaviest cannon on to the Butterberg, a hill west of the disordered Austrian units, and subjected them to such an intense cannonade that they were forced to withdraw.

Now came the decisive moment in the battle. The Prussian left flank was for a time exposed and Lucchese, whose cavalry – some 70 squadrons – had at last come up from the Austrian right wing, was ordered by Prince Charles to charge at this weak point.

As Lucchese's cavalry moved forward, it was seen by the Prussian Lieutenant-General George von Driesen, who was stationed near Radaxdorf, where he was on dead ground and thus undetected. Suddenly he launched his 40 or so squadrons to take the charging Austrians in their right flank. The battle had been won: Lucchese was killed and his cavalry scattered. Soon Driesen could wheel and take the Austrian infantry north of Leuthen in the rear.

As darkness descended – Lucchese's desperate and doomed charge had been

Prince Charles of Lorraine 1712–1780

The young brother of Francis I, Holy Roman Emperor, Prince Charles was, moreover, married to Marianne, the sister of Maria Theresa, the Emperor's wife. Prince Charles joined the Austrian Army in 1736 and subsequently saw service in an unsuccessful campaign against the Turks (1737–9). He led the Austrian Army against Frederick the Great, who beat him at Chotusitz in 1742 and again at the Battle of Hohenfriedberg in 1745. In all, Frederick defeated him five times.

Opinions vary as to Prince Charles's military abilities, his defenders claiming that his many defeats were occasioned by his bad luck in being in command against Frederick, a military genius; others maintaining he was incompetent and a personal disaster for the Austrian Army. Certainly, his rout at Leuthen prompted the court to seek his resignation, but he submitted it only after a letter from Maria Theresa herself; at the end of the war he went back to the Netherlands as governor.

Prince Charles was a tall, handsome, red-faced man with a heavy frame. He

Engraving of Prince Charles as Governor of the Austrian Netherlands.

was given to overeating and heavy drinking and was notoriously boastful; he was also inclined to have favourites and often quarrelled with his officers.

launched shortly after 16.00 on that cold, snowy December day – the Austrians finally broke and retreated in terrified disarray. Frederick and a strong escort thrust on to Lissa to gain the bridge, in this way successfully preventing the scattered Austrians from again re-forming for another battle behind the River Weistritz.

Frederick won the battle outright, and had he had a few more hours of daylight in which to consolidate his victory, the outcome of the war might have been decided, militarily at least. As with all battles until recent times, losses at Leuthen cannot be gauged with accuracy. It is thought that

the Austrians sustained losses in the region of 10,000, and some 12,000 men were captured. They also lost 131 guns and virtually all their baggage and wagons. Prussian losses have been put at roughly 6,380, including both killed and wounded.

Frederick was to suffer reverses, some calamitous, in the future, but the Battle of Leuthen, superbly orchestrated and annihilating in its impact, assures him a permanent position as a captain of genius. When exiled on St Helena, Napoleon was to write of the battle: 'Alone it is sufficient to immortalize Frederick, and place him in the rank of the greatest generals.'

Frederick's legacy to Prussia

Leuthen was the most brilliantly executed and complete of Frederick's victories but it by no means ended the war. In 1759 he was thoroughly beaten by an Austro-Russian force at Kunersdorf and in the following year Berlin was occupied; at this point, it is thought, Frederick seriously contemplated suicide. But within two years, in 1762, Elizabeth of Russia died and was succeeded by Peter III, an admirer of Frederick, who quickly took Russia out of the war.

This opened the way to Prussian victory, despite the country's being hedged in by enemies and outnumbered at least three to one. In 1763, the Peace of Hubertusburg was signed, under the terms of which Frederick kept his territorial conquests. Soldier-

ing, however, was not over for Frederick for, in alliance with Russia, his old enemy, he secured the virtual dismemberment of Poland, thereby incorporating vast areas of land into Prussia.

But it was his campaigning and his battles – notably Leuthen – during the Seven Years War that secured for Frederick his undisputed place among the small band of Great Commanders. Perhaps, however, his most enduring monument is that, despite the ravages Germany was to endure during the Napoleonic Wars, it was Frederick who first gave Prussia her ultimate identity. In retrospect, it is possible to see that under Frederick's despotic guidance Prussia must eventually emerge as the strongest military power in Europe in the nineteenth century.

George Washington *1732-1799*

W ashington's arrival at Boston on 3 July 1775 to take command of the Continental Army caused little stir; one soldier even wrote in his diary, 'Nothing happeng extrorderly'. But the event was of extreme significance, for over the next few years it was Washington who came to personify the Colonists' determination to gain independence, and it was through his military endeavours that they achieved it. As a soldier, Washington is best described as indispensable: when the Colonists had been crushed in a major engagement or had been destroyed here and there over the vast theatre of war, so long as Washington stood firm, they believed the struggle would continue.

Although the son of a Virginian gentleman, George Washington's education was minimal, and he was not sent to England for schooling as was common among the reasonably prosperous at the time. He left school when he was aged 15 and later became a self-taught surveyor. Part of his childhood was passed on one of the family estates on the Rappahannock River, nearly opposite Fredericksburg, but on the early death of his brother Lawrence, he inherited the estate he later called Mount Vernon, which was to be his home for the rest of his life. At the age of 20, he was created district adjutant in Virginia, made a major, and given responsibility for training the local militia.

Even when he was young, Washington's contemporaries held him in some awe, for he was always reserved and cool, and while he had friends, seems to have had no intimates. He was exceptionally tall for the time – 1.9m/6ft 2in or thereabouts – but was graceful and an accomplished horseman. His face, though slightly pock-marked, was serene and he radiated authority. Though just to his servants, invariably well-mannered, and honest and open with his friends, he was not generous and some, while impressed with his intellect, found him dull.

In 1759 he married a rich young widow, Martha Dandridge Custis, who had two small children. She was an attractive, kindly woman and Washington was devoted to her, but they made a slightly incongruous pair, since she was only about 1.5m/5ft tall, and the top of her head reached just to his chest.

George Washington was not a strategist of the first order, for he lacked military experience and had not been trained in warfare, and it is a high tribute to his latent skills that he quickly grasped the fundamental principles of warfare. He was elected Commander-in-Chief of the Continental Army, the main colonial force, on 15 June 1775, and at once found himself faced with an almost impossible task. Such troops as he had were undisciplined and untrained, their officers were insubordinate and inexperienced while against him was ranged the might of British arms.

It is as a military administrator that he stands highest, for he alone welded the enthusiastic but disorganized Continental Army into a victorious fighting unit. Above all he was persistent. Persistent in his pleadings with Congress for the necessities of war: arms, ammunition, and adequate clothing and resources for his men; and persistent in his resolve, despite his difficulties and numerical inferiority, to win the war.

After the war, Washington retired from the army and returned to his Virginian estates. The most celebrated man in the new republic, he later presided over the adoption of the 'Constitution of the United States' and on 30 April 1789 became the first president. He served two terms but then, weary of political intrigue, retired to his estate of Mount Vernon, where he died on 14 December 1799 and was buried.

George Washington at Princeton; the artist Charles Willson Peale has depicted the victor with a captured enemy cannon and flags; in the background can be seen Nassau Hall and troops of the British Army.
The most famous painting of the midwinter crossing of the Delaware by Washington's army is this picture by the German, Emanuel Gottlieb Leutze.

1732	*22 February* Born in Virginia, second son of a wealthy landowner.
1752	*December* Major, training Virginia militia.
1754	*April* Lieutenant-Colonel. *28 May* Beats French at Great Meadows. *4 July* Surrenders Fort Necessity; colonel.
1755	*9 July* Survives the Battle of Monongahela. *August* Commands Virginia militia.
1758	On Forbes expedition to Pittsburgh.
1759	Resigns commission.
1775	*15 June* Commander-in-Chief of the Continental Army. *3 July* Takes command at Boston.
1776	*4–18 March* Seizes Dorchester Heights and enters Boston. *13 April* Sets up HQ at New York. *27–30 August* Loses Long Island; retreats over East River. *15–16 September* Loses New York but holds Harlem Heights. *28 October* Loses White Plains. *16–20 November* Loses Forts Washington and Lee. *7 December* Retreats over the Delaware into Pennsylvania. *25–26 December* Crosses the Delaware, wins Trenton.

1777	*3 January* **Battle of Princeton.** *1 August* Meets Lafayette. *11 September* Loses Brandywine. *4 October* Loses Germantown. *19 December* Valley Forge, winter quarters and retraining.
1778	*28 June* Draws Monmouth.
1781	*22 May–19 October* Yorktown campaign effectively ends the war.
1783	*4 December* Enters New York. *23 December* resigns commission.
1789	*30 April* First president of USA.
1798	C-in-C for undeclared war with France.
1799	*14 December* Dies at Mount Vernon, aged 67.

Battle of Princeton/*3 January 1777*

BRITISH STRATEGY IN North America was, from the first, maladroit. The theatre of operations was vast and quite beyond the compass of a British army to subdue and occupy. A far more hopeful policy would have been to blockade the Colonists, since almost all lived on the coast or near to it.

Following the skirmishes at Lexington and Concord in April 1755, and Britain's costly victory at Bunker Hill on 17 June, full-scale war was unavoidable. The British abandoned Boston in March 1776, but on 2 July General Sir William Howe landed on Staten Island near New York with the first of nearly 32,000 troops. Against this force, George Washington could muster no more than 20,000 men.

After fruitless attempts to reach a peace agreement, Howe attacked Washington on 27 August and defeated him, but subsequently allowed him to escape to Manhattan Island. Washington's army was thoroughly demoralized and he soon withdrew from New York and retreated northward. Howe eventually moved in pursuit and on 16 November captured Fort Washington and four days later Fort Lee on the Hudson River.

This twin blow forced Washington to fall back to the Raritan River at the end of November. There he destroyed the bridges before retreating into Pennsylvania behind the Delaware River; he reached Trenton by 8 December. The British followed, but finding that all the rivercraft had also been destroyed along a 121km/75ml stretch, they abandoned the pursuit. This decision gave a respite to Washington's pessimistic army of Continental, or regular, troops and militia, now reduced by desertion and illness to 3,153.

The War of Independence 1775–83

This conflict arose, paradoxically, from Britain's defeat of France in the Seven Years War (1756–63). Once the French had been expelled from Canada, the 13 American colonies were free of threat, except from native Indians. Britain, however, with justice, expected the Colonists to make a financial contribution to their defence, but this taxation was deeply resented by the Colonists.

Moreover, the Colonists, though mostly of English descent, had grown apart from the 'Mother Country', and other immigrants – French, German, Dutch and Swedes – had joined their ranks. In sum, the Colonists comprised an agricultural society, unlike the more sophisticated British, who were governed by an aristocratic oligarchy and relied on commerce for the country's ever-increasing prosperity. A further cause for strife was that the British had established an Indian reserve west of the Alleghenny Mountains, which limited colonial expansion into the interior.

While the British deemed it only just that, through taxation, the Colonists should pay at least some of the upkeep of a garrison, the Colonists adopted a new cry: 'No taxation without representation.' Discontent grew, especially in Boston, and at length, on 5 March 1770, came the first inevitable clash – a riot developed in which British troops killed four Colonists. This was immediately dubbed the 'Boston Massacre' and resistance stiffened.

Britain had no option but to send troops to restore order; the Colonists, inflamed by revolutionary leaders, took to arms.

Howe, thinking that campaigning was over for the winter, left Major-General James Grant with some 12,000 men to hold the area, while he himself withdrew on 13 December to the comforts of New York. The British and Hessian allies went into winter quarters; most were stationed in Brunswick and Princeton, while the remaining troops were posted at strategic points along the Delaware from Bordentown to Burlington, a distance of about 129km/80mls. The 3,000 Hessians were thus overstretched, and their weakest point was at the village of Trenton. Command of the garrison here was given to Colonel Johann Rall.

Washington's disheartened and much-reduced army was rapidly ceasing to be an effective fighting force. Grant informed Rall on 21 December that 'the rebel army in Pennsylvania have neither shoes nor stockings, are in fact almost naked, dying of cold, without blankets and very ill supplied.' To rekindle his men's confidence and enthusiasm and make use of recent reinforcements, Washington resolved to attack the outpost at Trenton.

Washington decided to employ three columns in the assault. The main thrust, which he himself led, comprised about 2,400 infantry, 20 cavalry and 18 cannon, under two able young commanders – Majors-General Nathanael Greene and John Sullivan. The plan was for this force to cross the Delaware at McKonkey's Ferry, 12km/7½mls above Trenton, and take the village from the northwest. Meanwhile, Brigadier-General James Ewing would move 1,000 men (mostly militia) across the river at Trenton Ferry, opposite the village, and seize the south bank of the

When Washington attacked Trenton, his troops' morale was at a low ebb; in his own words, 'the game was pretty nearly up'. The capture of the Hessians, *right*, painted by John Trumbull, and the surrender of Colonel Rall, shown in the engraving, *left*, after a painting by A. Chappel, gave Washington's men new hope and led directly to their success at Princeton eight days later.

TO ALL BRAVE, HEALTHY, ABLE BODIED, AND WELL DISPOSED YOUNG MEN,
IN THIS NEIGHBOURHOOD, WHO HAVE ANY INCLINATION TO JOIN THE TROOPS,
NOW RAISING UNDER
GENERAL WASHINGTON,
FOR THE DEFENCE OF THE
LIBERTIES AND INDEPENDENCE
OF THE UNITED STATES,
Against the hostile designs of foreign enemies,

TAKE NOTICE,

The Continental Army

Washington's Continental Army was an attempt by the 13 states to match the European regulars they were fighting. It was founded in June 1775, when Congress raised 10 companies of riflemen from Maryland, Pennsylvania and Virginia and appointed generals to command them. Further battalions and two artillery companies were established as the war progressed.

Since Congress could not draft men for military service, a system of bounties and inducements was used to get and keep troops. In January 1776, $6.66 was paid to a man who enlisted with a good gun and bayonet, $4 to those without. On 26 June, Congress approved a $10 bounty for a three-year term; in September, this was raised to $20, plus 100 acres of land, for those who enlisted for the duration – the term Washington wanted. In October, a $20 suit of clothes was added.

Ironically, regular enlistments fell after 1776 because of the much better pay given to the militia by some of the New England states, who offered $33.33 above Congress's payment. Massachusetts almost tripled this sum, other states went even higher, all outbidding the Continental Army and creating a swarm of 'bounty jumpers' who would enlist, collect the payment, desert, re-enlist to be paid again, and so on.

Assunpink Creek, so as to block any Hessian retreat.

Colonel John Cadwalader was to take 2,000 men, mainly Pennsylvania militia, over the river farther south and attack Bordentown, to prevent the troops stationed there from going to the aid of Trenton. In the event, Ewing did not manage to cross the river, and Cadwalader could not ferry his cannon over.

The columns set off at about 14.00 on Christmas Day and by early evening had reached the Delaware. The weather was appalling: it was totally dark and a blizzard was blowing. Washington's column managed to cross the river in flat-bottomed boats; but owing to the conditions they did not complete the manoeuvre until 04.00, four hours behind schedule, and they still had a 15km/9ml march to Trenton. Once across the river, roughly half the force, under Sullivan, took the river road; the remainder, under Greene, the Princeton road to Trenton. Washington himself went with Greene's column.

An attack at first light was now out of the question and Washington had lost the element of suprise but, as he expected, the Hessians had been celebrating Christmas. The commander, Rall, having drunk himself almost to insensibility, lay in a stupor, and few of the pickets on the freezing winter night were fully alert. The battle opened at about 08.00 and was soon over – estimates as to its duration vary from 35 minutes to $1\frac{3}{4}$ hours.

Although Rall quickly roused himself, and the Hessians rapidly turned out and formed up, they were broken by artillery fire down the two main streets and were taken by flanking fire from Sullivan's men to the west. House-to-house fighting ensued, for in the icy weather most of the muskets had frozen up and were unusable. Sullivan's and Greene's men surrounded the village, and the Hessians had no alternative to surrender; of a force of 1,500, some 918 were taken prisoner.

Losses were light on both sides: only 4 Americans were wounded, it would seem, and 106 Hessians were killed or wounded; but their six brass 3-pounder guns were taken. The victory achieved precisely what Washington had wanted: his army became once more confident, optimistic and united.

Washington again withdrew across the Delaware, but his position was by no means secure, for as soon as the river was solidly iced over the British would be able to cross. Moreover, many in his army were due to depart on 31 December, the expiration date of their year-long term of enlistment. This problem he resolved by giving

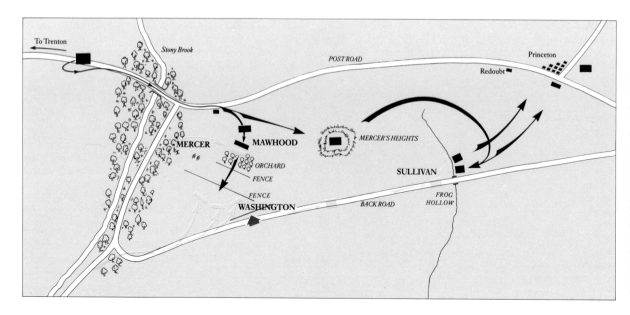

Washington's use of the tactic of indirect approach at Princeton was masterly. By leaving camp fires burning at Trenton to deceive the British, he was able to move his troops unmolested at night toward his true objective – Princeton. And once in position at Princeton he outnumbered his enemies, many of whom were preparing to attack the abandoned town of Trenton.

The supreme example of this tactic's use in modern times is Slim's plan for the capture of Meiktila/Mandalay during WWII.

The first shots in the Battle of Princeton were exchanged early on the morning of 3 January 1777 in Clark's Orchard (4). While on his way with the 17th Foot to reinforce Trenton, the British commander, Lieutenant-Colonel Charles Mawhood (6), had seen the advancing Americans and had turned back to engage them.

The Americans at first ousted the British from their positions behind the orchard fence (5), but when the 17th Foot charged, were driven back themselves and took refuge behind a second fence (7). During this charge, Brigadier-General Hugh Mercer, the American commander, was mortally wounded, adding to the panic and confusion in the Colonists' ranks. They were shortly further dismayed when they were fired on by two British cannon (3).

George Washington (2) galloped to the scene to rally the Americans, who were on the point of disintegration. Order was restored, and by then two 4-pounders (1) had been brought up on their left to counter the British guns opposite. Washington himself then led his once more steady men forward. He halted his grey horse only about 27m/ 30yds from the British line and gave the order to fire.

The British promptly returned the volley; miraculously Washington was not hit. But being outnumbered and their shorter front thus vulnerable to encirclement, they then retreated. Some made for their comrades at Trenton, the rest withdrew toward Princeton. The Americans followed and Washington's victory was soon complete, when the town fell.

The Prussian soldier/ writer Dietrich von Bülow later commented: 'The manoeuvres of the American General at Trenton and Princeton were masterpieces. They may be deemed models for the conduct of a general supporting a defensive war against a superior enemy.'

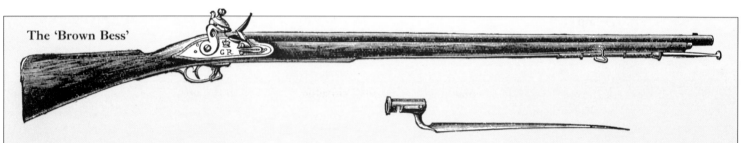

The 'Brown Bess'

Marlborough is traditionally credited with introducing this famous smooth-bore musket into the British Army in 1717. The original Long Land Service Pattern had a 116cm/46in barrel and weighed 5.3kg/11¼lb; about 1724 an iron ramrod was introduced. In 1768 the lighter, 106cm/ 42in barrel Short Land Service version came in, which needed just over half the Long Pattern's powder charge, thus reducing recoil. Light infantry carried a 96cm/38in cut-down variant of this model. All three versions were used in North America.

The Brown Bess was a robust 19mm/¾in calibre weapon, firing a 28g/1oz ball and carrying a 43cm/17in socket bayonet. A highly trained soldier could fire four or five unaimed rounds a minute. Maximum effective range was 73–91m/80–100yds and, on average, the musket misfired one in every six and a half shots.

a bounty of $10 to every man who re-enlisted for a further six weeks; even so, on 1 January 1777, Washington could muster only about 1,600 Continentals. He needed to defeat the British again without delay.

His plan for a second attack was strengthened by the fact that Cadwalader had succeeded in crossing the Delaware on 27 December and had occupied the evacuated Hessian post of Burlington. Washington therefore began to recross the Delaware on 30 December, and by 1 January had reoccupied Trenton. Meanwhile, the energetic, 38-year-old Major-General the Earl Cornwallis, hearing of the Trenton débâcle when about to sail for England from New York, had ridden 80km/50mls non-stop into New Jersey to take command of all British and Hessian forces there.

Uncertain where the bulk of the British Army lay, Washington sent strong detachments up the road toward Princeton to reconnoitre and guard his army from attack. When he learned that most of the enemy were at Princeton and Brunswick, these towns became his twin objectives.

On 2 January, 8,000 British troops and 28 guns appeared on the 18km/11ml long road between Princeton and Trenton, but Colonel Edward Hand, the American commander, fought a skilful delaying action against them, from Five Mile Creek through Trenton. The 'Second Battle of Trenton' ended in darkness with a cannonade across Assunpink Creek. But Cornwallis rejected advice to renew the attack at once with the words, 'We've got the old fox safe now. We'll go over and bag him in the morning.' And the British settled down in Trenton.

But that night, Washington left his campfires burning and, with gun carriages muffled, embarked on an enveloping move northeast toward his first target – Princeton. By first light on 3 January, after

a gruelling night march, advance units of Washington's 3,600-strong army were at Stony Brook, some 3km/2mls from the town itself.

The Princeton strongpoint comprising some 1,200 British troops was under the command of Lieutenant-Colonel Charles Mawhood. Unaware of Washington's movements, Mawhood left Princeton at dawn on 3 January with the 17th and 55th Foot, to move on Trenton. Only the 40th Foot remained in the town to guard the extensive supplies. As Mawhood crossed Stony Brook on the Post Road to Trenton, he became aware of enemy troops moving toward him. Thinking them to be defeated Americans fleeing from the previous day's clash, he turned about to cut them off.

Washington now prepared to deploy for an attack. Brigadier-General Hugh Mercer, with about 350 men, was ordered to destroy the bridge at Stony Brook to prevent British reinforcements from

The Battle of Princeton, too, was painted by John Trumbull. This artist had served in the Continental Army early in the war and had been George Washington's aide. In 1777 he resigned from the army and devoted himself to painting.

Trenton getting across. While this was attempted, the main body of American troops took the 'Back Road' to Princeton. Sullivan's force was well up the Back Road and within striking distance of the town, and Washington himself was farther back with the rest of Mercer's brigade when, at about 08.00, Mawhood's troops were at length sighted by Mercer. Mawhood had by then turned about, and Mercer, turning right to avoid being cut off, clashed with him in Clark's Orchard.

When all Mercer's men were in the orchard, they were fired on by 17th Foot on their left. The Americans immediately faced about left and promptly drove the redcoats from their positions behind a fence. Then battle was engaged in earnest, for each side brought up two field guns. The 17th Foot launched a ferocious charge that drove back the Continentals; during the action Mercer was mortally wounded. Washington, with Cadwalader's militia, hastened to the spot.

Although the Americans were on the verge of disintegration, they held when their two guns harried the British and prevented their further advance. The ranks were further steadied when Washington, Greene and Cadwalader, with no regard for their own safety, rode among the demoralized troops to rally them. Order restored, Washington himself led his men forward. About 27m/30yds from

the British line, he halted his grey horse and commanded them to fire. The outnumbered British returned fire, but then, aware of their vulnerability, fled: the 17th Foot toward Cornwallis in Trenton, the remainder making for Princeton.

The end of the engagement was now near. Sullivan, well up the Back Road, had halted as members of the 55th Foot, holding the commanding Mercer's Heights to his left, came down and joined the 40th Foot lining the brook at Frog Hollow. When Mawhood's troops were driven off by Washington, these men, too, abandoned their position and retreated to Princeton.

The Americans then entered the town, but some redcoats had occupied the sturdy Nassau Hall (today part of Princeton

University), intending to resist. However, a gun was brought forward, and after a few well-aimed shots the garrison surrendered. Some 190 prisoners were taken; the rest of the British made good their escape to the north. During the skirmish, which lasted 15 minutes or a little more, the Americans lost 40 men killed or wounded, the British 28 killed, 58 wounded and 187 missing.

Washington, knowing that Cornwallis was rushing reinforcements up from Trenton, could not hold the town. His troops were exhausted, so he was obliged to give up his plan to seize Brunswick and its supplies (including the $70,000 British war chest). Instead, his victorious army moved into winter quarters well north of Princeton, at Morristown.

Charles Cornwallis 1738–1805   Charles Mawhood ?–1780

The aristocratic Charles, Earl Cornwallis, had made the army his career, joining the Guards in 1756 at the age of 18. Unlike most soldier-aristocrats, he took his work seriously, studied the military arts and saw action during the Seven Years War. He volunteered to serve in North America, a surprising decision, since, though he was King George III's ADC, he had opposed the king's policies there. Cornwallis, however, was motivated primarily by loyalty to his country.

Again unlike the majority of his contemporary commanders, he paid great attention to his soldiers' needs and comfort; they in turn admired him. He was indisputably the most gifted tactical British commander in North America, despite being outwitted at Princeton and despite his final defeat and surrender at Yorktown.

Lieutenant-Colonel Charles Mawhood began his career as a cornet of dragoons

Major-General Charles Cornwallis

in 1752 and joined the 17th Foot in America as its lieutenant-colonel on 26 October 1775. He was a meticulous officer who followed orders to the letter, but was nevertheless capable of making quick, sound decisions.

But like many of the British officers, he held American soliders in low esteem and, particularly after Cornwallis had advanced on Trenton, felt his position in Princeton to be secure. So much so, that the night before the battle he was confident enough to call off his patrol southeast of Princeton, thereby allowing Washington to approach him unobserved the following morning. After Princeton, in March 1778, Mawhood won two minor actions in New Jersey. He died at Gibraltar when commanding the 72nd Foot there during the unsuccessful Great Siege of 1779–83 by the French and Spanish. His death was hastened by the terrible privations suffered by the garrison.

Independence achieved
The numbers engaged in the two battles, or more correctly skirmishes, at Trenton and Princeton were trivial when compared with those engaged in the French Revolutionary and Napoleonic Wars soon to begin in Europe, but the consequences of the two engagements were momentous.

The Americans regained their confidence and resolved to fight on, despite the fact that many of the Colonists, the 'Tories', remained loyal to the British Crown. Then, between 19 September and 7 October 1777, the Battle of Saratoga was fought on the west bank of the Hudson River, and the British, outmanoeuvred and defeated, surrendered.

This convinced the European powers, notably France, who still smarted from her defeat at British hands during the Seven

Years War, that it was in their interests to come to the Americans' assistance. Massive help was sent to the rebels, without which they must have failed. Before the Battle of Saratoga, American hopes of victory were slim; after it, triumph was assured. The Battles of Trenton and Princeton made Washington's reputation; as a result, Saratoga and ultimate victory became possible.

At a dinner given by his American captors after his surrender at Yorktown on the Chesapeake River in October 1781, Cornwallis replied to Washington's toast in elegant and appropriate terms: 'When the illustrious part that your Excellency has borne in this long and arduous contest becomes a matter of history, fame will gather your brightest laurels rather from the banks of the Delaware than from the banks of the Chesapeake.'

Napoleon *1769-1821*

N apoleon was more than one of the greatest commanders in history; he was also a statesman and law giver. He altered the map of Europe – dissolving the Holy Roman Empire in 1806; creating the kingdoms of Holland and Westphalia; and in 1809 annexing the Papal States to France, among much else. And he made himself Emperor of France and his brothers kings.

There was, however, little of the Frenchman about Napoleon, for he was born in 1769 at Ajaccio, Corsica, the son of a minor nobleman Carlo Bonaparte and his wife Letitzia, and Corsica was by language and tradition Italian. The island had, indeed, been ceded to France by Genoa only in 1768 and had Napoleon been born two years earlier he would not have been a French citizen. In childhood he seems to have been an assertive but introspective boy, much given to tantrums and ready to lie to achieve an objective. From an early age he was preoccupied with soldiering, and in 1779 was sent to the military school at Brienne, where his first task was to learn French.

In 1784 he went on to the *École Militaire* in Paris. He passed out in one year instead of the customary two and in 1785, when just 16 years old, was commissioned in the artillery. The young Napoleon's life was soon engulfed by the French Revolution, which gave him the opportunity for advancement. He first attracted notice in 1793, when he retook Toulon, which had been occupied by the British, thanks to his decisive use of artillery. He was only 24, but was promoted general of brigade.

Two years later in October 1795, when the Convention was attacked by a Parisian mob, Napoleon displayed that talent for quick decision followed by ruthless execution that was to be central to his career. Without qualms, he fired on the mob with eight cannon and dispersed it, killing about 100 people and wounding many more. The deed was done, he said, with 'a whiff of grapeshot'. He was given command of the Army of the Interior, and his future – glorious, terrible and ultimately doomed – opened before him.

Napoleon's military success has been attributed to many factors; sometimes it is explained solely by his 'genius', but his genius would have been unproductive had it not been based on other great qualities. He was hugely energetic and industrious, sometimes working for 16 hours a day (he adopted the bee as his emblem when he became emperor). He was meticulous and capable of grasping almost instantly the key move for success. He was also thorough in his campaign preparations: when supreme commander he was often found crawling about floors littered with maps, studying the minutest details. His astonishing success may be attributed above all, however, to his method of supply, whereby his troops lived off the land, to his use of speed of movement and his surprise attacks *en masse*. He also had the ability to pick able subordinates and to inspire adoration in his soldiers.

Although ruthless, Napoleon had undoubted personal charm and his empire brought French civilization to much of Europe and the New World. But the price was hardly worth paying. The number of killed and wounded in consequence of his wars was about four million, and the buildings destroyed and lives ruined cannot be computed. One of his generals once remarked, 'The Emperor is mad.' He meant, it is safe to assume, that Napoleon's ambitions were without limit and therefore unattainable. And so it proved, for he was eventually crushed at Waterloo and sent into permanent exile on the Atlantic island of St Helena.

Napoleon, mounted on Emir, watches the fighting on the second day of the Battle of Wagram; detail from a painting by Horace Vernet.
French guns were stamped with the Napoleonic cypher; detail from a captured bronze mortar at the Tower of London.
The emblem of the bee depicted here is taken from Napoleon's coronation robe.

1769	*15 August* Born at Ajaccio, Corsica.
1779	*15 May* Joins Brienne military school.
1784	Enters *École Militaire*, Paris.
1792	*6 February* Captain. *1 April* Elected lieutenant-colonel of a battalion.
1793	*23–25 February* La Maddalena raid. *16 September–19 December* Siege of Toulon, wounded. Promoted general of brigade.
1795	*5 October* The 'whiff of grapeshot'. *16 October* General of Division.
1796	*2 March* C-in-C Army of Italy. *12–28 April* Wins four battles, puts Piedmont out of the war. *10 May–17 November* Takes Lodi Bridge and Milan, wins six more battles.
1797	*14 January* Wins Rivoli. *2 February* Fall of Mantua. *7 April* Secures Austrian armistice.
1798	Egyptian Expedition to *August 1799*.
1799	*9 November Coup d'état* of Brumaire.
1800	*15 May–14 June* Crosses the Alps and wins Marengo.
1802	*25 March* Peace of Amiens. *1 May* Sets up St-Cyr Military Academy.
1803	*June* Prepares to invade England.
1804	*18–19 May* Proclaimed emperor; creates Imperial Guard and 18 marshals.
1805	*8 October–2 December* Wins Ulm and Austerlitz.
1806	*14–27 October* Wins Jena and enters Berlin. *18 December* Enters Warsaw.
1807	*7–8 February* Draws Eylau. *14 June* Wins Friedland. *7–9 July* Peace of Tilsit.
1808	Spanish campaign.
1809	*5–6 July* **Battle of Wagram.**
1812	Invasion of Russia.
1813	Last German campaign; loses at Leipzig.
1814	Campaign of France; wins 8 of 11 battles. *6 April* Abdicates; banished to Elba.
1815	The Hundred Days. *18 June* Loses Battle of Waterloo. *22 June* Second abdication.
1821	*5 May* Dies at St Helena, aged 51.

Battle of Wagram/5–6 July 1809

EARLY IN 1809, the Emperor Napoleon, who was campaigning in Spain, received disturbing news. The Austrians, whom he had crushed in 1805 at Ulm and later at Austerlitz when they were in combination with the Russians, were again mobilizing. He hastened back to Paris to organize their swift destruction.

By March 1809, Austrian mobilization was complete, and on 9 April their principal army began marching up the banks of the Danube into Bavaria, picking off various French outposts as they did so. Napoleon made immediate reply to this threat by himself assuming command of the Grand Army of Germany on 19 April. Napoleon then advanced upon, and soon occupied, Vienna.

This was, however, more impressive on paper than in practice, for Archduke Charles, younger brother of Emperor Francis I of Austria, had made little attempt to defend the city; instead, he stationed his army – some 95,000 men – north of the river. This was strategically prudent, since if Napoleon were to attack the Austrians – and attack was his habitual ploy – he would first have to cross the Danube, itself a formidable obstacle, and then fight a battle with his back to it.

Incredibly for a man of Napoleon's genius for meticulous planning and detailed reconnaissance, he had not first made sure where the Austrian Army was, and on 20 May took the gamble of crossing the river at Lobau Island, 7km/4mls below Vienna, on the assumption that it was far

Austria rearms

In 1809, Napoleon was master of the greater part of Europe. He had crushed an Austro-Russian army at Austerlitz on 2 December 1805 and, on 14 October 1806, routed the Prussians at the Battle of Jena. Then, at the Battle of Friedland (14 June 1807), Russia was again decisively defeated and withdrew from the struggle. Only Great Britain, the emperor's most resolute and persistent enemy, remained at war. Yet even at this high point of his fortunes, Napoleon can be seen in retrospect to have been doomed. Three factors were to ensure his downfall.

Admiral Lord Nelson's overwhelming victory at Trafalgar (21 October 1805) had left Napoleon's great empire isolated; moreover, Napoleon had at last overreached himself by involving the French in Spain, which became a fearful drain on his resources. There was a third factor and one which was to prove conclusive: every battle he won provoked great resentment in the defeated enemy, leading in turn to further battles, even greater resentment and yet more bloodshed.

Absolute victory was beyond Napoleon's compass and when, early in January 1809, he reached Paris from Spain, it was to find not only intrigues against him in the capital but disquieting news of Austrian rearmament. Napoleon's only option was to march rapidly against the Austrians and once more knock them out of the struggle.

removed. Even more surprising, he had constructed only a single improvised pontoon bridge across the 754m/825yds to Lobau Island in his eagerness to seek out the enemy. The archduke's counterstroke on 21 May came as an unwelcome surprise and placed the French bridgehead on the north bank in dire peril.

The two-day Battle of Aspern/Essling found the emperor outnumbered and outgunned two to one. Crucially, the flimsy bridge was broken at least five times by Austrian fireboats or the strength of the water itself, marooning Napoleon's 20,000 reinforcements on the south bank of the Danube and preventing the replenishment of ammunition.

By 14.00 on 22 May, Napoleon had no option but to order a retreat to the safety of Lobau Island. This was executed with difficulty and the pontoon bridge to the north bank was destroyed to prevent any Austrian pursuit, but there is no doubt that the emperor had been defeated for the first time in some 10 years. Losses were about equal – in the region of 22,000 – but the French had been thrown back from the north bank, and all Europe took note of it and rejoiced in the emperor's discomfiture. Furthermore, one of his best fighting marshals and closest friends, Jean Lannes, was mortally wounded.

Napoleon seems to have been paralysed in mind by this reverse, but his disbelief and dismay lasted no more than 36 hours. Then he applied himself, with his customary intensity and vigour, to replanning the

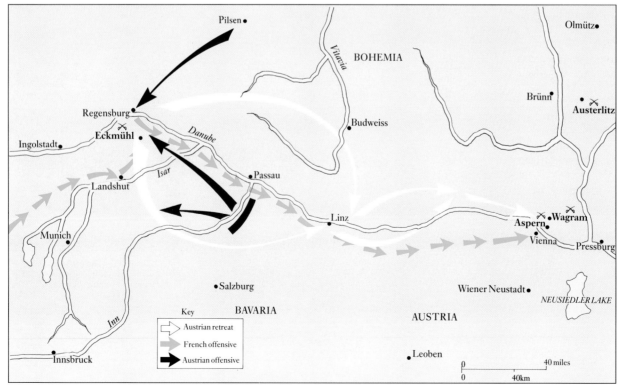

The Austrian Army marched into Bavaria on 9 April 1809, before the French Army of Germany was fully prepared. On 14 April Napoleon himself took charge and on 22nd brought the Austrians to battle and defeated them at Eckmühl. The Austrians retreated north of the Danube, while Napoleon marched east and took Vienna. In May, without knowing his enemy's precise whereabouts, Napoleon rashly took his army over the Danube. Archduke Charles promptly pounced and defeated Napoleon soundly at Aspern on 21–22 May; Napoleon withdrew to Vienna.

destruction of his enemy. Time, however, was not on his side, for news of Aspern/Essling was spreading throughout Europe and shortly there would almost certainly be uprisings against the French in Germany and elsewhere. Napoleon's situation was clear: he had to destroy the Austrians – and quickly. His activity became stupendous, a ceaseless flow of orders issuing from his headquarters.

By 25 May, the bridge from Lobau Island to the south bank of the Danube was repaired and firm; at once Napoleon moved all his 10,000 wounded to Vienna, where they received the best treatment then available. Next, with the utmost energy, he moved his army south, back over the Danube, save for Marshal André Masséna's 4th Corps, which was set to work building roads and erecting fortifications on Lobau Island. Two extra bridges were prepared for assembly and wooden piles driven into the river bed upstream to prevent fireboats destroying the bridges when they had been laid.

But above all, Napoleon was sending out messenger after messenger in search of reinforcements, no matter of what quantity. The underlying order in every message was the same – Hurry! Hurry! Hurry! Soon, the marshals and generals – almost all of whom were imbued with the Napoleonic concept of speed – were pouring across central Germany and from Illyria in the southwest to the small island of Lobau. By the beginning of July, Napoleon had some 160,000 men assembled at Vienna.

But there was another, no less feverish activity in Napoleon's preparations. The man who had started his career as a young artillery officer was now once again, in person, to deploy his favourite arm. By the beginning of July, he had assembled some 554 guns of all types.

Meanwhile, the Archduke Charles remained inactive. Though by no means an inconsiderable commander, his victory at Aspern/Essling had so surprised and elated him that he, too, became incapable of action. But whereas Napoleon's depression was temporary, Charles's euphoria seems to have degenerated into lethargy, which even included broaching the subject of peace with France with his elder brother Emperor Francis. Certainly he refortified the villages of Aspern and Essling, but beyond that he did no more than remove his army behind the River Russbach.

It has been suggested that his inactivity was deliberate and due to two expectations: that his younger brother, Archduke John, with a force of 13,000 men (originally from Italy) advancing westward from

Artillery at Wagram

Wagram was, at the time, the greatest artillery battle ever seen. Napoleon's 554 cannon fired 71,000 rounds in the two days, and Archduke Charles's 414 guns were scarcely less heavily used. After his defeat at Aspern/Essling, where he had only 144 guns against 280, Napoleon ransacked the arsenals and depots in Vienna and discovered 78 pieces, which went to Oudinot's, Masséna's and Davout's corps; more guns were ordered from France.

To offset the low morale and declining quality of his infantry, Napoleon restored two guns (3-, 4-, or 6-pounders) to each of 63 regiments, a support discontinued in 1801. And three Young Guard 4-pounder batteries, each with eight guns, were also formed in June 1809.

The heavy batteries on Lobau Island – 129 guns, including thirty 8-pounders and seventeen 30mm/12in mortars – were essential to Napoleon's plans, both for covering his troops and concealing where his bridgehead on the north bank would be. They made it impossible for the Austrians to fight as far forward as in May.

On the second day of Wagram, in the morning, Davout placed 12 guns so as to hit the Austrian 4th Corps in the flank and then virtually silenced their guns around Markgrafneusiedel with crossfire, prior to his own attack. The Lobau batteries helped slow down the Austrian right-wing offensive. By midday Napoleon was plugging his centre with General Lauriston's great battery of 112 guns, including many 12-pounders.

The Austrian artillery was divided into brigade (eight 3- or 6-pounders), cavalry and support (both four 6-pounders and two 7-pounder howitzers), and position batteries (four 12-pounders and two 7-pounder howitzers). Each infantry brigade had a position battery, while a division had a support battery, and the new corps two or three position batteries as a reserve. The organization was new, and the gunners less well trained than the French, but Archduke Charles had militarized artillery transport and, except for the 3- and 4-pounders, his guns were better supplied than the French.

Soldier of the artillery train (left) and foot artilleryman of the Imperial Guard (right). Napoleonic 12-pounders at the Tower of London.

Pressburg, would shortly reinforce him, and that disaffection with Napoleon's despotism would quickly cause rebellion in Germany. The former expectation was disabused when Eugène, Napoleon's stepson and Viceroy of Italy, while advancing to reinforce the *Grande Armée*, defeated Archduke John in a battle on the River Raab on 14 June and drove him eastward in retreat.

The latter prospect did not materialize in time because of Napoleon's ferocious activity; he was again ready to give battle to the Austrians before any major German insurrection could be organized. Thus Archduke Charles almost entirely squandered six weeks, except for incorporating *Landwehr* militia troops and more artillery pieces into his army.

Napoleon's plan was straightforward. On 30 June he made a feint with a division, covered by the fire of 36 guns, from the island of Lobau to its northwest side to distract the Austrians from his main crossing, eastward just below the village of Gross Enzersdorf. The main crossing began very late on 4 July, after a bombardment by artillery sited on Lobau Island. Napoleon's intention was to use the village as a hinge on which to wheel his army northwest, outflanking his foe's fortifications and splitting the main Austrian Army from that of Archduke John. The beauty of his plan lay in the fact that the bulk of the *Grande Armée* remained south of the Danube until the night of 3/4 July, while stores and guns had priority.

Archduke Charles, meanwhile, prey to

diverse advice from his generals and not certain of Napoleon's true intentions, had finally drawn up his army – now about 142,000 men – well out of French artillery range. Its right wing rested on the Bissamberg, and it then stretched southeastward behind the defensive line of the River Russbach. The villages of Aspern and Essling were only lightly defended. At 19.00 on 4 July Charles wrote to his brother John, 'The battle here on the Marchfeld will determine the fate of our dynasty . . . I request that you march at once, leaving behind all baggage and impedimenta, and join my left wing'.

During the night of 4 July and the early morning of the 5th, as Napoleon's army was crossing on 10 bridges from Lobau Island in a direction south of Gross

Napoleon's crossing of the Danube before Wagram was painted a year later by Joseph Swebach, called Fontaine, with a wealth of detail that reflects French pride in the achievement.

The emperor and his staff watch as a battery of 4-pounder guns crosses the pile-driven bridge to Lobau Island (the Danube has been narrowed from its actual 0.8km/½ml). The bridge has lanterns along it and even a sentry box at the south end. Up-river is a protective stockade to intercept any Austrian fireboats. The bridge and its pontoon neighbour, bearing a procession of ammunition limbers, broke at Schneidergrund Island before going on to Lobau, with a further 114m/125yd span from Lobau to the north bank proper.

There were no fewer than 10 bridges built across this channel between 30 June and 5 July.

On Napoleon's left are several pages, with some of his horses, and the turbanned Roustam, his Mameluke bodyguard.

Uniforms in 1809

The Napoleonic period was the golden age of the military tailor. Uniforms were as splendid as possible to raise the wearer's morale and strike awe in the enemy, rather than being regarded as practical clothing. One interesting exception stemmed from the 1809 campaign, when heavy losses incurred by the two French carabinier regiments (see 1 below) caused Napoleon to replace a blue coat and grenadier-style bearskin with breastplate and helmet, like those worn by the cuirassiers shown in the left foreground of the painting of the Danube crossing.

Every French infantry regiment had its

detachment of sappers or pioneers, *below*, under a corporal, four sappers for each of the four war battalions. They were chosen from the grenadier companies and therefore wore a bearskin, as well as being tall and bearded. The axe could be carried shaft up in a white leather case. Sappers also had their own type of sword with an elaborate eagle's or cock's head pommel. Such men did invaluble bridging and fortification work on the Danube in 1809.

Each battalion also had 12 drummers, *above*, two to a company, supervised by a corporal drummer on the regimental staff. It was the drummers who beat out the *pas de charge* as the signal for an attack.

1 Carabinier (1810).
2 Light cavalryman of the Imperial Guard, Napoleon's mounted bodyguard.
3 Marshal of the Empire, with baton.
4 Light infantryman of the line.
5 Officer of Dragoons of the Imperial Guard.
6 Austrian general wearing the Order of Maria Theresa.
7 Austrian fusilier.
8 Hungarian grenadier (18 battalions at Wagram).
9 Austrian lancer (2 regiments at Wagram).

Flying ambulances

As early as the end of 1792, the young French provincial doctor Dominique Jean Larrey, conscripted into the army only in March, was using flying ambulances of his own design with the Army of the Rhine. In August 1797, he formed a flying ambulance unit for Napoleon's Army of Italy.

This consisted of three divisions of 113 men, each led by a surgeon-major, with 14 other surgeons. There were 25 foot orderlies and 12 mounted orderlies who were also equipped to treat horses; these men wore red woollen sashes that could be used to carry the wounded. Each division had 12 light flying ambulances: eight 2-wheeled and four 4-wheeled.

The 2-wheeled ambulance resembled an elongated cube, with two small windows a side, and double doors front and back. Four rollers inside allowed the floor of the ambulance, with its leather-covered mattress, to be slid in and out, and two patients could be carried lying down. The side panels were padded to about 30cm/12in from the floor.

In 1809, at the time of Wagram, Larrey was inspector-general of medical services

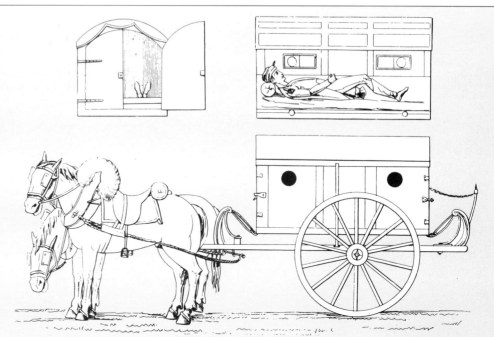

and the surgeon to the Imperial Guard. He gave his own account of the battle: 'With my flying ambulance I followed the movements of the Guard until the final moment...We dressed the wounded...on the field of battle, but when the numbers

These line drawings of a 2-wheeled flying ambulance appear in Larrey's own book, *Memoirs of Military Surgery and Campaigns*, which was published at Paris in 1812.

Enzersdorf, there was a thunderstorm, greatly hampering Austrian observation posts and almost muffling the sound of French movements. But thanks to Marshal Alexandre Berthier's impeccable staff, all proceeded as planned. By 10.00 on 5 July, most of the *Grande Armée* was over the river and in battle array, facing northwest in two curving lines. Marshal Louis Davout commanded on the right with his 35,000-strong 3rd Corps, Marshal Masséna on the left, having crossed with his 27,000 men on a 163m/178yd pontoon bridge that was swung into position under the emperor's personal supervision in under eight minutes.

By mid-afternoon, or a little later, the *Grand Armée*, which had made steady, though slow progress, formed a triangular shape. Davout faced the River Russbach, while Masséna, having taken Essling and Aspern with little difficulty, was at an angle of almost 45 degrees to his comrade, facing the Bissamberg. Another 18,000 troops and 48 guns under General Auguste Marmont and the Bavarian General Karl von Wrede were still crossing from the south bank of the Danube to Lobau Island.

At this point it would seem that the Austrians expected little further action that day; Napoleon, however, planned otherwise. He was in search of quick,

Etienne Macdonald 1765–1840

Etienne Macdonald was a Scot, whose father, after the Jacobite uprising on behalf of Charles Stuart ('Bonnie Prince Charlie' of legend and ballad), had escaped with the prince and then enlisted in the service of the French king.

Four years before the French Revolution, Macdonald, too, was commissioned in the French Army, but spent a great part of his time at the theatre and in dancing – his hobbies were collecting Etruscan vases and violin-playing. Later, however, he saw action and in 1793 was promoted general. In Italy, during the 1798–9 campaign, he conquered Naples, but lost the Battle of Trebia to the Russians.

Macdonald was 43 years old when, immediately after the Battle of Wagram, Napoleon promoted him marshal and made him Duke of Taranto. This was the only occasion on which Napoleon made one of his generals a marshal on the field – by a slip of the tongue creating him Marshal of France, rather than Marshal of the Empire as the other 25 were.

Etienne Macdonald is shown in this early portrait as General commanding the Army of Italy. In 1801 he fell from favour, but was recalled in 1809 and given command of part of the Army of Italy in support of the young Eugène. His promotion to marshal was a gesture of reconciliation, as well as recognition, by Napoleon.

Only four men, lying with knees bent, could be taken in the 4-wheeled ambulance; the artist has been carried away in this picture of Napoleon encouraging the wounded, *above*. Orderlies tending the wounded on the field of battle, *right*.

became too great I established an advanced dressing station . . . Before nightfall some 500 casualties were gathered . . . The majority had been gravely injured by cannon fire and required major surgery.' Even so, most wounded were not recovered for four or five days, suffering torments from fever, sunstroke and insects.

Austrian medical services were less well organized. The Josephenium medical academy at Vienna was in French hands; field hospitals were manned by semi-invalids and soldiers' wives, while casualty stations had just two staff surgeons and their assistants. Only in theory did each company, as well as battalion, have a surgeon.

Archduke Charles 1771–1847

The fifth son of the Habsburg Emperor Leopold II, Archduke Charles was, like Wellington and many other great commanders, a shy lad, lonely and often in poor health: he suffered from mild epileptic attacks all his life. He was small – little more than 1.5m/5ft tall – but was fearless in battle.

Even when young, he maintained that the Austrian Army was too content to conduct a defensive war and too concerned with preserving supply lines, unlike the French Army which foraged. Convinced that he could achieve more in the field than any other Austrian commander, he joined an intrigue to gain command of the army and in February 1796 was appointed Commander-in-Chief, aged only 24.

This was the year of his most accomplished victories at Amberg and Würzburg, when he drove General Jean Jourdan's army back over the Rhine. Nevertheless, his father and then his brother Francis feared that Charles might have political ambitions, and he was always accompanied on campaign by senior officers who could countermand his instructions.

Archduke Charles is portrayed as the victor of the Battle of Aspern in this contemporary English engraving.

Archduke Charles tried to remould the Austrian Army on 'modern' lines so he could beat, rather than merely contain, the French; in his view, Austria should achieve this reorganization before again fighting the French. In 1807–8 he abolished corporal punishment, established reserves and wrote enlightened infantry regulations that stated '. . . a soldier must be a nobleman'.

But Charles, often insecure and never able to take criticism calmly, quarrelled with old friends in his moments of self-doubt. This, taken with his plans which were political as well as military, alarmed the court, and meant he had to fight the 1809 campaign with his army still not as well organized as he had planned. There was too little time to teach his generals the precepts contained in his book *The Fundamentals of the Higher Art of War* or to get them used to his new corps organization. In these circumstances, his victory at Aspern/Essling was impressive; shortly after Wagram, however, he retired from military life because of political disputes with his brother Francis.

Battle of Wagram/4

At about 13.00 on 6 July 1809, Napoleon ordered General Etienne Macdonald to attack the centre of the Austrian line, hoping to achieve a breakthrough. This tactic, if successful, offers huge rewards: the enemy's front becomes divided, with the possibility of enveloping either or both sections of his army. If unsuccessful, as it was when Hannibal tried it at Zama, the attacking army can be severely disrupted. Macdonald's attack failed in its prime objective but was successful in preoccupying the Austrians while Napoleon executed decisive manoeuvres elsewhere.

General Etienne Macdonald's command of about 8,000 infantry, with cavalry support, attacked in a hollow square. This formation was highly vulnerable to artillery fire and, indeed, to infantry and cavalry attack. But by the time of Wagram French troops were inferior to those of Napoleon's earlier armies, so French commanders often deployed their men in these huge formations, hoping to direct them more easily than was possible with numerous smaller units.

An Austrian cavalry charge had been repulsed before the square attacked, and dead horses (3) littered the field, most brought down by artillery fire.

The flanks of the square were covered by carbineers (6) and cuirassiers on the left and Guard cavalry (2) on the right. Despite Macdonald's order to charge in support of the infantry, they refused to move, for they would take orders only from Napoleon.

Some protection was given to General Macdonald (5) by artillery units (4) in the rear; these killed and wounded many of the Austrian cavalry (1, 7) on their infantry's flanks.

Macdonald's men paid cruelly for their attack – pitiless hand-to-hand fighting reduced them to less than 2,000, a quarter of their original number. But their action held down the Austrians, allowing Masséna to retake Aspern on the French left, and Davout to push on to Wagram on the right.

Archduke Charles saw that these encircling moves made his position untenable and, to keep his army intact, retreated. The French, though victorious, were so weakened by their huge losses that they were unable to press home their advantage.

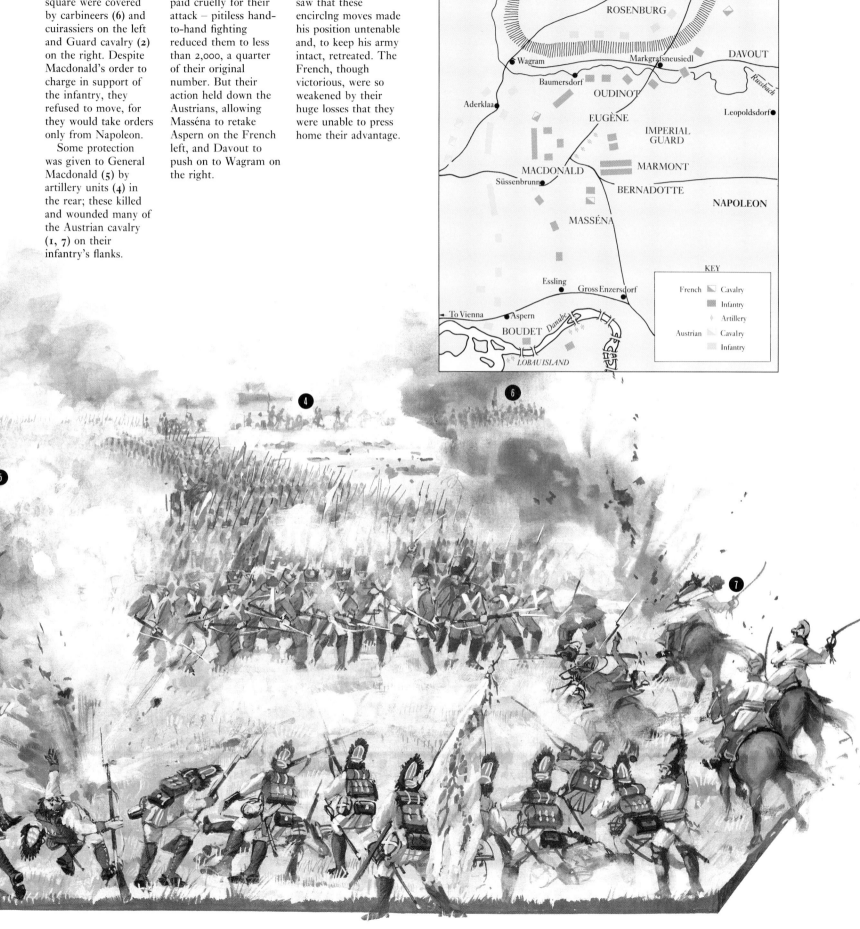

ARCHDUKE CHARLES

Russbach

ROSENBURG

DAVOUT

Wagram

Markgrafsneusiedl

Russbach

Baumersdorf

OUDINOT

Aderklaa

Leopoldsdorf

EUGÈNE

IMPERIAL GUARD

MARMONT

MACDONALD

Süssenbrunn

BERNADOTTE

NAPOLEON

MASSÉNA

Essling

Gross Enzersdorf

To Vienna

Aspern

Danube

BOUDET

LOBAU ISLAND

KEY

French		Cavalry
		Infantry
		Artillery
Austrian		Cavalry
		Infantry

overwhelming victory and at about 19.00 he ordered Marshals Davout and Jean Bernadotte (with his 18,000 men, mainly Saxons, in 9th Corps) to attack, with the idea of breaking the Austrian centre and left and enveloping these formations by taking Wagram and Markgrafneusiedl.

The assault failed, however, not least because Archduke Charles personally rallied his wavering and fearful men and organized a counter-attack. For reasons never fully understood, the French seem not to have pressed their attacks with their customary vigour. Eugène's Army of Italy rallied only when threatened by the bayonets of the Imperial Guard, and the unfortunate white-coated Saxons, mistaken for Austrians, were often fired on by

their own side. In any event, the advent of darkness shortly brought fighting to an end around a burning Wagram.

Since sunrise in early July is about 04.00, Napoleon quickly made his dispositions for fighting on the morrow. His plan was to reinforce his right flank, which would then turn the Austrians' left while other formations held the enemy centre. Masséna's corps was moved up to, and between, Sussenbrunn and Aderklaa. A mere division was allocated to defend Aspern on the left and the bridges to Lobau Island. The emperor snatched some sleep shielded by a pile of drums.

Archduke Charles also laid plans. These entailed a full-scale attack by two corps – 36,000 men – at dawn to smash the

French left, while at the same time Davout was to be attacked from the north. And the archduke got his blows in first.

From the moment that battle was rejoined at dawn on 6 July, along a 20km/12ml front, the fortunes of war swung first this way, then that. The village of Aderklaa, in the centre of the front, was swiftly taken by the Austrians, retaken by the French and then taken yet again by the Austrians – and all this by 08.00, so intense was the fighting. When, during this last action, Bernadotte rode ahead of his fleeing Saxons in an effort to halt them (they were also fired on by Masséna), a furious Napoleon, misunderstanding Bernadotte's action, dismissed him with the devastating words, 'Leave my presence

---

Napoleon's command structure

Napoleon enjoyed a well-integrated system of command. The army corps organization, in use by the French since 1800, meant that there were standing all-arms formations, commanded by marshals after 1804. These were, in effect, small armies with their own staffs, to which orders could be sent instead of to regiments or temporary wings.

By 1809 Napoleon had a 1:100,000 scale, hand-drawn series of maps, based on survey and triangulation and covering Europe west of Russia. He inherited a topographical bureau from the Revolution which was headed throughout his campaigns by the ex-artist Bacler d'Albe. Even in the field, a large table was set up every evening on which the coloured campaign map was spread. It was illuminated by candles, and a pair of dividers set at the normal day's march – 35–40km/22–25mls – lay alongside it; coloured pinheads denoted the different corps and armies.

There was also a statistical bureau that collected intelligence on foreign countries and compiled a book on enemy armies, which Napoleon carried with him.

On campaign Napoleon usually went to bed at 20.00, after dinner, and was woken at about 01.00 or 02.00 to receive reconnaissance reports. Orders went out before dawn, fair-copied on to huge sheets of paper with the place, date and time in the margin and the recipient's address at the top. The name and departure time of the dispatch rider were added, and all details entered in the archivist's daily register.

Napoleon had a separate general staff of perhaps 200 officers, under the indispensable Marshal Berthier, whose function included expanding and elaborating his orders and giving information to the topographical bureau on troop dispositions. For

liaison and special missions there were 8–12 adjutants-general and 12 orderly officers, all of whom spoke a foreign language and had served two years with the troops.

While Napoleon catnaps on the night of 5/6 July, surrounded by his battle HQ staff, Berthier is depicted writing dispatches in this painting by Roehn.

---

immediately and quit the *Grande Armée* within 24 hours!'

On the French right wing, the Austrians for an hour made some progress against Davout, while on Napoleon's left, although hours late, they pressed General Boudet's single division hard and began to threaten the bridges. At this moment – 10.00 or thereabouts – the archduke was in a potentially decisive position. General Count Johann Klenau's advance guard was as far east as Essling, having stormed Aspern, but Austrian commanders, were not trained to show initiative and all now paused to await orders.

Napoleon, however, was at his best and most inventive in danger. To quote Marmont: 'The Emperor remained perfectly calm although he read in the faces of his staff the anxiety caused by the victorious march of the enemy's right wing.' He immediately brought up a battery of more than 100 guns to give cover, while Masséna's troops marched south across the Austrian front to reinforce the French left. There they successfully contained the Austrian advance. Meanwhile, Marshal Jean Bessières' cavalry reserve charged repeatedly to gain time.

The crunch of the battle had come. Davout, on the French right wing, had taken Markgrafneusiedl, albeit slowly after heavy fighting, during which his horse was shot from under him. Shortly after midday, seeing the marshal's firing line beyond the village church, Napoleon judged the moment opportune to launch General Etienne Macdonald in an attack at the enemy centre, toward Gerasdorf, which was also at the junction of two Austrian corps.

Eight thousand French infantry, with cavalry support, then moved forward in massive concentration. They suffered cruel casualties – some historians estimate that they were reduced to less than a quarter of their original numbers – but their endeavour won the day, for on the left wing, while this blow was being administered, Masséna retook Aspern, and on the right centre the rest of the Army of Italy was pushing on to Wagram.

For the Austrians, the situation in the early afternoon – certainly by 14.30 – had become hopeless. Archduke Charles, lightly wounded himself, did not choose to allow his broken army to be destroyed. He withdrew (Archduke John arrived too late at 16.00) and it is confirmation of the equal struggle that he could do so in disciplined order, for the French had paid so grim a price for their victory that they were incapable of efficient pursuit and the Austrian Army escaped.

Losses on both sides were appalling. The second day's carnage from 16 hours' fighting with massed artillery surpassed the previous record bloodbath at Eylau in 1807. From start to finish, the French lost five generals killed, 6,806 officers and men, and 26,757 wounded. One man in every 17 casualties was an officer, an indication of how French leaders had sacrificed themselves leading poor-quality troops, for the ratio among the Austrians was about half this figure. The Austrians sustained 6,531 killed, including four generals, and 18,119 wounded, as well as 14,000–18,000 prisoners.

Napoleon and Marie-Louise were married on 2 April 1810 at the Louvre. It was a glittering occasion, as this painting by Rouget shows. The emperor was dressed in white satin with a jewel-encrusted cloak; the blonde, blue-eyed archduchess, only 18 years old, was weighed down by crown, dress sewn with diamonds and long heavy train. For a time the marriage was happy – indeed Napoleon neglected the war in Spain to remain with his wife until after his son was born.

Apogee of empire

At first glance, the Battle of Wagram seems to have been yet another of Napoleon's seemingly endless victories, since Archduke Charles sued for an armistice only five days later. Peace between France and Austria was signed at Schönbrunn in Vienna on 14 October 1809. Under the treaty's provisions, Austria paid a huge indemnity of almost 85 million francs, was obliged to reduce her army to 150,000 men and conceded considerable territory, including the Illyrian provinces, which came under French rule.

Moreover, Napoleon, who had divorced Josephine since she had not borne him a child, demanded – and in March 1810 was granted – the hand of Archduchess Marie-Louise, daughter of the Austrian emperor. She shortly gave birth to a son, whom Napoleon created King of Rome. His dynasty was, therefore, secure; and the parvenu, having married into one of the most ancient European houses, had to some extent legitimized his own position as self-styled emperor.

Yet Napoleon's very success at Wagram finally brought home to the demoralized European states the fact that his ambition was without limit, and they recognized that he could only be stopped if they united against him. Moreover, Napoleon was now 40 years old; his health was not as robust as it had been and his decisions not as quick. Sometime after 1805 he told his valet: 'One has only a certain time for war. I will be good for six years more; after that even I must cry halt.'

In addition, news from Spain was unsatisfactory, for Arthur Wellesley, the future Duke of Wellington, was inflicting defeats on Napoleon's marshals in his long campaign to drive the French out of the peninsula. Thus, at the moment when Napoleon seemed to be at his most powerful, there were already ominous signs presaging his eventual downfall. His 1812 Russian campaign was disastrous, and by August 1813, Great Britain, Sweden, Prussia and Austria were allied against him.

Duke of Wellington *1769-1852*

'T' he Duke'. Such was the Duke of Wellington's fame in the first half of the nineteenth century that these words meant only one man in Great Britain. Arthur Wellesley's early life, however, showed little promise of the glory to come. He was born in 1769, the same year as Napoleon, the third son of the Earl of Mornington, an Anglo-Irish landowner, and spent the first few years of his life in Dublin. But he never considered himself an Irishman. 'Because a man is born in a stable', he once remarked, 'that does not make him a horse.'

At the age of about seven, Arthur was taken to lodgings in London because of his father's financial difficulties and his preference for the capital rather than Dublin. Later he was sent to Eton College, from which he was removed as an economy measure after his father's death. Instead, the 15-year-old Arthur was sent to the School of Equitation at Angers on the Loire, which taught him French, horsemanship and good manners.

The future Duke of Wellington was a lonely, introspective boy who made no friends at school and was academically undistinguished. Shy, idle, and much given to daydreaming, there seemed no profession for which he was suited. As a last resort, his mother secured him a commission in the army in March 1787, but with little hope of his distinguishing himself. 'Arthur', she wrote, 'has put on his red coat for the first time today. Anyone can see he has not the cut of a soldier.'

Wellington in fact rose rapidly in rank, in part because of the patronage of his brother Richard, later the Marquess Wellesley. The decisive moment in his career came in June 1796, when he sailed with his regiment, the 33rd Foot, to India. He was given command of a division and saw action in Mysore and against an Indian warlord and robber Dhundia Waugh. Wellington's main achievement in India was to defeat, with only about 10,000 men, a force of 40,000 Mahrattas, a powerful, warlike people who were prominent in resistance to British rule. During these campaigns, Wellington learned the arts of warfare and how to move considerable bodies of men. He returned to England in September 1805 and it was then, while waiting for an appointment at the Colonial Office in London, that he met for the only time that other British hero, Vice-Admiral Lord Nelson. It was not until 1809 that he went, for the second time, to Portugal, where he was subsequently appointed Allied Commander-in-Chief in the Peninsular War. From that moment, his became a household name.

Wellington was a little under 1.8m/6ft tall, a strongly built man but not, like Napoleon, becoming overweight in middle age. His most notable features were his bright, clear blue eyes, a pointed chin and an immediately recognizable beaked nose. He exuded self-confidence and authority, which disguised his kindness of heart, for Wellington was responsible for many undisclosed generosities to old friends.

On campaign and in battle, Wellington displayed intense, unremitting energy, and for nearly three years in the Peninsula was in the front line with his army, usually sleeping in his clothes. Although he often wrote disparagingly of his men in moments of frustration, they respected and trusted him utterly; his officers never questioned his authority.

In battle, Wellington was the despair of his staff because they knew he was indispensable and yet he constantly exposed himself to danger, galloping from one threatened spot to another to encourage and sustain his troops by his cool bearing and to issue immediate orders. After Salamanca, Edward Pakenham wrote, 'Our chief was everywhere . . . he surpassed himself in the clearness and energy of his instructions . . .'. Another wrote from the Peninsula, '. . . *everything* depends on this one man.'

1769	*1 May* Born at Dublin, third son of the Earl of Mornington.
1787/ 1791	*7 March* Ensign in 73rd Foot; rises to captain in 58th Foot.
1793	*30 April* Major and, *30 September*, Commander of 33rd Foot.
1794	*15 September* Wins first action at Boxtel in Belgium.
1796	*3 May* Promoted colonel.
1797	*February* Lands at Calcutta, India.
1799	*March* Commands division in invasion of Mysore.
1802	*29 April* Becomes major-general.
1803	*23 September* Wins Assaye and, *29 November*, Argaum.
1805	Returns to England. *December* Takes a brigade to north Germany.
1807	*26 August* Wins Köge during the Copenhagen expedition.
1808	*25 April* Promoted lieutenant-general. *1 August* Lands in Portugal. *17 and 21 August* Wins Roliça and Vimeiro.
1809	*22 April* Lands at Lisbon. *12 May* Captures Oporto and, *27–28 July*, wins Talavera.
1810	*27 September* Wins Busaco. *12 October* Retreats into Lines of Torres Vedras, begun the previous year.
1811	*3–5 May* Wins Fuentes de Oñoro *31 July* Becomes a general.
1812	*22 July* **Battle of Salamanca**.
1813	*21 June* Wins Vitoria, promoted field marshal. *25–30 July* Battles of the Pyrenees. *8 September* San Sebastián falls. *7 October* Crosses into France. *10 November* Wins Nivelle and, *9–13 December*, Nive.
1814	*27 February* Wins Orthez, *20 March*, Tarbes and, *10 April*, Toulouse. *3 May* Created Duke of Wellington.
1815	*16–18 June* Waterloo campaign.
1818	Long political career begins.
1852	*14 September* Dies at Walmer Castle, Kent, aged 83.

Wellington was painted by Goya in August 1812. He wears the Spanish Order of the Golden Fleece; the Peninsular Gold Cross, not issued until 1813, was added later by Goya. Wellington's great victories are depicted around the edge of the Wellington shield, designed by Thomas Stothard and made c1834 by Benjamin Smith.

Battle of Salamanca/*22 July 1812*

FROM THE MOMENT of their occupation of Spain, the French were at a disadvantage, being in a hostile and inhospitable land. The Spaniards, ill-armed and little trained, resisted with fierce tenacity. The old fortresses of Saragossa and Gerona withstood all French attempts to take them, and at Baylen General Pierre Dupont was forced to surrender with his army of 17,000 men. Then, on 1 August 1808, the British Expeditionary Force under Wellington, then only Lieutenant-General Sir Arthur Wellesley, landed in Portugal and General Andoche Junot's army was forced to evacuate the country.

Wellington's 1812 Salamanca campaign was the third British advance into Spain from Portugal. In 1808 Sir John Moore had capitalized on Wellington's initial victory at Vimeiro in Portugal to advance via Salamanca to Spain's aid. Although this move ended in the harrowing retreat to Corunna and Moore's death in action there, it vitally dislocated Napoleon's plans to overrun Spain during the two months he took personal command after the initial French reverses.

In June 1809, Wellington, again in command, marched on Madrid with a Spanish army that proved little help. The British won a bloody defensive battle at Talavera but could get no farther. A concentration of French armies then forced Wellington to retreat to Portugal.

The next two years were spent securing that country as an impregnable supply base and training a Portuguese army by beating off Marshal André Masséna's determined invasion. This came to a halt before the secret Lines of Torres Vedras.

As a prelude to his 1812 campaign Wellington rapidly, if expensively, stormed the Spanish frontier fortresses of Ciudad Rodrigo and Badajoz, which he took on 7 April. He handed both to the Spaniards, which soothed their vanity, and he was now free to strike into Spain; particularly so, since it was at this moment that Napoleon ordered the withdrawal of 27,000 veteran troops from Spain for his Russian campaign.

The odds were still hopelessly against Wellington, however. His entire force comprised only 66,000 men and 54 guns, while against him was arrayed Marshal Auguste Marmont's 50,000-man Army of Portugal, Marshal Nicolas Soult's 60,000-strong Army of the South, and the Army of the North numbering about 40,000. In addition, King Joseph had a reserve of some 15,000 men in Madrid.

But the French armies were dispersed, and Wellington could attack separately either of the two barring the road into

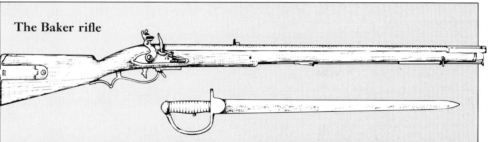

The Baker rifle

This weapon was designed by the London gunsmith Ezekiel Baker in 1800. It had a 75cm/30in barrel with quarter-turn rifling, and with sword bayonet, measured 1.75m/5¾ft overall; it weighed 5kg/11lb. It was accurate up to 274m/300yds but, like all rifles of the period, took 30 seconds to load (hence the 1807 withdrawal of rifles from Napoleon's army) and misfired as often as smoothbore muskets. At Salamanca it was used by the 95th Rifles (the Greenjackets), the 5th Battalion, 60th Regiment (the Royal Americans), in a total of more than 1,950 British, Brunswick and King's German Legion sharpshooters and some of the 4,300 Portuguese Caçadores.

Spain. He could go for Marmont in the north or Soult in the south, and beat one or other before they could combine. He chose to go for Marmont, Duke of Ragusa, bearing in mind the later harvest in the north (of significance because the French lived off the land) and that a siege train was on its way to that marshal.

On 13 June, Wellington crossed the frontier river Agueda with some 51,000 men, including 21,000 Portuguese and Spanish. Six of the seven infantry divisions contained British-officered Portuguese brigades, and there were two independent brigades. There were also five cavalry brigades, of which one was Portuguese and one King's German Legion, exiles from Hanover.

Marmont, with his foraging army of eight infantry divisions dispersed, could not offer immediate battle. With Napoleonic promptness, however, he fell back and ordered his army to concentrate. Wellington entered the university city of Salamanca unmolested four days later. There he waited, while besieging three fortified convents on the north bank of the River Tormes held by 800 men with 30 guns, in the hope of luring Marmont into an assault.

The outnumbered Marmont did not take the bait, however, and instead backed off on 22 June. When the British reduced the troublesome convents on the 27th, the Duke of Ragusa fell back some 48km/30mls to the River Douro, where – so long

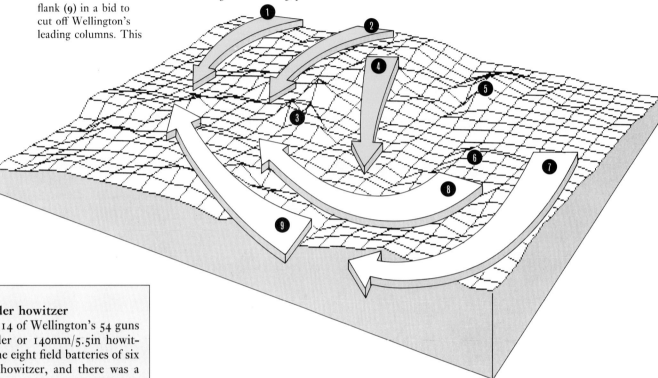

Thinking that the Allies were in full retreat to Portugal, Marshal Marmont abandoned his strong position on the Greater Arapiles (**6**) and extended his left flank (**9**) in a bid to cut off Wellington's leading columns. This produced a gap between the leading and the two following French formations (**7,8**). Wellington, on the Lesser Arapiles (**5**), then attacked with Pakenham's 3rd Division (**1**), which had been hidden from French view by low hills. He also made strong charges (**2,4**) either side of the town of Arapiles (**3**) at the gap in the French line.

The 24-pounder howitzer
At Salamanca, 14 of Wellington's 54 guns were 24-pounder or 140mm/5.5in howitzers. Each of the eight field batteries of six guns had one howitzer, and there was a reserve Anglo-Portuguese howitzer battery.

The howitzer was a low-velocity, high-trajectory weapon used for flinging 7.2kg/16lb shells on to hills or over obstacles. A crucial success was the wounding of Marmont at the Greater Arapiles. Two different types of howitzer existed, one for foot and one for horse artillery, of which there were three at Salamanca.
Respective barrel lengths; 84cm/33in, 68cm/26in; total weights: 1,156kg/2,548lb, 762kg/1,680lb; maximum range: 1,554m/1,700yds; effective range: 640m/700yds. Shellburst radius about 23m/25yds, but fuzes erratic.

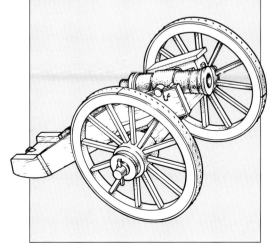

The armies' parallel march
Private Green of the 68th Foot, in 7th Division, was an eyewitness of the armies' parallel march on the morning of 20 July: 'I certainly expected that in a few minutes we should have been sharply engaged; but instead of this, the enemy broke camp, formed column, and marched to a ridge of hills, their bands and drums playing as though they were going to a general field day. I saw the head of their column ascend the hill and march in the direction of Ciudad Rodrigo. We marched in two lines parallel with them, having only to halt and front and we would be ready for them. We were not much more than a mile from each other, sometimes not so much; every now and then the enemy unlimbered their guns and fired on the British lines; but no execution was done, with the exception of one poor woman who was killed by a cannonshot. It was an extraordinary and grand sight to see the two armies drawn up ready for battle and manoeuvring the whole day without fighting; in the evening we reached the termination of the hill; then the enemy moved off and encamped in open country. I was immediately sent on advanced guard, which had received strict orders to keep a good lookout, for the enemy could not be more than four miles distant. I went on sentry and had frequently to put my ear to the ground to listen for them, a practice very common with the advanced guard of the army.'

as he could hold the river crossings from Toro to Tordesillas – Wellington's northward march could be contained. Wellington followed, and for 10 days in July, at the height of summer, the two armies watched each other across the Douro.

On 16 July the Salamanca campaign entered it decisive phase, when Marmont recrossed the river near Toro and probed at Wellington's left flank. Wellington responded to this feint, and the following day, Marmont, with some skill, force marched the mass of his army 48km/30mls eastward and crossed the river at the town of Tordesillas.

Wellington had been wrongfooted and retreated – to the dismay of his troops, who were confident they could beat the

Battle of Salamanca/2

French. Early on 18 July, he rode east with 2,500 cavalry to extricate Lieutenant-General Sir Stapleton Cotton's two detached divisions and cavalry brigade from the clutches of the whole Army of Portugal, which was marching swiftly west in two columns. Wellington himself, with two dragoon squadrons and two guns, had to take refuge behind the Light Division's outposts when French dragoons intercepted his over-bold reconnaissance.

His decision, however, was yet another example of his supreme mastery of the art of war. Wellington depended on his supply waggons, moving in great numbers along the Ciudad Rodrigo-Salamanca high road, to succour his army; Marmont's army had to live off the land or, more correctly, pillage to sustain itself. By retreating, Wellington was again withdrawing on, and thereby shortening, his supply lines, while luring Marmont into inhospitable terrain.

Moreover, the general was always conscious of the fact that he had under his command the only British army in the field; to lose it on a hazard would have dire consequences for the Allied cause.

For the better part of five days, the two veteran armies, almost always within cannon shot of each other and sometimes with

bands playing, marched southwestward in a unique parallel race. During the savage heat of Spanish high summer, with vultures hovering overhead, Marmont sought to cut off Wellington from his line of communication. During the 20th, the French drew slightly ahead. On the afternoon of the 21st, Marmont's army was the first to ford the River Tormes at Huerta and Encinas, to the east of Salamanca.

The Allied Army followed suit within hours, some units fording in a terrific thunderstorm that raged until midnight. Knowing that Marmont would soon be reinforced by 1,700 cavalry from the Army of the North and that King Joseph had set out from Madrid with 10,000-12,000 troops, Wellington decided to abandon Salamanca if really necessary and retreat to Ciudad Rodrigo.

British cartoonists satirized both armies at Salamanca as this pen and watercolour sketch, *above*, shows. The cowardly French cannot flee fast enough in the face of English gunfire, but a redcoat is not above rifling the pocket of a wounded enemy soldier while his companions fight.

The more peaceful pursuits of camp life are detailed, *right*, in the print of a scene of troops at a bivouac, painted in 1811 by Major T. St Clair. One man has his hair cut; a goat is being milked; and a sheep slaughtered for food, while a great cauldron is set over the fire. The relaxed orderliness reflects the efficient manner in which Wellington's army was organized and supplied.

Early on the 22nd the army's baggage train took that road. At the same time, petty skirmishing flared up 10km/6mls to the east between General Maximilien Foy's division and rifle-armed Brunswicker Oels near the ruined chapel of Neustra Senora de la Pena. Having seized the hill known as the Greater Arapiles, south of Wellington's apparent line of battle (and there are those who argue Wellington let him do so, being content himself with the Lesser Arapiles 732m/ 800yds to the north), Marmont then made a misjudgement that was to cost him dear.

Thinking that Wellington was a master of defensive strategy and nothing more, and believing that he was in full flight to his fastness in Portugal, the marshal, after a picnic lunch on the newly won hill had been interrupted by some British shells, accelerated his march to the Salamanca-Ciudad road. Soon after 13.00 he rode back to the Greater Arapiles, where he ordered his advance division under General Jean Thomières to move at maximum speed to envelop Wellington's retreating columns and force an 'advantageous rearguard action'.

In this way, a wide gap developed in the French line of advance between Thomières' 4,500 troops, with 30 guns, and the following 5,200-strong division of General Antoine Maucune, with 20 guns, which was stationed opposite the village of Arapiles. This situation had developed, together with heavy skirmishing and artillery bombardment of the village, by mid-afternoon, certainly before 16.00.

Wellington too had snatched a cold lunch, chicken or beef, only to be told by a spurring staff officer, 'My lord, the French are extending to their left.' 'The devil they are', he replied and remounted to return to the Lesser Arapiles. Once there, observing the situation through his telescope, he exclaimed 'By God, that will do.' His 4th and 5th Divisions would attack on either side of Arapiles, supported by 6th and 7th Divisions (hidden by low hills from Marmont's gaze).

The general then galloped west to Aldea Tejada. There the 'Fighting' 3rd Division, 5,800 troops newly under the command of Major-General the Honourable Edward Pakenham, his brother-in-law, had been placed in reserve. They had already marched 19km/12mls since 10.30, when Wellington had farsightedly moved them from the north bank of the Tormes. At about 15.00 Wellington told Pakenham: 'Edward, move on . . . take the heights in your front – and drive everything before you.' 'I will, my lord' was the laconic answer.

Private, 2nd Caçadores, 1812
By 1812 there were 12 regiments of the Portuguese Caçadores (Hunters), or light infantry, serving with Wellington's army. The soldier, *right*, is wearing the new uniform, introduced around 1811, of dark brown trousers and tunic braided with black. Regiments were distinguished by the colour of the cuff and collar facings and by the band on the top of the pointed gaiters. The number of the regiment appears on the front of the shako, which also bears a bugle horn badge, cockade and plume.

On the black leather belt and support strap are a sword bayonet and ammunition pouch, in which would be cartridges, made by filling a waxed paper tube with a powder charge. In the heat of battle this would obviate the necessity for loading ball and powder separately. The soldier carries one of the new-issue Baker Rifles, in the butt of which, in a small brass-mounted box, are ball ammunition and small tools.

Private, 11th Foot, 1812
The infantryman of the 11th Foot, the North Devonshire Regiment, *left*, is wearing the regulation red coat with regimental facings on collar and cuffs and double 'bastion' lace on the front. His blue-grey cold-weather trousers were standard by 1812; in hot weather they were exchanged for white linen or cotton. His shako bears a large regimental plate.

White leather cross belts support the square, black-lacquered canvas knapsack, with blanket rolled on top, and ammunition pouch. Slung across his right shoulder is a canvas haversack for carrying rations and a flat, round wooden water bottle. On fine laces around his neck and looped over a button, he has a small brush and steel picker with which to clean the lock and vent of his Brown Bess musket.

Wellington then hastened back to his position in the Allied centre to oversee a battle that was beginning to offer glittering prospects.

The gap between Thomières' leading formation and those behind was all of 1.6km/1ml; furthermore, another gap of roughly the same distance separated the centre divisions – under Maucune, Generals Bertrand Clauzel and Antoine Brenier – from those following in the rear, under Generals Jacques Sarrut, Claud Ferey and Foy. The two armies were roughly equal in strength – 48,500 French to 50,000 Allies – including 5,000 Germans, 18,000 Portuguese, 3,300 Spanish and 700 French royalists.

Although Wellington had about 1,000 more, and better mounted, cavalry, Marmont possessed a great superiority in guns, both in numbers and calibre. Thanks to Wellington having two able subordinates on sick leave and one detached, Marmont also probably had a better team of commanders, all of whom had served with him for at least a year.

The mass of Wellington's army was now concentrated facing south around the village of Arapiles, roughly opposite the left centre of Marmont's westward advancing army. On Wellington's left, facing east, were the all-redcoat 1st Division; the élite Light Division; and the King's German heavy dragoons under Major-General Georg von Bock: in all a

little over 10,000 men. They were fine, disciplined troops, ready and eager for the coming conflict.

The main battle began after 16.30, when Pakenham, following Wellington's earlier instruction, threw his 3rd Division, supported by the raking fire of 12 guns, and two cavalry brigades (1,200 men) at Thomières' scattered advance units. Their attack was wholly unexpected by the French and devastatingly effective, for they had thought the Allies in retreat, since for a long while their advance was hidden by woods.

Unruffled by a despairing charge on its right flank from the French hussars and

chasseurs and by wild volleys from Thomières' 1,400-strong 101st Line Regiment, 3rd Division marched to the crest of a slight rise and charged home to cries of 'Push on to the muzzle'. Their charge was carried with such force that the astonished and terrified French fell back on their advancing comrades. Half their number were cut down, their six guns and the precious eagle standard of the 101st taken, and their divisional commander killed.

As Pakenham's attack opened, Marmont, suddenly aghast, shouted orders for his left to be strengthened. But just as he prepared to mount his horse at the Greater Arapiles, he was severely wounded by a

Spain was united as never before against Napoleon's armies: every Spaniard became an assassin and any French soldier who separated from his fellows a target. French retaliation was brutal, villages were destroyed and all the inhabitants shot. The senseless slaughter, *above*, was depicted by Goya in a series of moving etchings, *The Disasters of War*.

No such horrors are depicted in this idealized 1814 print of Salamanca, *left*.

Wellington's supply system

Wellington was fond of the already old saying: 'In Spain large armies starve and small armies get beaten.' But in fact his army received frequent shiploads of ammunition and supplies – grain was imported from Morocco, Asia Minor and America – brought in to Portuguese ports, and Wellington had established an efficient depot supply system. By relying on these and on payment for food and transport, instead of the French method of requisitioning bordering on plunder, Wellington was able to keep his army concentrated for longer than his opponents and so beat them.

By 1812, he had 37 supply depots in Portugal and on the frontier, supervised by most of his 87 civilian commissaries and 255 clerks. He also had a new Commissariat Car Train of 1,300 carts, as well as the traditional ox-wagons, to convoy supplies between ports and depots. Each battalion and regiment had 13 or 14 mules and each division an additional 300–400 mules for its own transport. Muleteers were paid one Spanish dollar a day for themselves and one for each mule.

The Tagus River was navigable to Abrantes and the Douro to not far from Almcida, so water transport was also used.

A supply train following the British Army; print from a painting by Major T. St Clair, 1811.

There was a small Royal Wagon Train of perhaps 20 vehicles, which were employed as ambulances.

Wellington wrote of Marmont's logistics two days before Salamanca: 'The Army of Portugal has been surrounded for the last six weeks . . . scarcely a letter reaches its commander; but the system of organised rapine and plunder so long established in the French armies enable it to subsist at the expense of the total ruin of the country in which it has been placed.'

British howitzer shell. His second-in-command, the one-eyed senior divisional general Count Jean Bonet, was likewise put out of action. It was 20 minutes before Clauzel assumed command.

Meanwhile, Major-General Lowry Cole's 4th, and Lieutenant-General James Leith's 5th divisions, together with an independent Portuguese brigade, in all 14,000 infantry, moved forward.

Supported by 2,000 British cavalry and with 6th, 7th and Spanish divisions behind, totalling another 14,000 the entire force then attacked the French centre, which numbered only 12,000 infantry. Under intense fire and bayonet charges, Maucune's division broke. Then Wellington, riding between 5th Division's two lines, ordered Major-General Gaspard Le Marchant's heavy dragoons to charge at Maucune's retreating infantry. They cut through them with irresistable brutality and drove them back on Brenier's two leading regiments. Soon most men of both formations were either dead or disfigured beyond recognition by sabre slashes. Three French divisions had been beaten in 40 minutes.

Only on his left flank was Wellington deprived of absolute success. In a charge with unloaded muskets, to prevent their

stopping to fire, 2,600 Portuguese failed to take the steep and dominating Greater Arapiles and fled back to the Lesser Arapiles. At 18.00 the French centre, now under Clauzel's command, courageously counter-attacked. It was a Napoleonic bid to turn a lost battle.

Perhaps Clauzel assessed that 3rd Division was fought out, the British cavalry blown and that Cole's 5,200-strong 4th Division could be taken in flank from the Greater Arapiles. At any rate, he ordered a still undismayed Brenier (who had been wounded and captured at Wellington's victory of Vimeiro nearly 4 years before) to check 5th Division, while his own and Bonet's commands struck the 4th. Sarrut's intact division protected the gun-line southwest of the Greater Arapiles.

Clauzel's assault drove Cole's division back so fiercely that French officers were hacking at the retreating Anglo-Portuguese with their swords before the first line of Major-General Henry Clinton's 6th Division came up in support. Clauzel threw in General Pierre Boyer's dragoon division of 1,400 heavy cavalry, mounted on borrowed officers' chargers, to exploit his success. But Boyer's troopers, unused to their horses, lapped in vain around the Anglo-Portuguese squares.

Meanwhile, the Portuguese brigade of 5th Division had been switched to pour flanking fire into Clauzel's division. Both French divisions suffered heavily from converging artillery fire and the funnelling effect of the terrain. Eventually 6th Division charged Bonet's infantry from not more than 9m/30ft and routed them, with 1,500 casualties. Clauzel's command, its right flank exposed, joined the few survivors and those from Brenier's force in precipitate flight.

Wellington now rode to his left wing to order 1st and Light divisions to advance. Foy fought a skilful delaying action against the latter until an hour after sunset, while the light infantry of 1st Division's King's German Legion rushed to the top of the Greater Arapiles and captured six guns. Ferey's intact 5,600-strong division deployed along a wooded ridge southeast of the Greater Arapiles to fight the Army of Portugal's main rear-guard action. Most unusually for French infantry in the Peninsula, seven battalions were drawn up in a three-deep line, with a battalion square on each flank to cover it from cavalry, supported by artillery.

At 19.30, in the darkness, 6th Division advanced a second time. 'The face of the hill . . . was one vast sheet of flame, and

Wellington made superlative use of the tactic of feigned withdrawal at Salamanca, luring the French into over-confident pursuit in a bid to cut off his escape route to Portugal and safety. This caused their leading formations to become extended, giving Wellington the opportunity to turn and attack the French Army piecemeal.

His first move was to order Pakenham's 3rd Division, held in reserve, to attack the leading, now isolated formation under Thomières. Then, with 14,000 men of the 4th and 5th divisions, supported by 2,000 cavalry and 6th and 7th divisions, he attacked Maucune and Clauzel in the centre. The French broke, retreating eastward; at once Wellington ordered Le Marchant and his heavy dragoons to charge the fleeing infantry. The illustration captures this decisive moment.

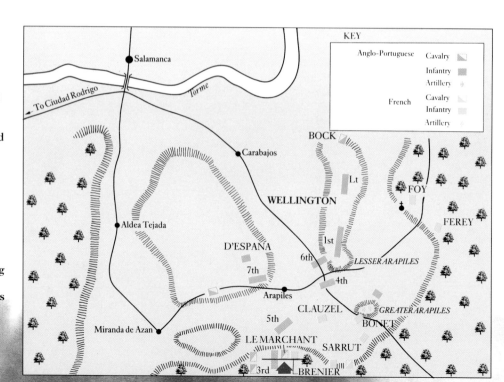

KEY

Anglo-Portuguese	Cavalry
	Infantry
	Artillery
French	Cavalry
	Infantry
	Artillery

Salamanca
To Ciudad Rodrigo
Tormes
Carabajos
BOCK
Lt
FOY
WELLINGTON
FEREY
Aldea Tejada
1st
D'ESPAÑA
6th
LESSER ARAPILES
7th
4th
Arapiles
CLAUZEL
GREATER ARAPILES
5th
BONET
Miranda de Azan
LE MARCHANT
SARRUT
3rd
BRENIER

Major-General Gaspard Le Marchant had nearly 1,000 dragoons arranged in two lines, the 5th Dragoon Guards and 4th Dragoons in front, and the 3rd Dragoons in support. They had already charged and destroyed two regiments of General Antoine Maucune's division, which had been trying to escape from an English infantry attack.

The two regiments had little opportunity to form squares before Le Marchant's charge cut them down. Those that could, fled. Le Marchant's horsemen pressed on at a gallop and crashed into Brenier's leading regiment, the 22nd Line (1).

Marshal Brenier's infantry, which had advanced in support of Maucune's shattered units, inflicted heavy casualties with musket fire on the charging cavalry – about a quarter of the 5th Dragoon Guards fell – but were unable to contain the fearful impact. Even the drummer (3), whose duty it was to sound the battle orders, was overwhelmed.

Musket fire and burning dry grass, ignited by sparks from the first volley, produced a dense, suffocating smoke cloud that added to the misery of the combatants and covered them with soot. Weapons and equipment discarded by the fallen French troops littered the ground and impeded the horses. Among them were the wicker baskets (6) that were filled with earth before battle and used like sandbags, especially around field guns.

Le Marchant himself (2) was in the midst of the mêlée, fighting like a common soldier. The carnage was some of the most terrible of the Peninsular War. The French infantry fought mainly with muskets and bayonets (5), but inflicted only slight damage on the British cavalry.

The dragoons, however, carried heavy cavalry swords (4), savage weapons that, unlike the curved sabres of the light dragoons, could sever limbs, crush rib cages and even decapitate. Those French soldiers not instantly killed with a single slash, suffered dreadful mutilation. Soon the entire area was strewn with corpses and Frenchmen in agony, hacked beyond recognition. Others, fleeing, were trampled to death by the battle-maddened horses.

Le Marchant's charge won the day for Wellington: the French left and centre were now broken and only the right remained. Most of that wing escaped, but Wellington's masterpiece had destroyed a French army and France never recovered her power in Spain.

Clinton's men looked as though they were attacking a burning mountain.' The first French volley alone wounded about 80 men of the 1/11th Foot; at the end of the day the brigade was left with only 618 men standing out of 1,464. Clinton vainly pushed his Portuguese troops against Ferey's stubborn line. All told, his command sustained 1,680 killed, wounded and missing, over one-third of Wellington's total losses. It was 5th Division turning Ferey's left that enabled the shattered but victorious 6th to take the position by about 20.30. Ferey, like Thomières, died trying to rally his men.

The indefatigable Wellington was still riding with the Light Division, as the then Major William Napier remembered: 'After dusk the Duke rode up alone behind my regiment [the 43rd] and I joined him; he was giving some orders when a ball passed through his left [pistol] holster and struck his thigh. He put his hand to the place and his countenance changed for an instant; but only for an instant; and to my eager inquiry if he was hurt, he replied, sharply, "No!" and went on with his orders.'

Only Foy's division, formed from the extreme French right, remained, and all it could do now was to cover the broken army's 13km/8ml retreat through the black mass of trees to the castle of Alba and its bridge over the River Tormes. Wellington had earlier placed a Spanish officer

Marmont's rapid promotion was largely due to the friendship and patronage of Napoleon. Marmont served at the siege of Toulon; in 1796 he was Napoleon's principal ADC and in 1798 commanded an infantry brigade in Egypt at the Battle of the Pyramids. In 1808 he was created Duke of Ragusa and won his marshal's baton at the Battle of Wagram in 1809, when he was only 34 years old. He became commander of the Army of Portugal in May 1811.

The fatal flaw in his character was his propensity for treachery. When, in 1814, Napoleon was forced to abdicate, Ney, Marmont and Macdonald took the Act of Abdication to Tsar Alexander. Ney pleaded for Napoleon's son to succeed him, which the Tsar agreed to recommend to the Allies. But by the second meeting next morning, Marmont with the large number of troops at his command had defected to the rival Bourbons, who in consequence were restored to the throne of France. Thus the Duke of Ragusa gave a new word to the French language: *raguser*, to betray.

Bertrand Clauzel, who had command of the Army of Portugal thrust upon him, was an extremely able career officer. He appears to have risen solely on merit,

Marshal Auguste Marmont 1774–1852

General Bertrand Clauzel 1772–1842

since he had not fought in any of the great battles of the *Grande Armée* and had therefore not attracted Napoleon's favour. He served in the Pyrenees and in Italy in the 1790s and also in the West Indies. He was made a general in 1802 and, after commands in Holland, Italy and Dalmatia, in 1809 served under Marmont in Austria; in the same year he was posted to Spain. In 1810, he became a Baron of the Empire and in 1813 a Count. He joined Napoleon during the Hundred Days and after the Restoration was exiled for some years.

THE STATIONERS ALMANACK for 1813.

SALAMANCA.

Prisoners of war

During the 1812 campaign, Wellington's army took 20,000 French prisoners, 7,000 at the Battle of Salamanca, who were marched through the city afterwards. At least 137 French officers were taken, who were given parole and might be exchanged if they fell ill or had performed an act of humanity for their captors. Men were placed either in the notorious 'hulks', or prison ships, of which there were about 50 at Chatham, Portsmouth and Plymouth, or in prisons, including Dartmoor, opened in 1806 and still a maximum security prison.

An allowance of 14 shillings a week was paid to captains and higher ranks, 11 shillings and eight pence to all below. Private funds could be transferred freely from France and vice versa.

By April 1810 there were 50,000 French prisoners in Britain and 10,000 British in France; by 1814 there were no fewer than 2,710 officers on parole at designated towns in England. Breaking parole resulted in imprisonment, and escape attempts incarceration in the 'Black Hole' – a 1.8m/6ft square punishment cell.

French prisoners are shown marching into Salamanca in this early 19th-century print.

in command of the fortress, in anticipation of precisely this French manoeuvre. For reasons wholly inexplicable, that officer had taken it upon himself to abandon the castle and to do so without informing his C-in-C. Thus the broken French Army managed to get across the bridge and escaped eastward. The victor's main pursuit was toward the fords near Huerta.

Nevertheless, the Army of Portugal was a broken force, with the loss of 14,000 men – half taken prisoner – including 7 generals out of 25, to Wellington's loss of 4,800, including 7 generals. The French also lost at least 1,700 horses, 2 eagles, 6 colours and 20 guns. Wellington had used the oblique order of attack, as Frederick the Great had at Leuthen, to overwhelming effect. Salamanca was the most decisive and the most aggressive of all Wellington's Peninsular victories to date, comprising, it was popularly said with pardonable exaggeration, 'the beating of 40,000 Frenchmen in 40 minutes'. Napoleon's armies had not suffered such a reverse in Spain since Baylen four years earlier.

Perhaps the greatest tribute came from Wellington's shrewd and able opponent General Foy, who wrote in his diary: 'This battle is the most cleverly fought, the largest in scale, the most important in results, of any that the English have won in recent times. It brings up Lord Wellington's reputation almost to the level of that of Marlborough.'

The later years

Wellington's victory at Salamanca, though decisive, did not end the Peninsular War; but the battle marked a turning point, much as Stalingrad was to do in World War II. It demonstrated to all Europe that Napoleon's brilliant marshals could be defeated and that the British were not to be driven into the sea a second time. Furthermore, France's grip on Spain had been weakened throughout the Peninsula.

Then news came from Russia. Napoleon and his *Grande Armée* had entered Moscow, but the city had burned down, and he was forced to retreat through the Russian winter. The French had been fighting for 20 years, since 1792, and now they were exhausted. The grim defeat in Russia, and the 'running sore' of Wellington's continued successes in Spain, combined to ensure Napoleon's temporary defeat. Wellington was created a duke by a grateful sovereign. But it was in 1815, after Napoleon's escape from Elba, that Wellington was able to administer the *coup de grâce* at Waterloo, the only battle in which he fought directly against Napoleon. This time there was no doubt where the final victory lay.

Wellington returned to England in 1818, to many more years of service to the British people, first as Master-General of the Ordnance then, in 1827, as Commander-in-Chief of the Army. Eventually, in 1828 at the age of 58, he joined that small band of men who have been their country's leader both on the battlefield and in peacetime, for he became Prime Minister.

But this was not a fruitful period of his life, for Wellington's aristocratic nature and soldier's taste for discipline made him distrust, and try to frustrate, reforms in an age that was clamouring for them. His ministry fell when he declared against extending the franchise. Later he served for a brief period as foreign secretary in 1831–2 and as a cabinet minister under Sir Robert Peel from 1841 to 1846.

'A celebrated commander on the retired list'

Robert E. Lee *1807-1870*

L ee did not doubt for one moment where his duty lay when the American Civil War threatened. 'If Virginia stands by the old Union, so will I', he told a friend. 'But if she secedes, then I will follow my native State with my sword and if need be with my life.' He did not support slavery, indeed he held it 'a moral and political evil in any country' and freed his own slaves before Emancipation; he did not consider secession to be the constitutional right of any state, but he had been reared to the belief that his principal loyalty lay with Virginia.

As the youngest son of a prominent but impoverished Virginian family, Lee's future was virtually preordained. In 1825, when he was 18 years old, he went to West Point, where he did well, graduating second in his class of 46, and entered the engineers. In 1831 he married Mary Custis, the daughter of George Washington's adopted son, thus reinforcing his early traditional loyalties. He served with distinction in the US Army for 31 years, notably during the Mexican War of 1846–8; Winfield Scott, the American Commander-in-Chief, called Lee 'the very best soldier that I ever saw in the field.'

By the outbreak of hostilities between North and South, Lee's reputation stood so high that on 18 April 1861 President Lincoln offered him command of the Federal armies. Lee declined. A day later, Virginia opted to leave the Union; Lee resigned his commission, abandoned his Washington home at Arlington and removed to Richmond. There he was at once offered command of all the forces, both military and naval, of Virginia. He accepted, though with few illusions as to what the future must hold.

A gentle, humorous man of kindly disposition and imposing presence, Lee was sustained by deep religious belief. He was held in the highest and most affectionate regard by his men, who cheered him even in the moment of his bloody repulse at Gettysburg. He was the greatest strategist to emerge during the war and was certainly one of the most aggressive commanders in history, with a highly developed ability to assess his enemy's dispositions and intentions from painstaking intelligence gathering and then to outwit him.

Yet Lee had his shortcomings. Once Jackson was laid low, Lee could not on his own pin down and entrap Hooker's demoralized army, any more than, with new and lesser corps commanders, he could achieve victory at Gettysburg. Perhaps most damaging of all, he was reluctant to give firm orders to his subordinate commanders. He preferred to follow, perhaps too closely, Winfield Scott's example of planning a battle but allowing his subordinates to work out the details for themselves; with the result that at Gettysburg the Confederate Army could be said to have had no Commander-in-Chief.

Given the circumstances of the war, however, Lee's was an impossible task, and his achievement in twice coming close to victory by invasion of the North, and in sustaining the conflict for four years, raises him to a high place among the great commanders of history. It was not until February 1865 that Lee was given overall command of the Confederate forces. Had this appointment been made earlier, and had Lee's brilliant lieutenant 'Stonewall' Jackson not been killed, the war might have ended differently – not in Confederate victory but possibly in Confederate independence.

There can be more fitting epitaph to Robert E. Lee than the words that appear under his bust in the Hall of Fame at Washington: 'Duty then is the sublimest word in our language. Do your duty in all things. You cannot do more. You should never wish to do less.'

Robert E. Lee; portrait dating from c1864.
The Battle Flag of the Confederate Army consisted of a dark blue cross, edged with white, on a red ground; the thirteen white stars on the cross represented the Confederate states. The 'Stars and Bars' was the First National Flag of the Confederacy, which was adopted on 4 March 1861.

1807	*19 January* Born at Stratford, Virginia, son of General 'Light Horse Harry' Lee.
1825	Enters West Point and, 1829, graduates into the engineers.
1846/ 1848	Chief engineer to Winfield Scott in the Mexican War. Makes three vital reconnaissances; wounded at Chapultepec; wins three brevet promotions (captain to colonel).
1852	Superintendent of West Point to 1855.
1855	Commands 2nd Cavalry in the West on and off to 1861.
1859	*18 October* Captures John Brown at Harpers Ferry.
1860	*20 February–19 December* Commands Dept of Texas.
1861	*18–23 April* Refuses Union command; resigns from US Army and is given command of Virginia's forces as major-general. *14 May* Brigadier-General CSA. *6 August–20 October* West Virginia campaign fails. *31 August* General CSA. *8 November* Heads Dept of South Carolina, Georgia and East Florida (coastal defence).
1862	*3 March* Recalled to Richmond as presidential military adviser. *1 June* Takes over Army of Northern Virginia. *26 June–2 July* Wins Seven Days and, *29–30 August*, Second Bull Run. *17 September* Draws Antietam. *13 December* Wins Fredericksburg.
1863	*1–6 May* **Battle of Chancellorsville**. *1–3 July* Loses Gettysburg.
1864	*5–20 May* Stops Grant at Wilderness and Spotsylvania. *3 June* Wins Cold Harbor. *18 June* Siege of Petersburg begins.
1865	*6 February* General-in-Chief of CSA. *2 April* Evacuates Richmond. *9 April* Surrenders at Appomattox Court House.
1870	*12 October* Dies at Lexington, Virginia, aged 63.

Battle of Chancellorsville/*1–6 May 1863*

WHEN VIRGINIA JOINED the Confederacy in 1861, President Jefferson Davis and his cabinet made Richmond the South's capital. This was a misjudgement, for the town was within 160km/100mls of Washington and offered an enticing target to the North, since its capture would be both a military and psychological victory of the highest order.

To take Richmond became the North's chief objective in the eastern theatre. However, the advancing Union Army of the Potomac, under Major-General Ambrose E. Burnside, met with disaster and heavy loss at Fredericksburg on 13 December 1862. Thus, in the spring of 1863, having suffered more than 70,000 casualties in seven months to the rebels' 48,000-odd, it faced the South's Army of Northern Virginia across the Rappahannock River. The former was commanded by Major-General Joseph Hooker, 'Fighting Joe', who had replaced Burnside on 26 January, the latter by General Robert E. Lee. Their numbers and equipment were far from equal: Hooker had at his disposal nearly 134,000 men, including 11,000 cavalry, and 413 guns; Lee little more than 60,000 (3,000 cavalry) and 220 guns.

Hooker's plan to destroy Lee's army was essentially sound and in some respects imaginative. Lee's force was mostly stationed at Fredericksburg, Hooker's a little northwest at Falmouth. Hooker ordered two corps, 40,000 men, under the able Major-General John Sedgwick, to cross the Rappahannock below Fredericksburg and hold Lee's army there. He himself moved secretly, with 42,000 men, up the river in a northwesterly direction and crossed it at Kelly's Ford, with the object of then turning east and taking Lee in flank and rear.

Hooker's remaining two corps, 35,000 men, were detailed to hold two other fords – Banks's Ford and United States Ford – and to garrison Falmouth. If necessary, these formations could be used to reinforce either of Hooker's two wings. Meanwhile, Major-General George Stoneman was to take most of his new cavalry corps, with 22 guns, and, preceding the main turning movement, raid Lee's rear lines of communication. This mediocre officer was, however, delayed by floods and crossed the Rappahannock only on the same day as Hooker.

Hooker's strategy was promising: he planned to make maximum use of his numerical superiority, combined with a powerful, unexpected encircling movement. This, he hoped, would either trap Lee's army in pincers, when it could be destroyed by weight of numbers, or force him to retreat on Richmond, whither Hooker could pursue him and, he hoped, end the war.

Jackson's successful turning manoeuvre (1) enabled him to penetrate the Wilderness forest and then burst upon the surprised and unprepared Federals, relaxing in the area of Talley's Farm (2), Wilderness Church (3) and Dowdall's Tavern (4). They fled (5) in the direction of Chancellorsville (6), where Hooker, the Federal commander, who had believed the Wilderness to be impassable, was unaware of the disaster that had befallen his soldiers.

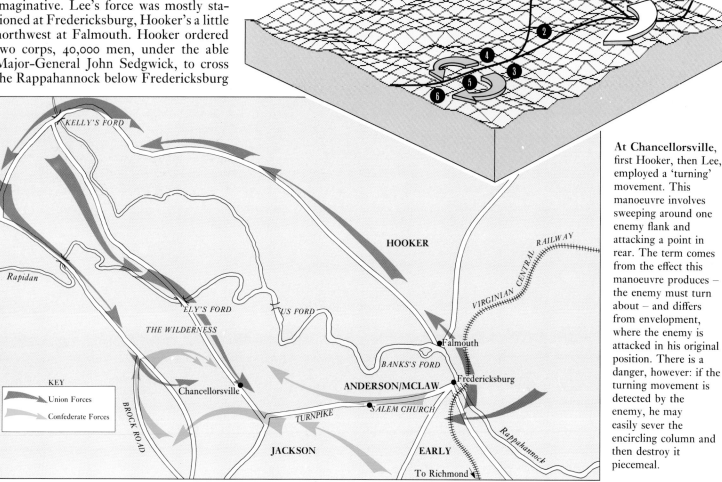

At Chancellorsville, first Hooker, then Lee, employed a 'turning' movement. This manoeuvre involves sweeping around one enemy flank and attacking a point in rear. The term comes from the effect this manoeuvre produces – the enemy must turn about – and differs from envelopment, where the enemy is attacked in his original position. There is a danger, however: if the turning movement is detected by the enemy, he may easily sever the encircling column and then destroy it piecemeal.

KELLY'S FORD

Rapidan

ELY'S FORD

US FORD

THE WILDERNESS

HOOKER

RAILWAY

VIRGINIAN CENTRAL RAILWAY

Falmouth

BANKS'S FORD

Fredericksburg

KEY

Union Forces

Confederate Forces

Chancellorsville

ANDERSON/MCLAW

SALEM CHURCH

BROCK ROAD

TURNPIKE

JACKSON

EARLY

Rappahannock

To Richmond

Union or secession?

It was the North's drive to capture the South's capital of Richmond, Virginia, that brought the Army of the Potomac and the Army of Northern Virginia face to face in May 1863 at Chancellorsville.

The differences that had provoked the American Civil War were given public voice during the presidential election of 1860, which was won by the Republican candidate, Abraham Lincoln. Slavery had been an issue of the election, but the principal debate had been on the right, claimed by the South, of individual states to secede from the Union. In his inaugural address on 4 March 1861, Lincoln made it abundantly clear that he sought only to prevent the extension of slavery to the Territories, great areas to the west that had yet to be granted statehood.

The new president observed: 'I have no purpose, directly or indirectly, to interfere with the institution of Slavery in States where it exists. I believe I have no lawful right, as I have no inclination, to do so.' A few moments later he set out his position on secession: 'Our national Constitution and our Union endure for ever. No State upon its own mere motion can get out of the Union.'

Nevertheless, the two propositions could not be divorced because more than 90 per cent of the black population lived in the southern states, and the question of slavery, ostensibly moral, was in fact regional. Civil war, though Lincoln eloquently denied the necessity for it, became inevitable.

At the opening of hostilities, the total population of the United States was some 31,000,000, but the South, with its plantation economy, did not possess the industrial strength of the North, its navy or its manpower. The best the South could hope for was rapidly to inflict such heavy defeats on the North that the latter would grow weary of the war and agree to Confederate demands for independence.

This might well have come about were it not for the single-minded strength of purpose of President Lincoln, who saw the position clearly: an inviolable Union, or secession and disintegration. The North's strategy quickly became clear. First they must deny the weaker South resources from abroad by a naval blockade of the east coast; then they must gain control of the forts and river routes in the west – notably the Mississippi – to split the Confederacy in two. Finally, they must take Richmond.

Communications and intelligence

The Army of the Potomac had first used balloons for reconnaissance in 1861, when about 52 officers and men operated a pair and carried out the first experiments in aerial photography and air-to-ground telegraphy. At Fredericksburg, Hooker had three stationary balloons observing Lee's defences, with couriers waiting underneath beside the cable men to retrieve messages that were attached to weights and dropped. After 09.00 on 1 May, when the fog lifted, the westward movement of Lee's troops was reported; and one or more balloons may have spotted the beginning of Jackson's flank march (interpreted as a retreat), but it is doubtful if Hooker received the report.

Hooker had a telegraph link from his Chief of Staff at Falmouth (north of Fredericksburg) to United States Ford. This was operated by the civilian-manned Military Telegraph Service, using ciphers that were never broken and reporting to the Secretary of War in Washington. By this time, 3,300 messages a day were being transmitted.

Under his direct control, Hooker also had flag and torch communication posts manned by the US Signal Corps, which had been formed on 21 June 1860, the first such body in the world. Each division usually had 12 signallers with telescopes, and relay stations were posted every 16km/ 10mls. The Confederate Signal Corps was established only on 29 May 1862.

During the Chancellorsville campaign, the weather, technical delays and the confined woodland terrain hampered Hooker's modern means of intelligence and communication, whereas Lee benefited from old-fashioned cavalry reconnaissance, having kept most of his mounted men with him.

Balloons were often used by the Union Army for observation. The *Intrepid*, *right*, is being filled with hydrogen converted from water by the generators on the left. A typical field telegraph station, *below*, linking points in the Union line, is hurriedly set up by the Telegraph Construction Corps.

Battle of Chancellorsville/4

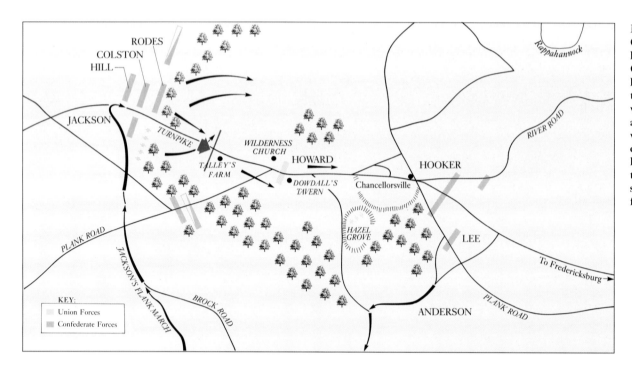

Major-General
Oliver Howard and
his superior,
General Joseph
Hooker, believed
that the heavily
wooded area known
as the Wilderness
was impenetrable to
cavalry, so they only
lightly defended
their encampment,
save for digging a
few trenches.

Stonewall Jackson and his Confederates (10) burst from the forest at about 16.00 on 2 May 1863, taking the Federal soldiers completely by surprise. Many had been asleep; others were cooking or eating a meal around Talley's Farm (9). Campfires, scattered in the ensuing chaos, caused numerous small fires.

Talley's Farm was situated at the junction of the Turnpike (5) and the Plank Road (8). This was so named because it was made from planks, each about 4.9m/16ft long and 5cm/2in thick, laid across baulks of timber. The Turnpike was no more than a road of trodden earth with gravel laid on top.

Near Dowdall's Tavern (6), Federal infantry in trenches (2) on both sides of the Turnpike put up a stubborn resistance. Other soldiers, bewildered and demoralized by the unexpected attack, promptly fled (3).

Fighting also took place around the Wilderness Church (1), where more of Howard's 11th Corps resisted. But the impact of Jackson's attack was so great that within minutes virtually the entire Federal force was in retreat. Supply wagons (4) and even some ambulances joined the headlong flight; so great was the haste that many vehicles turned over. Soon dead soldiers and horses littered the ground.

At Hazel Grove (7), Howard's headquarters, Federal troops also resisted but, like their comrades, these men were quickly swept back.

The Federal troops were in full flight, and had Jackson not been killed soon after, their line of escape across the Rappahannock River at US Ford would probably have been severed and the entire army then surrounded. This, in turn, might have so undermined the government in Washington that the South could have won the independence it sought.

Even so, the Battle of Chancellorsville was, as the historian Douglas Southall Freeman wrote, 'More nearly a flawless battle . . . than any that was planned and executed by an American commander.'

Hooker's personality, however, was such, that the signs of his imminent defeat could already be detected. His supreme confidence in his superior numbers and his delight with his encirclement plan induced in him a misplaced euphoria: 'May God have mercy on General Lee, for I shall have none', he is reported to have claimed. This led him to take no thought as to what Lee's ripostes might be. Furthermore, by sending his cavalry corps, save for one brigade and six horse artillery guns, to harass Lee's lines of communication to the south, he left himself heavily outnumbered in that important arm.

General Hooker began his flanking manoeuvre with three corps on 27 April. This movement continued throughout the 28th, when they were sighted by Confederate cavalry and the information passed on to 30-year-old General James 'Jeb' Stuart, Lee's outstanding cavalry division commander. The information was relayed to 'Marse Robert', as the soldiers called Lee, on the 29th. Since the reports were incomplete, and enemy numbers imprecise, Lee could not on the instant decide whether this was to be the main Federal attack. Taken all in all, he seems to have doubted it, but nevertheless sent Major-General Richard H. Anderson with his 6,700-strong infantry division and 16 guns to cover the Confederate left flank.

During the morning of the 29th Lee was more concerned with the activities of Sedgwick on his right flank. Most of his senior commanders – notably Lieutenant-General Thomas 'Stonewall' Jackson of 2nd Corps – advocated descending on Sedgwick before he had fully deployed. Lee, the supreme strategist of the Civil War, was unconvinced and declined to commit his outnumbered army until he could accurately ascertain the meaning of Hooker's movement to his left.

The situation was much clearer to Lee on 30 April: Hooker's three corps, having crossed the Rappahannock, got over its tributary the Rapidan during the day and forced two Confederate brigades to fall back from their positions at United States Ford. By that evening, Hooker's force was in the region of Chancellorsville, 22km/ 14mls west of Fredericksburg.

Lee's situation was unenviable. He had learned that Hooker's cavalry was moving in force to his rear, with the object of destroying the Virginian Central Railway and cutting his lines of communication with Richmond. Moreover, to his left, right and front there were enemy armies, two of which were separately equal in strength to his own. As Sir Winston Churchill was to write: 'Nothing more

The fine quality of the picture, *above*, by Matthew Brady, of Union 12-pounders shows it is not an action shot. The same is true of the Federals serving a Parrott gun, *right*.

Civil War weaponry

The Springfield, or US rifle musket model 1861, predominated in both armies. It measured 1.4m/4ft 4in, weighed 4.4kg/ 9¾lb, was of 15mm/0.58 calibre and had a 45cm/18in bayonet. Maximum effective battle range was about 457m/500yds and rate of fire 1 or 2 rpm, but due to the percussion cap, this was not affected by wet or windy weather. The South imported 100,000 British-made 14mm/0.577in calibre 1855 Enfield rifle muskets, which took Springfield ammunition.

Lee's cavalry favoured the famous 9mm/ 0.36in Colt Navy revolver weighing just 1.1kg/2¼lb; the British Webley double-action muzzle-loading revolver; shot guns,

and the 1856 British bolt-action breech-loading Terry carbine, carried by Jeb Stuart. As well as Colt revolvers and the standard 0.9m/3ft sabre, Union horsemen had the 1848 lever-action breech-loading Sharps carbine and the 1860 Spencer repeating magazine carbine.

Artillery was divided into smoothbore (12-pounder, light and howitzer) and rifled (10- and 20-pounder Parrott, ordinance) pieces. Hooker possessed 70 per cent rifled cannon, which were longer-ranged and more accurate than smoothbore, to Lee's 40 per cent, with better ammunition in general. The most favoured cannon was the 1856 12-pounder Napoleon light smooth-bore.

hopeless on the map than his position on the night of the 30th can be imagined, and it is this which raises the event which followed from a military to an historic level.'

On the evening of the 30th, Lee was giving thought to withdrawal, for although this would inevitably entail some

losses, he could be certain of evacuating his whole army. Then, on 1 May, Hooker ordered an advance along the Turnpike and Plank Road east toward Chancellorsville. As he moved into the Wilderness forest, he ran into Anderson's units, under Jackson's orders, which promptly attacked him. Hooker, thinking himself

about to be engaged by the entire Confederate Army, temporarily lost his nerve, as he later admitted, and fell back on defensive lines which he had constructed before Chancellorsville. Thus, to Lee's astonishment, Hooker abandoned the initiative; Lee promptly seized it.

Lee decided to split his small army and deal with Hooker first. He therefore sent Major-General Lafayette McLaw's division of 6,600 men to support Anderson's men, who had now dug in; together they could guard his rear when he advanced. He left only 10,000 men and 45 guns, under Major-General Jubal A. Early, to hold Sedgwick at Fredericksburg, and bodly marched on Hooker with the rest of his small force.

His plan was to encircle Hooker's right flank and for this task he had his close associate and ablest subordinate, Stonewall Jackson, who volunteered to take his whole corps. The two generals sat down on a log and worked out the details together. A guide had been found who could lead Jackson's corps along the paths winding through the Wilderness to the Wilderness Tavern. While Jackson was executing this manoeuvre, Lee, with only 13,000 men and 24 guns against some 50,000, held Hooker's attention in the centre with skirmishes and probes. This would, he hoped, give Jackson the full day he needed to march across the Federal front and get in position for a flank attack.

Jackson started to move his force of nearly 32,000, including 1,450 cavalry and 112 guns, at about 07.00 on 2 May; the march of 24km/15mls took until early evening to complete. Crucial to the plan was that it should be unobserved by the Federals, only little more than 3km/2mls away, but a gap in the forest revealed the manoeuvre to them – fortuitously as it turned out, since Hooker took it to be a move to cover a Confederate retreat.

The Wilderness was a region of wild forest, brush and brambles, crossed by a few narrow tracks; the scrub was so dense that Hooker had deemed it a sufficient barrier to guard his right flank. At about 12.30, troops who had detected Jackson's

As the war went on, the dress of the Confederate soldiers became a mixture of their own uniforms, items taken from Federal prisoners and civilian clothes. But their rifles, here methodically stacked, received constant careful attention.

men started to harass the Confederate wagon trains with rifle and cannon fire. Two Union divisions advancing to attack the column came up against Jackson's rearguard, who, aided by one of Anderson's brigades, fought valiantly before withdrawing into the protection of the Wilderness.

All this information was brought to Hooker and his flanking 11th Corps commander, Major-General Oliver Howard, but they refused to believe what was evident to the officers on the spot. Their interpretation was that the Confederates were merely skirmishing to draw attention from Lee's force in the centre, which they were still convinced would retreat. Furthermore, since evening was drawing on, Hooker decided to remain in his strong

Lieutenant-General Thomas J. Jackson 1824-63

A man of contradictions, Jackson, like many great commanders, showed little early aptitude for warfare, and his time at West Point was undistinguished. But he continued to learn about the military art throughout his life, enhancing his reputation with each campaign.

He has come down to posterity with the sobriquet 'Stonewall', earned at First Bull Run in 1861, when Brigadier-General Barnard E. Bee, seeing his own men waver, pointed with his sword and cried, 'Look, there is Jackson, standing like a stone wall!' Jackson's matchless Shenandoah Valley campaign followed in March-June 1862.

Jackson was nearly 1.8m/6ft tall, with a brown beard and striking blue eyes. His personal habits were austere – he neither smoked, drank alcohol, nor gambled, and was a staunch, Bible-reading Presbyterian.

Reminiscent of the partnership between Marlborough and Eugène, Jackson's association with Lee was one of the most successful in military history. General Robert E. Lee, the strategist, could always see what should be done in battle; Jackson, the tactician, could always do it. Lee said of him, 'Such an executive officer the sun never shone on. Straight as the needle to the pole, he advances to the execution of my purpose.'

Jackson's death was a grievous blow to Lee, who often said: 'I know not how to replace him.' Indeed, he could not; and without Jackson, Lee was at his least effective at Gettysburg in July 1863. The magnitude of Jackson's loss was neatly summed up by a surviving Confederate general: 'The death of the Southern Confederacy dates from Chancellorsville.'

Stonewall Jackson *by Thomas Nast*

This peaceful scene of camp life, showing the inspection of Union troops at Cumberland Landing, Pamunkey, Virginia, was photographed by Alexander Gardner, who was renowned for his pictures taken during the Civil War. The picture first appeared in the book *Incidents of War*.

defensive position until the morning, when the situation should be clearer. Had he instead thrown his full strength at Lee, he must at the very least have driven Lee farther from Jackson and toward Sedgwick, who was about to push Early off the Fredericksburg defences. But Hooker remained inactive.

Jackson was now nearly in position, since he had turned Hooker's flank by about 17.00. He was now opposite Lee, 6km/4mls away to the east; between them lay the right wing of the Federal Army. Jackson was shortly to spring a total surprise on the enemy.

When Jackson reached the Plank Road, he sent the 1,600-strong 'Stonewall' Brigade of Virginian troops to secure the point where it was joined by the Germanna Plank Road. This manoeuvre would guard his rear as he swung around to attack Howard in flank. Then he moved his main force to the Turnpike, about 1.6km/1ml farther on, where he deployed.

Brigadier-General Robert E. Rodes's division was formed up behind a screen of sharpshooters in the first rank, with behind it that of Brigadier-General Raleigh E. Colston, and then Major-General Ambrose P. Hill's 'Light' Division. Some 26 guns were deployed, with the rest behind in column of advance.

Some time shortly before 18.00 on 2 May, Jackson, mounted on his sturdy Little Sorrel and with his watch in his hand at which he frequently glanced, turned to Rodes, mounted on his right, and asked him if he were ready to attack. Rodes assured him that he was. 'You can go forward then', said Jackson; with this laconic remark began one of the outstanding attacks of the Civil War.

The evening quiet was broken by a bugle call, echoed by responses left and right. The Confederates thrust through the gloomy woods for a few moments, their clothing ripped by the clinging brambles; then they emerged into the open, gave voice to the terrifying 'rebel yell' and fell upon the enemy.

Surprise was total. The 10,500 infantry and 34 gun crews of Howard's 11th Corps were eating their supper or relaxing, and some were already asleep under the trees, when Jackson's 'foot cavalry' burst upon them from the camouflage of the Wilderness. At this particular moment and point, the Confederates were, unusually, numerically superior, and they drove the Federals into disarray within an hour.

Night was beginning to fall but Jackson saw, with the eye of a great tactician, a superb opportunity before him. He was less than 1.6km/1ml from the road to United States Ford, the Federals' only line of retreat; if he could mount one final

The Blue and the Grey

Few armies from the same nation could have presented a greater contrast than the North's Army of the Potomac and the South's Army of Northern Virginia. In Hooker's words, the former 'was the finest army on the planet', superbly equipped in all respects, while its enemy has well been called an 'army of ragged individualists.'

Of 1,080 US Army officers in 1861, only 313 joined the South; Lee's generals, 31 per cent were West Pointers to Hooker's 42 per cent. Union troops were volunteers and included the 15,000 pre-war regulars, although the unpopular draft was introduced in August 1862, while the South had had conscription since April of that year. Sickness and desertion were chronic problems for both sides: Lee had 22,414 sick and 5,953 absent without leave on 31 March 1863, for example.

By 1863, the colourful variety of uniforms had long since merged into standard Union blue, with képi, and Confederate grey – or merely butternut due to the shortage of dyes – with a slouch hat. 'Johnny Reb', to give the Confederate soldier his nickname, was always needing shoes and equipment, and his best source for all *matériel* and food was captured items. In 1862 Lee's army took 75,000 small arms and 155 guns: half its 220 guns at Chancellorsville had been captured.

Both sides had started the war with the same US Army ration, but while the North did not suffer deprivation, in April 1863 Lee recorded the South's daily ration as 0.5kg/18oz flour, 113g/4oz bacon, a few peas and occasional dried fruit, and 4.5kg/10lb rice for each 100 men every third day.

Lack of transport for distribution and inefficient use of it by the Commissariat, rather than lack of food, was the South's perennial handicap. One of Lee's constant worries was to provide sufficient good horses for the cavalry (whose scouts were his eyes) and to draw the guns, and to feed them. Forage was so desperately short in the late spring of 1863 that Lee was forced to send his artillery to the rear and to delay bringing up reinforcements.

The Confederate infantry colonel, *below left*, wears a slouch hat, grey full-dress coat and red silk sash. His rank is denoted by the three embroidered gold stars on his collar and by the width of the gold braid on his sleeves.

Specially chosen NCOs generally acted as standard bearers in the Confederate Army. The sergeant, *left*, wearing a forage cap similar to the French képi and red wool sash, is carrying the Virginia State Flag.

effort, he could cut off the entire enemy army. But his force, though exultant in victory, was now dispersed in the maze of the Wilderness and disorientated by the deepening shadows. Jackson, impatient to get his conclusive manoeuvre under way, decided he must himself see the exact position to his front and rode forward with some of his staff officers.

The party had gone only a short way before it came under sharp rifle fire and it is thought Jackson was wounded; they turned back in haste toward Confederate lines. But the confusion and darkness were such that a group of men from 18th North Carolina Regiment, believing themselves under attack by Union horsemen, opened fire at about 20 paces. Three officers fell, and Jackson sustained three bullet wounds in his arms and shoulder. Out of control, his horse galloped close to a tree; Jackson was knocked off but was caught as he fell.

Almost immediately afterward, Union artillery wounded the next in command, General Hill, and command devolved upon General Rodes until, a little later on Jackson's order, he handed it over with good grace to General Jeb Stuart. Jackson died eight days later, after the amputation of his left arm, from pneumonia and the loss of blood.

Shortly after being shot, Jackson had become unconscious, and no officer other than the wounded Ambrose Hill knew his plans. Thus the Confederate's great opportunity was lost. Stuart re-formed the men of Jackson's corps who, although they had eaten and rested little for 30 hours or so, were enraged by their beloved leader's wounding and fought with renewed fury. The following day, 3 May, they again attacked the Federal line, driving it back in the bloodiest day's fighting of the battle. They succeeded in joining up with Lee, but Jackson's imaginative encircling movement had not been implemented.

The suddenness and audacity of the attack by the Confederates entirely demoralized Hooker, who had been so confident of victory. Then, at about 09.00, a solid shot from a 25-gun battery on the Hazel Grove height hit a pillar of Chancellorsville House, on the verandah of which Hooker was standing. He seems to have been stunned by flying masonry, possibly concussed, and passed the rest of the day in an ineffectual daze. All he could think about, and order, was retreat.

With Jackson's removal from the scene, this was now possible, for Hooker had 76,000 men and 244 guns to hold off Lee while his army got back over the Rappahannock River. Few doubted that Jackson could have prevented this.

Major-General Joseph Hooker 1814–79

Following General Ambrose E. Burnside's costly defeat at Fredericksburg in December 1862, Joseph Hooker was appointed to command the Army of the Potomac in January 1863. But even in his letter of promotion, President Lincoln expressed misgivings: 'there are some things in regard to which I am not quite satisfied with you.' Lincoln had in mind Hooker's inordinate ambition and counselled him, 'Beware of rashness . . .'.

Although he had been a handsome youth in his West Point days, by 1863 the Massachusetts-born Hooker was extremely red-faced, with lustreless eyes and the walk of an old man, Both were probably the consequence of his addiction to alcohol, a weakness that aroused contempt in his men. He was also disliked by his fellow officers for his ambition and his superior, pompous manner.

Hooker did, however, possess considerable ability. He was a good organizer and, having taken over Burnside's demoralized army, at once set about reinvigorating it. He instituted a course of training, resupplied and re-equipped the army, gave it cap badges and 'Hooker's girls' (official prostitutes) and devised a fair rota for leave – all of which restored morale. Moreover, his plans at Chancellorsville were fundamentally sound and thought out in considerable detail.

Major-General John Sedgwick 1813–64

But Hooker had one failing that negated all his talents: he had an overweening belief in his own abilities. Thus while he had been a competent divisional and corps commander for the Army of the Potomac in the early stages of the Civil War, when he was subject to a superior's orders, he took no notice of advice and warnings when he was in supreme command.

Shortly after Chancellorsville he resigned and was replaced on 28 June by Major-General George G. Meade. After his resignation, Hooker continued to serve in the Union Army in the western theatre.

At Chancellorsville Hooker had been fortunate in one respect at least. His left wing was under John Sedgwick, a redoubtable and experienced West Pointer who had served in the war against the Seminole Indians in Florida, in the Mexican War and in various other frontier disturbances. A man of great personal bravery – he was twice wounded in 1862 – and resolve, he retrieved his force over the Rappahannock after Hooker's defeat at Chancellorsville.

A stern disciplinarian, Sedgwick was nevertheless affable and was judged the best-loved commander in the Union Army. He was shot by a Confederate sniper while on reconnaissance and supervising the siting of artillery during the Spotsylvania campaign in 1864.

On the afternoon of the 3rd, confident that Stuart could pin down Hooker's 80,000 troops entrenched at Chancellorsville, Lee turned his attention to the hapless Sedgwick. On Hooker's orders of 21.00 on 2 May, this general and his men had crossed the Rappahannock and taken the hitherto impregnable heights opposite Fredericksburg from Early, who had retreated down the Telegraph Road. They had also driven back Brigadier-General Cadmus M. Wilcox's brigade as far as Salem Church.

From midday on 4 May, however, Sedgwick's position was unpleasantly transformed. With the main army in retreat, he found himself with the river to his rear, Early back in his old defences, and faced at Salem Church by McLaw's and Anderson's divisions from Lee's army. But the Confederate soldiers, who had displayed such courageous endurance, were now exhausted and were slow taking up position. Nevertheless, Lee got the attack going by 18.00 and pressed it into the night, his artillery shelling Banks's Ford.

Sedgwick was beaten but, after losing 4,600 men, he managed to extricate the rest of his force, during the small hours of 5 May, over the pontoon bridges which had been moved to Banks's Ford. There he was joined by Hooker and the rest of the Army of the Potomac early on 6 May.

The Federals lost more than 17,000 men of their total of 134,000, as well as 13 guns, the Confederates nearly 13,000 out of 60,000, including almost a quarter of Jackson's corps, and 8 guns. They did, however, capture 20,000 rifles. While the Federals sustained the greater loss, the percentages – about 13 and 22 respectively – were disproportionate, and Lee would have increasing difficulty in finding replacements, whereas the North would not.

The **spirited** naif painting, *left*, shows General Sickles' men covering the retreat at Chancellorsville.

Negroes served in the Federal Army, *below*, and as non-combatants with the Confederates. To the surprise of the North, many negro slaves in the South remained on the plantations, helping the women to run them while the men were away at war.

Gettysburg: the turning point

The military initiative was now firmly in Lee's hands and he planned his long-delayed invasion of Pennsylvania. There was, however, a dire problem in the western theatre, where Vicksburg on the Mississippi River was in danger of falling to Major-General Ulysses S. Grant. It was suggested that Lee might go to its relief but he saw the situation clearly: either Virginia or Mississippi was in danger of being lost; better to risk the loss of Vicksburg while he threatened Washington.

His plan – to bring the Army of the Potomac to battle, destroy it and thereby gain Southern independence – was accepted by the Confederate War Cabinet eight days after the Battle of Chancellorsville. On 3 June 1863, Lee's northward advance began. Hooker – then still in command of the Army of the Potomac – proposed marching on Richmond, but Lincoln forbade him, rightly saying that the true objective of the Union

Army was to destroy Lee. Thus the two armies began their northerly march that was, on 1 July 1863, to bring them to the fateful field of Gettysburg.

That most terrible of Civil War battles was, in a strict sense, indecisive. Of the North's 93,000 troops, some 23,000 were killed, wounded, captured or missing; the South lost 20,000 out of 75,000 – but the South had no way of replacing that number. The day after the battle's end, 4 July, the Confederate garrison at Vicksburg was finally starved into surrender. Lee took his troops down the Shenandoah Valley to their earlier positions behind the Rappahannock and Rapidan rivers, knowing that, however long fighting continued, the war was lost. Almost two years later, after Appomattox, Lee said: 'If I had had Jackson at Gettysburg I should have won the battle, and a complete victory there would have resulted in the establishment of Southern independence.'

Viscount Allenby *1861-1936*

During the Palestine campaign a signal was frequently sent from GHQ to corps staff – 'B.L.', meaning 'Bull Loose'. The 'bull' in question was General Sir Edmund Allenby, and the message warned that he had set out once again to see some section of his command, perhaps a depot, a hospital or a forward line. His staff needed as much warning as they could get of his impending arrival, for Allenby was quick to find fault and was given to frequent outbursts of temper, often brought on by a seemingly trivial error or omission on the part of a subordinate. Yet these eruptions, which usually left the unfortunate object of his rage white-faced and speechless, soon subsided; nor did Allenby ever hold a grudge for long. To those who served him loyally and to the best of their ability he was generous with praise.

Allenby's troops held his abilities in high regard but, save for those who knew him well, had little affection for him. Indeed, throughout much of the British Army Allenby was unpopular. It was not only his unpredictable temper and his tiresome, peevish irritability, but also his apparent air of aloof superiority that turned men against him. This was a false impression, as those who knew him well have testified; but it took hold and Allenby, who never sought praise or advancement for himself, was denied much of the military credit that was rightly his due.

Throughout his life, Allenby was motivated above all by a sense of duty. He always obeyed his superiors' orders, no matter how he judged them, and expected his subordinates to give him the same unquestioning obedience. It is perhaps for this reason that he was more successful as overall commander in Palestine than he had been on the Western Front in France. Once he was sure of his staff's loyalty and obedience, he left them unsupervised while he occupied himself with visiting all parts of his command without warning.

Allenby's early life seems to have been idyllic. He was born at Brackenhurst Hall in Nottinghamshire, one of six children; here there were woods to roam and fields to play in. Later he was sent to Haileybury school, where he became imbued with that sense of duty and service that was so greatly to influence his military conduct; subsequently he went to the Royal Military College at Sandhurst. He did well, though not outstandingly so, and in 1882 was commissioned into the cavalry and was to spend his entire career until May 1915 in that arm.

He was a large, strong young man, physically tough, and self-disciplined. His interests were diverse, notably sport, travel and reading, but above all he had an abiding fascination with botany and ornithology, which he had acquired as a child. Indeed, as Field Marshal Viscount Wavell said in his biography of Allenby, 'War was to him a tedious, distasteful business which interfered with enjoyment of the quiet and beautiful fruits of the earth.'

It is difficult to assess Allenby's standing as a commander, for his unpopularity denied him full recognition and there were always those ready to denigrate his achievements. Thus his period in France during World War I has been stigmatized a costly failure. Wavell refutes this and goes so far as to claim that Allenby was 'the best British general of the Great War'. Indeed, he makes the point that Allenby was the same type of man as Wellington – lacking the common touch but always realistic, insistent on good administration, and supremely gifted in his ability to conceal his intentions from the enemy and strike with maximum surprise. There can hardly be higher praise for a commander than such a comparison.

Field Marshal Viscount Allenby, as he had then become, was portrayed in pastels by Eric Kennington and the drawing first published in 1926 in Seven Pillars of Wisdom. *The book's author, T.E. Lawrence – Lawrence of Arabia – greatly admired Allenby and after their first meeting described him as 'a very large and superior general'.*
Silhouette of a Desert Mounted Corps trooper.

1861	*23 April* Born at Brackenhurst Hall, Nottinghamshire, son of a country gentleman.
1881	Royal Military College, Sandhurst.
1882	*10 May* Second Lieutenant, 6th Inniskilling Dragoons, South Africa.
1884/ 1888	Bechuanaland and Zululand expeditions; promoted captain.
1889	Adjutant, Inniskilling Dragoons.
1896/ 1897	Staff College; promoted major in *May*.
1898	Adjutant to 3rd Cavalry Brigade in Ireland.
1899/ 1900	Boer War: leads squadron, then regiment in relief of Kimberley and to Pretoria.
1901	*January* Commands flying column to end of war, without reverse.
1902	Colonel and CO 5th Royal Irish Lancers.
1905	Brigadier-General commanding 4th Cavalry Brigade.
1909/ 1910	Major-General and Inspector-General of Cavalry.
1914	*4 August* Commands BEF cavalry division, then Cavalry Corps as, *9 October*, lieutenant-general.
1915	*6 May* Takes over 5th Corps then, as general, *October*, Third Army.
1917	*9 April–3 May* Battle of Arras, initial success. *28 June* Takes over Egyptian Expeditionary Force. *29 July* Only son killed on Western Front. *31 October–7 November* **Battle of Beersheba**. *9 December* Fall of Jerusalem.
1918	*19 February–4 May* Jordan Valley operations. *19–30 September* Wins Battle of Megiddo. *1–26 October* Takes Damascus, Homs, Tripoli and Aleppo.
1919	*25 March* Special High Commissioner for Egypt. *July* Field Marshal. *October* Created Viscount.
1925	*14 June* Resigns and leaves Egypt.
1936	*14 May* Dies at London, aged 75.

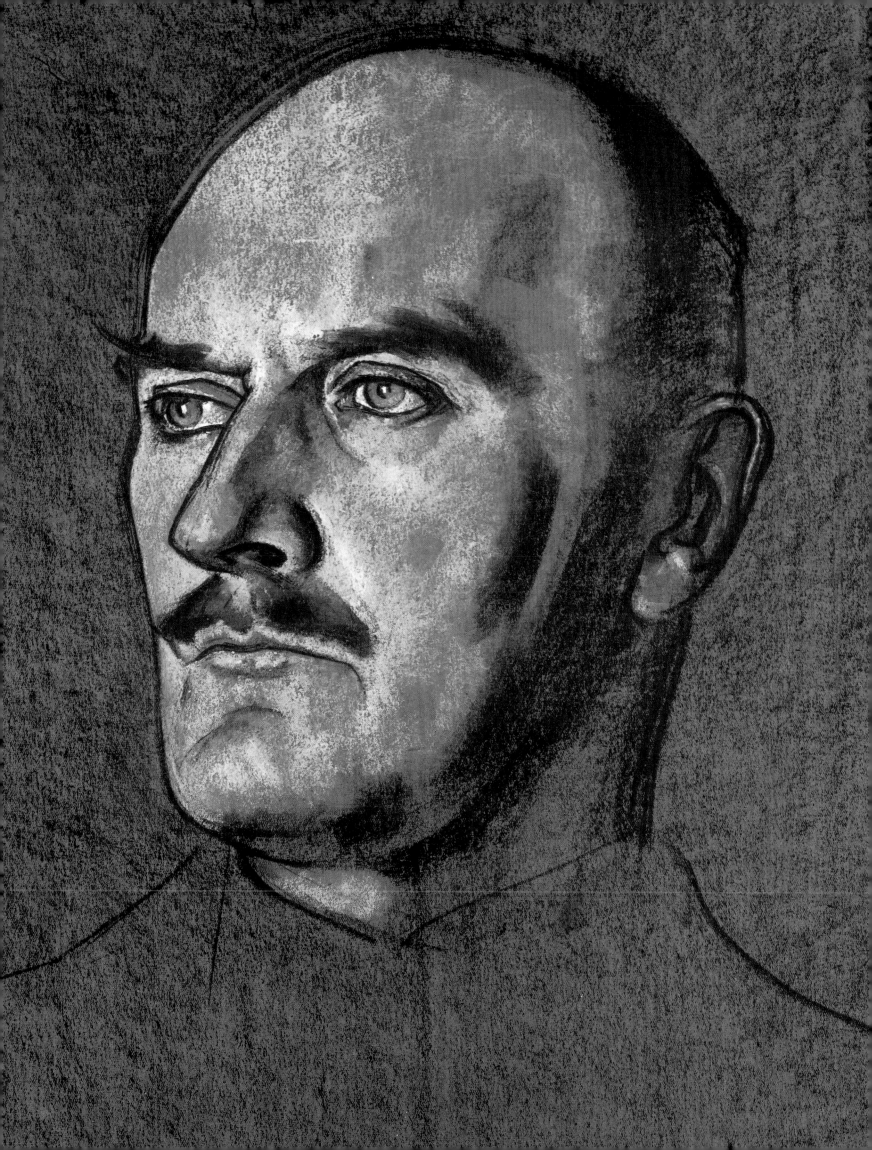

Battle of Beersheba/*31 October–7 November 1917*

IN THE AUTUMN of 1917, the rival armies in the Near East were unequal in expertise, resources and numbers. The Allied force – British, Anzac and Indian troops, with their Arab allies – was led by General Sir Edmund Allenby, an experienced army commander, resolute and militarily gifted. The men under his command were seasoned, fit, well trained, properly fed and clothed and with an abundance of weapons and ammunition.

The Turko-German command was divided in its counsels; and the Turkish Seventh and Eighth armies were ill fed, ill clothed, under strength and short of military supplies. Deserters were many.

The Turks, however, had a number of advantages, high among them their strong defensive position on the line between Gaza on the coast and Beersheba, 40km/ 25mls inland to the east. Most telling was the indomitable, stubborn nature of the Turkish soldier, who, despite his many deprivations, remained long-suffering and prepared to sacrifice himself in battle. The Turkish Army, was therefore, formidable and, though outnumbered roughly two to one, could not easily be overcome.

The Turks and Germans were also faced with a fundamental strategic problem. They well knew that strong reinforcements were being dispatched to Allenby in Palestine and that an offensive was in preparation. They had earlier lost Baghdad, capital of Mesopotamia and the eastern terminal of the Berlin-Baghdad rail line, and needed to recapture it.

Here, then, was their dilemma. If they reinforced their army in Palestine, they must abandon their proposed march on Baghdad; if, however, they moved on Baghdad, they risked the British smashing through the Gaza-Beersheba defensive line. This would allow them to sweep northward virtually unopposed and take Aleppo, thereby severing the Baghdad rail line and isolating Turkish troops in Mesopotamia.

It was not until about the middle of October that a decision was reached to send the *Yilderim* (Lightning) Army to Palestine to frustrate Allenby's impending attack. By then it was too late, although two Turkish divisions – the 19th and 26th – had been conveyed by rail from Aleppo to the Gaza-Beersheba defensive line and were in place before the battle opened; and another, the 20th, was close behind. But, even in total, they were inadequate to contain the ensuing blow.

There was another disadvantage to Turkey, the result of miscalculation and defective intelligence: neither the Turks nor their German masters believed it

The Palestine offensive

Allied military strategists during World War I were divided on a central issue and came to be known as 'Westerners' and 'Easterners'. The former held that the key to victory lay on the Western Front and that all resources in men and munitions should be sent to France in order to destroy Germany, the principal enemy. The latter held that in static, trench warfare the Germans could not be beaten, even at terrible cost, and advocated instead first destroying their weaker allies, especially Turkey, then Germany herself.

The decision of the British War Cabinet in June 1917 to reinforce the Allied Egyptian Expeditionary Force, with the object of conquering Turkish-occupied Palestine, was therefore of the first importance. The early months of 1917 had not been encouraging for the Allies: true, the US had entered the war but her effort could not yet be felt; but Russia had collapsed and German submarine warfare was by now at its height.

The British Prime Minister, Lloyd George, needed an Allied, preferably British, victory for reasons of home morale. There were, in addition, sound strategical reasons for an Allied offensive in Palestine, for following the Russian collapse, many Turkish formations had been released for service there. To strike first was therefore militarily prudent and General Sir Edmund Allenby was deputed by Lloyd George to take Jerusalem 'as a Christmas present for the British nation.'

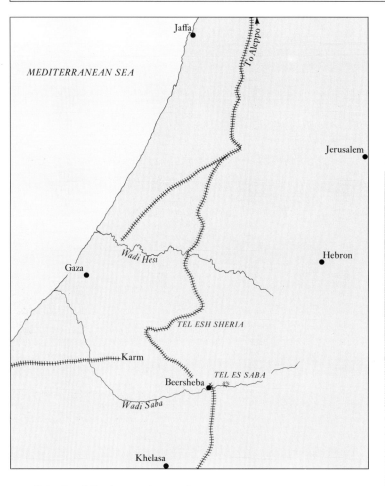

possible for Allenby to throw the greater part of his force at the Beersheba flank. They were convinced he would attack at Gaza, with possibly a sea-borne landing north of the town to cut Turkish communications and take their army in rear.

The obvious route of invasion into Palestine was, indeed, along the coast road to Gaza, for it eliminated the problem of water supply and would enable formidable

Each machine-gunner in the DMC led a packhorse, which carried parts of the dismantled guns on its back; this one, *opposite*, is a 7.6mm/0.303in Vickers. During the action munitions were brought up by camel trains, *right*.

Desert Mounted Corps

In July 1917 Allenby formed three cavalry divisions into the Desert Mounted Corps, which became his main arm of mobile warfare. To Chauvel's Anzac Mounted Division was added the Australian Mounted Division, made up of the 3rd and 4th Australian Light Horse brigades and the British 5th Mounted Yeomanry Brigade. The 6th, 8th and 22nd Yeomanry brigades were formed into the new Yeomanry Mounted Division. Almost all these men were veterans of Salonika or Gallipoli. In reserve were the mixed British/Anzac Imperial Camel Brigade and the 1,000-strong Indian Imperial Service Cavalry Brigade. Each division had a 12-gun unit of Royal Horse Artillery 13-pounders in support.

For the Beersheba operation, each DMC trooper had three days' rations of bully beef, biscuits and groceries. Two saddle bags held 8.6kg/19lb of grain for the horse: two days' mobile ration. A third day's fodder was carried in the general service wagons of each regiment, which also had a lighter wagon for technical stores and cooking utensils. The corps could thus support itself for three days without relying on the main wagon trains that shuttled between them and the advance ration dumps that had been set up by the corps truck column.

naval support to be brought to bear. Against this strategy had to be weighed the solid defences around Gaza that had already twice thwarted the British, in March and April. In the centre of their line, Turkish defences were also strong, but the Turkish left was weaker, and the terrain around Beersheba gave opportunity to Allenby's cavalry, of which he had a massive preponderance.

As early as July, Lieutenant-General Sir Philip Chetwode, one of Allenby's corps commanders who had served with him in France, had outlined a plan, which in its essentials Allenby accepted.

On 22 October, Allenby issued precise battle orders. Chetwode, with 20th Corps (47,000 infantry and 214 guns) was to make the main blow at Beersheba from the southwest; meanwhile, the Australian Lieutenant-General Sir Harry Chauvel's Desert Mounted Corps (11,000 cavalry and 28 guns) was to storm Beersheba from both east and northeast. These assaults, in tandem, were ordered for 31 October.

Four days earlier, 21st Corps' 218 guns, on the British left by the coast, were to mount and steadily increase the shelling of Gaza and its defences. Allenby hoped that this, particularly when supported by naval bombardment, would persuade the Turks that his objective was Gaza. To enhance this impression preparations were deliberately shown to be underway for a sea-borne landing at Wadi Hesi, 11km/7mls to the north of Gaza.

These and other stratagems, such as that of a staff officer luring the Turks to chase him and then dropping a blood-stained haversack containing bogus plans for an attack on Gaza, did indeed deceive the Turks and Germans. Even when Allenby's flank movement was detected on 29 October, they took it to be no more than a diversionary movement.

Allenby's orders contained an explicit instruction: Beersheba must be taken on the first day to prevent the Turks understanding his strategy and reinforcing their left wing. In outline, the plan was to concentrate the main blow of four divisions and two mounted divisions against the Turkish left, capture Beersheba and its water supply intact, then to roll up the Turkish left flank toward Gaza, while leaving the cavalry free to go northwest to seize the water supplies on the Wadi Hesi. While this last action was in progress, the Turks' attention would be held by bombardment of, and probes against, Gaza.

Allenby's full strength on 30 October, immediately before the battle, was roughly 58,000 infantry and cavalry combined on the right wing, together with 242

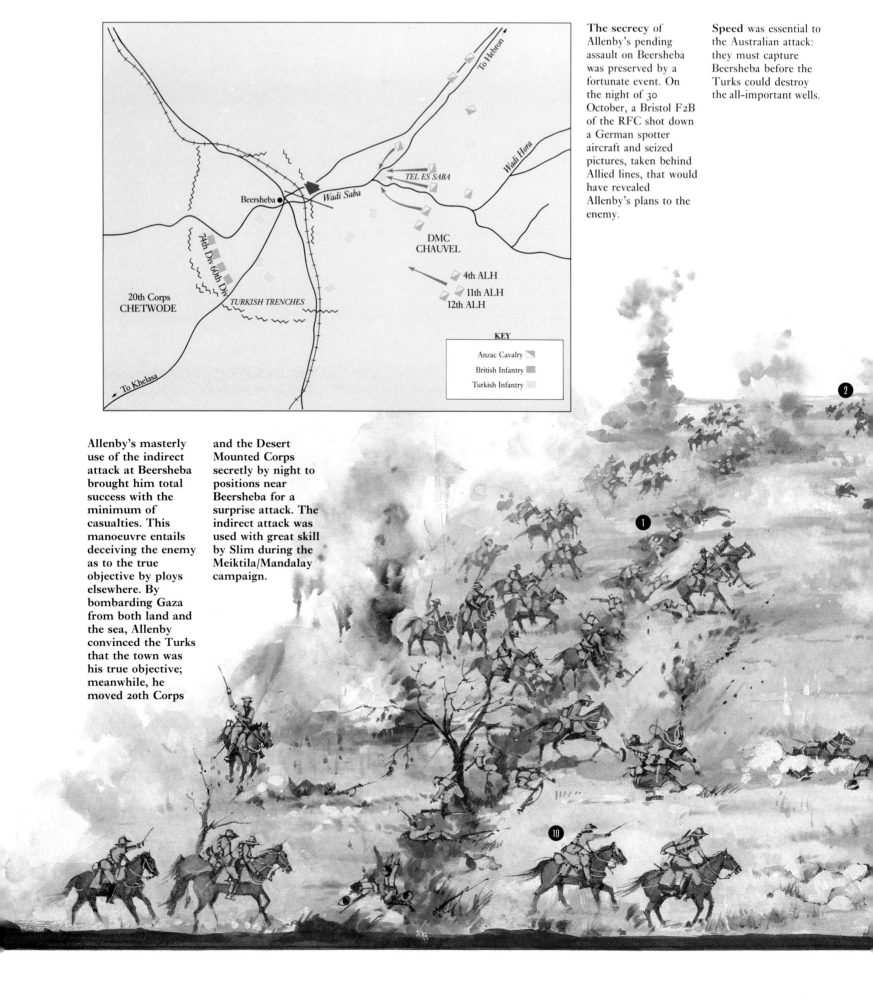

The secrecy of Allenby's pending assault on Beersheba was preserved by a fortunate event. On the night of 30 October, a Bristol F2B of the RFC shot down a German spotter aircraft and seized pictures, taken behind Allied lines, that would have revealed Allenby's plans to the enemy.

Speed was essential to the Australian attack: they must capture Beersheba before the Turks could destroy the all-important wells.

Allenby's masterly use of the indirect attack at Beersheba brought him total success with the minimum of casualties. This manoeuvre entails deceiving the enemy as to the true objective by ploys elsewhere. By bombarding Gaza from both land and the sea, Allenby convinced the Turks that the town was his true objective; meanwhile, he moved 20th Corps and the Desert Mounted Corps secretly by night to positions near Beersheba for a surprise attack. The indirect attack was used with great skill by Slim during the Meiktila/Mandalay campaign.

Map labels:
To Hebron
Wadi Hora
TEL ES SABA
Beersheba
Wadi Saba
74th Div 60th Div
DMC CHAUVEL
20th Corps CHETWODE
TURKISH TRENCHES
4th ALH
11th ALH
12th ALH
To Khelasa

KEY
Anzac Cavalry
British Infantry
Turkish Infantry

The attack on the town of Beersheba and its defences was made from the southeast by 400–500 men of the 12th (**2**) and 4th (**9**) regiments of the Australian Light Horse. The cavalry received the order to charge at 16.30, about half an hour before sunset. The 11th Regiment was in reserve, with the 5th and 7th Mounted brigades farther back but coming up fast in support.

Each regiment deployed in three successive lines of a squadron each, with 274m/300yds between them and 4.6m/5yds between each of the horsemen. The Australians did not carry swords, so they charged with drawn bayonets (**10**). The cavalry was supported by two batteries of horse artillery in their rear, which fired on Turkish earthworks and on Beersheba (**4**) itself, setting some areas on fire (**5**).

Casualties were few among the cavalry when they overran the first Turkish trench (**1**), for the Turks, astonished at the speed and ferocity of the charge, failed to alter their rifle sights. Most of their bullets passed harmlessly over the heads of the Light Horse, and the Turks' shallow trench was quickly overwhelmed.

A second trench (**3**), lay beyond the first. This was more formidably defended and as much as 3m/10ft deep and 1.2m/4ft wide. As the cavalry came up at full gallop to this next objective, a number of horses and men were brought down by rifle fire and sporadic Turkish artillery shots from batteries (**6**) in Beersheba.

At the second trench, many of the Australians dismounted and attacked the Turks with their bayonets. Some 40 Turks perished before the rest surrendered. Australian troopers (**8**) meanwhile pressed on toward Beersheba and were later reinforced by their comrades.

As darkness fell, the cavalry galloped across the Wadi Saba (**7**) into the town itself, charging along the streets and brushing aside all opposition. Beersheba was firmly in Australian hands by 18.00, by which time about 1,200 Turkish prisoners had been taken and 14 guns.

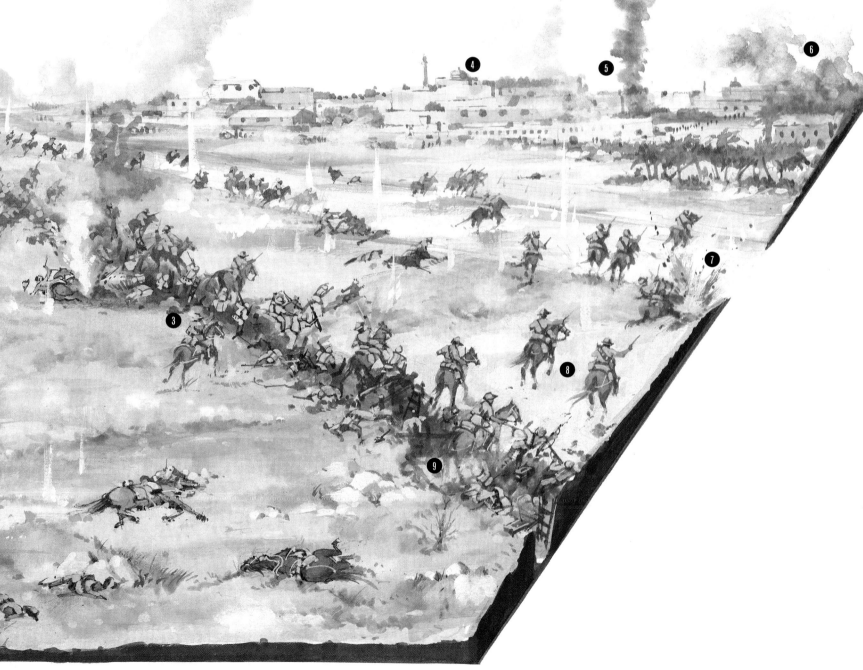

Bristol F2B fighters

Allenby recognized that air supremacy must be wrested back from the German pilots who had been supporting the Turks since July 1916, and his shopping list of reinforcements for Palestine included 60-odd aircraft. By October he had four Royal Flying Corps squadrons, as well as No.21 Kite Balloon Company, facing Gaza.

The mainstay of Allenby's air superiority was the fast, manoeuvrable, two-seat Bristol F2B, which arrived in September 1917 and played a large part in preventing Turkish disruption or reconnaissance behind his lines.

Engine: 186kW/250hp Rolls-Royce Falcon III; ceiling: 11¼ mins to 10,000ft; speed: 192kmh/119mph at 6,500ft; armament: one fixed Vickers 7.6mm/0.303in gun on the nose, one movable Lewis 7.6mm/0.303in gun in rear seat.

General Erich von Falkenhayn 1861–1922

General Kress von Kressenstein 1870–1948

By 1917 Turkey was in a parlous state, principally because many of her best units had been sent to fight with Germany against Russia and Romania. In March, Baghdad fell to the Allies, but in the same month the Russian collapse after the Revolution began to release many Turkish soldiers for service in Palestine. In order to boost Turkish morale, the German High Command sent General von Falkenhayn to Turkey in May 1917 to devise a strategy for the recapture of Baghdad.

Von Falkenhayn was a robust, widely experienced commander. He had been Chief of the General Staff from September 1914 until August 1916, when, after the long, unsuccessful assault on the fortress of Verdun, he was replaced by Hindenburg and Ludendorff. Falkenhayn then played a distinguished part in the brilliantly executed German conquest of Romania.

In the Palestine campaign, his plans were gravely disrupted by incessant and bitter disputes between Enver Pasha of the Turkish High Command and Jemal Pasha, the Governor of Syria. He was fortunate, however, in his immediate subordinate, General Baron Kress von Kressenstein, an experienced and inventive officer – a kind of World War I Rommel – who was in command of the Turkish Eighth Army facing Allenby in the Gaza-Beersheba line.

guns. The centre was only lightly held, but on the left, facing Gaza, there were in 21st Corps about 36,000 men and 218 guns of all types. Turkish figures are imprecisely known, but most authorities agree that they had nine infantry divisions, comprising some 45,000 men, 1,500 cavalry and about 300 guns.

Beersheba was no more than a large, sprawling Arab village; it had, however, a water supply and a railway station, on a line running north to south. Nevertheless, the Turks, under German instruction, had prepared defences all around the town, but these were in single line only and could quickly be overcome by resolute assault. Allenby's objective was to seize the town with a quick, overpowering and unexpected blow before the Turks could destroy the town's wells.

Chauvel had been given two tasks: he was to cut and hold the road from Beersheba to Hebron and Jerusalem to the northeast to prevent reinforcements coming down and severing that escape route from the town. Then he was to attack Beersheba. Meanwhile, two British infantry divisions were to attack from southwest of the town between the Khalasa to Beersheba road and the Wadi Saba.

First, however, Allenby had to move this great concentration of men, undetected if possible, from his left to his right flank. This he did in stages: the troops moved by night and spent the day in wadis. In this deception, he was greatly

aided by having air superiority. During the night of 30/31 October, some 40,000 troops started to move eastward for the assault on Beersheba, which was defended by no more than 5,000 Turks, with 16 guns and about 10 machine-guns. Only thorough reconnaissance had made this movement over featureless and roadless country possible.

At about 12.00 on 31 October, the main defences were seized, with little loss, but the British were still some 6km/4mls from the town itself. The Desert Mounted Corps, by their night ride, were now to the east of Beersheba. There was, however, a strong defensive position between it and the town, a small hill – Tel es Saba – which nevertheless dominated all the eastern approaches to Beersheba. It was stoutly defended and was not taken until about 15.00, or a little later.

Chauvel subsequently ordered three regiments of Australian Light Horse to drive directly at Beersheba and, as darkness fell, this 1,600-strong cavalry unit charged through the Turkish defences and penetrated the town. In this manner, not only was Beersheba taken but, most important, its water system and wells.

The next object was to roll up the Turkish line from their left. A delay had always been envisaged, however, during which to improve the water supply in Beersheba, so as to provide sufficient for 20th Corps and its animals, and to bring up the Corps' guns. During this period,

the Turks were to be kept fully occupied by an attack by 21st Corps. This attack, launched on the night of 1/2 November over a 5km/3ml front succeeded – 550 prisoners, 3 guns and 30 machine-guns were taken – but with severe loss, for some 2,700 men were killed, wounded and missing. This made starkly clear the difficulties that would have been encountered had Gaza been Allenby's first objective.

A further delay to Allenby's attack from Beersheba occurred when the flank guard on his right wing became heavily engaged with Turkish reinforcements, hastily sent into the hills north of Beersheba in the mistaken belief that the British planned to rush up the Hebron road to Jerusalem. Chetwode and Chauvel in turn miscalculated, for they judged these reinforcements to be intent on recapturing the vital wells at Beersheba.

Allenby, who had planned the renewed attack for 4 November, drove to 20th Corps headquarters at Beersheba to investigate the reasons for the delay. Convinced by his commanders on the spot that a further pause was necessary, he consented to postponing the attack until the 6th. The attack then went as planned, and the 10th, 60th and 74th divisions smashed the Turkish left flank.

Now, however, shortage of water again played a part. Since all its transport had to be transferred to 21st Corps on the coast for a final assault, 20th Corps could not move far from its water supply at Beersheba and was obliged to halt yet again. Nevertheless, by 7 November, after stubborn fighting by both sides, Allenby had driven back the Turkish reinforcements and taken Tel esh Sheria, a commanding hill northwest of Beersheba.

The battle was won, for the endangered Turks had no option but to retreat and when, on the morning of 7 November, 21st Corps probed into Gaza they found the town abandoned. This citadel had held up the British advance into Palestine for some eight months; now at last it had fallen, and so Allenby could pursue his defeated enemy.

Allenby's great victory may be said to derive from three interlocking factors: careful and detailed preparation for the masterstroke; success in deceiving the enemy as to his intention, and his ability to solve, in barren terrain, the problem of water supply by his swift and decisive capture of Beersheba.

Allenby had been determined that no fighting should take place in Jerusalem itself, and his attack centred on the Turkish defences west of the city. A sharp British assault on 8 December dismayed the Turks, who withdrew overnight, and on the 11th Allenby walked into Jerusalem through the Jaffa Gate.

'A Christmas present for the British nation'

Allenby was now poised to pursue his enemy up the coast road. Pursuing a defeated army is, however, more complex and potentially more costly than may at first appear, for a broken army retreats toward its supply bases while the pursuers distance themselves from their own. Moreover, those in retreat are obliged to move swiftly, while the exhausted victors can all too easily follow at a more leisurely pace. Allenby understood this and ordered the pursuit to be pressed with maximum speed.

But the mounted troops were hampered by the problem of water supply and with their occupation of Jaffa on 16 November, the pursuit temporarily ended. Allenby had nevertheless broken the Gaza-Beersheba line, advanced some 80km/50mls and taken about 10,000 prisoners and some 100 guns. On 18 November, despite the advent of the rains and warnings to be cautious from the British War Cabinet, Allenby renewed his advance, and the two Turkish armies before him were now driven 32km/20mls apart. Allenby's plan was to reach the Jerusalem-Nablus road north of the former and, by cutting it, force the Turks to abandon the city. Jerusalem fell on 9 December 1917, and two days later Allenby entered the city by the Jaffa Gate; he was on foot and accompanied by no more than 20 officers, among whom was Major T.E. Lawrence.

The capture of Jerusalem caught the imagination of the world but did not of itself end the war in the Near East. However, in the following months, British troops advanced through Mesopotamia, while British and Arab forces pushed up through Palestine. On 1 October 1918 Damascus was occupied, and on the 31st, Turkey concluded an armistice with the Allies.

Tomoyuki Yamashita *1885-1946*

T he son of a country doctor, Yamashita was first destined for a career in medicine, but his parents decided to enter him for the army. He passed out of the Hiroshima Military Academy with honours in 1908 and was commissioned into the infantry. Later he earned a place at the Japanese Staff College, where he completed his course with distinction in 1916.

Promotion came rapidly: in 1919 Yamashita was posted as Japanese Military Attaché to Switzerland and later to Vienna. In 1940 he was appointed Inspector General of the Japanese Army Air Force and visited Hitler and Mussolini to study German and Italian weaponry and tactics.

Yamashita was a complex man, an amalgam of contradictions. His hobbies were gardening and fishing, yet his obsession was preparing for a war against the Anglo-Saxons that he believed to be not only just but inevitable. A deeply religious man of integrity, he nevertheless became increasingly involved in the various military intrigues of the 1920s and '30s, when a number of cliques vied with each other for the power that would come with the formation of the military government they all sought.

Yamashita joined the so-called 'Imperial Way' group, in contrast to Hideki Tojo, the War Minister, who was a leading member of the 'Control Faction'. The two men detested each other and, throughout his career, Yamashita was aware that any military failure or political indiscretion would bring about his immediate dismissal.

In 1936, 'The Young Officers' Rebellion' was staged by those who claimed the politicians were reducing rather than enlarging and modernizing Japan's armed forces. The revolt was suppressed, but Yamashita strongly urged leniency for the men involved, leading his superiors to believe – not without reason – that he had sympathy for their cause. He was, therefore, posted to North China, where fighting was in progress, and during the next two years repeatedly exposed himself to fire, seeking an honourable death, since he feared he had earned the displeasure of the Emperor. This was but one manifestation of his attachment to the *samurai* code. He believed implicitly that the punishment for failure or dishonour was death, and for this reason, after the war, accepted his death sentence as a war criminal with equanimity.

Late in 1945, he was put on trial before a US military commission in Manila. The prosecution's case centred on well-documented atrocities against Filipinos and Allied prisoners in the Philippines committed by Japanese sailors during the defence of Manila, which were, properly, a naval responsibility. How far Yamashita was to blame is hard to establish, as was the extent of his responsibility for the early excesses of the Japanese after the fall of Singapore, but the prosecution maintained that, as Commander of the Fourteenth Area Army, he should have taken steps to prevent the murders, whether or not he had the authority to do so.

The trial was unprecedented for it was the first time an enemy general had been tried and convicted not only for actions taken, but also for actions not taken, during a war; it set the pattern for all trials of war criminals. Yamashita was stripped of his military status and sentenced to death by hanging on the express command of General Douglas MacArthur. Paradoxically, General Masaharu Homma, who had returned to civilian life, was executed as a military man, by firing squad. Yamashita's last words before he was hanged on 23 February 1946 are thought to have been: 'I pray for the Emperor's long life and prosperity for ever.' That prayer had been the guiding principle of his life.

General Tomoyuki Yamashita, photographed at Manila in the Philippines while awaiting trial for war crimes. His resigned attitude is summed up in his remark: 'In war someone always has to lose. What I am really being charged with is losing the war.'
The Rising Sun – symbol of Japanese might.

1885	*8 November* Born at Osugi Mura, Shikoku Island, South Japan.
1900/	Hiroshima Military Academy.
1908	Commissioned into 11th Infantry Regiment.
1916	Graduates from Staff College as captain.
1919/	As lieutenant-colonel, Military
1921	Attaché in Switzerland and Germany.
1921/	At Tokyo Imperial HQ and Staff
1926	College instructor.
1926/	As major-general, Military
1929	Attaché in Vienna.
1930	Commander of 3rd Guards Regiment in Tokyo.
1936	*February-March* Key mediator in Young Officers' Revolt.
1937	*November* Becomes lieutenant-general.
1938/	Commands 4th Division in
1940	Northern China.
1940/	*July* Succeeds Tojo as Inspector-
1941	General, Army Air Force. *December-June* Heads military mission to Germany; meets Hitler and Mussolini. *6 November* Appointed commander of Twenty-fifth Army for invasion of Malaya. *8 December* Landings in Thailand and Malaya; *11–12* breaks through Jitra Line; *26* crosses Perak River unopposed.
1942	*2 January* Outflanks Kampar position; *7* breaks through Slim River position and *11* enters Kuala Lumpur. Destroys Indian brigade and *22* crosses River Muar. *February 8–15* **Battle of Singapore**. *17 July* Leaves to command First Area Army in Manchuria.
1944	*October* Defends Philippines with Fourteenth Area Army.
1945	*2 September* Surrenders. *29 October–7 December* Found guilty of war crimes at Manila.
1946	*23 February* Hanged at Manila, aged 60.

Battle of Singapore/8–15 February 1942

ON 7 DECEMBER 1941, Japan launched her attack on the American naval base of Pearl Harbor in Hawaii. Simultaneously she struck, without declaration of war, in three directions: against the Dutch East Indies and the Philippines to gain essential war materials; into the Pacific Ocean toward the Solomon Islands; and into southeast Asia through Burma and Malaya.

Malaya offered bountiful rewards, for the peninsula produced 38 per cent of the world's output of rubber and more than 60 per cent of its tin – two commodities that the Japanese war machine lacked. The supreme objective was, however, the capture of Singapore at the foot of the Malay Peninsula. This great British naval bastion was more than a fortress; considered impregnable, it was the outstanding symbol of Western might in Asia.

The task of seizing the glittering prize of Malaya and Singapore was entrusted to Lieutenant-General Tomoyuki Yamashita by the Japanese supreme command. He was hurriedly appointed only a month before the invasion, but his Twenty-fifth Army was a well-equipped, well-trained formation comprising three divisions – some 70,000 fighting men – two-thirds of whom were veterans of up to three years campaigning in China. This gave him a total strength, with auxiliaries, of 110,000 men. It was a sign of Yamashita's confidence that he turned down the offer of five divisions and opted to use only three. Few victorious commanders have actually forsworn extra troops.

The Twenty-fifth Army was supported by 3rd Air Division with 459 aircraft, plus 159 naval aircraft, greatly outnumbering the 158 aircraft available to the RAF. Furthermore, three specially trained, independent engineer regiments were allocated to each division, at Yamashita's insistence, to ensure that bridges could be rapidly built over the many rivers, enabling the Japanese to advance at maximum speed. Yamashita also had 6,000 bicycles per division, each carrying 40kg/88lb of equipment, which meant his troops could move speedily along jungle paths and through the rubber plantations, as well as on the roads. Speed was the essence of Japanese strategy, so as to deprive the British of time to reinforce the defences of Singapore.

Yamashita's plan, completed in less than a month, was both simple and potentially deadly. While part of his army moved from Indo-China westward through Siam (Thailand) and seized the narrow neck of the Malay Peninsula, Japanese landings were to be made at Patani on the east coast and at Singora,

Japan prepares to strike south

In October 1941, General Hideki Tojo, Japanese war minister and leader of a military political group dedicated to war, was appointed prime minister. His plans for war against the Anglo-Saxons, never disguised, were supported by many influential service officers.

Japan's expansionist policies can be traced back to at least 1895, when she seized Formosa (Taiwan). Later, America's isolationist policies gave her the chance for further, unmolested encroachment in eastern Asia: in 1931 she invaded Manchuria and in 1937 attacked China.

These and other conquests alarmed the Western powers, notably the USA, who in 1938 imposed an embargo on the export of certain manufactured goods to Japan, later including scrap iron and – crucial to the Japanese war machine – oil. By 1941, the Japanese realized that they must either withdraw from the lands they had conquered to placate America, or go to war. The advent of Tojo as prime minister ensured that the latter would be chosen.

The decision was made even more alluring by events in the West. When Hitler's blitzkrieg tactics rapidly brought about the fall of western Europe in May–June 1940, and when Great Britain, standing alone, was threatened with German invasion, all her colonies in the east, as well as those of France and Holland, became vulnerable to Japanese attack.

Yamashita's overland attack from the north of the Malay Peninsula to capture Singapore is an example of the strategy of indirect approach on an enormous scale. Its aim is to launch a massive blow at the point unexpected by the enemy, while distracting him with threats elsewhere. This calls for the aggressor to have greater numbers or better armed, better disciplined troops – Yamashita had the latter. The British had long assumed that any attack on Singapore would come from the sea and they could not contain Yamashita's swift advance.

Japanese soldiers, *right*, usually had 6.5mm Long Meiji 38 rifles, weighing almost 4kg/9lb, with bayonets fixed for close fighting.

Opposite:
Sappers rapidly repaired the Johore Causeway, blown up by the retreating British, enabling transports to cross to Singapore Island, *above*. Bicycle troops made their way quickly along Malaya's good roads, *below*.

KEY

Japanese advance

0   50 miles

with overwhelming superiority in the air and at sea – repeatedly reinforced his invading army with subsidiary landings behind British lines on both sides of the peninsula, using captured vessels as well as his original landing craft.

The Japanese 5th and 18th divisions drove southward toward Alor Star in the west of the peninsula and Kroh in the centre, often, due to Japan's chronic shortage of rubber, riding tyreless bicycles along Malaya's well-paved roads. At Jitra they inflicted a crushing defeat on the British and the 11th Indian Division after which, retreat was their only real option. The British never regained their balance and the farther and faster they retreated, the lower became their morale.

Time and again, Yamashita's tactics were to commit a limited number of troops in frontal attacks, usually supported by tanks and often at night, then deploy the bulk of his available force to attack in flank and rear. This kept the Japanese advance at maximum momentum, while British troops, soaked with the ceaseless rain, exhausted, hungry and dispirited, could only obey as best they might the orders of their superiors – which were always to fall back to new defensive positions.

In the first week of 1942, the British and their allies were again decisively defeated at their defensive positions on the River Slim. On 11 January, Kuala Lumpur fell, and after that there was uninterrupted flight to the supposed safety of the island of Singapore and its fortress. Meanwhile, further Japanese reinforcements were

somewhat to the north of it. South of Patani, another force was to land at Kota Bharu. These and other lesser invasions began on 8 December 1941, only hours after Japanese carrier-borne bombers had attacked the American naval base of Pearl Harbor at the other side of the Pacific.

Yamashita, who had arrived in Saigon from Manchuria with no more special equipment than a rush mat, was fortunate in having an able chief of staff, General Sosaku Suzuki. His brilliant if idiosyncratic chief of operations and planning was Colonel Masanobu Tsuji, who since January 1941 had done much preparatory work on jungle warfare with the 'Taiwan Army Research Section'. On the other hand, Yamashita faced the hostility of his superiors, including Field Marshal Count Terauchi and Prime Minister Tojo.

British commanders, who had forseen the possibility of a Japanese attack on Malaya, although by no means its precise details, had planned to forestall such a move by an advance northward into Siam codenamed 'Matador'. This operation could not be implemented, however, since British scruples forbade such a move unless the Japanese had first violated Siam's neutral status.

'Matador' was, therefore, put into effect too late, for by the early morning of 10 December Japanese 5th Division had already landed at Singora, under Yamashita's eye, and had crossed the peninsula to the west coast, where it was advancing rapidly into the Kedah. There now ensued a British retreat, contested but always outmanoeuvred, down the west coast of Malaya. Meanwhile Yamashita –

(Map labels: Singora; Japanese 5th & 8th Divs; Patani; SIAM; Jitra; Kedah; Alor Star; Takumi Force; Kota Bharu; Kroh; George Town; PENANG; Butterworth; Gong Kedah; Krian; Perak; Taiping; Kuala Trengganu; Ipoh; MALAYA; Kuala Lipis; Telok Anson; Slim; Kuantan; Kuala Selangor; Serandah; Kuala Lumpur; Port Swettenham; STRAIT OF MALACCA; Port Dickson; Endau; Malacca; Muar; Muar; Parit Sulong; Johore Bahru; Singapore)

Japanese Type 95 light tank
This was Japan's standard light tank, produced from 1935 by Mitsubishi and kept in production until 1942–3. Despite its token armour and cramped fighting compartment for the crew of three, it proved lethal in Malaya and Singapore, together with smaller numbers of Type 89 and 97 medium tanks with 57mm/2¼in guns.

Yamashita had about 228 tanks in the four regiments of 3rd Tank Brigade, and in spite of losing 2nd Regiment at the end of January 1942, still had 150 tanks for the Battle of Singapore. The British were repeatedly surprised and overrun by rapid tank attacks down the main roads, sometimes at night. They had only 18 light tanks right at the end of the campaign, and the troops guarding Singapore had not had

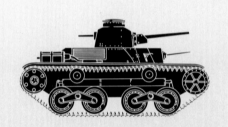

pre-war training in anti-tank tactics. Their 2-pounder guns, mines and anti-tank rifles (some in armoured cars) were seldom well-employed.
Weight: 7.4 tons; **road speed:** 40kmh/25mph; **range:** 242km/150mls; **armament:** one 37mm/1½in gun on rear of turret, two 7.7mm/0.3in machine-guns, one on rear of turret, one on hull.

Vickers Wildebeest MkIII torpedo-bomber
This obsolete, single-engine biplane, with a crew of two or three, was the oldest operated by the RAF in Malaya, or indeed anywhere. Yet, in conjunction with the Singapore fortress guns, it was supposed to repulse any Japanese naval attack. Nos 36 and 100 Squadrons had 24 Wildebeest aircraft between them, in which they vainly but bravely attacked Japanese transports off Kota Bharu on 8 December 1941 and Endau on 26 January 1942. They helped to hit six ships, but not in stopping the landings.

Ironically, on the latter occasion, on which 10 Wildebeeste were shot down, they carried 113kg/250lb bombs instead of torpedoes because of the shallow water; flying at 1,000ft, their slowness hampered the fighter escort. These aircraft were also used in night raids on Japanese troops and against motor transport in central Johore.
Speeds: 220kmh/137mph and 159kmh/99mph cruising at 5,000ft; **range:** 1,561km/970mls with weapon load; **armament:** two 7.7mm/0.303in machine-guns; **bombload:** one 50cm/18in torpedo or up to 848kg/1,870lb of bombs.

landing at Singora and were brought up by rail, unfatigued, to the front.

Johore, immediately north of the island of Singapore, was now in peril. General Sir Archibald Wavell, supreme commander of the Allied forces in Java, knew that its fall would render Singapore untenable, and already commanders on the spot were speaking of destroying ammunition and stores so that the Japanese should not be able to benefit from them. Churchill took a different view and cabled, in these dire days of near despair, 'the obvious method is to fire the ammunition at the

enemy . . . Firing away the ammunition is the natural and long-prescribed course when the fall of a fortress is imminent'.

The Japanese onslaught – they had advanced some 805km/500mls in eight weeks – had brought them within sight of the island of Singapore, some 32km/20mls wide and 16km/10mls deep. Only the narrow strait – in places no more than 966m/1,100yds across – stood between them and the humiliation of the British by the capture of their great eastern fortress.

On the night of 30/31 January, the GOC Malaya, Lieutenant-General

Arthur Percival, issued orders for the evacuation of the mainland by all his troops to Singapore island. He had at his disposal some 85,000 men – more than enough, in theory, to repel the Japanese. A third of this number, however, were newly landed reinforcements; they were insufficiently trained and had not seen action. The main portion of his force was exhausted and demoralized by their long, ceaseless retreat down the Malay Peninsula. All – NCOs and other ranks, officers and divisional commanders – sensed the imminence of defeat. Churchill had repeatedly cabled, urging stubborn resistance to the end. But the troops on the spot lacked confidence in their ability to do so.

With typical boldness, Yamashita had decided to establish his HQ in the superb vantage point of the Sultan of Johore's Green Palace. He argued that the British would not believe that such a prominent building would be used, and he was right. On its east side there was a five-storey observation tower, with a glazed roof, reached by an iron spiral staircase. For a week he and his staff lived here on dry and tinned food, happy in the knowledge that British fire would deter unnecessary visitors.

On the morning of 8 February, the Japanese, assembled in strength in the

camouflage of plantations northwest of the island, subjected it to bombardment by 440 guns. Then, at 22.45, 15,000 men of the 5th and 18th Japanese divisions began crossing the Johore Strait in 300 small craft, led by armoured landing craft. Both divisions had had experience of amphibious operations since the time of the landings in China in November 1937, and 4,000 China veterans were included in the first wave of Japanese troops.

Their initial target was 22nd Australian Infantry Brigade, west of the River Kranji. Though the Australians fought stoutly, they were heavily outnumbered, and the Japanese, despite great loss of men and landing craft, quickly took the village of Ama Keng. When Yamashita saw the blue signal flares announcing success only 10 minutes after the crossing, he shed tears of joy. The next morning, the Japanese were able to attack Tengah airfield, some 8km/5mls inland.

There was one obvious position for the defenders to try to halt the Japanese advance – between the sources of the Kranji and Jurong rivers. This gap Percival plugged by pulling back 22nd Australian Brigade and bringing forward 44th Indian Brigade.

At sunset on 9 February, Yamashita and his staff crossed the strait on a raft, made from three boats lashed together, and moved to a tent set up in a rubber plantation north of Tengah airfield. This new command post was soon connected by telephone and submarine cable to the Green Palace. First to see Yamashita ashore was a group of prisoners of war.

On the night of 9 February, however, the Imperial Guards Division crossed the Johore Strait in the causeway area and mounted an independent attack on 27th Australian Brigade. Initially it was feared that Yamashita's leading regiment had been annihilated in petrol set ablaze by the defenders. Later the report was found to be false, and Yamashita was furious when he found they had merely disregarded the normal rule of having a staff officer in the front line to send back intelligence.

The Japanese had, however, secured their landing site and thus a gap opened between the Australians and the line held between the headwaters of the Kranji and Jurong rivers.

Reinforcements from the British 18th Division and elsewhere were rushed to the danger spot. But by the night of 10 February the Japanese, whose momentum of advance had been gathering, were on the point of taking the 580ft/117m high village of Bukit Timah, 'Tin Mountain', with a column of about 50 tanks.

Senior private of the Imperial Guard carrying a Model 99 light machine-gun.

145

'Force Z'

In the autumn of 1941, the British Prime Minister Winston Churchill advocated sending a small force of capital ships to Singapore to make a show of strength and, it was hoped, to deter any Japanese attack. Two major ships were chosen: the battle-cruiser *Repulse*, which had been completed as long ago as 1916, and the battleship *Prince of Wales*, completed only in 1941.

The two vessels, escorted by destroyers, were to have been accompanied by the new aircraft-carrier *Indomitable*, but she had run aground during her trials in the West

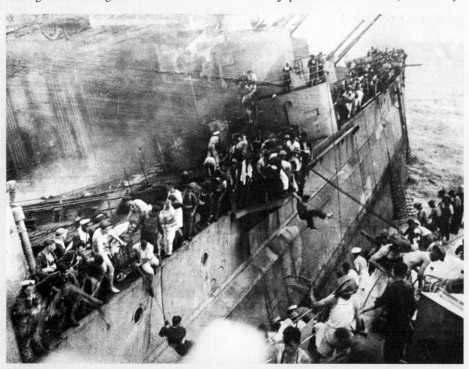

Indies and was undergoing repairs. 'Force Z' was nevertheless ordered to Singapore.

Repulse, commanded by Captain William Tennant, who had been Senior Naval Officer ashore during the evacuation of Dunkirk, and *Prince of Wales*, under Captain John Leach, together with four destroyers, sailed into Keppel Harbour on 2 December. On 8 December the Japanese invaded Malaya.

Vice-Admiral Sir Tom Phillips, the Commander of the British Eastern Fleet, decided to dispatch 'Force Z' north to strike at enemy ships as they landed troops on the east coast. On the night of 8 December, therefore, the great ships and their escorts headed toward Singora. This plan was perilous without air cover.

The following day, thick cloud obscured the position of the ships but, early in the evening, the weather cleared and they were spotted by a patrolling Japanese aircraft.

The element of surprise, on which Tom Phillips had counted, was lost; without air cover he was obliged to return to safety.

Shortly after this, Phillips received information that the Japanese were landing at Kuantan, farther south. He altered course but found no Japanese ships; unknown to him, however, his vessels had been spotted by an enemy submarine. Phillips then probed north again to investigate some barges that had been sighted earlier. Finding nothing, he once more turned south.

But Japanese naval aircraft, alerted by their submarine, soon appeared in the sky. The bombers went first for *Repulse*, which sustained a direct hit. Then, 20 minutes later, a second formation assaulted *Prince of Wales* with both bombs and torpedoes, and further formations arrived.

After about an hour and a half of bombardment, *Repulse* went to the bottom; less than an hour later, *Prince of Wales* followed her. Many sailors were taken off by the escorting destroyers, but Phillips and Leach went down with *Prince of Wales*. The Japanese bombers, now dangerously low on fuel, turned homeward.

This was the first time capital ships had been sunk at sea by air attack alone. The Japanese had demonstrated a terrible lesson of modern warfare: even a capital ship, no matter how strongly armoured and heavily armed, was so vulnerable to air attack if not accompanied by an aircraft-carrier as to be almost a sitting target.

Chinese guerrilla forces

One of the major mistakes of Yamashita's opponents was not to mobilize the highly motivated Malayan Chinese against the Japanese in sufficient time or number, either for conventional or guerrilla operations. Lieutenant-Colonel John Dalley of the Federated Malay States Police Force had suggested creating a guerrilla network in 1940, but not until mid-December 1941, after the Japanese had invaded, was he asked to do so.

His force of 200 men, with British officers, started training at Number 101 Special Training School in Johore in mid-January 1942. By the time of the Battle of Singapore, 'Dalforce' numbered 4,000 guerillas, who operated on Singapore Island. These men were used, often in company detachments, to patrol mangrove swamps where landings might be made; two of the four companies supported the Australians. They were chronically short of weapons, for the small arms intended for 'Dalforce', including light machine-guns, were lost when the liner *Empress of Asia* was sunk by Japanese bombers on 5 February, while on her way from India to Singapore.

After the surrender, the Japanese made 'Dalforce' the excuse for their savage treatment of the Chinese population, but this behaviour was instigated by the military police rather than by Yamashita.

Many of the Chinese were Communists, and they continued to operate on the mainland in guerrilla bands, sometimes under the leadership of British or Australian soldiers who had been left behind, and using abandoned equipment. Eventually they became the nucleus of the Malayan People's Anti-Japanese Army, which was 7,000 strong in 1945. This in turn became the anti-British Malayan Revolutionary Liberation Army of the 1948–60 guerrilla war that precipitated the granting of independence to Malaya.

The Japanese were now thrusting southeast between Bukit Timah and the MacRitchie Reservoir, on which the city of Singapore depended for its water supply, and which had been Yamashita's target all along. Meanwhile, they had repaired the causeway across the Johore Strait, which had been demolished by the Australians, and units of the Japanese Imperial Guards were nearing the village of Nee Soon in the north of the island.

Yamashita tried to secure an early end to the campaign on the evening of 11

British and Indian officers, *left*, pause on the verandah of a Chinese house to check their position during British exercises in Malaya. The Chinese played only a minor part in the defence of Singapore, as this picture of a roof-watcher shows, *below*. They could have been mobilized to much greater effect.

continue to inflict maximum damage on enemy for as long as possible by house-to-house fighting if necessary.' Wavell reported this exchange to Churchill who, though earlier so demanding of fighting to the finish, wished to spare useless loss of life. He later wrote: '... when it was certain that all was lost at Singapore I was sure it would be wrong to enforce needless slaughter, and without hope of victory to inflict the horrors of street fighting on the vast city, with its teeming, helpless, and now panic-stricken population.' He signalled to Wavell: 'You are of course sole judge of the moment when no further result can be gained at Singapore, and should instruct Percival accordingly.'

February by having a communiqué air-dropped in a message tube on the outskirts of Singapore city. It began, 'In the spirit of chivalry we have the honour of advising your surrender ...'; Percival sent no reply.

On 12 February, 3rd Corps was obliged to withdraw to a line holding the Seletar and Peirce Reservoirs and eastward to the village of Paya Lebar, then swinging south to Kallang airfield on the island's southern shore. By 13 February the hopelessness of the British position was generally recognized, and plans for evacuating troops by sea to Java were implemented. All who could be of most use in the war – some 3,000 nurses, technicians, and soldiers and officers with special qualifications or experience – were also dispatched in whatever small ships and vessels were available. Most fell victim to Japanese warships and aircraft or were captured.

Meanwhile, in the city of Singapore itself all was turmoil and despair. It was

now within Japanese artillery range and corpses littered the streets. Over the city hung a cloud of dark smoke, augmented by repeated detonations as the fixed guns of the defences, bombs and aircraft fuel were destroyed. The great naval base itself was largely blown up.

Over all hung the terrible spectre of water shortage. The Japanese had captured all the reservoirs that fed the city and could now either cut off supplies or pollute them. Surrender was thus inevitable. On 13 February, Percival signalled to Wavell: 'Enemy now within 5,000 yards of sea-front, which brings whole of Singapore town within field artillery range ... In opinion of commanders troops already committed are too exhausted either to withstand strong attack or to launch counter-attack . . . it is unlikely that resistance can last more than a day or two.'

The following day, 14 February, General Wavell signalled back: 'You must

At this, Wavell signalled Percival: 'When you are fully satisfied that this [fighting] is no longer possible I give you discretion to cease resistance.'

On the morning of 15 February, the Japanese commander toured the Alexandra Hospital to apologise for the illegal massacre of patients and staff the day before, opening tinned peaches with a bayonet and handing them out himself. Yamashita's field guns were down to 100 rounds of the 1,000 apiece with which they had begun the battle, and British fire was still intense. But Percival also had ammunition shortages, and his commanders unanimously opposed any attempt to recapture the reservoirs.

At 18.10 the same day, Percival surrendered to Yamashita, who asked through his American-educated interpreter: 'Does the British Army surrender unconditionally?' and received the brief answer 'Yes'. When Percival asked for 24 hours' grace

Battle of Singapore/4

Before attempting to cross the Johore Strait to the island of Singapore, Yamashita made a feint to mislead the enemy by landing in the east on Pulau Ubin Island. He quickly occupied it during the night of 7 February; artillery was then brought over to shell Changi fortress on the extreme easterly point of Singapore Island.

Nearly 450 Japanese guns opened fire on the British defences before the main crossing of Johore Strait (2) began. Fire was laid along the entire north and northwest coast to confuse the British as to the planned landing sites. Much damage was done. Many machine-gun positions were destroyed, together with pillboxes and wire defences, but undamaged machine-guns (8) cost the Japanese heavy casualties when the first units landed.

On the night of 8/9 February, units of the Japanese 5th and 18th divisions assembled in their landing craft. These had been hidden in the dense cover of the rubber plantations and were brought to the water's edge only at the last moment. The causeway (6) linking Singapore Island with the mainland had been partially destroyed by the retreating British.

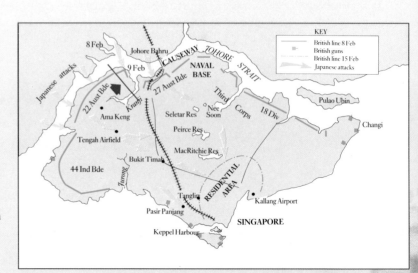

The crossing of Johore Strait began shortly after 24.00, as soon as all the Japanese troops had been embarked. Each division had 50 motor boats (1) and about 100 collapsible launches (3). The latter, powered by an outboard motor capable of 8 knots, were constructed of plywood sections with connecting rubber joints. Most were about 4.6m/15ft long and could be quickly assembled by one man.

The invading Japanese were stubbornly opposed by men of the heavily outnumbered 22nd Australian Brigade (9), among them A and C Companies of 2nd Battalion. In the first wave, the Japanese threw in some 4,000 men, against whom the Australians could muster no more than 2,500, for they had been badly hit by the artillery barrage. Japanese soldiers were hampered by the muddy shore, broken defences and mangrove roots, but they soon managed to gain a foothold.

Yamashita's HQ in the top of the tower in the Imperial Palace (4) at Johore Bahru overlooked the strait, which was only 549m/600yds wide at that point. He was able to watch the action unfolding before him.

The right wing of 5th Division (5) landed near the mouth of the Sarimbun River, where many small islands (7) proved a serious impediment.

The Japanese had overwhelming air superiority throughout the Malaya/Singapore campaign. This was of particular advantage when they invaded Singapore Island, for British aircraft had not been able to reconnoitre Japanese assembly points, so they did not know where the blow would fall. Air raids on Singapore city and docks, also, reduced the British will to resist and hampered their counter-attack.

Lieutenant-General Arthur Percival 1887–1966

Within a month of enlisting at the outbreak of World War I, Percival had been commissioned in the infantry, where his personal courage won him an impressive list of decorations, notably the Distinguished Service Order, the Military Cross and the *Croix de Guerre*.

In 1923 he enrolled at Camberley Staff College and quickly distinguished himself. Promotion came rapidly, and in 1939, while serving with 1st Corps in France, he became a major-general. During 1936–7 he had been Chief of Staff in Malaya and, partly for this reason, he was promoted to acting lieutenant-general and appointed GOC Malaya in April 1941, when it was clear that a Japanese invasion threatened.

Percival, a tall, slight man, was an outstanding staff officer; but his personality seemed, except to those who knew him intimately, uninspiring. Most of the soldiers who served under him in Malaya did not even know what he looked like – a fatal flaw in a commander. Percival was at a great disadvantage

during the Malayan campaign. He was appointed too late to have had time to grasp the situation thoroughly and make a personal impact on his subordinates; he was heavily outnumbered, both at sea and in the air; he was deluded by his staff into assuming that jungles and mangrove swamps were impenetrable to the enemy, and his communications systems were so inadequate that often

the best, indeed only, means of transmitting orders to the front was by rail. Worst of all, Percival had no experience of field command above a 1918 battalion. He could commit his plans clearly and concisely to paper but could not adapt them on the field when changing conditions disrupted them.

Despite his difficulties, history has not dealt either kindly or justly with Percival. Given the situation in Malaya, it is improbable that any other commander could have averted the disaster. But it remains a curious paradox of military history that of the two greatest disasters to befall British troops in World War II – Dunkirk and Singapore – one was considered heroic, the other ignominious.

Percival was released from captivity, emaciated but mentally unimpaired, at the end of the war and, at General MacArthur's special invitation, was on board the USS *Missouri* in Tokyo Harbour to watch the Japanese sign the instrument of surrender.

before signing the document, Yamashita agreed – but with a cruel proviso: 'Then, in that case,' he said, 'up to tomorrow morning we will continue the attack. Is that all right, or do you consent immediately to unconditional surrender?' He received the same answer – 'Yes'.

Percival and his troops went into barbaric captivity, but it was typical of Yamashita's practicality and restraint that only a small detachment of Japanese troops was sent into Singapore, although Yamashita himself tellingly drove down the roads lined by the conquered army. On 17 February he ordered: 'The Army will not hold a celebration. Instead of a triumphal entry ceremony, a ceremonial commemoration service for the dead will be solemnized on 20 February . . .'.

The Japanese had taken roughly 80,000 prisoners, half of whom were British or Australian, together with some 750 guns and 65,000 small arms, thousands of locomotives and motor vehicles and 10 light aircraft. They themselves had lost more than 30 tanks and perhaps 50 aircraft for more than 200 belonging to the RAF. Their total casualties during the campaign were stated by the Japanese to be 3,507 officers and men killed and 6,150 wounded. British losses are estimated at roughly three times that number, and in all, about 130,000 people were taken prisoner.

The guns of Singapore

It is still widely believed that the guns of Singapore pointed the wrong way. True, they were sited to defend key installations from sea-borne attack, but they did also fire inland, but their effect was lessened by having mainly armour-piercing ammunition and very few high-explosive shells.

Altogether the two coastal artillery regiments had 13 main and 11 minor batteries. The former mustered five 38cm/15in guns and six 23cm/9.2in guns, manned by the

British. In addition, there were 18 Indian-manned 15cm/6in guns. These crews had no radar but fired on map references.

Landing places, roads, Tengah airfield, Johore Bahru and its railway, Japanese tanks and artillery were all targets. On the last night, 14/15 February 1942, three of the Indian-manned batteries sank an unidentified 8,000-ton ship off Keppel Harbour. The next morning, the guns set on fire 200,000 tons of fuel oil.

During the last days of Singapore, Civil Defence workers, *left*, struggled to control the fires, caused by Japanese bombing, that consumed large areas of the city. Down at the docks, *below*, more volunteers laboured to preserve the community's only remaining way of supply and escape.

The entire campaign, ending in total domination, had taken the Japanese little more than 70 days. Churchill, ever the realist, accounted it 'the worst disaster and largest capitulation in British history.'

The most remarkable aspect of the conquest of Singapore was, however, the treatment of the victor. There had been celebratory paper-lantern processions up and down Japan, but Yamashita, who had hoped to be sent on to invade Australia, or to Burma or India, was not even summoned home to give the traditional personal report he had prepared for the emperor. Instead, he lingered on at Singapore until July, while his troops helped to overrun Sumatra and Burma; then he was ordered back to Manchuria to take command of the First Area Army on the Russian border.

Prime Minister Tojo similarly sidelined Lieutenant-General Shojiro Iida, conqueror of Burma in April 1943, and never re-employed Lieutenant-General Masaharu Homma, victor in the Philippines by May 1942. Tojo was mortally afraid of popular, victorious commanders, and it was not until he fell in 1944, that Yamashita was rescued from his Manchurian exile, to be given the hopeless task of holding the Philippines archipelago in the face of the very kind of naval and air superiority he had enjoyed in Malaya and Singapore. In a fitting full circle, Yamashita emerged from the Philippines jungle to surrender the same day the Royal Navy again dropped anchor at Singapore on 2 September 1945.

Japan at her zenith
Even before the capture of Singapore, the Japanese had been advancing westward against Burma, with the ultimate objective of cutting the 'Burma Road', the route by which provisions and weaponry were sent to Generalissimo Chiang Kai-shek in China.

With the capture of Malaya and Singapore, Japan gained a base for her fleet, southern airfields and – of infinite importance to her war effort – roughly half of the world's total output of rubber and tin. Furthermore, all these gains represented equivalent losses to the Allies. Perhaps the most important gain to Japan, however, was psychological: the belief in Western invincibility was shattered, British prestige brought low. Japan could now claim to be the liberator of eastern Asia from Western domination.

Within six months of Japan's first attack, she had occupied most of Burma, all the Dutch East Indies, the Solomon Islands and the greater part of New Guinea. Moreover, having sunk the *Repulse* and the *Prince of Wales* and sunk or severely damaged every ship in Pearl Harbor, of which there were about 90, Japan had achieved naval supremacy in the Pacific.

Japan's triumph was shortlived, however, for even in the days immediately following her capture of Singapore, her eventual doom might be detected by the farsighted. Two events – one yet to come, the other already past – would ensure this. The British and Indian forces, by a supreme effort of physical and mental will, held the Japanese advance on the borders of India, bringing Japan's westward advance to a halt.

Most important of all, Japan's attack on Pearl Harbor, despite immediate appearances, had been a failure, for she had not achieved what should have been her principal aim: the destruction of American aircraft-carriers. Four US carriers – *Lexington*, *Enterprise*, *Saratoga* and *Yorktown* – together with strong cruiser formations, had all been at sea at the time of Japan's attack and were still operational in the Pacific.

Japan's sole hope of success lay in rapid, overwhelming victory, so inducing American, British and Commonwealth peace overtures. When this was not forthcoming, the Japanese were faced with ever-growing American strength in weapons, aircraft, ships and manpower. In June 1942, having overrun most of the southern and western Pacific, and needing to protect the oil and raw materials she had seized, Japan devised an elaborate plan to ambush and destroy what remained of the US Pacific Fleet at Midway atoll in roughly the centre of the ocean.

In the event, the Japanese were outmanoeuvred and lost four of their aircraft-carriers within the space of 24 hours. The tide of war had turned and the Japanese scarcely won another battle.

Erwin Rommel *1891-1944*

U nbeknown to him, Erwin Rommel was chosen by the July 1944 plotters to be Germany's head of state after they had killed Hitler. And no wonder, for he was the best-known and most charismatic German general of World War II. Unusually for a high-ranking German officer, Rommel came from a solid middle class background rather than the upper class that Prussian military tradition demanded – his father and grandfather were schoolmasters. He first saw action in World War I, during which he distinguished himself, winning both the Iron Cross and the *Pour le Mérite*, Prussia's highest military award.

When Hitler came to power, Rommel believed that he might well prove Germany's saviour, eradicating the ignominy of the Treaty of Versailles after World War I and eliminating the dreaded prospect of a communist government. Rommel's relationship with Hitler was complex. At first he admired him, almost held him in awe, but he was never afraid to speak his mind in Hitler's presence. He was fascinated by the man's hypnotic, messianic personality and the way he always reached decisions by intuition rather than reasoned argument. Most telling of all for Rommel was Hitler's phenomenal memory, which enabled him, at will, to reel off a mass of statistics pertaining to the whole spectrum of government and the German war machine.

In 1940, Rommel was appointed to command 7th Panzer Division, which he led to spectacular success during the invasion of France. Dr. Goebbels's propaganda ministry turned him into a national hero, and his later appointment to command of the Afrika Korps made him an instantly recognizable figure of world renown. Even his enemies in North Africa demonstrated their respect by dubbing him 'The Desert Fox'.

The officers and men of the Afrika Korps idolized Rommel, despite his being difficult to work with. He was by nature impatient and insisted on his orders being obeyed without question. Sometimes he was insensitive in his criticism of subordinates, but he was always generous in his praise of those who served him well. In battle, wishing to oversee everything, he concerned himself with details, which are not the proper province of a commander. On the other hand, he was fearless, and masterly at handling his troops. One of his greatest achievements was to weld the Afrika Korps into a confident, proud unit with its own special identity.

In 1943, Rommel was appointed to inspect German coastal defences along the Atlantic Wall; then, early in 1944, he was given command of Army Group B – all German forces from the Netherlands to the Loire – under Field Marshal Gerd von Rundstedt, Commander-in-Chief West. Rommel's blunt reports of the deficiencies of the western defences were not what Hitler wanted to hear, and he became increasingly impatient with his 'favourite general'.

As the war continued, many of the top commanders, Rommel included, became convinced that Germany should seek peace with the Allies. Then, on 20 July 1944, an abortive bid was made to assassinate Hitler with a bomb placed in his eastern headquarters. General Otto von Stülpnagel, who was deeply implicated in the plot, while under anaesthetic after a failed suicide attempt, mentioned Rommel's name. Coupled with further hints, innuendoes and misquoted or invented conversations, this falsely incriminated Rommel in Hitler's deeply suspicious mind. On 14 October, Rommel, who was convalescing after being severely wounded in an RAF attack in Normandy in July, was given the option of being tried before a people's court, with terrible consequences for his family if he were found guilty (as was certain), or of committing suicide, in which case his family would be spared. Rommel chose the latter option; he was driven to a lonely wooded spot, took the poison provided for him and died almost instantly.

Desert victor: General Erwin Rommel on the road to Cairo.
The palmtree and swastika, badge of the Deutsches Afrika Korps.

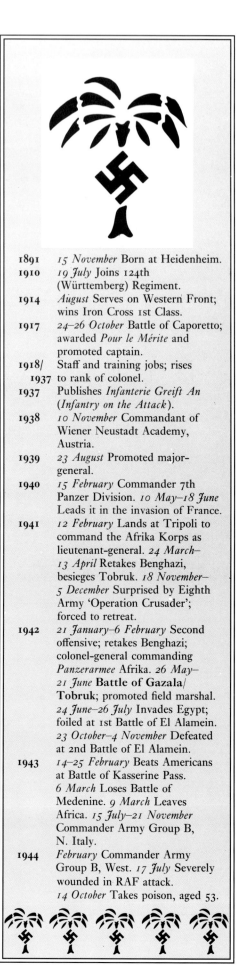

1891	*15 November* Born at Heidenheim.
1910	*19 July* Joins 124th (Württemberg) Regiment.
1914	*August* Serves on Western Front; wins Iron Cross 1st Class.
1917	*24–26 October* Battle of Caporetto; awarded *Pour le Mérite* and promoted captain.
1918/ 1937	Staff and training jobs; rises to rank of colonel.
1937	Publishes *Infanterie Greift An* (*Infantry on the Attack*).
1938	*10 November* Commandant of Wiener Neustadt Academy, Austria.
1939	*23 August* Promoted major-general.
1940	*15 February* Commander 7th Panzer Division. *10 May–18 June* Leads it in the invasion of France.
1941	*12 February* Lands at Tripoli to command the Afrika Korps as lieutenant-general. *24 March– 13 April* Retakes Benghazi, besieges Tobruk. *18 November– 5 December* Surprised by Eighth Army 'Operation Crusader'; forced to retreat.
1942	*21 January–6 February* Second offensive; retakes Benghazi; colonel-general commanding *Panzerarmee Afrika*. *26 May– 21 June* **Battle of Gazala/ Tobruk**; promoted field marshal. *24 June–26 July* Invades Egypt; foiled at 1st Battle of El Alamein. *23 October–4 November* Defeated at 2nd Battle of El Alamein.
1943	*14–25 February* Beats Americans at Battle of Kasserine Pass. *6 March* Loses Battle of Medenine. *9 March* Leaves Africa. *15 July–21 November* Commander Army Group B, N. Italy.
1944	*February* Commander Army Group B, West. *17 July* Severely wounded in RAF attack. *14 October* Takes poison, aged 53.

Battle of Gazala/*26 May–22 June 1942*

ALTHOUGH MAJOR-GENERAL Neil Ritchie, Commander of the 125,000-strong British and Commonwealth Eighth Army, and his immediate superior, General Sir Claude Auchinleck, Commander-in-Chief, Middle East, had laid plans to attack Rommel at the Gazala Line west of Tobruk, it was evident by May 1942 that Rommel could pre-empt this strategy. Ritchie therefore deployed his army in a defensive formation.

Ritchie knew that Rommel's object was to capture Tobruk. To frustrate this, he constructed lines of minefields, interspersed with 'boxes' of infantry and artillery, protected by barbed wire and mines. These boxes stretched intermittently from Gazala on the Mediterranean coast to Bir Hacheim, a desert fortress some 64km/40mls south, held by units of the 1st Free French Brigade. A little to the southeast of this was a box held by 3rd Indian Motorized Brigade. These boxes, Ritchie judged, could simultaneously fulfil two functions: they could prevent engineers of Rommel's *Panzerarmee* from clearing the defensive minefields unmolested and provide strongholds that an advancing enemy must first subdue.

Ritchie divided the Gazala Line into two sections. His right flank, from Gazala on the coast to the 'box' at Sidi Muftah, together with South African units in Tobruk itself, were allocated to 13th Corps under Lieutenant-General William Gott. The front from Sidi Muftah to Bir Hacheim, the most southerly point on the Allied line, was entrusted to Lieutenant-General Willoughby Norrie, commanding 30th Corps, who also commanded the tank formations to the rear of the defence line. Behind the Gazala Line, farther east, were more boxes, notably at El Adem.

This militarily orthodox development contained a number of deficiencies, notably Ritchie's expectation that because his troops were firmly entrenched, the fighting would follow the same static pattern as that in World War I. On his right flank he was protected by the sea, but on his left the Gazala Line simply ended, with undefended tracts of desert stretching away to the horizon. And if a path were cleared through the minefields, Axis forces could penetrate his defences.

What would Rommel do? He had under his command the Deutsches Afrika Korps (DAK) – comprising 15th and 21st Panzer Divisions – 90th Light Division, and Ariete and Trieste Divisions of the Italian 20th Corps, as well as four Italian infantry divisions. In all, he had 113,000 troops, his largest-ever force in the desert. Rommel's tank strength was 560 as compared with Ritchie's 994, but only some 167 British tanks were the latest MkIII Grants, the remainder being inferior to German Panzer IIIs and IVs. In the air, the Axis had 704 aircraft to 320 British.

Rommel had two options: he could either attack in the north along the coast and make straight for Tobruk – which the British thought more likely – or he could undertake a long flanking movement, swinging around south of Bir Hacheim and then coming northeast behind the Gazala Line. In the event, he chose the latter option.

Rommel's great enveloping movement, beginning on the night of 26 May, comprised three parallel prongs. The first prong, the Italian 20th Corps, was ordered to move south, then swing northeast to destroy 3rd Indian Motorized Brigade and take Bir Hacheim. Meanwhile, the centre prong, comprising the 15th and 21st Panzer Divisions, would go farther east, then turn northward, to get behind the Allied line. The third prong, 90th Light Division, would make the same movement but in a wider arc, aimed at British 7th Armoured Division near Bir Beuid.

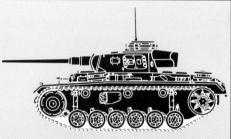

Panzer MkIIIJ
Rommel received 19 of these tanks just prior to his attack at Gazala. They had face-hardened armour and carried a crew of five.
Weight: 22.3 tons; desert speed: 19kmh/12mph; range: 175km/108mls; armament: one long-barrelled 50mm/2in L/60 gun with a 2kg/4½lb shell that could penetrate any British tank and two 7.9mm/0.30in machine-guns.

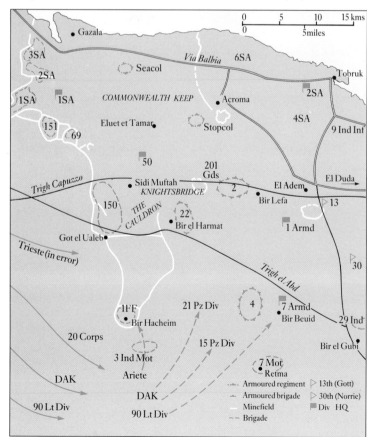

Among the most expert examples of the envelopment of a single flank is Rommel's at the Battle of Gazala. Here the tactic met with complete success, for he had first deceived the British into thinking that he would make for Tobruk – his obvious objective – by the direct route along the coast road. His long drive south enabled him to roll up the British left flank, thereby forcing them into retreat and allowing him to capture Tobruk.

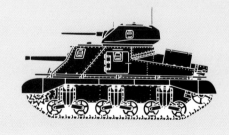

Grant MkIII
In early 1942, the Eighth Army had 242 of these robust American-made tanks, which carried a crew of six. Their chief drawback was that the main gun in a WWI-style sponson had limited traverse.
Weight: 26.75 tons; desert speed: 16kmh/10mph; range: 193km/120mls; armament: one 75mm/3in gun with 6.3kg/14lb shells, up to four 7.9mm/0.30in machine-guns.

Prelude to Gazala

To restore his military credibility after his abortive attack on France in June 1940, the Italian dictator Mussolini resolved to over-run British-held Egypt from his North African colonies. Marshal Graziani launched his attack on 13 September with some 236,000 men, 1,800 guns, 340 tanks and 150 combat-ready aircraft. Against this was arrayed General Archibald Wavell's small contingent of about 36,000 men.

Within three days the Italians had taken Sidi Barrani. Reinforced by three tank battalions from the Home Forces, Wavell counter-attacked in December. The British covered the 900km/560mls to Benghazi in eight weeks, capturing 130,000 prisoners.

Hitler, appalled at this reverse to his ally, early in 1941 authorized the despatch of Panzer formations to Libya, under the command of Lieutenant-General Erwin Rommel, who had led 7th Panzer Division during the blitzkrieg on France. Rommel at once took operational command.

The ensuing campaigns did not achieve a decisive victory for either side, and the desert 'frontier' shifted back and forth for more than two years. In May 1942, Rommel's 15th and 21st Panzer Divisions, 90th Light Division and two divisions of the Italian 20th Corps were drawn up opposite the so-called Gazala Line, running north-south a little to the west of Tobruk. Rommel knew that the British Eighth Army's reinforcements heralded an offensive; he also knew that Hitler was now preoccupied with the war in Russia. These two facts rightly led him to believe that this was his last chance to take Cairo and the Suez Canal; failure now would mean the expulsion of the Axis from North Africa.

In mid-afternoon on 26 May, armoured cars of Eighth Army reported sighting massed German transport, including Panzer formations, on the move. This crucial information never reached 30th Corps because a wireless watch had not been ordered. Ritchie himself, stationed at Gambut to the rear, remained ignorant of Rommel's movements. Eighth Army, therefore, did not move, although around midnight Rommel and his Panzers were already level with Bir Hacheim, ready to begin their encircling manoeuvre.

Early on the morning of 27 May, however, 7th Motorized Brigade, in the incomplete Retma box, had a brutal awakening. At about 08.00, the full weight of the thrust by 90th Light Division bore down upon the box and swept it aside. At almost the same time, Ariete Division knocked out 3rd Indian Motorized Brigade. Rommel's next objective, as he drove at speed up the eastern side of the Gazala Line, was 4th Armoured Brigade. Ritchie now belatedly realized where the main assault was coming from.

It was too late for Allied motorized

A Panzer MkIII tank, *left*, equipped with a 55mm gun.

Rommel, shown here with Major-General von Bismarck (left) and Colonel Fritz Bayerlein, made his battle plans up at the front: one of his great strengths as a commander.

The crew of this Grant MkIII, *left*, are well protected against the dust – a hazard to both men and their equipment.

units to concentrate in force. The 15th Panzer Division smashed into 4th Armoured Brigade while it was still off balance and destroyed many of its tanks. Furthermore, 7th Armoured Divisional HQ was silenced and its commander, Major-General Frank Messervy, temporarily taken prisoner; so Norrie in the north had only an outline knowledge of the disaster that had occurred. However, as a precautionary measure, he moved his HQ east to El Adem and sent 22nd Armoured Brigade south in support of Messervy.

As so often, Rommel was too fast for his

Battle of Gazala/2

Rommel, having turned the enemy's left flank, thrust north across the hot, featureless desert. But as he advanced, so his supply lines lengthened because he had not succeeded in taking Bir Hacheim, the 'box' manned by 1st Free French Brigade, in the extreme south of the Allied line. He determined, therefore, to break through the British minefields in the centre of the Gazala Line from the east, since by doing so he would more than halve the length of his own supply lines. Between him and his base in the west lay the box manned by the British 105th Infantry Brigade. Rommel unleashed his attack on it on the morning of 31 May 1942.

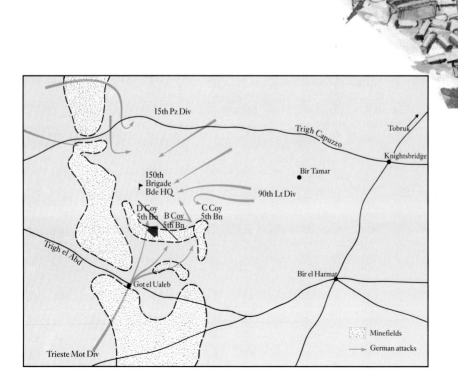

In the desert there are no natural defensive features, so each of the 1.6km/1ml square 'boxes' along the Gazala Line had been turned into a veritable castle, with minefields and barbed wire protecting its perimeter. Each box was supplied with ammunition, stores, food and water to withstand several days' siege.

The all-arms garrison of 150th Brigade box in 'The Cauldron' was made up of two battalions of the Green Howards and one from the East Yorkshire Regiment – tough and determined men from the mining and ship-building towns of northeastern England. They were supported by tanks and men from 1st Army Tank Brigade.

Inside the box, each company of about 100 men formed a further self-contained defensive area, with Matilda I tanks (2) and guns of all types. This area, too, was surrounded by mines, and more barbed wire, and sandbags protected trenches and gun pits.

After three days of bombing and shelling, on the morning of 1 June, only 13 British tanks were still serviceable; there were six 140mm/5$\frac{1}{2}$in guns left, with 20 rounds each, and twelve 25-pounders (7) with less than 100 rounds between them. Most of the 2-pounder anti-tank guns and the new 6-pounders (6) had been destroyed.

In scorching heat and stifling dust thrown up by mortar and artillery fire, Rommel's attack was closing in on the last of the defenders: B and C Companies of the Green Howards. German Panzer III tanks (1) took part in the attack, and half-tracks and armoured cars (4) crammed with soldiers brought up troops for the final onslaught. German infantrymen quickly found paths through the minefields and advanced on the few machine-gun positions still in operation. At one point, Rommel himself (5) led a platoon of panzer grenadiers into the attack.

Knocked-out guns and tanks, piles of spent shell cases, dead and wounded lay everywhere, but the British remained in their well-camouflaged and skilfully sited positions. Rommel's men had to battle for each separate gun, trench and dugout. Fierce hand-to-hand fighting took place with hand-grenades, rifles and bayonets (3).

The final post was eventually overrun at about 14.00, and Rommel himself called on the whole of 150th Brigade to surrender. The Germans took 3,000 prisoners, 101 tanks and armoured cars and 124 guns of all types, as well as small arms and equipment.

The men of 150th Brigade proved a stubborn enemy. Always generous in his praise of a valiant adversary, Rommel later wrote that his troops had had to fight their way 'against the toughest British resistance imaginable. The defence was conducted with considerable skill and, as usual, the British fought to the last round.'

Desert conditions were appalling: just before the capture of 150th Brigade box, Rommel's men were down to half a cup of water a day. When troops came across a well, *top*, they relished the chance to wash off the sweat and grime, but even so they were frugal with the precious water. Added to the natural hardships – scorching sun, cold nights, sand storms, lack of water – was the hazard of vast mine 'marshes' laid by the Allies all along the Gazala Line. This DAK man, *right*, has dug away the sand to reveal a British plate mine.

enemies. He drove into 22nd Armoured Brigade before it was fully prepared and forced it back to the Sidi Muftah-Knightsbridge area, where the 150th Infantry Brigade box guarded two important east-west desert tracks – Trigh Capuzzo and Trigh el Abd.

Until this juncture, all had gone as Rommel planned; now, however, difficulties began to accumulate. Allied tank crews fought ferociously and were shortly reinforced by other armoured units, and problems of supply – notably fuel – were beginning to tell. Despite this, Rommel determined on a further advance when, by the evening of 28 May, his tanks were refuelled and regrouped. But he could not now capture Tobruk by a direct thrust, so he adjusted his tactics.

Rommel had erred in not ensuring the early capture of Bir Hacheim. This meant not only that his supply lines were by now extremely long but that they constantly increased as he advanced. He therefore decided to penetrate the British minefields in the centre of the Gazala Line from the east, so greatly reducing the distance to his supply bases. By early evening on 31 May, he had completed the exercise and was in

the minefields, with tracks cleared. While Ritchie believed Rommel to be trapped, he crushed 150th Brigade box near Sidi Muftah on 1 June and gained control of the key central sections of the Gazala Line.

Rommel remained unmolested in this bridgehead – dubbed 'The Cauldron' – while he reorganized his army for another attempt on Tobruk. The Allies could not agree on what move to make. Ritchie, after interminable debates with his subordinate commanders, finally resolved to attack Rommel in The Cauldron. But the major attack was not mounted until early on 5 June, by which time Rommel's dispositions were complete.

First to go in were the infantry, 10th Indian Brigade, who initially made good progress. This advance was squandered by 22nd Armoured Group's slowness in coming to their support. By the time they did, the infantry had been checked with heavy loss, and the tanks, which overtook the infantry, came under such intense fire from *Panzerarmee* artillery and massed anti-tank guns that they, too, retreated.

Eighth Army losses were cripplingly heavy, and the attack, after brave but futile attempts to break through, petered out. In

two days, Ritchie lost more than 150 tanks, nearly 100 field guns, 36 anti-tank guns and virtually all of 10th Indian Brigade, together with some 3,000 Axis prisoners. Rommel's losses are not precisely known but appear to have been light. On the same day, he launched his counter-attack; 21st Panzer and Ariete thrust east, while in the south 15th Panzer moved northeast. Everywhere they made sustained progress.

Only one impediment still remained to Rommel's renewed thrust toward Tobruk: the Free French garrison at Bir Hacheim in the extreme south. The box had already been assailed for 10 days but was now attacked by every unit that Rommel could spare from The Cauldron. Bombardment greatly intensified, and the Luftwaffe, though repeatedly attacked by the RAF, also turned its full power on the French. By 10 June the RAF had lost 75 aircraft and the Axis nearly 60.

Ritchie, seeing the hopelessness of the French position, gave Bir Hacheim's commander, General M.P. Koenig, permission for the garrison to break out on the night of 10/11 June. Rommel, though his army was depleted and exhausted, now indisputably held the initiative, for he was master of the southern half of the Gazala Line. Ritchie had little option but to pull his left flank back to the Trigh Capuzzo, so creating a defensive line running parallel with the sea from the Gazala Line to El Adem.

This line was attacked by Rommel on 11 June. By nightfall, his 123 tanks were across the Trigh Capuzzo east of El Adem: South African and other troops holding the Gazala Line in the north faced either encirclement or retreat along the Via Balbia, running close to the Mediterranean shore. The Gazala garrison was, therefore, hastily withdrawn to Tobruk.

The British had now to decide whether to evacuate Tobruk or abandon it to siege. Once again the wrong order was given: hold Tobruk. The consequence was that, while the bulk of what remained of Eighth Army escaped eastward to the Egyptian frontier, Tobruk was encircled by Rommel on 18 June. On the morning of the 21st, a white flag was hoisted over the garrison's H.Q. Ritchie laid desperate plans to hold Rommel at Mersa Matruh, but his dispositions were as unimaginative as those at Gazala, and on 25 June General Auchinlek relieved him of his command.

Since the fighting began on 27 May, Rommel had taken 45,000 prisoners and had reached the last Allied defensive position before Cairo and the Suez Canal – a line from the impassable Quattara Depression in the south to a small railway junction called El Alamein on the coast.

General Ritchie was much criticised for his handling of Eighth Army during the Battle of Gazala. Shortly after the disastrous outcome, he was relieved of his command by General Sir Claude Auchinleck, C-in-C, Middle East – the man who had insisted on appointing him in November 1941.

Certainly, Ritchie, as a reliable staff officer, lacked experience of high command (both Gott and Norrie, his corps commanders, were superior in rank and experience). He was, therefore, trapped between his inexperience and the presence in Cairo of his C-in-C who, becoming alarmed at the battle's progress, bombarded him with suggestions. Ritchie had, too, been unable to impose his authority and personality on Eighth Army. All this resulted in Ritchie conducting the battle

Major-General Neil Ritchie 1887–1983

General Sir Claude Auchinleck 1884–1981

as if by committee: he sought the opinions of those above and below him and then resorted to lengthy discussions at different HQs as to the course to follow. Rommel, on the other hand, made his decisions quickly and alone,

up at the front with his spearhead.

It is, perhaps, fair to say that the cause of the Gazala débâcle lay more with Auchinleck's choice of Ritchie than with the man himself. He was personally brave, meticulous and frank; he was, however, slow to make up his mind and totally lacked imagination. Though he conducted the battle in a way that might have earned the plaudits of the academic military strategist, this was his greatest weakness because he was pitted against a commander who always was ready to improvise and adapt and who disregarded textbook rules.

Ritchie continued to serve throughout World War II, and in 1944–5 his abilities were demonstrated to full effect as a corps commander in General Sir Miles Dempsey's Second Army in northwest Europe.

Turn of the tide
Immediately Hitler heard of the fall of Tobruk, he promoted Rommel to field marshal – at 50 the youngest in the German Army; Germany was exultant.

On the other side, the retreat to El Alamein, a mere 113km/70mls from Alexandria, demoralized the British. Churchill decided to make the journey to the desert front to appraise the situation for himself; he was dismayed at the seriousness of the crisis and the low morale of the troops, even though Rommel had been fought to a stalemate in July at the First Battle of El Alamein.

On 18 August, Auchinleck was relieved of his command and replaced by General Sir Harold Alexander; command of the Eighth Army was given to Lieutenant-General Bernard Montgomery. The Eighth Army itself was heavily resupplied, and the two new commanders quickly re-established its morale and confidence. Soon Alexander and Montgomery were able to execute Churchill's original order: 'To take or destroy the German-Italian Army.'

Rommel at Tobruk, above left. *Hitler presenting Rommel with his field marshal's insignia in September 1942*, right.

The Eighth Army inflicted a crushing defeat on Rommel at the Second Battle of El Alamein (23 October–4 November) and drove him back along the coast to Tripoli, which they reached on 23 January 1943. Rommel was now trapped between the Eighth Army in the east and an Allied force, under Lieutenant-General Dwight D. Eisenhower, which had recently landed in French North Africa to his west.

Rommel pleaded vainly for the evacuation of North Africa. On 10 March, he again put the case to Hitler at his HQ in the Ukraine; again he was refused. Ill and suffering great mental fatigue, Rommel was sent on sick leave. On 5 May, the last Axis troops surrendered, and the way was open for an Allied invasion of first Sicily and then the Italian mainland.

Erich von Manstein *1887-1973*

Born Erich von Lewinski, of Polish extraction, von Manstein was adopted by his mother's sister and her husband, General von Manstein, and took their family name. He passed out of the Cadet Corps in 1906 and later saw service during World War I, notably at Verdun and the Battle of the Somme. After the war he held various staff appointments and on the outbreak of World War II in 1939 was made Chief of Staff to von Rundstedt's Army Group A in the Polish campaign.

The military historian Basil Liddell Hart has described Erich von Manstein as 'the Allies' most formidable military opponent, a man who combined modern ideas of manoeuvre, a mastery of technical detail, and great driving power.' He first came to prominence in the late autumn of 1939 when Hitler called for plans for the attack on the Low Countries and France. The most favoured plan was essentially the same as that employed in 1914 – a powerful thrust through the Low Countries that could then turn southwest to envelop Paris. But von Manstein had devised his own plan, which entailed the Germans making an unexpected principal thrust through the Ardennes, a heavily wooded, mountainous region of Belgium, generally regarded as impenetrable by armour.

Von Manstein's repeated advocacy of this strategy irritated his superiors, and in January 1940 he was appointed commanding general of 38th Infantry Corps, stationed in the German interior. Although this was promotion, it was clearly designed to remove a troublemaker from the centre of strategic planning. However, some of von Manstein's associates arranged for him to talk personally to Hitler in Berlin on 17 February 1940. Von Manstein later wrote that Hitler 'was surprisingly quick to grasp the points . . . and he entirely agreed with what I had to say.' His plan was adopted, with the results known to history: France fell within seven weeks, and the British Expeditionary Force was driven from Europe by way of Dunkirk. Paradoxically, von Manstein's own corps played only a secondary role in the campaign.

The German invasion of the USSR in 1941 gave von Manstein what he most craved: command of a panzer corps. Later, commanding Eleventh Army, he successfully broke into the Crimea, and in the summer of 1942 captured the great Soviet bastion and port of Sevastopol. For this he was promoted field marshal.

Von Manstein is mainly renowned for these two great strategic exploits, but his military genius was given its greatest scope after the German disaster at Stalingrad. With Paulus's surrender of the Sixth Army, there was real danger of a general collapse on the German southern flank. Von Manstein's great hour had come: by his inspired and immaculately executed flank counterstroke, he recaptured Kharkov and threw back the Soviet advance in disarray. But in the huge tank battle at Kursk shortly afterward, von Manstein was beaten by sheer weight of Soviet numbers. Thereafter, all he could do was to fight well-executed withdrawals – always hampered by Hitler's orders never to give ground.

Von Manstein was among the extremely few German commanders who were prepared to confront the Führer, put their views and refuse to be browbeaten. Others, more sycophantic, were amazed by his outspokenness. But by the spring of 1944, Hitler had tired of his brilliant but troublesome field marshal, and von Manstein was retired - though with more civility than Hitler usually showed when relieving generals of their command. On 24 February 1950, von Manstein was sentenced by a British war crimes court to 18 years imprisonment, later commuted to 12 years. He was, in fact, released on 6 May 1953.

Erich von Manstein appears in this photograph as a colonel-general, wearing the Iron Cross and the ribbon with crossed swords and oakleaves of the Knight's Cross. He was promoted to field marshal by Hitler on 4 July, after Sevastopol fell to the Germans. The Tiger MkI heavy tank, used for the first time in the Battle of Kharkov, was a powerful and efficient weapon.

1887	*24 November* Born at Berlin.
1906	Enters 3rd Guards Regiment.
1914/ 1918	First lieutenant and regimental adjutant; sees action before going to War Academy. Staff posts.
1927	Promoted major.
1933	Promoted colonel.
1935	Head of Operations Department of the General Staff.
1937	Major-General and Deputy Chief of the General Staff.
1938	Commands 18th Division at Leignitz.
1939	*August* Chief of Staff to C-in-C East. *October* Chief of Staff to von Rundstedt's Army Group A.
1940	*24 February* The 'Manstein Plan' adopted, but he is removed to command 38th Infantry Corps. *June* Promoted general.
1941	*22 June–12 September* Leads 56th Panzer Corps in invasion of North Russia. *13 September* Takes command of Eleventh Army. *26–30 October* Invades Crimea; start of the siege of Sevastopol.
1942	*15 January* As colonel-general retakes Feodosia. *8–18 May* Retakes Kerch Peninsula. *7 June– 4 July* Captures Sevastopol; promoted field marshal. *27 November* given Army Group Don with brief to relieve Stalingrad. *12–23 December* Relief drive fails.
1943	*20 February–18 March* **Third Battle of Kharkov.** *4–17 July* Battle of Kursk. *14 September– December* Retreats behind and loses line of the Dnieper River.
1944	*4 January* Fails to get withdrawals approved by Hitler, but *6–17 February* evacuates Korsun pocket. *23 March–1 April* Extricates First Panzer Army. *31 March* Dismissed by Hitler.
1950	Sentenced to 18 years imprisonment on two charges of war crimes.
1953	*6 May* Released from prison.
1959	Publishes his memoirs, *Lost Victories.*
1973	*10 June* Dies at Irschenhausen, West Germany, aged 85.

Third Battle of Kharkov/*20 February–18 March 1943*

FIELD MARSHAL ERICH von Manstein was appointed Commander of the newly redesignated Army Group South on 14 February 1943; he found the German position on the southern front alarming in the extreme. Not least of his problems was the great disparity in numbers and resources between the opposing armies.

On 23 January, along the whole 700km/435ml front from the Sea of Azov in the south to Kharkov in the north, there were just 495 German tanks to 5,000 Russian. In March, von Manstein himself estimated that he had only 32 divisions in Army Group South; against this, the Russians could deploy 341 formations, including armoured brigades and rifle divisions. Although Russian formations, in general, comprised fewer fighting men than did the German, the ratio was about seven to one in Russia's favour, and her lines of communication were much shorter.

In these circumstances, von Manstein concluded that the battle on the southern front in the winter of 1942–3 would be a decisive one. The result would depend on whether the Russians managed to trap the German forces against the Black Sea and the Sea of Azov, or whether the Germans could prevent such a deadly envelopment.

To the Russians their most promising strategy was obvious. Much of the Axis force in the south comprised Romanian, Italian and Hungarian armies, infinitely inferior to German formations. If these, sited between the Russian South-West Front, or Army Group, (under General Nikolai Vatutin) and the Voronezh Front

(commanded by General Filipp Golikov), could be broken by westward thrusts, then the German south wing might be cut off and boxed in on the coast.

In response, von Manstein was intent on making a strategic withdrawal; that is, retreating but, in doing so, luring the Russians forward in the mistaken belief of a general German retreat, even disintegration. Then, with the power of a coiled spring released, he could hurl the foe back with maximum losses.

On 15 January the Russians on the Voronezh Front mounted a great offensive. The Second Hungarian Army, though more resolute than the Italians and Romanians, was nevertheless swiftly broken, and Russian units drove through the gap formed, which was about 282km/175mls wide. Their onrush was such that by the end of January they had captured Kursk and, to the south of it, had crossed the River Donets below Kharkov.

Although the German Caucasus armies had been successfully withdrawn, von Manstein faced encirclement, for all the indications were that the prongs of the Russian thrust were aimed at Zaporozhe, north of the Sea of Azov. This city was Army Group South's main supply base and also served as von Manstein's HQ.

To order a strategic withdrawal, von Manstein had first to secure Hitler's permission. The Führer's reluctance to

---

Su 76 self-propelled gun

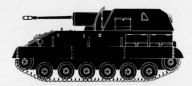

This Russian self-propelled gun, based on a modified T70 tank chassis, was the first to come into service, in December 1942. Its open top and high silhouette did not make it an ideal tank destroyer, indeed its four-man crews nicknamed it the '*Suka*', or bitch, but it was used in large numbers as an assault gun by the infantry.

Weight: 11.2 tons; **road speed:** 44kmh/27mph; **road range:** 265kml/165mls, cross-country range: 160km/100mls; **armament:** one 76.2mm/3in gun.

T70 light tank

The two-man Russian light tank was an upgraded version of the T60 and replaced it as a light reconnaissance tank from March 1942 until production ceased in October 1943; during this time, more than 40 per cent of Soviet tanks were T60s or T70s. It lacked hitting power and cross-country performance when compared with similar German tanks.

Weight: 9.2 tons; **road speed:** 45kmh/28mph; **road range:** 360km/225mls, cross-country range: 180km/112mls; **armament:** one 45mm/1in Model 38 gun, one 7.6mm/0.3in machine-gun.

Tiger MkI heavy tank

A formidable five-man heavy tank, this was used in quantity during Manstein's counter-stroke in the Donets Basin. In March, 2nd SS Panzer Corps employed them at Kharkov; for the first time Russian T34s had met their match, and the effect on the Red Army was demoralizing.

Weight: 56 tons; **road speed:** 37kmh/23mph, cross-country speed: 19kmh/12mph; **road range:** 116km/73mls, cross-country range: 67km/42mls; **armament:** one 88mm/3½in KwK36, two 7.92mm/0.3in MG34 machine-guns.

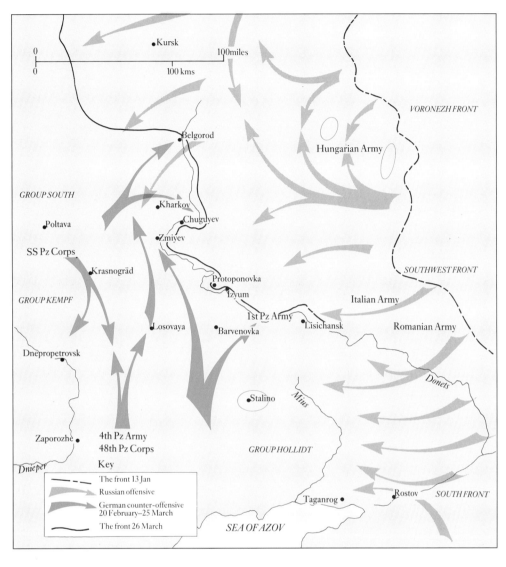

Von Manstein's use of the strategy of feigned retreat during the Kharkov campaign was flawlessly executed and resulted in total success; Wellington too was successful when he employed it at Salamanca. There is, however, a potentially grave danger in this manoeuvre, since it entails inducing the enemy to leave a strong position while retreating to terrain more favourable to oneself. A retreating army can easily panic, unless it is confident, well disciplined, and led by a commander the troops trust.

be right in holding this as a general strategic principle? Most of his commanders in the East, other than von Manstein, feared to disagree with him to his face.

But after the defeat at Stalingrad, Hitler lost interest – albeit briefly – in the Eastern Front. He was preoccupied with events elsewhere, for by February 1943, when the Russians recaptured Kharkov, he was confronted with other reverses and impending problems. In January, Montgomery's Eighth Army had entered Tripoli and the days of the Afrika Korps were numbered; on 9 February, Hitler's Japanese allies had been forced to evacuate Guadalcanal; and now he had to make what preparations he could to prevent an Allied invasion of western Europe.

On 6 February 1943, the Führer visited von Manstein at his headquarters, when the proposed withdrawal was discussed. Hitler was attentive and reasonable; he agreed – or so von Manstein understood – to whatever his commanders in the East thought appropriate, though still viewing

give up any captured territory in the face of counter-attacks was much criticised after the war, notably by defeated German generals. They claimed that the 'little corporal', by his insistence on never retreating and his constant interference with strategic planning, caused calamitous decisions to be taken.

Certainly Hitler, whose sole experience of battle had been during the trench warfare of World War I, was imbued with the concept that every metre of captured ground should be fought for and, if at all possible, held. But there was more to it, for when the German advance had been brought to a halt before Moscow in December 1941, he forbade any retreat at all, despite appeals from his senior commanders. He was proved right, for the line held, despite cruel winter conditions; had he authorized a retreat, even of limited extent, it would almost certainly have degenerated into wholesale flight. He reasoned that his judgement had been proved correct once, so why should he not

Henschel 129 B2 'Tank buster'
This single-seat, specialist ground-attack aircraft came into service with the Luftwaffe from January 1942. It was plagued by the unreliability of its twin, French-made Gnome-Rhône engines and its lack of manoeuvrability. Von Manstein had about 50 Henschels to support his counter-offensive at Kharkov.

Speeds: 417km/253mph and 315kmh/196mph cruising at 9,845ft; range: 690km/429mls; armament: one 30mm/1¼in M103 cannon, two 20mm/⅘in and two 13mm/½in machine-guns; later up-gunned to a 37mm/1½in, then 75mm/3in cannon.

Third Battle of Kharkov/2

The third battle for Kharkov itself took six days. General Hausser launched his attack early on **9 March 1943, and by 11 March men from 2nd SS Panzergrenadier** Regiment had pushed into the centre of the city.

Snow lay in patches, and the Germans (2), armed with rifles and MP40s were still wearing their heavy sheepskin parkas. The Panzer MkIVs (1) advanced slowly up the broad boulevards, with their tramlines (4) and overhead wires, Cratered roads, burning buildings and Russian T34 tanks (6) bore witness to the intense fighting that took place for every street corner.

Russian soldiers, fighting for their city and for their lives, resisted ferociously. Slit trenches, dug in the open squares (5), were manned by machine-gun crews, and the huge blocks of flats and offices, although apparently hardly touched, were largely shells. Devastated internally by three separate bouts of house-to-house fighting, they now provided shelter for deadly Russian snipers (3).

The German panzers eventually took the railway station on 12 March, and on 15 March the fighting ended when the tractor factory was overrun. Kharkov soon became once again a major German supply and communications centre.

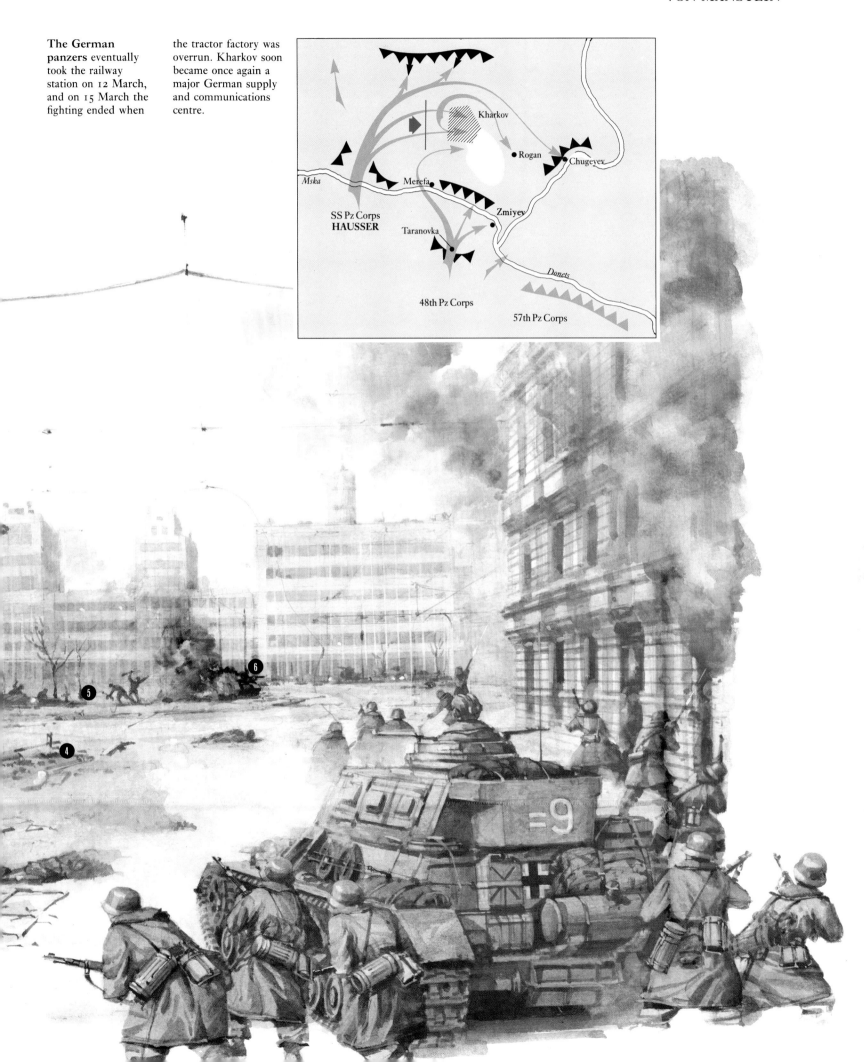

Kharkov

Rogan

Chugeyev

Mska

Merefa

Zmiyev

SS Pz Corps
HAUSSER

Taranovka

Donets

48th Pz Corps

57th Pz Corps

retreat with strong disapproval. Von Manstein could, therefore, put into effect his plans for strategic withdrawal.

Drawn up at his headquarters, they were safe from the Russian 'Lucy ring' – an espionage network that operated through Switzerland and reported direct to Moscow – which normally knew what was happening at Hitler's HQ. Furthermore, the field marshal could count on his subordinates' tactical flexibility and initiative in response to his signals.

Meanwhile, the Russians, certain they had victory within their grasp, were pressing forward at maximum speed. They failed, however, to read the significance of an ominous sign: of the many prisoners they had taken, few were German.

Events now moved quickly. The First Panzer Army had withdrawn from the Caucasus and abandoned Rostov; the army detachment under General Hollidt moved eastward from its positions on the lower Donets and took station on the River Mius; 48th Panzer Corps, under General Kempf, likewise withdrew from the River Donets and moved to positions north of Stalino in the Dombas industrial region.

On 16 February, Army Detachment Kempf, to avoid envelopment from the north at Belgorod, was obliged to abandon Kharkov. The jubilant Russians exploited the wide gap they had opened up between Army Detachment Kempf and formations on the Donets at Izyum. They pushed on through Losovaya, and by 21 February advance Russian tanks reached the River Dnieper, almost within sight of the German main base at Zaporozhe.

Von Manstein, in these seemingly dark days, was content, for the Russians were doing precisely what he had hoped and planned: the farther they advanced, the

Tank battles raged throughout Kharkov. Here two Tiger MkI tanks and a self-propelled Marder gun, *above*, blast their way into the city.

Red square, in the centre of Kharkov, *right*, was in reality a vast circular plaza, ringed by huge buildings. The illusion they give of permanence is belied by the devastated area around them – the result of countless bombing raids and the three battles the ravaged city had endured.

more punishing would be the counter-attack. By retreating, he was, in fact, drawing the over-confident Russians into a potential death pocket, for Army Detachment Kempf was firmly stationed at Krasnograd, and by 21 February Army Detachment Hollidt and First Panzer Army were on the River Mius and to the north of Stalino. The SS Panzer Corps, brought up from France, was also ready, with battalions of the new Tiger tank.

Von Manstein's counter-attack opened on 22 February with about 350 tanks. Five panzer divisions, in a coordinated movement and enjoying massive air support, struck northward at the advancing Russians' left flank. Manstein worked well with his Luftwaffe commander, Colonel-General Baron Wolfram von Richthofen (cousin of the World War I air ace), who had provided close air support to blitzkreig advances from the beginning of

the war. While 48th Panzer Corps struck toward Barvenovka, 17th Panzer Division took Izyum and Protoponovka on the River Donets, and the SS Panzer Corps, thrusting through Losovaya, established contact to the north with Army Detachment Kempf. The euphoric Russians were taken wholly by surprise.

The terrain was almost flat and the rivulets criss-crossing it frozen, enabling German armour to move at their maximum speed. Some Russian formations eluded the trap, but most were savaged. By 6 March, many Russian armoured units were encircled; 23,000 men had been killed or wounded, 615 tanks destroyed, and more than 1,000 artillery guns of all sorts captured, along with 9,000 men. Forty-eighth Panzer Corps raced north and reached the eastern outskirts of Kharkov, while the SS Panzer Corps advanced north directly on the city.

Meanwhile, the First Panzer Army, thrusting between Izyum and Lisichansk, had also defeated the Russians and thrown them back across the Donets.

On 3 March, the intense cold of winter loosened its grip, but the ensuing thaw brought with it mud – the most serious impediment to tank movement. Though time was, therefore, now on the Russians' side, German formations were still able

Filipp Golikov was a small man with a round face and a shaved head. He commanded the Sixth Army during the Soviet invasion of Poland in 1939, but was most competent as a staff officer and served as such during the winter war against Finland in 1940. He subsequently became head of Soviet Military Intelligence – but came to the disastrous conclusion that Germany would not attack the USSR.

After Germany's invasion of Russia in 1941, Golikov was sent to London and Washington to solicit aid for the hard-pressed Russians. In 1942 he was posted to the Bryansk Front, but was shortly dismissed as defeatist when he said it would be impossible to contain the German advance at Stalingrad. He was, nevertheless, posted to command the Voronezh Front in 1943. From the end of 1943 to 1950 he was responsible for repatriating those few German prisoners of war who had survived the Soviet camps.

Nikolai Vatutin graduated from Frunze Military Academy in 1929 and, having survived Stalin's purges of army officers in the 1930s, served as an

to make progress. The SS Panzer Corps, under Hausser, encircled Kharkov by driving north of it and attacking the city from both north and west.

Hausser's victory has, however, been the subject of much criticism by military historians to this day. Many suggest that he attacked the city from the west too soon and that he did so purely for reasons of personal prestige. By doing this, it is said,

**General
F.I. Golikov
1900–80**

**General
N.F. Vatutin
1901–44**

adviser to the Soviet Supreme Command. He distinguished himself in high command at Stalingrad and the great tank battle of Kursk in 1943. He was also involved in the campaigns to recapture Kiev and the Ukraine, during which he was severely wounded in an ambush by Ukrainian Nationalist partisans. Despite surgery, he died six weeks later, on 15 April 1944, aged 42.

he embroiled himself in punitive street fighting, whereas a firm encirclement of the city would have ensured its fall with little German loss and would also have prevented Russian units from escaping eastward to Chuguyev.

The debate continues because Hausser's radioed orders from Colonel-General Hermann Hoth's Fourth Panzer Army were imprecise: Hausser understood the message to mean that he was empowered to take Kharkov from the west if he thought this feasible. Believing this to be the case, he duly launched his attack. There was heavy street fighting for more than four days, but Kharkov was once more in German hands by 15 March. The great city fell, in von Manstein's words, 'without difficulty', and he added in understatement, the Germans 'succeeded in cutting off the retreat of considerable numbers of the enemy across the Donets.'

After the German disaster at Stalingrad, von Manstein's achievement in stabilizing the German front must rank as one of the greatest (if not the greatest) achievements of command during World War II. He had executed a successful withdrawal – probably the most demanding and dangerous manoeuvre to confront a commander – trading space for time and eliminating the peril of encirclement. He had then launched a masterly counter-attack, with local armoured and air superiority, that caused the Russians immense losses in men and material. Most important of all, he had re-established the German front from Taganrog to Belgorod as a virtually straight defensive line and, at little cost, had retaken the fourth largest city in the USSR. And all that when his opponents possessed a considerable numerical advantage. Few generals have achieved so much in so short a time.

'Operation Citadel'

The disaster of Stalingrad was in large measure redressed by the German success at Kharkov. Three Soviet armies and a tank corps had been destroyed and the German line was firmly re-established. It was a measure of Stalin's deep anger that he brought in Marshal Georgi Zhukov, the victor of Stalingrad, to shore up the front and find out what had gone wrong.

A decisive factor in the struggle had, however, been revealed. The Germans had won a great campaign victory against considerable odds; but the USSR was capable of replacing its losses, Germany was not. Although the Kharkov counter-offensive had completely broken the Soviet advance, the balance in trained manpower and *matériel* was moving inexorably in Russia's favour. By early 1943, the USSR had hundreds of giant factories safely sited in the interior, and their output was augmented by massive consignments of war material from Great Britain and the USA.

After Kharkov, the Germans could hope at best for stalemate, and to achieve even this they needed a further decisive victory. The opportunity presented itself in July at Kursk, a bulging Soviet salient to the north of Belgorod. If this could be 'pinched out', many thousands of Soviet soldiers would be captured and the eastern base of the bulge would provide a gap through which German armour could penetrate unopposed. Von Manstein had wanted to do this as the third phase of his counter-stroke, in May when the ground had dried out, but the plan, 'Operation Citadel', was implemented only on 5 July and was quickly frustrated by Russian numerical superiority.

This was the end of German hopes in the East. As General Walther Warlimont, Deputy Director of the German Operations Staff, was to write: 'Operation Citadel was more than a battle lost; it handed the Russians the initiative and we never recovered it again'. German defeat in the East could not be averted.

William Slim *1891-1970*

E ven as a youth, William Slim was fascinated by soldiering, but his military ambitions were frustrated by the social conventions of the early 1900s, for his father was an ironmonger of modest means. Someone of his background had no prospect of becoming an officer; yet being middle class precluded his entering the army as a private and then striving for promotion.

In 1903, when Slim was about 12 years old, the family moved to Birmingham, where Slim was educated at a Roman Catholic school; later he was employed as a clerk, but his craving for a life in the army persisted. In 1912, displaying an early example of his determination to overcome bureaucratic obstacles using whatever means were to hand, Slim succeeded in joining the Birmingham University Officer Training Corps. He was not a student there, but through his undergraduate brother he managed to get himself enrolled. The young man had judged, with tragically accurate foresight, that Great Britain and Germany would shortly go to war and that his OTC training would then enable him to gain a commission in the army. In 1914, at the outbreak of hostilities, he duly became a second lieutenant in the Royal Warwickshire Regiment.

Slim saw action at Gallipoli, where he was badly wounded, and later served in France and Mesopotamia; in 1919 he transferred to the Indian Army. From 1926 onward he held mainly staff appointments and supplemented his income by writing short stories; but in the early months of World War II, by then a brigadier, he commanded troops again in Syria, Persia and Iraq. Then, in March 1942, he was given command of the 1st Burma Corps, after the fall of Rangoon and in the early stages of the grim Allied retreat through jungles and over mountains as the Japanese overran Burma. Late in 1943 a new army, the Fourteenth, was formed, and Slim was appointed its commander.

The morale of the triumphant Japanese was high, that of the defeated British, Indian and Burmese troops correspondingly low. It is a tribute to Slim's abilities as a commander that in such circumstances he was able to implant in his men the belief that they were in every respect superior to the Japanese and could beat them. Slim later compared the Japanese soldiers to ants: ruthless and bold when their plans went well, but becoming totally confused if these were disturbed.

Slim combined in high measure the attributes of a strong character – epitomised by his determined, jutting chin – and friendly good humour. His troops felt not only affection for their commander but also complete confidence in him; every man knew that in a battle under Slim's command he had at least a chance of remaining alive. As one soldier wrote: 'He was a wonderful person, a real bulldog, and made you feel you would follow him anywhere.'

His achievement in welding a defeated, demoralized army into a united, confident fighting instrument was matched during World War II only by Montgomery with the Eighth Army. Once he had revitalized his army, he set about planning the reconquest of Burma. But the demands of the war in Europe meant that this was low on the Allied list of priorities, and again it was only by disregarding red tape and going right to the top that he succeeded in obtaining the supplies and air support he needed. The key to reinforcement in the difficult terrain in Burma was air transport, and Slim used it to better effect than any other commander.

In August 1945 Slim was appointed Commander-in-Chief Allied Land Forces, South-East Asia. In 1948 he became Chief of the Imperial General Staff, and in 1953 Governor-General of Australia, where his sound common sense and affability soon overcame initial local resentment that this high office should be held by anyone other than an Australian.

General Sir William Slim in March 1945, the time of the Meiktila/Mandalay campaign. The medal and ribbon of the Burma Star.

1891	*6 August* Born near Bristol.
1912	Joins Birmingham University Officer Training Corps.
1914	*22 August* Commissioned in the Royal Warwickshire Regiment.
1915	*13 July–9 August* Serves at Gallipoli.
1917	At capture of Baghdad: wins the Military Cross.
1919	*May* Captain in the Indian Army.
1920	*27 March* Posted to 6th Gurkha Rifles. Fights on NW Frontier.
1926	Mainly staff appointments begin.
1939	*23 September* Brigadier commanding 10th Indian Brigade.
1940	*6 November* Takes, then abandons, Italian-held Gallabat in Sudan.
1941	*22 January* Wounded in Eritrea. *15 May* Temporary major-general commanding 10th Indian Division in Iraq. *1 July–17 September* Invades Syria and Persia.
1942	*13 March* Commander 1st Burma Corps. Retreat from Burma.
1943	*14 April–26 May* Extricates 14th Indian Division from Arakan. *16 October* Appointed to command Fourteenth Army.
1944	*4–24 February* Repulses Japanese attack in Second Battle of Arakan. *7 March–22 June* Wins Battles of Kohima/Imphal. *14 December* Knighted by General Wavell.
1945	*14 January–28 March* **Battle of Meiktila/Mandalay.** *30 March–3 May* Pursuit to Rangoon. *1 July* Promoted general. *16 August* Becomes C-in-C Allied Land Forces SE Asia. *9–12 September* Supervises landings in Malaya; at Japanese surrender in Singapore.
1948	*1 November* Chief of the Imperial General Staff.
1949	*4 January* Promoted field marshal.
1953	Governor-General of Australia.
1956	Publishes *Defeat into Victory*.
1970	*14 December* Dies in London, aged 79.

Battle of Meiktila/Mandalay/*14 January–28 March 1945*

DURING JULY 1944, the Japanese 15th Army, broken at the battles of Imphal and Kohima, began to retreat into Burma. Their exhausted troops, many ill and starving, could only hope that the British pursuit would be abandoned as the monsoon progressed. They were disabused of this expectation swiftly. Lieutenant-General William Slim, commander of the victorious British-Indian Fourteenth Army, spurred on by Admiral Lord Louis Mountbatten, Supreme Allied Commander, South-East Asia, maintained the momentum of his pursuit, despite the hindrance of heavy rain, which averaged 406mm/16in a month and sometimes reached 508mm/20in a week in the jungle of the Arakan.

Though conditions were equally bad for both armies – mud, streams turned into raging torrents, mosquitoes and leeches ever present – Slim's troops were well provided with food, medical supplies and ammunition. Moreover – a factor later to be of crucial importance – the Allies now had undisputed mastery of the air.

There were, in effect, three fronts in the Burma War. To the south, on the Bay of Bengal, lay the huge, jungle-covered hill area of the Arakan, criss-crossed with rivers and islands and the scene of earlier fighting as the Japanese tried to drive on Calcutta. On the central front, now eastward of Imphal and Kohima, lay the 260,000-strong Fourteenth Army, consisting of eight divisions and three independent brigades of British, Indian, Gurkha and African troops, plus two brigades of tanks. To the north, close to the Chinese frontier, was a conglomerate Allied force comprising three Chinese divisions and two American battalions, thrusting southeast from Ledo.

The Japanese were by now reduced to about 100,000 men in 12 weak divisions, two of which were from the so-called 'Indian National Army' – captured soldiers who had been persuaded to renounce their allegiance to Great Britain and fight for the Japanese. They had also one tank regiment with 20 tanks, 7 battalions of Hung San's Burma National Army and numerous auxiliary troops. In the air they had only 64 aircraft to the Allies' 1,200.

In the autumn of 1944, the Allies devised two possible strategies for the recapture of Burma, codenamed 'Capital' and 'Dracula'. The former envisaged an advance to the line Pakokku–Mandalay–Lashio, to begin in mid-November. The latter entailed capturing Rangoon by seaborne and airborne assaults, after which these troops would drive northward to effect a junction with the Fourteenth

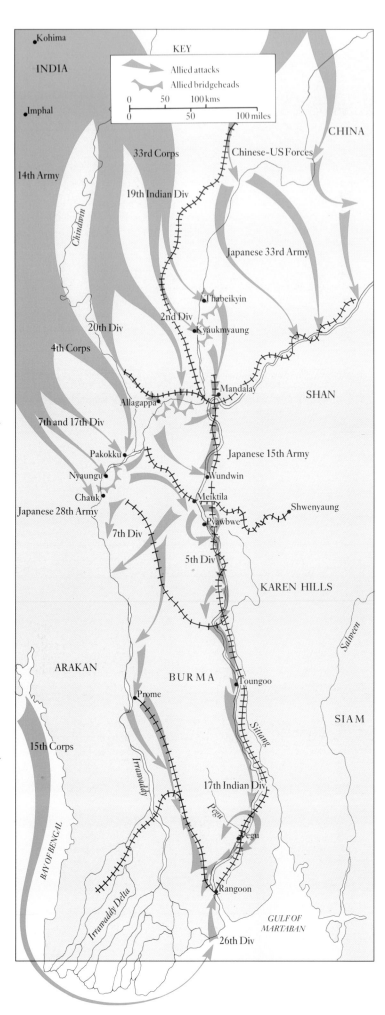

The indirect attack, deceiving the enemy by secondary probes as to the true objective while manoeuvring troops into position for the main thrust – has often been employed, but seldom with such success in modern times as in General Sir William Slim's application of it during the Meiktila/Mandalay campaign. For this tactic to prove decisive, speed, surprise and, ideally, numerical superiority are needed – all of which Slim achieved.

Napoleon was a master of this ploy, and Frederick the Great used it to deadly effect at Leuthen. In inferior hands, however, and particularly if opposed by a watchful commander, this manoeuvre can bring disaster, for the main thrust may be cut off, isolated and then eliminated.

Japan's drive on India

In the six months immediately following her attack on Pearl Harbor on 7 December 1941, Japan made massive territorial gains in the Dutch East Indies and the Philippines. In March-April 1942 her armies overran Burma and drove the British, Indian and Burmese formations westward over the River Chindwin into Assam. Just within the Indian border they formed a defensive line, pinned on Imphal, which was situated in the only area flat enough for airfields. Moreover, the one serviceable road in the region passed north through Imphal to Kohima, then northwest to Dimapur. From there a railway line ran north into India, allowing supplies and reinforcements to be brought up to the Allied front.

The Japanese were well aware of the strategic importance of Imphal and Kohima; they knew, too, that the British were planning a counter-offensive early in 1944. To forestall this, the Japanese decided to attack, with the eventual intention of breaking into India and seizing Calcutta. Their lines of communication were, however, dangerously overextended, while the British were well provisioned by the railway line and by air drops.

Partly for this reason, between April and July 1944, the Japanese were decisively beaten at the twin battles of Kohima and Imphal and suffered some 60,643 casualties, as well as the loss of 120 tanks, about 90 guns and 100 aircraft.

After these crucial battles, the initiative passed irrevocably into Allied hands. The recapture of Burma by the Fourteenth Army was not in serious doubt; the question was where it would strike.

Army, so severing the Japanese lines of communication in Burma.

By October 1944, however, it was evident that German collapse in western Europe could not be brought about until 1945 and it would be impossible to provide sufficient men, shipping and aircraft to implement Operation Dracula. Operation Capital was necessarily resolved on, which in effect meant that the ensuing battles would largely be the responsibility of Slim's Fourteenth Army, supported by a southward drive on his left flank, as far as Lashio, by General Stilwell's American-Chinese force.

Before the campaign opened, however, there were a number of changes in command on both sides. Following the defeats at Imphal/Kohima, the Japanese Burma Area Army commander, Lieutenant-General Masakazu Kuwabe, had been replaced on 30 August by 66-year-old

The importance of air supply

Fourteenth Army used 750 tons of supplies daily in December 1944; by March 1945 this had increased to 1,200 tons. Slim's ability to supply his divisions by air was the keystone to his reconquest of Burma – between 2 January and 21 May they received 210,000 tons of supplies by air, 16.7 per cent of which were air-dropped or parachuted in. The British, Canadian and American crews never had more than 400 aircraft available, and aircraft flew up to 150 hours a month – often as many as three sorties a day. As well as supplies, 31,000 reinforcements were flown in and 40,000 casualties taken out.

The economical range for a fully laden Dakota was only 402km/250mls, so forward airfields were essential. Those captured at Meiktila were at once brought into use.

Thabukton airfield

17th Indian Div

99th Bde
(flown in to Thabukton)

48th Bde

63rd Bde

255th Tank Bde

Japanese 18th Div   Wundwin

NORTH LAKE

Pagoda

KYIGON

9th Bde (flown in)

Airfield

Kanna

Magyigon

MEIKTILA

Point 860

SOUTH LAKE

Japanese 49th Div

Point 799

KEY

British attack 28 Feb – 3 March

Japanese defences

Japanese counter-attack 14 – 23 March

Pyawbwe

By late morning on 1 March 1945, on a hot, dry day of brilliant sunshine, 48th Indian Infantry Brigade was advancing from the northwest to the centre of Meiktila. About two-thirds of the way down the eastern shore of North Lake stood a beautiful pagoda, already held by Indian troops. From a terrace below it, General Sir William Slim watched a typical action.

Some 20 or 30 men of the Gurkha Rifles were trying to flush out a group of Japanese soldiers in well-concealed bunkers (5), who were barring their progress into the town (4). This lay some 0.8km/½ml distant across open ground, cut up by water channels and traversed by the railway line (6).

Fairly close to the pagoda (1), the Gurkhas lay flat or crouched low behind the cover afforded by the rough ground, clumps of bushes and a spinney of trees (2). They were under heavy machine-gun fire from the concealed Japanese.

The Gurkhas returned fire on the enemy position with Bren-guns. A single Sherman tank (7) fired one or two shots, then lobbed some smoke grenades just in front of the Japanese bunkers. Under cover of the screen, the Gurkhas ran forward (3), diving for shelter as the smoke cleared, and a few enemy shells burst harmlessly on the edge of the lake.

The tank opened fire on the bunkers again, and under cover of sustained bursts of machine-gun fire and further smoke laid by mortars (8), the Gurkhas dashed forward. Three men with tommy-guns thrust them into the small open mouths of the bunkers and opened fire. At once about 20 Japanese soldiers ran from the bunkers, zigzagging toward the town; they were shot down by two bursts of fire from the Gurkhas.

Ten minutes later the two platoons of Gurkhas moved forward to carry out another operation. Similar actions took place all over Meiktila in the four days of hard fighting it took to gain possession of this important centre.

Lieutenant-General Heitaro Kimura, an energetic, highly imaginative strategist. That same day Lieutenant-General Shihachi Katamura replaced the disgraced Mutaguchi at the head of Fifteenth Army.

On the Allied side, Stilwell – known to his troops as 'Vinegar Joe' because of his acerbic disposition – was recalled to the USA after he had quarrelled with General-issimo Chiang Kai-shek. In his place, Lieutenant-General Dan I. Sultan was given command of ground troops in the northern sector.

Slim's strategy was originally to fight Kimura's Thirty-third Army (under Honda) and his Fifteenth Army (under Katamura) on the plains around Shwebo, where he could deploy his great superiority in tanks. Kimura, however, was quick to grasp the dangers inherent in his position. Instead of fighting with his back to the River Irrawaddy, with all that that augured for his potential destruction, he gave the order to retreat to the east bank – a decision hitherto almost unknown from a senior Japanese commander. His strategy was eminently sound, for he would be close to his supply depots and the Irrawaddy is a great natural barrier which he had every hope of holding against attacks by Fourteenth Army, which he could then destroy when increasing supply problems forced it to retire to the River Chindwin.

The three Japanese armies, each roughly equivalent in strength to a British corps, were soon positioned on the east bank of the river with the 25,400-strong Thirty-third Army in the north; the 21,400 men of Fifteenth Army in the centre and Twenty-eighth Army, under General S. Sakurai, in the south.

Slim and his Fourteenth Army were faced with the awesome prospect of forcing a passage, without proper landing craft, over one of the world's greatest rivers, which was guarded at all possible crossing points by a highly trained, fanatical enemy led by a most resourceful commander. He therefore devised a new strategy; it was simple, bold and highly imaginative.

About 128km/80mls behind the River Irrawaddy lay Meiktila, the principal Japanese base in central Burma. It included airfields, hospitals, supply dumps and road and rail links with Mandalay and Rangoon. If Slim could capture this, he might so disrupt the Japanese in good open tank country as to force them into general retreat. He resolved, therefore, to make more than one crossing but to disguise, if he could, his main thrust until the last moment. Slim decided to make a strong feint north of Mandalay with 33rd Corps while later making his main thrust south of it and straight at Meiktila. After that, in his staff's phrase, it was SOB, 'Sea or bust', to get to the port of Rangoon before the monsoon broke, and before Operation Dracula was mounted. On 18 December he gave his corps commanders orders for 'Extended Capital'.

This entailed the complex and hazardous task of moving a great formation – in the event, 4th Corps under Lieutenant-General Frank Messervy – from his left flank to his right without the Japanese knowing what he was about. Here Allied air superiority played a crucial role, for it enabled Slim to deprive the Japanese of effective air reconnaissance. Thus, when Slim's southern attacks went in, Kimura was for a long time in ignorance of his true intentions and still thought that 4th Corps was northwest of Mandalay. A dummy headquarters for 4th Corps was established in the north, one of many deceptions to delude Kimura and his staff.

Slim made his opening moves on the night of 9 January 1945, when the 19th Indian Division of 33rd Corps, commanded by Lieutenant-General Sir Montague Stopford, started to cross the river at Thabeikyin about 96km/60mls north of Mandalay. On the night of 13/14 January, 62nd Brigade established a bridgehead a few miles south of this at Kyaukmyaung. The Japanese rapidly came to the conclusion – as Slim had planned and hoped – that this was the main British attack, and Kimura ordered reserves to the sector, even taking some troops from Meiktila.

Despite these reinforcements, British bridgeheads held and expanded and Allied tanks were rapidly brought in. On 12 February another 'bamboo and bootlace'

Valentine II MkIII bridgelaying tank
In 1943–4 the Valentine tank was used mainly for training by the British Army, but this specialized adaptation was of enormous operational importance on the Burma front. The gun turret of the 17-ton tank was replaced by the No 1 scissors bridge, operated with hydraulic arms and rams. The bridge, which was 10.4m/34ft long by 2.9m/9½ft wide, proved invaluable for spanning countless *chaungs* – river beds – on Fourteenth Army's way through Burma.

Slim's two Indian tank brigades, and 15th Corps in Arakan, each had an independent Royal Armoured Corps bridging troop equipped with the bridgelayers. The tank was a crucial factor in Fourteenth Army's rapid advances.

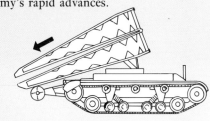

Japanese 47mm anti-tank gun

This was Japan's most modern, Type 01 (M41) anti-tank gun in 1945. It replaced in part the obsolete Model 94 37mm/1½in gun. Its widely split trail, independently sprung wheels and low silhouette made the 47mm extremely stable. It could fire high explosive as well as armour-piercing shells, but by Western standards it was not powerful, lacking penetration. There were also too few to provide the establishment figure of four per battalion or six per regiment, and they had to be supplemented by field and anti-aircraft guns, as well as by suicide tactics. However, it is thought that the 47mm may have accounted for 11 of the

tanks lost by Fourteenth Army around Meiktila.

Muzzle velocity: 834mps/2,735fps; range: 457m/500yds; ammunition: 1.4kg/3lb shell with a penetration at 457m/500yds of 50mm/2in – only 70 per cent as great as that of the British 6-pounder at the same range.

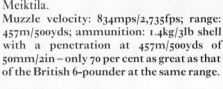

crossing was effected at Allagappa, just south of Mandalay, reinforcing Kimura's belief that these operations represented Slim's main thrust.

Meanwhile, Messervy's 4th Corps, west of the Chindwin, was speeding south toward the Irrawaddy. His plan was to capture Pakokku by mid-February and then drive rapidly in a direct line to Meiktila. As his various units advanced toward the river, they set about improving the roads – even employing 10 elephants in the task – so that they could be used by tanks, and building airstrips.

Messervy decided to cross the Irrawaddy, not at the obvious Pakokku but at Nyaungu, the narrowest point, although even here the river was still over 1.2km/¾ml wide. To deceive the enemy, he intended to make two subsidiary crossings, south and north of his main blow. During the night of 13/14 February, Messervy began his main crossing. Napalm was deployed for the first time in Burma and a bridgehead was quickly established near Nyaungu, which was captured on the 16th. His 7th Indian Division then took Pagan and Pakokku.

The general situation was already moving in Slim's favour, for by the third week of February he had, in total, four divisions and a tank brigade over the river and had suffered only light casualties, given the difficulty of the operation and the ferocity of Japanese resistance in the northern sector of the front.

British troops used flamethrowers to flush out and kill Japanese 'human bombs'. It was precisely this terrible attitude to war, which had grown up on both sides, that persuaded US President Truman that, paradoxically, lives would be saved if he unleashed the murderous power of the atom bomb.

Japanese suicide squads

Japanese soldiers had been indoctrinated with the *samurai* code of total obedience to commands and always to seek honourable death in battle rather than to surrender. Many went further; they would fight not only to their last bullet but then with whatever was to hand. At Meiktila, they used sharpened bamboo stakes, and in one of the Irrawaddy bridgeheads, officers assailed British tanks with drawn swords.

As the British advanced, only isolated pockets of resistance remained, but the Japanese continued the fanatical struggle by using *nikuhaku kogeki*, human destruction squads. Soldiers crouched alone in rows of foxholes, each clasping a large bomb between his legs and holding a heavy stone with which to strike the fuse when a tank passed over his hideout. At the appropriate moment, bomb, tank and soldier were all blown apart. Allied troops found this practice awesome and abhorrent, but soon learned to seek out the Japanese and kill them before the tanks went in.

Mandalay Hill, a rock outcrop some 244m/800ft high, was taken on 11 March after two days hard fighting. From their lookout among the temples and pagodas on its slopes, men of the 19th Indian Division watched the battle for Fort Dufferin.

Kimura had been taken completely by surprise, but even after the southern crossings he continued for some time to believe them merely diversionary Chindit-style operations and thought that 4th Corps was still in the north, poised to attack near the earlier crossing points in what he called 'the battle for the Irrawaddy shore'. Because Kimura had been moving reserves north, 33rd Corps was hard pressed, and 4th Corps needed to strike quickly at Meiktila.

On 21 February, 4th Corps' veteran 17th Indian Division, commanded by Major-General David Cowan, and the 255th Indian Tank Brigade's Shermans began the dusty drive on Meiktila. Astonishingly, the Japanese even now did not believe this to be more than a secondary offensive, since a garbled intelligence report had put the number of tanks at 200 and not the more accurate figure of 2,000. On 26 February Thabutkon airfield, some 16km/10mls from the town, was captured,

Fort Dufferin, the last stronghold held by the Japanese, was built in 1858. Its 6m/20ft high brick walls, backed with immense embankments of earth, enclosed 3.2km²/1¼sq mls of parkland. A moat 61m/200ft wide lay all around it. Despite bombing and constant attempts to breach the walls with gun fire, the garrison only abandoned the fort on 19/20 March, creeping out through drains from the moat. A few days later General Slim held an official flag-raising ceremony in the fort.

and within four days the Dakotas of 1st US Air Commando Group had flown in 99th Brigade and a stream of much needed supplies.

Major-General Kasuya, commander of the Meiktila area, is thought to have had 3,000–4,000 troops at his disposal; these he put to work digging defensive ditches. Every available man – including cooks, 500 hospital patients and male nurses – was armed and every gun (about 50) brought up. Meiktila would not be easy to take, not least because there was a large lake to the north and another to the south of the town and all the approach roads could be covered by artillery.

Cowan began investing the town on 28 February. While he distracted the Japanese by using his 48th and 63rd Brigades in a show against Meiktila's western defences, he sent his tank brigade and its two motorized battalions north of the city, with orders to bypass it and then turn south and west to capture the airfield sited east of the town. Having gained his objective, and supported by heavy air attacks, 255th Tank Brigade stormed Meiktila from the east. Meanwhile, attacks on the western and southern sides were pressed home.

The Japanese put up fanatical, suicidal resistance during four days of relentless street fighting. Every house window, every ditch, bomb crater or pile of rubble, and the many hastily constructed bunkers, were manned by Japanese soldiers, all intent on honourable death, never surrender. The prolonged, gruesome struggle of house-to-house and often hand-to-hand fighting came to an end on 3 March, when the Japanese were finally overcome. Roughly half the garrison had been killed and half wounded; of Kasuya's total force, only 47 were taken prisoner.

Kimura, though both astonished and appalled by the loss of Meiktila, responded with his usual decisiveness and speed. He rapidly assembled a relief force of about 12,000 men, supported by 9 tanks and 70 guns, and sent them south under Lieutenant-General Masaki Honda from Thirty-third Army. However, while the British formations were coordinated and accustomed to working together, Honda's force, gathered from five different divisions, was difficult to unify.

Despite the ferocity of Japanese attacks,

their first objective – the recapture of the airfield to prevent reinforcements and supplies reaching the British – was denied them. During 15–18 March, 9th Brigade was actually flown in to Meiktila at the cost of only 22 casualties and one Dakota. By late March it was evident that the Japanese, though fighting with maniacal courage, had lost most of their guns and no longer posed a threat. When Honda ordered a retreat on the 28th, Meiktila was firmly in Slim's hands.

Meanwhile, on 26 February, at almost exactly the moment that Kimura had been obliged to turn south to recover Meiktila, Stopford's 33rd Corps in the north, with opposition to it much reduced, began to drive on Mandalay. The Japanese were brushed back everywhere and, by 8 March, though fighting with the same courageous desperation as their comrades had in the south, they were reduced to only two strongpoints in the city – Mandalay Hill and Fort Dufferin. After intense fighting, the former fell on 11 March, the latter, after heavy bombardment, nine days later on 20 March.

In the Battles of Meiktila/Mandalay, the Allies sustained some 18,055 casualties (more than at Kohima/Imphal) of whom 2,667 were killed. At least 27 tanks had been lost or hit. Kimura's army, on the other hand, had ceased to exist as a fighting force, losing 12,913 men, 6,513 of whom were killed, about 150 guns and 13 tanks.

Kimura's position was now virtually hopeless: he could only reinforce one front by depleting the other, and both were essential to him. His only option was to retreat eastward, with all the suffering and loss of life that that would entail. Meanwhile, Slim, who held the east bank of the Irrawaddy, from Mandalay south to Chauk, and the main road and railway lines leading south, was 544km/338mls from a glittering objective: Rangoon, on the Gulf of Martaban. Only one thing could deprive him of the prize: the advent of the monsoon. Speed was essential and Slim decided to take the risk. Since there was some prospect of his not reaching Rangoon before the May rains began, Mountbatten reinstated a sea-borne and airborne landing at the city and its port, or as Slim later put it, 'a hammering at the back door while I burst in at the front.'

Slim's southward march was both remorseless and swift. There were two routes to Rangoon: down the parallel road and railway lines and down the left bank of the River Irrawaddy to their west. His plan was that 4th Corps should take the road/rail route, 33rd Corps that of the river; in this way he intended to trap the

The monsoon usually set in at the end of May, turning the dusty hard-baked earth into a quagmire. Vehicles slithered off the roads, and the only way to move equipment such as these 40mm/1½in anti-aircraft guns, *above*, was to manhandle it. After taking Meiktila and Mandalay, Slim drove rapidly on Rangoon in an all-out effort to reach it before his army was caught by the monsoon and bogged down.

By 21 May, Slim's army had received 38,600 tons of supplies brought by vessels plying the Chindwin and other inland waterways. Here, *above*, a convoy of amphibious trucks – DUKWs – directed by flag signals, is taking reinforcements and supplies to forward British troops. The dock area of Rangoon, *left*, was devastated by Allied and Japanese bombing, so in early June Allied ships had to anchor in the harbour to offload.

retreating Japanese between his two advancing forces.

All went according to plan. The 7th and 20th Divisions, driving down the great river, reached and entered the town of Prome on 2 May. Meanwhile 4th Corps, led by 255th Tank Brigade, took Pyawbwe on the railway route; on 22 April they reached Toungoo and then moved on to Pegu, the capture of which would seal the only Japanese escape route eastward.

Advance troops reached Pegu on 29 April – the day on which the monsoon broke, early. Time was now running out. The Japanese, fully conscious of this, rushed every available man to hold Pegu, but on 2 May, 17th Division broke through and seized the town. Cowan's men then braced themselves for the final 45km/28ml advance to Rangoon.

That same day – 2 May – was also the day for the amphibious attack on Rangoon. During the previous 48 hours, Allied bombers had assailed the fortifications at Elephant Point, a defence system guarding the seaward entrance to Rangoon, and Gurkha paratroopers were dropped near it. But the city had by then been abandoned by the Japanese: believing that a sea-borne attack was no longer envisaged, the garrison had earlier left to help hold Pegu.

Soon the amphibious force, having landed without meeting resistance, joined up with the 17th Division at Pegu and the 20th at Prome. The Second Battle of Burma was effectively over. In five months, Slim had driven the Japanese out of all their earlier areas of conquest and the dispirited, demoralized, starving Japanese Army could only retreat eastward as best it might. Most found lonely deaths in their trek to what they hoped would be safety.

General Heitaro Kimura 1878–1948

On 30 August 1944, after the Japanese had been decisively beaten at the Battles of Imphal and Kohima, General Heitaro Kimura was appointed Commander Burma Area Army. He had previously been Vice-Minister of War under General Tojo. His was a virtually impossible task: his troops were demoralized and in retreat, many were sick, and they were all on pitifully reduced rations.

It in no way detracts from Slim's imaginative and masterly handling of the Meiktila/Mandalay/Rangoon campaign to state that his opponent was at a great disadvantage. Not only was Kimura's army inferior in numbers and *matériel*, but ironically, as Slim too had

General Heitaro Kimura surrenders his sword to General Sir William Slim.

found, the Burma theatre was of secondary concern to his High Command. Burma was the farthest outpost from Japan; it was difficult to defend and of little economic value. Kimura, therefore, far from being strongly reinforced, was actually stripped of about a third of the 30,000 replacements sent between June and October 1944.

A lesser general might have been overwhelmed, but Kimura's defence of Burma was stubborn and militarily sound. It says much for his courage and strategic grasp that he was prepared to retreat – a manoeuvre abhorrent to the Japanese mind – over the great barrier of the Irrawaddy River. There he had at least some prospect of holding the British advance.

His failure to do so must be attributed largely to his stricken army and his inadequate resources. That he fell into Slim's trap and believed Mandalay not Meiktila to be the principal Allied objective was due to his almost total lack of air reconnaissance and to faulty Intelligence. Certainly, he was quick to recognize Slim's brilliance and called his attack on Meiktila 'the master stroke'. Slim also held Kimura's abilities in high esteem and after the war, wherever he lived, prominently displayed his *samurai* sword.

Kimura took part in the surrender ceremony on 12 September 1945 at Singapore and was hanged as a war criminal in 1948.

The eclipse of Japan

The loss of Burma was a serious, though not in itself fatal, blow for the Japanese. 'The Fourteenth Army', Churchill was to write, 'under the masterly command of General Slim, fought valiantly, overcame all obstacles, and achieved the seemingly impossible.' He signalled to Lord Mountbatten on 9 May 1945, 'In honour of these great deeds of South-East Asia Command His Majesty the King has commanded that a special decoration, the "Burma Star", should be struck and the ribbons will be flown to you at the earliest moment.'

The Japanese reverse in Burma was brought about in part because at that stage of the war the theatre had become of low priority to their High Command. Some units had actually been transferred to other, more crucial defensive sectors, for by early 1945 Japan faced the prospect of an invasion of her mainland.

The sea battles of the Coral Sea, Midway and Leyte Gulf had together eliminated the Japanese navy and merchant fleet, while in the air the Allies' overwhelming superiority left the mainland

easy prey. Three-quarters of Tokyo and large parts of other Japanese cities were laid waste by air bombardment, but their fighting spirit was undiminished.

It was in these circumstances that US President Truman authorized the use of atomic bombs – one on Hiroshima on 6 August 1945, a second on Nagasaki on 9 August – that brought about Japan's unconditional surrender on 2 September, thereby saving both Allied and Japanese lives.

Thus the British Fourteenth Army and other formations both British and American were not called upon to suffer the terrible losses an invasion of Japan would have entailed. The fall of Rangoon marked the virtual end of fighting in Burma, for by the time the monsoon lifted, the atomic bomb had brought World War II to an end.

Douglas MacArthur *1880-1964*

T he troops will be home by Christmas': thus General Douglas MacArthur after his great victories at Inchon and Seoul. The unfortunate words, an expression frequently uttered by Allied optimists during the early months of World War I, reveal much of MacArthur's character, for his victory against 'impossible' odds made him so overconfident as to cloud his military judgement. He was more than 70 years old at the time and could not – or would not – comprehend the concept of limited war in a nuclear age as opposed to total victory.

His strategy called for an advance to the Yalu River, after which the United Nations force would bomb China, if necessary with atomic bombs. This was hardly a realistic strategy for the 1950s and it was one which President Harry S. Truman's Democratic government could not countenance. MacArthur paid the price for his outdated and autocratic posturing: he was recalled and spent the last years of his life as a private citizen although, as a five-star general, he remained on the active list.

Douglas MacArthur was born in Little Rock, Arkansas, the son of Lieutenant-General Arthur MacArthur, a Civil War hero who had led the 4th Wisconsin Infantry in an epic charge during the Battle of Chattanooga in 1863. Douglas MacArthur went as a matter of course to West Point, from which he graduated in 1903 with an outstanding scholastic record. Like Lee, he went into the engineers and won distinction in Mexico. He served in the Philippines and Japan; in France with outstanding bravery during World War I; and, again like Lee, in 1919–22 as Superintendent of West Point, where he modernized the military training.

In common with many senior commanders during World War II – among them Montgomery and Mark Clark – MacArthur was a 'showman', always surrounded by an entourage of staff, reporters and cameramen. His corncob pipe, his sunglasses and the rows of faded gold braid on his Philippines Field Marshal's cap, which he had designed himself, were all intended to make him instantly recognizable.

MacArthur commanded the defence of the Philippines after the Japanese attack on Pearl Harbor on 7 December 1941; when further defence of the islands became impossible, he left, on the orders of US President Roosevelt, for Australia, where he assumed command of all Allied forces in the Southwest Pacific. From his Australian base, he directed the New Guinea Campaign and, between October 1944 and July 1945, the campaigns that ultimately liberated the Philippines. These great military achievements raised him to international status.

Appropriately, it was MacArthur who accepted Japanese surrender on board the USS *Missouri* in Tokyo Bay on 2 September 1945. He was then appointed commander of the Allied powers in occupied Japan. In this capacity, he demonstrated his great gifts as commander-administrator: he restored harmonious relations between the USA and Japan, liberalized Japan's Press and education, and secured the vote for women.

His great achievements and virtually vice-regal powers in Japan led him to regard himself as omnipotent, so making conflict inevitable between himself and the US Commander-in-Chief, the President. This finally came about during the Korean War. MacArthur, after his triumph at Inchon, could not see that if, as he wished, the UN force did indeed attack Communist China, the USSR might well invade western Europe while the Americans were embroiled in the Far East. In his view, war could be conducted in only one of three ways: 'Either pursue it to victory; surrender to the enemy and end it on his terms; or what I think is the worst of all choices – to go on indefinitely, neither to win or lose.'

General Douglas MacArthur accompanied the Marines at Inchon and later toured the front to encourage their drive on Seoul.
The general's battered cap, corncob pipe and sunglasses, which are preserved at the Douglas MacArthur Academy of Freedom, Brownwood, Texas.

1880	*26 January* Born at Little Rock, Arkansas.
1893	West Texas Military Academy.
1903	Graduates from West Point. Serves in the Philippines.
1914	*May* Veracruz reconnaissance, Mexico.
1917	Colonel and chief of staff to 42nd Division on Western Front.
1918	*26 June* Brigadier-General. *30 July* Commands 84th Brigade. *10 September–16 October* St Mihiel and Meuse-Argonne. *5–22 November* Commands 42nd Division.
1919	*12 June* Appointed youngest-ever Superintendent West Point.
1925	Youngest US major-general, in command Manila, Philippines.
1930	General and US Army Chief of Staff.
1935	Military adviser to Philippines.
1936	Field Marshal, Philippines Army.
1937	*December* Retires from US Army.
1941	*26 July* Recalled; given command of US Army Far East. *19 December* C-in-C US Far East forces; *22–31* evacuates Manila.
1942	*9 January–8 February* Repulses Japanese attacks on Bataan. *12–17 March* Leaves Corregidor, awarded Congressional Medal of Honor and made Supreme Commander Allied Forces SW Pacific in Australia.
1943	*22 January* Papua cleared of Japanese. New Guinea/New Britain operations.
1944	*29 February–27 April* Admiralty and Hollandia operations isolate Japanese 18th Army. *20 October–25 December* Retakes Leyte. *15 December* General of the Army.
1945	*9 January* Invades Luzon and, *5 July*, announces liberation of the Philippines. *5 April* Commander of US Army, Pacific. *2 September* Conducts surrender ceremony in Tokyo Bay.
1950	*7 July* C-in-C UN Command South Korea. *15–29 September* **Inchon Landings** and recapture of Seoul.
1951	*11 April* Relieved of commands.
1964	*5 April* Dies at Washington, aged 84.

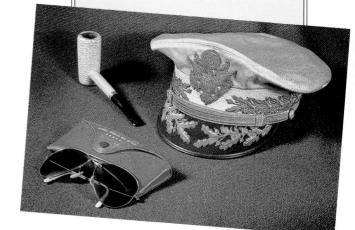

The Inchon Landings/*15–29 September 1950*

GENERAL DOUGLAS MACARTHUR'S plan to win the war in Korea, codenamed 'Chromite', centred on an audacious amphibious landing far in the enemy's rear. This at first met with strong objection from the US Joint Chiefs of Staff, in particular from General Omar N. Bradley, then its chairman, who regarded amphibious assaults as no longer necessary in the atomic age. Others argued that to take the Marine Brigade away from the Pusan perimeter was breaking one of the cardinal rules of war – dividing an army in the face of superior numbers – despite the fact that this was precisely what the Confederate hero Robert E. Lee had done at Chancellorsville, his most perfect victory.

MacArthur persisted, however, and eventually, on 28 August 1950, received permission to implement his plan. He was reinforced for this purpose with 26,000 Marines. These were organized in Japan as 10th Corps, comprising the veteran 1st Marine Division and the army's 7th Infantry Division.

It was not in MacArthur's strategic thinking to use Eighth Army, pinned down in the southeast of Korea, around

The Korean Conflict

When the Japanese surrendered at the end of World War II, they were obliged to give up control of occupied Korea; their troops north of the 38th Parallel surrendered to the USSR, those south of it to the USA. In 1948, these occupied zones were handed over to civilian governments, the Communist north becoming known as the People's Democratic Republic of Korea, the free south as the Republic of Korea.

Animosity between the two quickly became intense. The USSR provided the North with instructors and equipment and, the moment they were ready, the 120,000-strong North Korean People's Army, with 150 Russian T34 tanks, poured across the border. The unprovoked attack on 25 June

1950 took the South by surprise; their lightly armed army of 95,000 men was quickly driven back and soon held only a small area around Pusan in the southeast.

The United Nations presented North Korea with an ultimatum, calling for an immediate cease-fire and their withdrawal behind the 38th Parallel. It was ignored. Then the United Nations ordered its first peacekeeping force into action. The USA provided most of the troops, with strong support from the United Kingdom and the Commonwealth. In all, 17 countries contributed men to the United Nations force, which was placed under the command of the distinguished United States general, Douglas MacArthur.

Pusan, in a slow and costly slog up the peninsula, where in any case they might be overwhelmed by the enemy's numerical superiority. Far better, in his view, to strike in the enemy's rear and force him to fight on two fronts simultaneously. The place he chose for his assault was Inchon.

To MacArthur the advantages of taking the port and town of Inchon were convincing. First and foremost, it was only 29km/18mls to the west of the South Korean capital, Seoul, through which all enemy supplies had to pass on their way south to the Pusan perimeter. Second, just north-

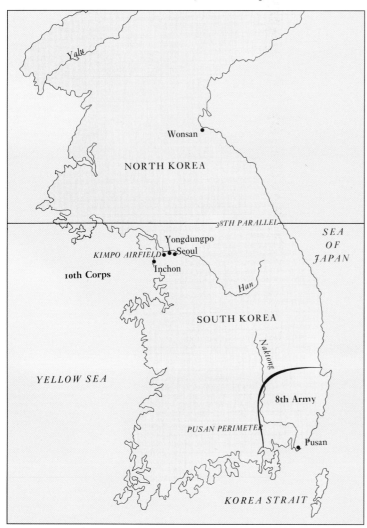

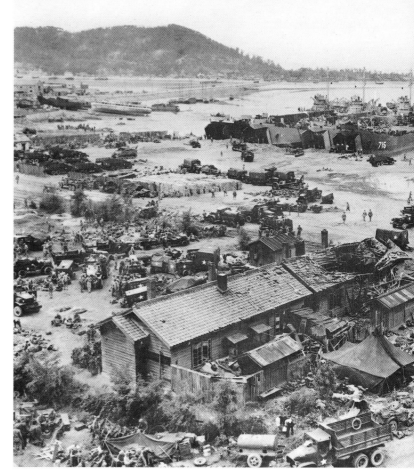

Landing craft

Less than a year before Inchon, General Omar N. Bradley, Chairman of the US Joint Chiefs of Staff, predicted that 'large-scale amphibious operations . . . will never occur again.' The US Navy had reduced its Pacific War fleet of 610 amphibious ships to 91 by 1950, decommissioning 510 landing craft in 1948 alone.

But General MacArthur, who had made 87 successful, often unopposed, landings in the Pacific during 1942–5, was convinced of the viability of his plan. He had fortunately insisted on the despatch of a tiny amphibious force to Japan for training in May 1950. This became the nucleus of the Inchon armada: most of the equipment and many of the men had taken part in earlier landings under MacArthur.

As well as navy-manned vessels, the Military Sea Transportation Service provided ships or chartered them; 30 of the 47 tank landing ships used were Japanese-manned craft soon converted from their civilian roles. The Advance Attack Group that captured Wolmi-Do was carried in three destroyer escorts, rebuilt as high-speed transports, and a Landing Ship (Dock) – an LSD. LSDs transported landing craft for vehicles and personnel (LCVPs) and utility landing craft (known as tank landing craft in World War II), which landed 10 tanks on the first day. Three medium rocket landing ships (LSMRs) each put down a barrage of 2,000 127mm/5in rockets in 20 minutes before the troops went in.

At Blue Beach, the assault was carried out in the 172 LVTs of 1st Marine Amphibian Tractor Battalion. Brought into service in 1943, these armoured 'amtracs' (known as Alligators or Buffaloes) could carry 40 men or 4.5 tons at 5.7 knots in the water or 43kmh/27mph on land. There was also a 75mm/3in howitzer version.

east of Inchon was Kimpo airfield; and finally, once Seoul was taken, MacArthur would have accomplished a turning movement on a vast scale and would have forced the enemy to face about.

MacArthur's resolve was inflexible, but there were serious problems to be overcome – indeed some senior officers thought the operation impossible. For the sole approach route to Inchon by sea was along Flying Fish Channel, a hazardous passage with strong currents. Moreover, on only one day in September – the 15th – would the tides be high enough for a landing, and even then for only three hours in the morning and evening. And between high tides, great expanses of impassable mud flats were exposed, stretching in places 5km/3mls out to sea.

There were other problems: some of the landings had to be made against the quays and walls of Inchon, rather than on the more usual flat beach; the landing troops would be overlooked on both sides by hills, and there was the further danger that September was the typhoon season. Indeed, on 3 September a typhoon did strike, causing damage to ships and equipment that it took MacArthur's men more than 24 hours to repair. All in all, the plan did not look auspicious and the US Joint Chiefs of Staff gave MacArthur authority to undertake it with nervous reluctance.

During the days before the landings, heavy air and naval bombardments were made at a number of places, including Inchon, to confuse the enemy. Then, in the early hours of 15 September, the leading ships of the 230-strong armada got into position at the entrance to Flying Fish Channel to catch the early high tide.

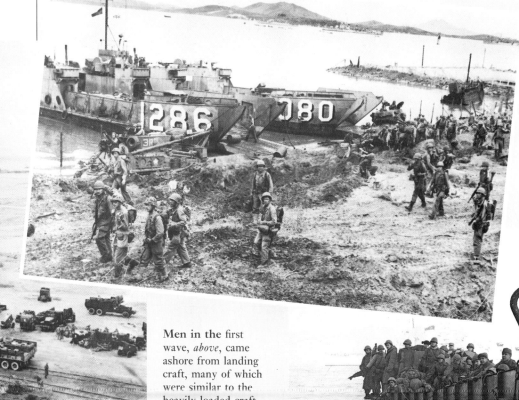

Men in the first wave, *above*, came ashore from landing craft, many of which were similar to the heavily loaded craft *right*; escort ships lay well out. Red Beach, *left*, was a scene of intense activity shortly after the first Marines landed, with landing craft being unloaded, stores assembled and trucks and jeeps moving off.

At Inchon, Douglas MacArthur used a 'turning' movement on a massive scale. The manoeuvre entails getting behind the enemy and forcing him to turn about. Both Hooker and Lee attempted this at Chancellorsville; Lee succeeded.

MacArthur's daring but perilous plan was to hold the North Korean Army's attention at Pusan while landing in force at Inchon; then the United Nations' forces would be in position both in front and rear of the enemy.

The North Korean High Command, unsuspecting of a UN landing at Inchon, had left the area lightly defended. Despite manned pillboxes and sporadic artillery and mortar fire, they inflicted few casualties among the invading marines, while they themselves were quickly ferreted out of their positions. On Day One, 12,000 US

Marines were landed, at a cost of 196 casualties; the North Koreans, of whom there were some 2,000, suffered 300 prisoners taken, with many more killed and wounded. The remainder retreated.

Men of the 1st and 2nd Battalions 5th Marines were ferried to Red Beach from the troop carriers (2) in LCVPs (5) – Landing Craft Vehicle and Personnel. These vessels could carry some 35 men.

Following earlier naval and aerial bombardments, many buildings were ablaze, notably butane tanks (6) in the harbour area. Dense smoke blew along the front, affording the Marines some cover.

Carrier-based Corsairs (1) strafed the landing zone until the last few minutes before the Marines

went ashore. These F4U fighter-bombers were capable of 726kmh/451mph.

The bows of the vessels landing the Marines were still about 1.2m/4ft below the level of the sea wall, although it was high tide, and the men had to use hooked ladders to climb ashore (4). The first units were landed by 17.24. Behind the LCVPs were LSTs (3) – Landing Ships Tanks – which brought in both men and equipment.

North Korean machine-gunners and other soldiers with mortars in dugouts (7, 9), who had earlier fired on the ships, were now demoralized by the bombardments and offered half-hearted resistance. By 24.00, the Marines who landed at Red Beach had taken all their objectives – the three commanding heights of British Consulate

Hill, Observatory Hill (8) and Cemetery Hill. The road to Seoul was now open.

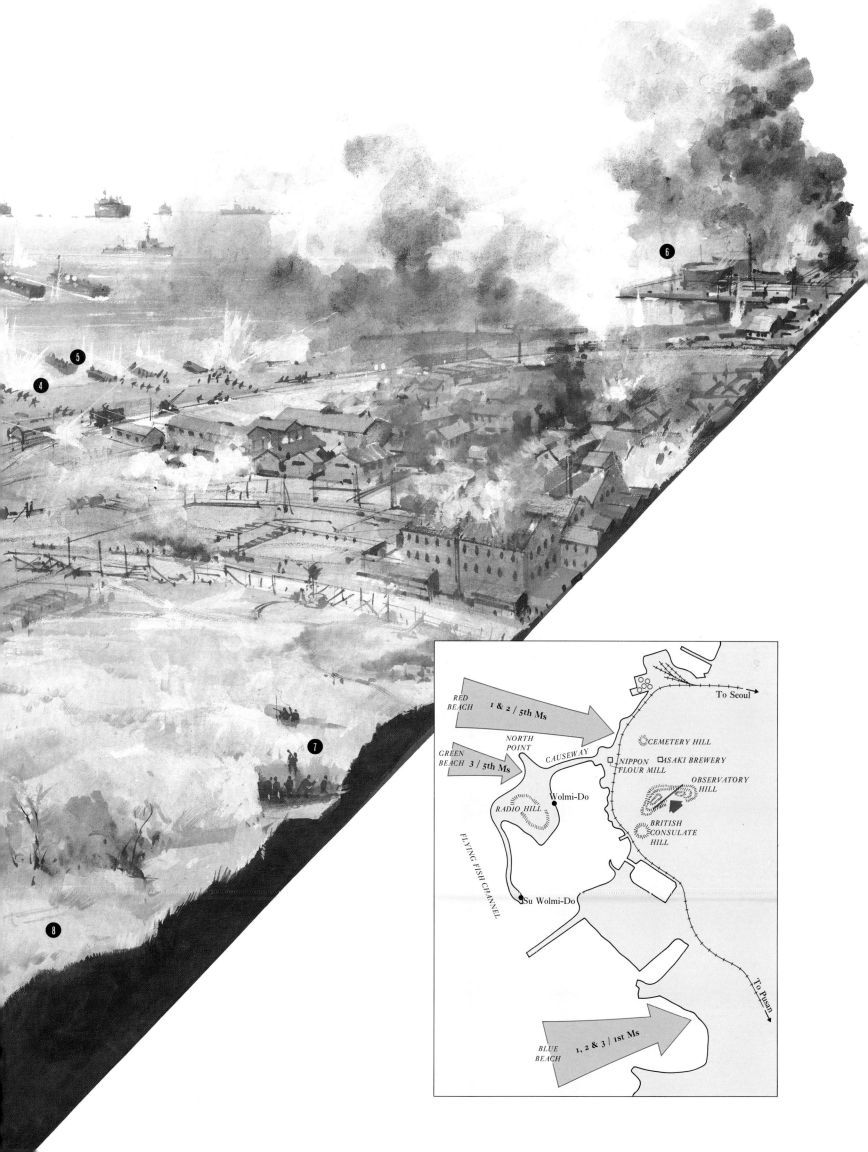

RED
BEACH   1 & 2 / 5th Ms

To Seoul

NORTH
POINT   CAUSEWAY

GREEN
BEACH   3 / 5th Ms

CEMETERY HILL

NIPPON
FLOUR MILL   ASAKI BREWERY

OBSERVATORY
HILL

Wolmi-Do

RADIO HILL

BRITISH
CONSULATE
HILL

FLYING FISH CHANNEL

Su Wolmi-Do

To Pusan

BLUE
BEACH   1, 2 & 3 / 1st Ms

Landings were to be made on three beaches – 'Red', 'Green' and 'Blue'. The first objective was to take Wolmi-Do, a small, fortified island connected to Inchon and the mainland by a causeway. The town and airport were then to be seized, after which 10th Corps was to turn eastward and take Seoul. While this attack was in progress, Eighth Army would advance northward from Pusan.

At about 06.33 on the morning tide of 15 September, 3rd Battalion of 5th Marines landed on Green Beach. Two further battalions of 5th Marines – the 1st and 2nd – came in on the evening tide and at 17.24 landed on Red Beach, facing Inchon itself. At about 18.00, the three Battalions of 1st Marine Regiment, 3,850 men, landed at three points on Blue Beach, south of Inchon; their task was to take the road and rail routes to the town from Seoul. Then Landing Ships (Tanks) (LSTs) brought in engineers and bulldozers to Red Beach to repair damage caused to the port.

The early morning assault on Wolmi-Do, at Green Beach on its west coast, went according to plan. One company of Marines, immediately on landing, turned right and stormed Radio Hill, a dominant feature rising to about 107m/350ft. Mean-

while, on the west coast, two platoons moved south to deal with Su Wolmi-Do, a small island joined to Wolmi-Do by a causeway. Other units pushed up to North Point and also eastward, to gain and hold the causeway to the mainland.

The North Korean raw marine conscripts, with a few 76mm/3in guns, who had been subjected to intense bombing, napalm, rocket and shell fire for the better part of a week, offered only sporadic resistance, save on Su Wolmi-Do, where a small pocket of men fought stubbornly. Both islands were in Marine control by 11.15, but by then the tide had gone out, and the troops who had landed at Green Beach were temporarily cut off from the fleet. Seventeen Marines had been wounded but none killed. Soon after 08.00 a triumphant MacArthur signalled his armada: 'The Navy and Marines have never shone more brightly . . .'.

At 14.30 ships of the fleet started to bombard Inchon itself. Then, at 17.24, the tide once more high, 1st and 2nd Battalions of 5th Marine Regiment landed on Red Beach. The men had to clamber up ladders propped against the sea wall, for their landing craft, despite the flooding tide, were some 1.2m/4ft below its top.

The Marines' immediate objectives were to take British Consulate Hill to their right, Observatory Hill ahead of them and Cemetery Hill to their left: three commanding heights running north to south through Inchon. By 24.00 all three were in Marine hands, troops were safely within Inchon town and LSTs were delivering equipment to Red Beach. However, some weapons on the incoming LSTs, firing ahead of them, in the confusion wounded 23 Marines fighting on Red Beach and killed one.

On Blue Beach, where 1st Marine Regiment landed from amphibious tractors at 18.00, all was chaos. Visibility was extremely poor because smoke from the burning Inchon combined with rain to produce the effect of thick fog. And then some landing vehicles of the second wave became grounded on mud offshore and their complement of Marines had to struggle to land as best they could. Despite this, the Marines of 1st Regiment had Blue

Beach firmly in their control shortly after 01.00 on 16 September. Moreover, Kimpo airfield to the north had been taken. On Day One, 13,000 troops and their equipment had been landed at a cost of 196 casualties. Of the 2,000 defenders, around 300 had been taken prisoner.

Early on the 16th, MacArthur and his staff left their headquarters in USS *Mount McKinley* to visit the scene, and he ordered an immediate advance on Seoul. This, the second part of the campaign, was likely to prove more difficult because the capital had been turned into a veritable fortress. The overall plan was for a two-pronged attack. The 1st Marines would

advance to the Han River and to Yongdungpo, the 5th would sweep north and east, then attack Seoul from the northwest and north.

Now, however, came a period of alarm for MacArthur. Eighth Army opened its offensive northward on 16 September, the day after the landings at Inchon, but at first made little headway against stiff resistance. If it could not break out, MacArthur's entire strategy would be in danger of ruin. However, Eighth Army finally managed to cross the Naktong River, and a week after the offensive began the North Korean People's Army began to disintegrate and fall into rapid retreat.

Seoul itself fell to 10th Corps on 27 September after a struggle that levelled most of the city. The North Korean People's Army fled over the 38th Parallel and MacArthur, on President Truman's authority, could advance to the Yalu River, the north's frontier with China, and place the entire peninsula, once more united, under United Nations control.

In two weeks MacArthur had defeated 44,000 North Korean troops piecemeal, killing 14,000, capturing 7,000 and destroying 50 T34 tanks. His Marines alone had taken or destroyed 52 guns and mortars and captured 7,658 infantry weapons, as well as recapturing a large amount of US equipment. The price of all this was 566 killed and 2,713 other casualties among his 71,339 men.

Choi Yong Kun 1903–1972

MacArthur's opponent at Inchon, Choi Yong Kun, was born at Pyungan Pukto, Korea, in 1903. After having attended two military academies, he fought in the Northern Expedition of 1927 and took part in the Canton Communist riots in December that year. He led a guerrilla unit against the Japanese after they occupied Manchuria in September 1931.

In August 1936 he became an officer in the Korean People's Revolutionary Army; promotion came quickly and in February 1948 he was appointed its commander-in-chief. He was subsequently make a vice-marshal and was Minister of National Defence between 1953 and 1957; then, from 1957 until his death, he served as President of the Presidium of the Supreme People's Assembly.

US Marines, *below left*, bring up amphibian trucks and tractors to cross the Han River in the drive on Seoul.

An F4U Corsair, *left*, being loaded with 45kg/100lb bombs on the flight deck of USS *Philippine Sea*. These aircraft, fast and with a range of more than 621km/1,000mls were used at Inchon to soften up defences prior to the landings.

Marines, *right*, conduct a methodical, often dangerous search for North Korean snipers among the ruins of a building in Seoul.

Uneasy truce
MacArthur's rapid advance into North Korea, sanctioned by the United Nations, proved a foolhardy move. Misleading and inadequate intelligence reports had lulled both MacArthur and the US Joint Chiefs of Staff into thinking that Communist China would not intervene. In the event, on 26 November 1950, 180,000 Chinese 'volunteers' thrust across the frontier and drove the United Nations forces rapidly southward. The line was temporarily stabilized at the 38th Parallel; but on 1 January 1951 the Chinese and North Korean armies, in freezing conditions, advanced again and shortly recaptured Seoul.

Soon, however, the North's attack lost impetus. Seoul was retaken by United Nations forces on 14 March, and the line once more stabilized along the 38th Parallel. General MacArthur, who had been disregarding many orders from the Joint Chiefs of Staff, now insisted that the North should again be invaded and full-scale war against Communism undertaken, if necessary using

atomic weapons. 'There is no substitute for victory' he wrote on 20 March. President Truman relieved him of all his commands on 11 April and replaced him by General Matthew B. Ridgway.

After suffering a number of failed offensives, the Communists agreed to peace talks. Since their purpose was to gain time while they reinvigorated their army, the negotiations proved prolonged: they started on 10 July 1951 and agreement was not reached and an armistice signed until 27 July 1953, during which time fighting continued.

After three years of fierce conflict, a demarcation line was drawn between North and South along the positions of the two front lines. An uneasy truce has been maintained ever since. Casualties in the bitter war were unusually high: the US alone lost more than 54,000 dead and 103,000 wounded; losses for the North and South Koreans are not precisely known but it is estimated that each suffered some 10 times that number.

Moshe Dayan *1915-1981*

J ust as I can hardly remember when it was that I began milking cows, so it's hard to remember the exact time I first began handling Father's carbine.' Thus General Moshe Dayan, recalling his boyhood, for throughout his life he was deeply involved both in developing Israel and in the young state's struggle to survive against surrounding and more numerous Arabs.

Dayan was the child of Ukrainian Jewish parents, who had left Russia to settle and farm in Palestine, where he was born in 1915. He attended Senior Agricultural School in Nahalal, but his hankering for the soldier's life was soon evident: in 1929, then aged 14, he joined the *Haganah*, the underground Jewish Army. This was the period of British administration of Palestine and clashes between the Arab and Jewish settlers were already frequent. By 1937, Dayan, then a sergeant, was commanding a mobile unit of the legal Jewish Settlement Police under the British Army. In the following year he saw action countering Arab raids into Israeli territory under Captain Orde Wingate, the future leader of the Chindits in the Burma campaign of World War II. He later readily admitted his tactical debt to Wingate's example and expertise.

In June 1941, his great chance came to prove himself as a commander in the field when the Allies invaded Lebanon and Syria, at the time under the control of Vichy France. In an early engagement, however, Dayan lost the sight of his left eye when a bullet penetrated the binoculars he was using. Despite lifelong discomfort and several operations, Dayan became reconciled to the eye-patch he was now obliged to wear and turned it, like Churchill's cigars, Montgomery's hats and Patton's ivory-handled pistols, into his immediately recognizable trademark.

In later life, Dayan was to serve as Minister of Agriculture in 1959 and Minister of Defence in 1967. He embodied Israeli national fighting spirit through five wars. He was, however, personally blamed for Israel's unpreparedness in the Yom Kippur War of 1973, when Israel was unexpectedly attacked during its most sacred religious festival, and in consequence had to resign in May of the following year, together with the prime minister, Golda Meir.

It is the Sinai campaign of 1956, however, that raised Dayan to the small class of great commanders. He, almost alone among senior Israeli officers, recognized that the war in Sinai would not be like battles fought in World War II. While Rommel's, Montgomery's and von Manstein's tank commanders would probably have reacted aggressively, the Egyptians were more likely to lose nerve and cohesion if crossroads and other strategic sites were taken and Egyptian strongpoints bypassed and left in rear of his advance. In this estimate he was in general correct.

Dayan was a 'fighting general' who liked to be up front with his leading formations. During the Sinai campaign he moved rapidly from one crucial sector to another – always as a source of inspiration to his men but not always to the comfort and serenity of the local commanding officer.

In the Sinai campaign, Dayan revealed not only his strategical and tactical gifts but also his political and diplomatic acumen. He wanted to bring about the collapse of the Egyptian Army but not the death of its men, for that would only intensify the hatred long held and deeply ingrained of Arabs for Jews. In this he was proved right and his policies bore fruit when, as Foreign Minister, he was influential in negotiating a peace with Egypt that did much, at least temporarily, to dissipate tension in the area.

Moshe Dayan, photographed in 1973 during the Yom Kippur War. Despite the buccaneering appearance given by his eye-patch, Dayan was more than just a soldier. One of his main interests was archaeology, and even at the height of the Sinai Campaign he found time to dig in the sand at sites where artefacts might possibly be unearthed. The Star of David, symbol of the state of Israel.

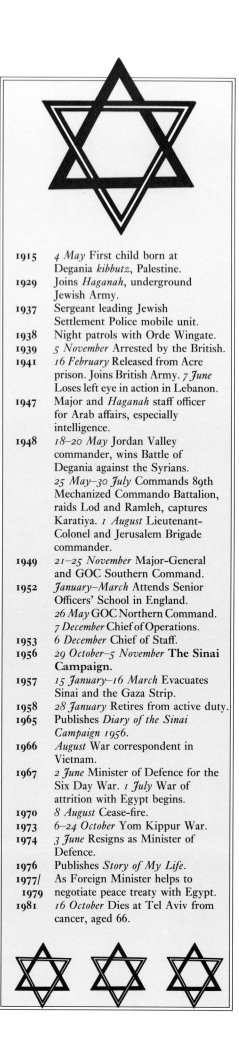

1915	*4 May* First child born at Degania *kibbutz*, Palestine.
1929	Joins *Haganah*, underground Jewish Army.
1937	Sergeant leading Jewish Settlement Police mobile unit.
1938	Night patrols with Orde Wingate.
1939	*5 November* Arrested by the British.
1941	*16 February* Released from Acre prison. Joins British Army. *7 June* Loses left eye in action in Lebanon.
1947	Major and *Haganah* staff officer for Arab affairs, especially intelligence.
1948	*18–20 May* Jordan Valley commander, wins Battle of Degania against the Syrians. *25 May–30 July* Commands 89th Mechanized Commando Battalion, raids Lod and Ramleh, captures Karatiya. *1 August* Lieutenant-Colonel and Jerusalem Brigade commander.
1949	*21–25 November* Major-General and GOC Southern Command.
1952	*January–March* Attends Senior Officers' School in England. *26 May* GOC Northern Command. *7 December* Chief of Operations.
1953	*6 December* Chief of Staff.
1956	*29 October–5 November* **The Sinai Campaign.**
1957	*15 January–16 March* Evacuates Sinai and the Gaza Strip.
1958	*28 January* Retires from active duty.
1965	Publishes *Diary of the Sinai Campaign 1956.*
1966	*August* War correspondent in Vietnam.
1967	*2 June* Minister of Defence for the Six Day War. *1 July* War of attrition with Egypt begins.
1970	*8 August* Cease-fire.
1973	*6–24 October* Yom Kippur War.
1974	*3 June* Resigns as Minister of Defence.
1976	Publishes *Story of My Life.*
1977/ 1979	As Foreign Minister helps to negotiate peace treaty with Egypt.
1981	*16 October* Dies at Tel Aviv from cancer, aged 66.

The Sinai Campaign/*29 October–5 November 1956*

ISRAELI STRATEGY IN the Sinai Campaign was complicated by the need to attain several objectives if total success were to be achieved. Paramount was the need to deceive the Egyptians into thinking that early actions were merely retaliatory raids and not the outbreak of war. This problem was aggravated by the difficulty of movement, for roads were few and often inadequate in Sinai; the northern part of the peninsula was desert, while the mountainous south was virtually impassable.

Israeli aims were, first, to neutralize rather than destroy the Egyptian Army and to exterminate all *fedayeen* (self-sacrifice) terrorists operating from hideouts in the Gaza Strip. There was a third, all-important objective: to capture Sharm El-Sheikh in the south of the peninsula.

This town overlooks the Straits of Tiran, on the west side of which lay Egyptian-controlled Sinai and on the east, the small island of Tiran. Between the two, the channel navigable by ocean-going ships was only 198m/650ft wide. Thus the Egyptians, with a few well-sited guns, were able to dominate the strait and prevent vessels from moving into the Gulf of Aqaba and north to the Israeli port of Eilat. If the Egyptian stranglehold could be broken, Eilat could become a thriving Israeli trading centre.

There was, however, a serious problem facing the Israeli general staff. The only serviceable road to Sharm El-Sheikh ran along the west, not the east, coast of the Sinai Peninsula. It followed that, in order to make Sharm El-Sheikh secure once it had been captured, Egyptian forces must be driven out of the area and the whole peninsula occupied.

To achieve all these objectives Dayan devised an audacious strategy. The first move, on the afternoon of 29 October 1956, was for four Israeli Mustang fighters to fly 2.7m/12ft above the ground in a daring manoeuvre to sever Egyptian telephone lines in Sinai with their wings and propellors.

Then a battalion of 202nd Paratroop Brigade, numbering 395 men, took off in 16 Dakotas to drop near, and take, the eastern entrance to the Mitla Pass, a long mountain defile only some 48km/30mls from the canal. To avoid detection on Egyptian radar screens, the planes flew low across the desert, only in the last moments rising to a height at which their parachutes could be safely opened.

Their landing, Dayan rightly judged, would be seen by the Egyptians as merely a raid. This impression was given further weight by other paratroop brigade units being assembled on the Jordanian border

Nasser's threat to Israel

The seeds of the conflict known to Israel as the 'Sinai Campaign', and to Great Britain and France as 'Suez', were sown in 1920 when Great Britain was given a mandate for Palestine by the League of Nations. Relations between the Arabs, who deemed the country to be theirs, and the Jewish settlers were always tense and often erupted into armed conflict. On 14 May 1948, the independent state of Israel was established and a major war soon broke out, for surrounding Arab countries were bitterly opposed to its formation. Troops from Egypt, Syria, Iran, Jordan and Lebanon invaded Israel, but a cease-fire was quickly imposed by the United Nations.

The ensuing armed peace was repeatedly broken by isolated engagements, and the volatile situation exacerbated by the importance attached to the area by the great powers. The USA, Great Britain and France supported Israel, the USSR the Arab states.

Then on 26 July 1956, Egypt's president, Colonel Gamal Abdul Nasser, nationalized the Suez Canal Company which operated the international waterway. Massive consignments of arms had recently been sent to Egypt by Czechoslovakia, and Israel feared invasion. Her fears were increased when, shortly afterward, Egypt and Syria established a joint military command.

Egypt's military build-up, her illegal nationalization of the canal and subsequent blockade of Israel's shipping through the Straits of Tiran, created an intolerable situation for Israel. The UN failed to act to free the canal, and Israel, Great Britain and France resolved to mount an offensive to return it to international control.

The precise details of the plan are not know, but Israel was to seize the Sinai Peninsula, then halt some 16km/10mls east of the canal. Great Britain and France would then launch air attacks and amphibious landings to occupy the canal zone.

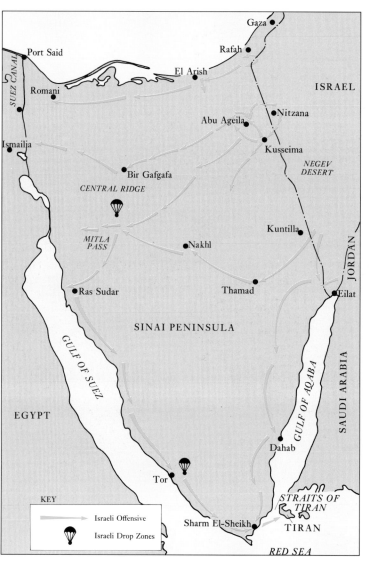

Dayan's campaign in Sinai was based, as was Slim's in the Meiktila/Mandalay campaign, on the indirect approach. By dropping paratroopers at Mitla Pass, deep in Egyptian-occupied territory, he held the enemy's attention while making his main attack along the Gaza Strip and toward Sharm El-Sheikh. The danger with this tactic is that the troops in the first attack may be cut off and destroyed. Dayan appreciated this but judged – correctly – that the Egyptians, assuming the drop to be only a raid, would not use aircraft against his paratroopers.

Dayan was well liked by his troops. This group of men, photographed near the Red Sea, displays a so-called 'Spandau'-type German WWII MG42 machine-gun which they have probably captured, since after 1945 the Czechs made these weapons and sold them to Egypt.

as a feint. At all costs, the true objective – Sinai – must be hidden for as long as possible from the Egyptians.

Meanwhile, the commander of the paratroop brigade, Lieutenant-Colonel Ariel Sharon, with the relief forces for the airborne drop, thrust across the Negev Desert toward Kuntilla to support the isolated paratroopers dropped at the Mitla Pass. Twenty-four hours had been allocated for this advance to Mitla, although Dayan thought that, given the terrain, in which vehicles could quickly sink up to their axles in the sand, 48 hours was more realistic. The attack in the centre was underway, but there remained the prize of Sharm El-Sheikh in the south and the large concentration of Egyptian troops in the northeast.

Why the Egyptian High Command concentrated their greatest numbers and fire-power within the strip of land running from El Arish to Gaza is uncertain. Rafah itself is no more than a village possessed of water wells, but with ridges that could be manned and gunned. However, farther

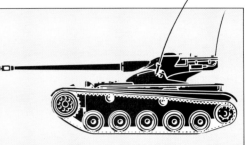

AMX 13 light tank
The Sinai campaign was conducted mainly with World War II weapons; on the ground a notable newcomer was the three-man French AMX light tank. Designed in 1949, the AMX entered service in 1951, and there are still some 327 in the French Army today.

It was a fast, light, low-silhouette air-transportable tank, ideal for rapid desert advances and reconnaissance. The Israeli Army had about 100 AMXs: one squadron in each of 202nd Paratroop Brigade and 27th and 37th Armoured Brigades, and a whole battalion in 7th Armoured Brigade, were equipped with them.

Weight: 14.5 tons; road speed: 69kmh/43mph, cross-country speed: 40kmh/25mph; armament: one long-barrel high-velocity 75mm/3in gun, automatic loading, mounted on an oscillating turret, one 7.5mm/0.3in machine-gun.

west lay the Central Ridge, of which Mitla formed the most southerly point, and there a stiff, even if costly stand could have been made. Probably the Egyptian High Command thought that by placing the bulk of their eastern forces in the Rafah region they posed a strong deterrent to

Israeli aggression; in the event, they were merely offering most of their best units as hostages to attack.

Sharon, meanwhile, took Kuntilla, which fell with little resistance, and then drove on to Thamad, which in turn fell within an hour but only after stiff fighting. Speed was the essence of Israeli strategy and, while this second battle was being fought, other units of Sharon's command thrust on to the next Egyptian garrison on their westward drive – Nakhl. This fell within the space of 20 minutes, and by 31 October, less than 30 hours after the first advance and now 290km/180mls west of its starting point, Sharon's force was able to rejoin the parachute battalion that had earlier landed at the eastern end of the Mitla Pass.

By this preliminary manoeuvre, the Israelis had secured their southern axis, roughly across the centre of Sinai, and

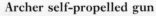

Archer self-propelled gun
Prominent among Egyptian weapons was the British-made Archer self-propelled anti-tank gun. This married the Valentine tank chassis to the excellent 17-pounder, 76mm/3in anti-tank gun with limited traverse. Top speed was 32kmh/20mph.

First produced in March 1944, 655 Archers were built. The Egyptians had 50 in 1956, 40 of which were captured by the Israelis in Sinai, with 35,000 rounds of ammunition. They had played a noteworthy part in the defence of Abu Ageila and Rafah.

The Sinai Campaign/2

The Gaza Strip was an important objective for the Israelis for two reasons. Most of the Egyptian troops were concentrated in the area, which offered the prospect of their ready encirclement, and a thrust along the coast to the Suez Canal would secure the Israeli Army's flank.

Most of the area was flat, featureless desert. Near Rafah, however, was a deep belt of hard earth ridges which had been fortified by the Egyptian 5th Brigade to form a cluster of interdependent strongpoints.

The Israeli attack on Egyptian positions west of Rafah began at 05.25 on 1 November 1956. In fortified sites on a number of the mounds, some up to 46m/150ft high, the Egyptians had installed anti-tank guns (9), usually in concrete bays.

The Egyptian defensive area contained some 20 hills. Each of these heavily entrenched strongpoints was surrounded by coiled and apron barbed wire fences (8), between which land mines had been laid.

Two Israeli companies stormed Hill 25 (6), then moved against its twin summit (7) along a communicating trench.

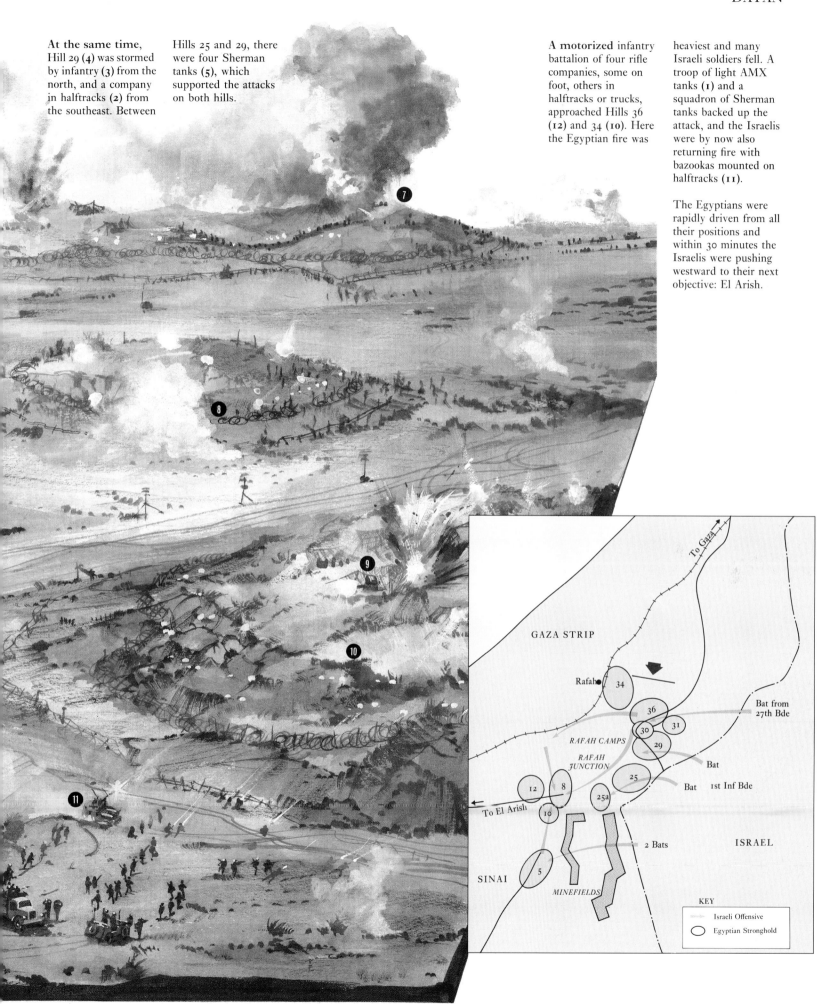

At the same time, Hill 29 **(4)** was stormed by infantry **(3)** from the north, and a company in halftracks **(2)** from the southeast. Between

Hills 25 and 29, there were four Sherman tanks **(5)**, which supported the attacks on both hills.

A motorized infantry battalion of four rifle companies, some on foot, others in halftracks or trucks, approached Hills 36 **(12)** and 34 **(10)**. Here the Egyptian fire was

heaviest and many Israeli soldiers fell. A troop of light AMX tanks **(1)** and a squadron of Sherman tanks backed up the attack, and the Israelis were by now also returning fire with bazookas mounted on halftracks **(11)**.

The Egyptians were rapidly driven from all their positions and within 30 minutes the Israelis were pushing westward to their next objective: El Arish.

GAZA STRIP

To Gaza

Rafah

34

36

30   31

29

RAFAH CAMPS

RAFAH
JUNCTION

12   8

25

25a

Bat from
27th Bde

Bat

Bat   1st Inf Bde

To El Arish

10

2 Bats   ISRAEL

SINAI

5

MINEFIELDS

KEY

Israeli Offensive

Egyptian Stronghold

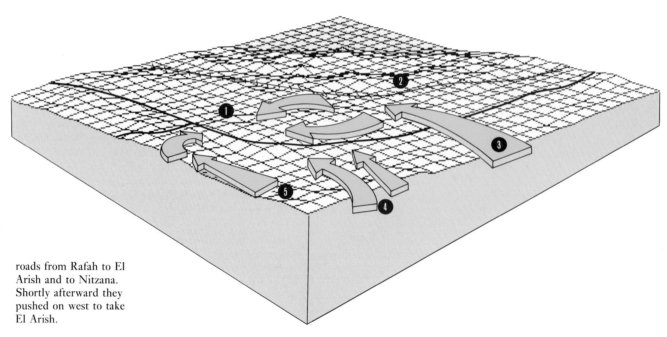

The earth mounds fortified by the Egyptians lay in the environs of Rafah (2). The Israelis attacked the hills with two formations, a battalion from 27th Brigade (3) and two battalions of 1st Infantry Brigade (4). While this fighting was in progress, two battalions of the 1st Infantry Brigade (5) struck south, then joined their victorious comrades at the junction (1) of the roads from Rafah to El Arish and to Nitzana. Shortly afterward they pushed on west to take El Arish.

overlapped Egyptian forces in the northeast. Meanwhile, two battalions of 4th Infantry Brigade had advanced some 17km/11mls over the border to capture the crossroads at Kusseima. Units of the brigade were quickly sent southwest to join Sharon's troops at Nakhl.

Now, however, came a disruption of Dayan's strategy, for Colonel Asaf Simhoni, GOC Southern Command, decided to commit the élite 7th Armoured Brigade, including its 100 tanks, to capturing the Abu Ageila position a day earlier than ordered. This was against Dayan's explicit instructions, for he was still mindful of the need to disguise his movements as being far short of outright war. But the order had been given and, though furious, he had no alternative but to agree to the attack being maintained.

Abu Ageila fell within an hour, with Israeli air support fighting off the Egyptian armour that moved south in support from El Arish. Meanwhile, on the central axis, Israeli forces had begun to drive Egyptian 1st Armoured Brigade back through Bir Gafgafa to Ismailia on the Suez Canal itself. At the same time, on 31 October, Sharon at the Mitla Pass became the second commander to disobey Dayan's orders.

The sharpest battle of the campaign ensued, during which 38 Israeli soldiers were killed and some 120 wounded. Ariel Sharon, commander of 202nd Paratroop Brigade, had been ordered to hold the eastern end of the Mitla Pass but forbidden to take it. He nevertheless asked permission to send forward a reconnaissance group; this was granted, but with it came a new order forbidding entry into the pass. Sharon, possibly because he wished to enjoy some of the credit that victorious Israeli commanders were earning elsewhere, ignored the order and sent a strong column forward.

At once it was subjected to intense fire from Egyptian troops hidden in caves on either side of the pass. Fighting lasted for about seven hours and additional Israeli troops had to be sent to extricate their comrades. Once more outraged by a subordinate's ignoring his orders, Dayan nonetheless recorded in his *Diary*: 'I regard the problem as grave when the unit fails to fulfil its battle task, not when it goes beyond the bounds of duty and does more than is demanded of it.'

By 1 November, central Sinai was clear of Egyptian troops. There remained two Israeli tasks: to subdue the north from

Israeli troops wait at a rendezvous, *below*; desert conditions were arduous and vehicles easily became scattered or stuck in the sand.

The victorious column, *below left*, has halted by a sign pointing to Nakhl, which they have just overrun.

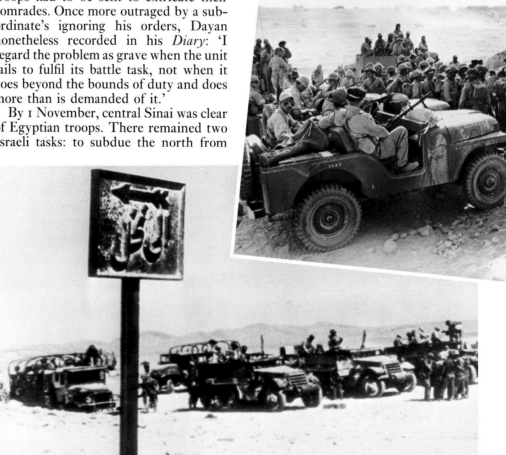

Gaza to El Arish and to capture Sharm El-Sheikh. A little before 24.00 on 30 October nearly 3,000 soldiers of 1st 'Golani' Infantry and 27th Armoured brigades had begun crossing the northern border. Their object was to assault Rafah from the northeast, cut off the Gaza Strip and then push on westward to take El Arish. Sustained bazooka attacks and painstaking clearance of minefields resulted in the two brigades meeting at the Rafah Junction.

Dayan himself was up with 27th Armoured Brigade and at the reunion recorded that 'We fell into each other's arms in the classic tradition of a Russian movie.' Within half an hour, 27th Brigade was on its way to El Arish; this town, which the Egyptians had evacuated, was occupied on 2 November. By the evening of that day, the brigade had advanced to Romani, 16km/10mls east of the Suez Canal, its designated halting place.

At 06.00 on the same day, as scheduled, a reinforced 11th Infantry Brigade struck at Gaza. Its Egyptian governor almost immediately surrendered, and an Israeli military government was established in the Gaza Strip.

Of all Dayan's objectives only Sharm El-Sheikh in the south remained. At 05.00 on that same day – 2 November – 9th Brigade, comprising 1,800 men and 200 vehicles, set off through trackless and waterless wastes along the Gulf of Aqaba, Sinai's eastern shore. Time and again the vehicles sank immobile into the sand and had to be dug out; at one point it seemed that the expedition must fail. But by endurance and will-power the advance continued; on the 3rd they reached Dahab and by the 4th were on the outskirts of Sharm El-Sheikh.

General Abd Al-Hakim Amer 1919–67

Born in Astral in Minya Province in 1919, Amer attended the Cairo Military Academy and was commissioned in 1939. In 1948 he served, as did the future president Nasser, in the first Arab-Israeli war. From this period stemmed his long and close association with Colonel Nasser.

Amer, who was said to have a 'gentle, warm and impulsive nature', played a leading role in the military coup that overthrew King Farouk of Egypt in 1952. This brought General Neguib and Colonel Nasser to power and in the following year Amer was made chief of staff. In 1956 he was appointed commander-in-chief of the joint military command established by Egypt and Syria. Then, in 1964, he was made first vice-president to Nasser and deputy supreme commander, with power to rule for 60 days if the president were disabled or killed.

Amer's distinguished career came to an abrupt end after the fiasco of the Six Day War in 1967 and he was relieved of all his posts. Later in the same year he was arrested with 50 officers and two

former ministers for allegedly plotting Nasser's overthrow. On 14 September he was given, like Rommel, the choice of standing trial, which would inevitably have ended in his execution, or of taking poison. Again like Rommel, he chose the latter option.

To support them, other Israeli forces made a simultaneous advance down the west coast from Mitla to Ras Sudar, and two paratroop companies were dropped at Tor on 2 November. On the 5th, after a grim advance of 332km/200mls, with strong air force back-up, 9th Brigade took Sharm El-Sheikh; by 09.30 the last Egyptian outpost in Sinai had surrendered.

Thus, 'Operation Kadesh' had achieved all its objectives within the political timetable. The Israeli Army had thrown 35,000 Egyptian troops and 200 tanks out of Sinai, and it stood, as agreed with its allies Great Britain and France, 16km/10mls east of the Suez Canal. The following day the Anglo-French amphibious assault troops went in at Port Said.

Aftermath of the Sinai Campaign

The British, French and Israeli attempt to regain control of the Suez Canal by force was severely criticised by member countries of the United Nations, which – at the behest of the USA and the USSR – imposed a cease-fire to commence on 6 November 1956. The following year, Israel relinquished her impressive territorial gains in the Gaza Strip and Sinai to a United Nations emergency force, but only after she had first secured guaranteed access to the Gulf of Aqaba.

Nonetheless, border incidents, both on the Israeli frontier with Egypt and those with Syria and Jordan, continued. In May 1967, Egypt's President Nasser asked for the withdrawal of United Nations forces from Egyptian territory, remobilized and closed the Gulf of Aqaba. On 5 June 1967, Israel crippled the Arab air forces with intense air assaults. Within 72 hours, Israeli armoured units again controlled the Sinai Peninsula, had thrown the Jordanians out of Jerusalem and gained the strategically important Golan Heights. This – the so-called 'Six Day War' – was brought to a close under United Nations pressure on 10 June.

In 1973, however, the Arab states, on the most sacred Jewish festival of Yom Kippur, attacked Israel from both Egypt and Syria. Taken by surprise, the Israelis were at first driven back but quickly recovered balance, and some of their units actually crossed the Suez Canal and gained a foothold on its west bank. Their losses, however, both in men and weaponry, were heavy and led to Dayan's leaving his post as Minister of Defence. US pressure induced Israel to give up her captured territory.

Further outbreaks of full-scale war have been avoided but acute tensions between Jews and Arabs in the Middle East remain. In retrospect it is evident that the Sinai Campaign did nothing to lessen this inherent friction. But for Israel there was one considerable gain from the superbly orchestrated strategy: hitherto rightly regarded by the world as a small nation, probably unviable, she was recognized as a resolute power, determined to hold her territory against more populous enemies and therefore worthy of support. The 1956 war was not only a military triumph but a significant step in Israel's search for security.

BIBLIOGRAPHY

This list comprises a selection of those books consulted by the Publishers in the preparation of *Battles of the Great Commanders* and also suggestions for further reading. The number following each entry indicates the commander to whom the book chiefly refers. Alexander (1); Scipio (2); Genghis Khan (3); Henry V (4); De Córdoba (5); Gustavus Adolphus (6); Turenne (7); Marlborough (8); Frederick (9); Washington (10); Napoleon (11); Wellington (12); Lee (13); Allenby (14); Yamashita (15); Rommel (16); Von Manstein (17); Slim (18); MacArthur (19); Dayan (20).

Alexander, Bevin *Korea: The First War We Lost* Hippocrene Books, New York, 1986 **(19)**

Allen, Louis *Burma: The Longest War 1941–1945* J.M. Dent, London & Melbourne, 1984 **(18)**

Barber, Noel *Sinister Twilight: The Fall & Rise Again of Singapore* Collins, London, 1968 **(15)**

Barnett, Correlli *The Desert Generals* George Allen & Unwin, London, 1983 **(16)**

Belfield, Eversley *Knight's Battles for Wargamers: Oudenarde, 1708* Charles Knight, London, 1972 **(8)**

Belloc, Hilaire *The Tactics & Strategy of the Great Duke of Marlborough* Arrowsmith, London, 1933 **(8)**

Boatner, Mark Mayo *Cassell's Biographical Dictionary of the American War of Independence 1763–1783* 1966 **(10)**; *Cassell's Biographical Dictionary of the American Civil War 1861–1865* 1973 **(13)**; Cassell, London

Bradbury, Jim *The Medieval Archer* The Boydell Press, Woodbridge, Suffolk, 1986 **(4)**

Brent, Peter *The Mongol Empire* Weidenfeld & Nicolson, London, 1976 **(3)**

Cagle, Malcolm W. & Manson, Frank A. *The Sea War in Korea* Arno Press, New York, 1980 **(19)**

Carell, Paul *The Foxes of the Desert* Macdonald, London, 1960 **(16)**; *Scorched Earth: Hitler's War on Russia* Vol 2 George Harrap, London, 1970 **(17)**

Carlyle, Thomas *History of Friedrich II of Prussia called Frederick the Great* Vol 7 Chapman & Hall, London, 1888 **(9)**

Carver, Michael *Tobruk*, 1964; *Dilemmas of the Desert War: A new look at the Libyan Campaign 1940–1942* 1986; B.T. Batsford, London **(16)**

Catton, Bruce *The Centennial History of The Civil War: Never Call Retreat* Doubleday, New York, 1965 **(13)**

Chandler, David G. *The Campaigns of Napoleon* Weidenfeld & Nicolson, London, 1966 **(11)**; *Marlborough as Military Commander* B.T. Batsford, London, 1973 **(8)**; *Napoleon*, 1974; (Ed) *Napoleon's Marshals*, 1987 **(11)**; Weidenfeld & Nicolson, London.

Churchill, Winston S. *Marlborough, His Life & Times* Vol 3 George Harrap, London, 1936 **(8)**; *The Second World War* Vols 1–6 1948–1954 **(15, 16, 17, 18)**; *The American Civil War* 1961 **(13)**; Cassell, London

Clark, Alan *Barbarossa: The Russian–German Conflict 1941–1945* William Morrow, New York, 1965 **(17)**

Cockayne, T. Oswald *The Life of Marshal Turenne* Longman, Brown, Green & Longman, London, 1853 **(7)**

Curtin, Jeremiah *The Mongols: A History* Little Brown, Boston, 1908 **(3)**

Dayan, Moshe *Diary of the Sinai Campaign 1956*, 1967; *Story of My Life* 1978; Sphere, London **(20)**

Deane, John Marshall, (Ed) D.G. Chandler *A Journal of Marlborough's Campaigns During the War of the Spanish Succession 1704–1711* Society For Army Historical Research, London, 1984 **(8)**

De Gaury, Gerald *The Grand Captain: Gonzalo de Córdoba* Longmans Green, London, 1955 **(5)**

Duffy, Christopher *The Army of Frederick the Great* David & Charles, London, 1974 **(9)**; *Siege Warfare: The fortress in the early modern world 1494–1660*, 1979; *Frederick the Great: A Military Life* 1985 **(9)**; Routledge & Kegan Paul, London

Dupuy, Trevor N. *The Military Life of Gustavus Adolphus: Father of Modern War* Franklin Watts, New York, 1969 **(6)**; *Elusive Victory: The Arab-Israeli Wars 1947–1974* Hero Books, Fairfax, Virginia, 1984 **(20)**

Earle, Peter *The Life and Times of Henry V* 1972 **(4)**; *Robert E. Lee* 1973 **(13)**; Weidenfeld & Nicolson, London

Falls, Cyril (Comp) *History of the Great War: Military Operations, Egypt & Palestine – from June 1917 to the end of the war* Part I HMSO, London, 1930 **(14)**

Fletcher, C.R.L. *Gustavus Adolphus and the Struggle of Protestantism for Existence* G.P. Putnam's Sons, New York, London, 1890 **(6)**

Flexner, James Thomas *George Washington in the American Revolution (1775–1783)* Leo Cooper, London, 1972; *Washington: The Indispensable Man* Collins, London, 1976 **(10)**

Fortescue, J.W. *A History of the British Army* Vol 1 Macmillan, London, 1920 **(7)**; *Wellington* Ernest Benn, London, 1960 **(12)**

Fowler, William 'Kharkov 1943' *War Monthly* Issue 33 Marshall Cavendish, London, 1976 **(17)**

Fox, Ralph *Genghis Khan* John Lane, The Bodley Head, London, 1936 **(3)**

Fox, Robin Lane *The Search for Alexander* Allen Lane, London, 1980 **(1)**

Freeman, Douglas Southall *Robert E. Lee: A Biography* Vols 1 & 2 Charles Scribner's Sons, New York, 1934 **(13)**; *George Washington: A Biography* Vol 4 Eyre & Spottiswoode, London, 1951 **(10)**

Fuller, J.F.C. *Decisive Battles: Their influence upon history and civilisation* Vol 1 1939, Vol 2 1955, Eyre & Spottiswoode, London; *The Decisive Battles of the United States* Hutchinson, London, 1942 **(10)**; *The Generalship of Alexander the Great* Eyre & Spottiswoode, London, 1958 **(1)**

Gardner, Brian *Allenby* Cassell, London, 1965 **(14)**

Glover, Michael *Wellington As Military Commander* Sphere, London, 1973 **(12)**

Gough, J.E. *Fredericksburg and Chancellorsville* Hugh Rees, London, 1913 **(13)**

Griffith, Paddy (Ed) *Wellington – Commander: The Iron Duke's Generalship* Antony Bird, Chichester, Sussex, 1985 **(12)**

Grousset, René *Conqueror of the World* The Orion Press, New York, 1966 **(3)**

Gullett, H.S. *The Australian Imperial Force in Sinai and Palestine 1914–18* Angus & Robertson, Sydney, 1923 **(14)**

Hamilton, J.R. *Alexander the Great* Hutchinson University Library, London, 1973 **(1)**

Hammond, N.G.L. *Alexander the Great: King, Commander and Statesman* Chatto & Windus, London, 1981 **(1)**

Hart, Basil Liddell *Greater than Napoleon: Scipio Africanus* William Blackwood, London, 1926 **(2)**; *A History of the World War 1914–1918* Faber & Faber, London, 1934 **(14)**; *The Rommel Papers* Collins, London, 1953 **(16)**

Harwell, Richard *Washington* An abridgement in one volume Eyre & Spottiswoode, London, 1970 **(10)**

Haswell, Jack *James II: Soldier and Sailor* Hamish Hamilton, London, 1972 **(7)**

Heinl, Robert Debs Jr. *Victory at High Tide* The Nautical & Aviation Publishing Company of America, Annapolis, Md, 1979 **(19)**

Henderson, G.F.R. *Stonewall Jackson and the American Civil War* Vol 2 Longmans, Green, London, 1906 **(13)**

Herzog, Chaim *The Arab–Israeli Wars* Arms & Armour Press, London, 1982 **(20)**

Hibbert, Christopher *Agincourt* Batsford, London, 1978 **(4)**

Holmes, Richard & Kemp, Anthony *The Bitter End* Antony Bird, Chichester, Sussex, 1982 **(15)**

Horne, Alistair *Napoleon: Master of Europe* Weidenfeld & Nicolson, London, 1979 **(11)**

Hozier, H.M. *Turenne* Chapman & [H...] London, 1885 **(7)**

James, G.P.R. *The Life and Time[s] Louis the XIV* Vol 2 Henry G. Bo[...] London, 1851 **(7)**

Jarman, Rosemary *Nawley Crisp[...] Day: The Glory of Agincourt* Coll[...] London, 1979 **(4)**

Johnson, Robert Underwood & B[...] Clarence Clough (Eds) *Battles [...] Leaders of the Civil War* Vol 3 [...] Century Co, New York, 1888 **(13[...])**

Keegan, John *The Face of Battle* Jo[...] than Cape, London, 1976 **(4)**

Ketchum, Richard M. (Ed), *The Am[er]ican Heritage Picture History of [...] Civil War* Doubleday, New Y[...] 1960 **(13)**; *The Winter Soldiers* M[c]donald, London; Doubleday, [...] York, 1973 **(10)**

Kingsford, Charles Lethbri[...] ** *Henry V: The typical mediaeval [...]* G.P. Putnam's Sons, London, 1901 **(4)

Kirby, S. Woodburn (et al) *Histor[y of] the Second World War. The [...] Against Japan: The Loss of Singa[pore]* Vol 1 1957 **(15)**; *The Reconquest [of] Burma* Vol 4; 1965 **(18)**; HMS[O] London

Lamb, Harold *Ghenghis Khan: Conqueror, Emperor of all Men* Ban[...] Books, New York, 1963 **(3)**

Langley, Michael *Inchon: MacArth[ur's] Last Triumph* B. T. Batsford, Lond[on] 1979 **(19)**

Lazenby, John F. *Hannibal's War[: A] military history of the Second P[unic] War* Aris & Phillips, Warmins[ter,] Wiltshire, 1978 **(2)**

Leasor, James *Singapore: The Ba[ttle] That Changed the World* Hodder [&] Stoughton, London, 1968 **(15)**

Leckie, Robert *The Korean War* Ba[rker] & Rockliff with Pall Mall Press, L[on]don, 1963 **(19)**

Lewin, Ronald *Slim the Standa[rd] bearer: A Biography of Field Mars[hal] the Viscount Slim* Leo Cooper, L[on]don, 1976 **(18)**; *The Life & Death of [the] Afrika Korps: A Biography* B[...] Batsford, London, 1977 **(16)**

Lindsay, Philip *King Henry V: [A] Chronicle* Ivor Nicolson & Wats[on,] London, 1934 **(4)**

Longford, Elizabeth *Wellington: [The] Years of the Sword* Weidenfeld [&] Nicolson, London, 1969 **(12)**

Luttwak, Edward & Horowitz, D[an] *The Israeli Army* Allen Lane, Lond[on] 1975 **(20)**

Macdonell, A.G. *Napoleon & [His] Marshals* Macmillan, London, 1[...] **(11, 12)**

Mackenzie, Franklin *The Ocean [and] The Steppe: The Life and Times of [the] Mongol Conqueror Genghis Khan* V[in]tage Press, New York, 1963 **(3)**

Manchester, William *American Caes[ar:] Douglas MacArthur 1880–1964* Arr[...] Books, London, 1979 **(19)**

nstein, Erich von *Lost Victories* Methuen, London, 1958 (**17**)

rsden, E.W. *The Campaign of aaugamela* Liverpool University ress, Liverpool, 1964 (**1**)

tthews, Geoffrey *The Re-conquest of Burma 1943–45* Gate & Polden, Aldershot, Hampshire, 1966 (**18**)

lenthin, F.W. von *Panzer Battles 1939–1945: A study of the employment f armour in the Second World War* Cassell, London, 1955 (**17**)

n-at-Arms Series* Various titles Osprey Publishing, London, 1975–1986

itary Uniforms* Blandford, London & oole, Dorset, 1969–1985

ford, Nancy *Frederick the Great* Hamish Hamilton, London, 1970 (**9**)

ntrose, Lynn & Canzona, Nicholas A. *U.S. Marine Operations in Korea 1950–1953: The Inchon-Seoul Operation* Vol 2 Historical Branch G-3 Headquarters U.S. Marine Corps, Washington, 1955 (**19**)

pier, W.F.P. *History of the War in the Peninsula and in the South of France 1807–1814* George Routledge, London, 1882 (**12**)

an, Charles *A History of the Peninsular War* Vol 5 Clarendon Press, London, 1914 (**12**); *A History of the Art of War in the Middle Ages* 1924 (**4**); *A History of the Art of War in the Sixteenth Century* 1937 (**5**); Methuen, London

en, Frank *The Campaign in Burma* HMSO, London, 1946 (**18**)

ker, Geoffrey *The Thirty Years War* Routledge & Kegan Paul, London, 1984 (**6**)

Perkins, James Breck *France Under Mazarin* Vol 2 G.P. Putnam's Sons, London, New York, 1886 (**7**)

Perrett, Bryan *Tank Tracks to Rangoon: The Story of British Armour in Burma* Robert Hale, London, 1978 (**18**)

Petre, F. Loraine *Napoleon & The Archduke Charles: A history of the Franco-Austrian Campaign in the valley of the Danube in 1809* The Bodley Head, London, 1909 (**11**)

Playfair, I.S.O. (*et al*) *History of the Second World War. The Mediterranean & Middle East: British fortunes reach their lowest ebb* Vol 3 HMSO, London, 1960 (**16**)

Polybius (Trans. Paton, W.R.) *The Histories* William Heinemann, London, 1976 (**2**)

Potter, John Deane *A Soldier Must Hang: The biography of an oriental general* Frederick Muller, London, 1963 (**15**)

Prasad, S.N. (*et al*) *Official History of the Indian Armed Forces in the Second World War 1939–1945: The Reconquest of Burma* Vol 2 Combined Inter-Services Historical Section, India & Pakistan, 1959 (**18**)

Prawdin, Michael *The Mongol Empire* George Allen and Unwin, London, 1940 (**3**)

Prescott, William H. *History of the reign of Ferdinand & Isabella, the Catholic Kings of Spain* Richard Bentley, London, 1842 (**5**)

Preston, R.M.P. *The Desert Mounted Corps* Constable, London, 1921 (**14**)

Purcell, Mary *The Great Captain: Gonzalo Fernández de Córdoba* Alvin Redwood, London, 1963 (**5**)

Rathbone, Julian *Wellington's War* Michael Joseph, London, 1984 (**12**)

Rees, David *Korea: The Limited War* Macmillan, London, 1964 (**19**)

Renault, Mary *The Nature of Alexander* Allen Lane, London, 1975 (**1**)

Roberts, Michael *Gustavus Adolphus: A History of Sweden 1611–1632* Vol 2 Longmans Green, London, 1958; *Gustavus Adolphus & the Rise of Sweden* The English Universities Press, London, 1973 (**6**)

Rothenberg, Gunther E. *Napoleon's Great Adversaries: The Archduke Charles and the Austrian Army 1792–1814* B.T. Batsford, London, 1982 (**11**)

Rousset, Camille (Ed) *Recollections of Marshal Macdonald, Duke of Tarentum* Richard Bentley, London, 1892 (**11**)

Quintana, Don Manuel José *Memoirs of Gonzalo Fernández de Córdoba, styled The Great Captain* Edward Churton, London, 1851 (**5**)

Rutherford, Ward *The Biography of Field Marshal Erwin Rommel* Bison Books, London, 1981 (**16**)

Scullard, Howard H. *Scipio Africanus in the Second Punic War* Cambridge University Press, Cambridge, 1930; *Scipio Africanus: Soldier & Politician* Thames & Hudson, London, 1970 (**2**)

Seaton, Albert *The Russo-German War 1941–1945* Arthur Barker, London, 1971 (**17**)

Selby, John *Stonewall Jackson as Military Commander* B.T. Batsford, London; D. Van Nostrand, Princeton, 1968 (**12**)

Slim, William *Defeat Into Victory* Cassell, London, 1956 (**18**)

Swinson, A. *Four Samurai: A quartet of Japanese Army Commanders in the Second World War* Hutchinson, London, 1968 (**15**)

Taylor, F.L. *The Art of War in Italy 1494–1529* Cambridge University Press, Cambridge, 1921 (**5**)

Teveth, Shabtai *Moshe Dayan* Weidenfeld & Nicolson, London, 1972 (**20**)

Tsuji, Masanobu *Singapore: The Japanese Version* Constable, London, 1962 (**15**)

Vladimirtsov, B. Ya *The Life of Genghis-Khan* Benjamin Blom, New York, London, 1969 (**3**)

Walker, C.C. *Jenghiz Khan* Luzac, London, 1939 (**3**)

Wavell, A.P. *The Palestine Campaigns* Constable, London, 1932; *Allenby: Soldier and Statesman* White Lion Publishers, London, 1974 (**14**)

Wedgwood, C.V. *The Thirty Years War* Jonathan Cape, London, 1964 (**6**)

Weygand, Maxime *Turenne, Marshal of France* George Harrap, London, 1930 (**7**)

Wigmore, Lionel *Australian Army in the war of 1939–45: The Japanese Thrust* Series I Australian War Memorial, Canberra, 1957 (**14**)

Wylie, John Hamilton *The Reign of Henry the Fifth* Vol 2 Cambridge University Press, Cambridge, 1919 (**4**)

Young, Peter & Lawford, J.P. *Wellington's Masterpiece: The Battle & Campaign of Salamanca* George Allen & Unwin, London, 1973 (**12**)

Ziemke, Earl F. *Army Historical Series. Stalingrad to Berlin: The German Defeat in the East* United States Army, Washington, 1968 (**17**)

CKNOWLEDGEMENTS

publishers are grateful to the staff of The Imperial War Museum, don; The London Library; The School of Oriental and African lies, London, and The Royal Geographical Society, London, for assistance.

litional four-colour artworks: Richard Hook/Linden Artists
e artworks: Janos Marffy
ps: Richard Prideaux, Technical Art Services; Adam Willis
nputer maps: Chapman Bounford
ex: Valerie Lewis Chandler

ure credits

eft; r = right; t = top; c = centre; b = bottom

ichael Holford; 9 Photoresources; 11t Scala; 11b Sonia Halliday; Peter Newark's Historical Pictures; 12b Lauros-Giraudon; 14 ish Museum; 15 Scala; 18t British Museum; 18b BBC Hulton ure Library; 19 British Museum; 20 Robert Harding Picture rary; 21 Scala/National Museum, Naples; 23t British Museum; 23b sell Collection; 27 Michael Holford; 28 Aldus Archive; 29 iothéque Nationale, Paris; 31t The MacQuitty International ection; 31b Victoria & Albert Museum; 34–35 Aldus Archive; 36–

37 The Bridgeman Art Library; 39t Victoria & Albert Museum; 39b British Library; 42 British Library; 43t Giraudon; 43b British Library; 44 Arxiu Mas; 45 Roger-Viollet; 47 Mansell Collection; 50 BBC Hulton Picture Library; 51 Mansell Collection; 53 The Royal Collections, Stockholm; 55 Mary Evans Picture Library; 58t Krigsarkivet, Stockholm; 58b Mansell Collection; 61 Reunion des Musées Nationaux, Paris; 63 Mary Evans Picture Library; 66 Mansell Collection; 67 Roger-Viollet; 68 Mansell Collection; 69 National Portrait Gallery, London; 70 Royal Armouries; 71–72 Peter Newark's Historical Pictures; 72–73 Michael Holford; 75 Mansell Collection; 78 National Army Museum; 79t Mansell Collection; 79b Robert Harding Picture Library; 80 Bildarchiv Preussischer Kulturbesitz; 81 Schloss Charlottenburg, Berlin; 83 Bildachiv Preussischer Kulturbesitz; 86 Ullstein; 87 BBC Hulton Picture Library; 88 Peter Newark's Western Americana; 89 Pennsylvania Academy of the Fine Arts – Gift of the Executors of Elizabeth Wharton McKean Estate; 91tl Library of Congress; 91tr BBC Hulton Picture Library; 91b The Bettmann Archive/BBC Hulton Picture Libary; 94t Mary Evans Picture Library; 94b The Bettmann Archive/BBC Hulton Picture Library; 95 Mansell Collection; 97 Bulloz; 99t Annie Horton; 99b Royal Armouries; 100 Victoria & Albert Museum; 101tc Robert Harding Picture Library; 101tb Peter Newark's Historical Pictures; 102b Bulloz; 103tl Jean-Loup Charmet; 103tr Roger-Viollet; 103b Mansell Collection; 106–107 Bulloz; 108 Victoria & Albert Museum; 109 National Gallery, London;

112t Mansell Collection; 112b, 114t Fotomas Index; 114b BBC Hulton Picture Library; 115 Fotomas Index; 118t BBC Hulton Picture Library; 118b, 119t National Army Museum; 119b Mansell Collection; 121 Peter Newark's Western Americana; 123, 126t BBC Hulton Picture Library; 126b Peter Newark's Western Americana; 127 Robert Hunt Library; 128t Peter Newark's Western Americana; 128b BBC Hulton Picture Library; 129–130 Peter Newark's Western Americana; 131 BBC Hulton Picture Library; 133 National Portrait Gallery, London; 134–135 Robert Hunt Library; 138 Topham; 139 Robert Hunt Library; 140 USN/MARS; 141–143 Robert Hunt Library; 144–145 Imperial War Museum; 146 Topham; 147 Robert Hunt Library; 150 Photo Source; 151t Popperfoto; 151b Robert Hunt Library; 153, 155 Imperial War Museum; 155r Robert Hunt Library; 158t Robert Hunt Library; 158b Imperial War Museum; 159tl Photo Source; 159tr Popperfoto; 159b Robert Hunt Library; 159br Ullstein; 161 Robert Hunt Library; 163 Topham; 166t Photo Source; 166b Robert Hunt Library; 161t Novosti; 167r Topham; 168 Burma Star Association; 169 Popperfoto; 171t Topham; 171r, 174 Imperial War Museum; 175–177 Popperfoto; 178t Imperial War Museum; 178c&b Photo Source; 179 Imperial War Museum; 180 Peter Newark's Historical Pictures; 181 Popperfoto; 182–183 Robert Hunt Library; 183 Popperfoto; 186t TRH/US Navy; 186b, 187 TRH/DOD; 189, 191 Popperfoto; 194c BIPAC; 194b, 195 Topham.

INDEX